NURSE PRACTITIONER'S
LEGAL REFERENCE

P9-ARS-435

NURSE PRACTITIONER'S
LEGAL REFERENCE

SPRINGHOUSE

Springhouse, Pennsylvania

STAFF

Publisher
Judith A. Schilling McCann, RN, MSN

Editorial Director
David Moreau

Creative Director
Jake Smith

Clinical Manager
Joan Robinson, RN, MSN, CCRN

Editor
Julie Munden

Clinical Editor
Gwynn Sinkinson, RN, MSN, CRNP

Copy Editors
Jaime Stockslager (supervisor), Kimberly A.J. Johnson, Pamela Wingrod

Designers
Arlene Putterman (associate design director), Joseph John Clark, Donna S. Morris

Cover Illustration
Roy Scott

Projects Coordinator
Liz Schaeffer

Electronic Production Services
Diane Paluba (manager), Joyce Rossi Biletz

Manufacturing
Patricia K. Dorshaw (manager), Otto Mezei (book production manager)

Editorial Assistants
Beverly Lane, Beth Janae Orr, Elfriede Young

The procedures described and recommended in this publication are based on research and consultation with legal, medical, and nursing authorities. To the best of our knowledge, these procedures reflect currently accepted clinical practice; nevertheless, they can't be considered absolute and universal recommendations, nor can they be considered legal advice. For individual application, all recommendations must be considered in light of the unique circumstances of each legal or administrative situation. The authors and the publisher disclaim responsibility for any adverse consequences from following the suggested procedures without first seeking legal advice, for any undetected errors, or for the reader's misunderstanding of the text.

© 2001 by Springhouse Corporation. All rights reserved. No part of this publication may be used or reproduced in any manner whatsoever without written permission except for brief quotations embodied in critical articles and reviews. For information, write Springhouse Corporation, 1111 Bethlehem Pike, P.O. Box 908, Springhouse, PA 19477-0908. Authorization to photocopy items for internal or personal use, or for the internal or personal use of specific clients, is granted by Springhouse Corporation for users registered with the Copyright Clearance Center (CCC) Transactional Reporting Service, provided that the fee of $.75 per page is paid directly to CCC, 222 Rosewood Dr., Danvers, MA 01923. For those organizations that have been granted a photocopy license by CCC, a separate system of payment has been arranged. The fee code for users of the Transactional Reporting Service is 1582550972/01 $00.00 + .75.

Printed in the United States of America.

NPLR- D N O S A J J M A M
03 02 01   10 9 8 7 6 5 4 3 2 1

Library of Congress
Cataloging-in-Publication Data
Nurse practitioner's legal reference.
    p.; cm.
    Includes bibliographical references and index.
    1. Nurse practitioners—Legal status, laws, etc.—United States. 2. Nursing—Law and legislation—United States. 3.3 Nurses—Malpractice—United States. 4. Nursing ethics—United States. I. Springhouse Corporation.
    [DNLM: 1. Nurse Practitioners—legislation & jurisprudence—United States. 2.Ethics, Nursing—United States. 3. Legislation, Medical—United States. 4. Legislation, Nursing—United States. WY 33 AA1 N775 2001]
    RT82.8 .N8646 2001
    344.73'0414—dc21   00-069694
    ISBN 1-58255-097-2 (alk. paper)   CIP

Contents

Contributors

Susan Barrow, RN, MSN, JD, is an associate professor of nursing and director of the Nursing Center for Caring Arts at Truman State University as well as an associate attorney at Oswall, Cotley and Templeton, P.C. in Kirksville, Mo. She's a member of the American College of Legal Medicine, the American Bar Association, the Missouri Bar Association, the Medical-Legal Committee of the MBA, Sigma Theta Tau, the American Nurses Association, and the Missouri Nurses Association.

Deborah Becker, MSN, CRNP, CS, CCRN, is an assistant program director of the adult acute nurse practitioner program at the University of Pennsylvania School of Nursing in Philadelphia. She's a member of the American Association of Critical Care Nurses, the Association for Acute Care Nurse Practitioners, and Sigma Theta Tau.

Penny S. Brooke, APRN, MS, JD, is the professor and coordinator of service-learning at the University of Utah College of Nursing in Salt Lake City. She's a member of the American Association of Nurse Attorneys, the Utah State Bar Association, the National Association of College and University Attorneys, the Campus-Community Partnership for Health, and Intermountain Therapy Animals.

Jacqueline M. Carolan, RN, BSN, JD, is an attorney with Fox, Rothschild, O'Brien, & Frankel in Philadelphia. She's a member of the Philadelphia Bar Association and the Pennsylvania Bar Association.

Joseph T. Catalano, RN, PhD, is a professor of nursing at East Central University in Ada, Okla. He's a member of the American Nurses Association and its Committee on Human Rights and Ethics. He's also a member of the Oklahoma Nurses Association and the American Association of Critical Care Nurses.

Amy Darby, RN, BSN, MA, JD, is an associate at Sidley & Austin in Chicago. She's a member of the American Bar Association.

Joseph L. DuFour, RN, MS, CS, FNP, is a lecturer at State University of New York at New Paltz and a practitioner at Family Practice in Glen Falls, N.Y. He's a member of the New York State Nurses Association, the New York State Coalition of Nurse Practitioners, and Sigma Theta Tau.

Ginny Wacker Guido, RN, MSN, JD, is associate dean and director of graduate studies at the College of Nursing, University of North Dakota in Grand Forks, N.Dak. She's a member of the American Nurses Association, the North Dakota Nurses Association, the American Association of Critical Care Nurses, the Society of Law, Medicine, and Ethics, the National League for Nursing, and Sigma Theta Tau.

Ann Helm, RN, MS, JD, is a nurse-attorney at Plaintiffs' Medical Legal Consulting in Lafayette, Ore., and Judge Advocate General with the United States Air Force Reserves. She's a member of the American Association of Trial Attorneys, the Oregon Association of Trial Attorneys, the Oregon State Bar Association, and Oregon Women Lawyers.

Cathy A. Klein, RN, MSN, PNP, APP, MSEd, JD, is an attorney-at-law at Cathy A. Klein, RN, PC, in Denver, Colo. She's a member of the American Nurses Association, the Colorado Nurses Association, the American Bar Association, the Colorado Bar Association, the Denver Bar, the American Trial Lawyer's Association, and the Colorado Trial Lawyers Association.

Michelle J. Lespasio, RN, NP, JD, is a nurse practitioner attorney with Corporate Medical Service, Incorporated, in Woburn, Mass. She's a member of the Massachusetts Coalition of Nurse Practitioners, the Massachusetts Association of Women Lawyers, and Sigma Theta Tau.

Deborah M. Lessard, Esq., RN, is an attorney in private practice in Mechanicsburg, Pa. She's a member of the American Bar Association, the Pennsylvania Bar Association, the American Nurses Association, and the Pennsylvania State Nurses Association.

Patricia Sokol, RN, BSN, JD, is completing an internship at the American Medical Association in Chicago. She's a member of Sigma Theta Tau.

Jerelyn Peixoto Weiss, RN, MS, FNP, JD, is a medical legal consultant in private practice in White Plains, N.Y. She's a member of the California and New York Bar Associations, the New York Coalition of Nurse Practitioners, and the National Health Lawyers Association.

Susan E. Ziel, RN, BSN, MPH, JD, is an attorney-at-law at Krieg, DeVault, Alexander, & Capehart, LLP in Indianapolis, Ind. She's a member of the American Bar Association, the American Health Lawyers Association, the American Nurses Association, the Breast Health Awareness League, the Executive Women in Health Care, the Health Care Compliance Association, the Healthcare Financial Management Association, the Indiana Medical Group Management Association, the Indiana State Bar Association, the Medical Group Management Association, and the Mental Health Association for Hamilton County.

Foreword

As a nurse practitioner (NP), you play an integral role in the delivery of health care. How you make decisions and deliver that care to your patients is greatly impacted by the ever-changing health care marketplace. More than ever, you are faced with difficult legal and ethical dilemmas that can adversely affect your practice. The challenges that you encounter may raise numerous questions that have important ethical and legal ramifications, for example:

● Are you entitled by your state nurse practice act to be an independent NP?
● What do you do if the pharmacist refuses to fill the prescription without a physician's signature?
● How do you ensure the rights of patients who are HIV-positive or have AIDS?
● Does having professional liability insurance make you more vulnerable to malpractice lawsuits?

Nurse Practitioner's Legal Reference will answer the legal and ethical questions that you face as an NP. Although schools of nursing prepare you for the role of providing competent care for your patients, most have neither the expertise nor the time to prepare you for the array of legal and ethical issues that arise when caring for patients. This handy reference addresses — concisely and completely — issues that confront NPs who are new in their role as well as those who have been honing their skills for several years.

Chapter 1 provides a general overview of the NP's role, introducing various laws that govern NP practice, including nurse practice acts, federal and state definitions of collaborative practice, and the legal significance of standards of NP practice. An area of common overlap and potential liability for the NP — distinguishing NP practice from medical practice —. is also discussed.

Your legal risks and responsibilities on the job are the focus of chapter 2. You'll read about prescribing medications, admitting privileges, risk management strategies, and your role in research-based practice. Discover your potential liability in caring for special patient populations, such as minors, abused patients, mentally ill or developmentally disabled patients, and suspected criminals. Learn about your responsibilities to report abuse, write orders for restraints, and submit evidence in criminal cases.

Chapter 3 covers legal issues on the job, such as collaborative practice and the employment relationship, and provides extensive information about contracts. You'll learn about working as an independent contractor, the necessity for contracts, how to protect yourself legally, the basic components of a contract, and what to do when you encounter conflicts. You'll also find step-by-step guidelines that walk you through the process of successfully negotiating your contract.

Chapter 4 discusses your legal risks while off duty, including the giving of health care advice and practicing in disaster settings. It also explains what you should do if you're in a position of working outside of your scope of practice — a legal predicament faced by many NPs.

Chapter 5 covers all aspects of malpractice — what constitutes malpractice, defenses that protect the NP should a malpractice suit be filed, and helpful pointers on how to avoid malpractice liability. This chapter also discusses the role of professional liability insurance and how to defend yourself if you go to trial.

Chapter 6 reviews various aspects of documentation, from the legal significance of documentation to documenting controlled substances and telephone triage. It also addresses legal concerns in the 21st century, such as facsimiles, e-mails, and telemedicine.

Chapters 7 through 9 present the basics of ethical decision making, ethical conflicts in clinical practice, and ethical conflicts in professional practice. The role of law versus ethics, the value of ethical theories, and how to act as a patient advocate are discussed in Chapter 7. Chapter 8 explores such issues as a patient's right to die, organ transplantation, and genetic screening and engineering. In Chapter 9, you'll read about patient autonomy, maintaining privacy and confidentiality, and some emerging ethical challenges for NPs.

Chapter 10 focuses on patients' rights and responsibilities, including informed consent, privacy, and confidentiality. Chapter 11 discusses recent developments in the health care marketplace and how they will directly impact your nursing career.

Each chapter incorporates a review of relevant court cases, describing legal precedents of the case as well as pertinent legal tips for NPs. Throughout the book, numerous case studies focus on an NP "caught" in a dilemma; you'll discover how the dilemma is resolved and what she learns or gains from the situation. Rounding out this invaluable reference are a comprehensive glossary of legal and ethical terms, three helpful appendices, an index of

critical court cases, and a general index to help you quickly locate the information you need.

Nurse Practitioner's Legal Reference is an authoritative reference on NP law and ethics. You will not want to be without this comprehensive source of information as you negotiate through challenging career opportunities, face difficulties in ensuring patients' rights, and conquer ethical decisions that could affect your practice. It's an indispensable reference that all practicing NPs and those studying to become an NP can use with confidence for years to come.

Ginny Wacker Guido, RN, MSN, JD
Associate Dean and Director, Graduate Studies
College of Nursing
University of North Dakota

Chapter One

NURSE PRACTITIONER PRACTICE AND THE LAW

LIKE ANY OTHER health care professional, a *nurse practitioner (NP)* wants to retain existing privileges, find new opportunities for professional security and advancement, increase economic benefits, and improve access to quality health care for all patients. To realize these goals, NPs must understand and negotiate within the legal responsibilities and limits currently defining their practice. This is a particularly critical and complex task for NPs, given the considerable variation in NP authority and autonomy found across the United States. This variation is caused, in part, by a lack of uniformity in the laws and regulations defining NP practice. In addition, it's caused by the multitude of informal and less transparent requirements imposed on NPs by nonregulatory entities, such as hospitals and health plans.

This chapter provides fundamental information on the laws that directly govern nursing. It includes a detailed discussion of the *nurse practice act* — the state law that regulates nursing. You'll find coverage of how nursing law is applied in court and about the role of your state board of nursing.

You'll learn about *standards of care* and how these standards may be used as evidence during *malpractice* litigation.

This chapter also explains the many legal issues that impact an NP's practice, both directly and indirectly. It provides a basic understanding of such topics as scope of practice, the regulation of NP practice, and the types of regulation that NPs can face. While the chapter covers these subjects in some detail, it isn't exhaustive. Practice location particularities that may affect an NP's ability to practice aren't reviewed. Thus, it's imperative that you research and become familiar with the subtle rules and regulations that affect your individual practice. Methods to access this information are discussed throughout the chapter.

Understanding the NP

The nursing and health care communities broadly recognize an NP as a *registered nurse (RN)* with advanced academic and clinical experience. These qualifications enable the NP to diagnose and manage most common and many chronic illnesses, either independently or in collaboration with a physician. The title *advanced practice nurse (APN)* is used to identify RNs who have advanced education or a master's degree in a clinical specialty. APNs include NPs, *clinical nurse specialists (CNSs), certified nurse-midwives (CNMs),* and certified registered nurse-anesthetists (CRNAs). Depending on the specialty area, NPs regularly perform functions that formerly were physicians' exclusive responsibilities. They're specially trained to make independent judgments about a patient's condition. In addition to performing basic nursing tasks, NPs evaluate patients, perform advanced therapeutic procedures, assess changes in patients' health status, and manage patients' medical care regimens.

For legal purposes, however, the definition of an NP is established by state law. Often, this definition isn't a concise statement, but rather a list of credentials an individual must hold in order to provide NP services. Practice credentials can include licensure, educational requirements, and certification. They may vary from state to state but are designed to ensure quality and protect the public.

LICENSURE
Each state has the jurisdiction to determine the requirements for licensure for NPs. All states require NPs to hold state licenses as RNs and provide coverage of the NP under their current RN license process. Only three states (California, Florida, and New York) provide either dual licenses or separate certificates for the NP. Each nurse practice act contains licensing laws; these laws establish qualifications for obtaining and maintaining a nursing license.

EDUCATIONAL REQUIREMENTS
In 1994 the American Association of Colleges of Nurses took the position

that all APNs, including NPs, must have a master's degree to be certified. As of January 1, 1999, the Health Care Finance Administration (HCFA) released regulations that would require NPs to hold a master's degree in order to be eligible for reimbursement. Most of the national NP organizations have required a master's degree for national certification for the last 5 years.

CERTIFICATION
NP certification may be obtained from a nongovernmental agency or association after meeting predetermined qualifications. These qualifications may include graduation from an accredited program, passing scores on a qualifying examination, or completion of a given amount of work experience. NPs may seek certification either to satisfy their state's mandate or to provide tangible recognition of professional achievement in a defined functional or clinical area of nursing.

For example, the American Nurses Credentialing Center of the *American Nurses Association (ANA)* and other professional organizations certify RNs with master's degrees based on predetermined standards that include passing a written examination and completing minimum clinical practice time in the specialty area.

Regulating NP practice

The rules governing nursing practice are created by numerous shareholders in health care. Although the regulation of health care professionals is generally left to the states under their broad authority to protect the health and well-being of their citizens, three distinct sources of law dictate NP practice:
● statutory law, which emanates from Congress (federal law) or state legislatures (state law); nurse practice acts are statutory laws

● administrative law, which concerns administrative agencies, boards, and commissions legislated by Congress or by the state legislature (such as a state board of nursing or the HCFA of the U.S. Department of Health and Human Services)
● judicial law, which is derived from judicial opinions.

These three types of regulatory laws can prove harmful or helpful to the NP who faces disciplinary action for any violation of her state's nurse practice act. (See *Understanding types of law,* pages 4 and 5.)

LIMITS OF ADVANCED PRACTICE NURSING

Historically, the majority of APNs were allowed to practice only under a physician's direction or with his orders. Without a physician's order, she could perform only traditional nursing tasks. This has changed significantly. NPs' legal authorization to practice has expanded over the years by state nurse practice acts, statutes, and judicial law.

Because expanded roles for nurses are rapidly changing, questions about scope of practice frequently lack clear-cut answers. Many questions about scope of practice are still being addressed by legislation. For example, many state legislatures are currently writing practice guidelines regarding authority to diagnose and treat. Joining an NP organization is one way of staying informed about current issues facing NPs in your specialty or your region.

It's always important to be aware of the legally permissible scope of your nursing practice as it's defined in your state's nurse practice act. Never exceed its limits. Otherwise, you're inviting legal problems.

NURSE PRACTICE ACTS

Each state has a nurse practice act, which is designed to protect the public by broadly defining the legal scope of nursing practice. Your state's nurse practice act is the most important law affecting your NP practice. Every NP is expected to care for her patients within defined practice limits; if you give care beyond those limits, you become vulnerable to charges of violating your state nurse practice act. Every NP should know and understand the nurse practice act of the state where she's employed. For a copy of your state's nurse practice act, contact your state nurses' association or the state board of nursing. (See *State nurses' associations,* pages 6 to 9.)

Nurse practice acts tend to be broadly worded, and the wording varies from state to state. Understanding your nurse practice act's general provisions will help you stay within the legal limits of NP practice.

Interpreting the nurse practice act isn't always easy. One problem stems from the fact that nurse practice acts are statutory laws. Any amendment to a nurse practice act, therefore, must be accomplished by means of the inevitably slow legislative process. Because of the time involved in pondering, drafting, and enacting laws, amendments to nurse practice acts lag well behind the progress of changes in NP practice.

Scope of practice

Your *scope of practice* — the professional nurse activities, including the action or legal boundaries of those activities — are defined under each state's nurse practice act. Can the NP diagnose, treat, prescribe medications for, and manage the care of patients? All of these issues are addressed in each state's nurse practice act, and detailed answers are found in the rules and regulations promulgated by each state's board of nursing.

In some states the medical board also develops rules and regulations

Understanding types of law

Statutory law

Written law, known as ***statutory law,*** is passed by a legislative body and often referred to as a statute or an "act." The U.S. Constitution is at the top of the hierarchy of enacted law, followed by federal law and then state law. The importance of this structure is that a lower authority can't grant privileges or responsibilities denied at a higher level. However, a lower authority may authorize responsibilities not specifically denied at a higher level, or set forth more stringent criteria for nursing responsibilities allowed at a higher level. Consequently, a state may not enact a law that conflicts with a federal law, and similarly, a law passed by the U.S. Congress that contradicts the Constitution may be declared void by a court.

Statutory law may be amended, redefined, or repealed. An amendment adds or repeals portions of an act or its associated regulations. Amendments become part of the act with the same legal force as the original act. While amendments permit legislatures to modify an act to keep it current, these changes can be difficult to track, making it harder to identify the most current version of a law.

Another facet of statutory law includes redefinition. The rewriting of the fundamental provision of an act, redefinition can, for example, reverse a definition of a nurse practitioner's (NP's) scope of practice that prohibits diagnosis or ordering of diagnostic tests. This changes the basic premise of the act without amending or repealing it.

Finally, a repeal is a declaration by law that either a portion of an act or an entire act is removed from the laws of the state or the United States. When a legislature changes or expands an existing law, it must also repeal sections that conflict with the changes. For example, if a state legislature decides to grant or expand NPs' prescriptive authority, it must repeal any sections of the nurse practice act that declare it unlawful for NPs to prescribe before it can enact the new provision into law.

Administrative law

Administrative agencies, boards, and commissions deal with ***administrative law*** that's legislated by Congress or the state legislatures. For NPs, the most important administrative agency is the state board of nursing created under the provisions of each state's nurse practice act. Because Congress and state legislatures can't realistically implement their many laws, this task is frequently delegated to the board of nursing, which oversees and enforces the laws. Administrative agencies are given the authority to carry out the specific intentions of the statutes by creating rules and regulations that enforce statutory laws.

Position statements and declaratory rulings may also be issued by the board of nursing to guide nurses on a particular issue. They're less formal than rules and regulations (which in most states require public hearings), but are equally binding.

Because of the increasingly complex nursing and medical procedures, formal or informal guidance is available from the board of nursing. Through official position statements or opinion letters as well as general statements, the state's board of nursing helps define the boundaries of nursing practice.

Judicial law

Judicial law is made by courts and interprets dispatched legal issues. For example, the courts are regularly called on to decide if a specific action constitutes medical practice.

Don't assume, however, that courts always ignore the difference between medical practice and expanded nursing roles. A case on this point is *Hernicz v. State of Florida, Department of Professional Regulation* (1980). It involved an NP who examined and treated two patients without a sponsoring physician's approval in a state where NPs must have sponsoring physicians. The state board of nursing suspended his license, and the court decision upheld the suspension.

Understanding types of law *(continued)*

Institutional policy

Institutional policies may be more (but not less) restrictive than statutes, rules and regulations, and other higher authorities. For example, your state's nurse practice act may permit NPs to perform a certain procedure, but your facility may prohibit it. As an employee of the health care facility, you're bound by your employer's policies.

The scope of NP practice defined by institutional policies can vary considerably within the same state, and even within the same facility. For example, NPs working in a trauma unit may be authorized to insert chest tubes while NPs working in the primary care clinic aren't.

Policies that originate at the bottom of the hierarchy are generally the easiest to change. To change an institutional policy, for example, you'd work through the appropriate administrative chain of command. If, on the other hand, the source is a state or federal law, you would need to initiate legislative action to produce change. This is commonly a laborious and time-consuming process.

---

that affect NPs. This is done because until recently many NP responsibilities were considered part of the physician's role. A state's nurse practice act may provide separate definitions, eligibility criteria, and scope of practice for each type of APN, including NPs, CRNAs, CNMs, and CNSs, or it may address these areas in general terms that apply to all APNs. Some state nurse practice acts don't address the responsibilities of APNs, and thus NPs, within the act itself, but have promulgated rules and regulations that define the scope of practice for NPs. For example, the nurse practice act may merely declare that APNs are recognized by the state and that they must hold current certification from a national certifying authority. Yet, the state board's rules and regulations may define regulations concerning prescriptive authority and independence of practice. Ultimately, the state's board of nursing helps define the boundaries of nursing practice. (See *Defining the boundaries of NP practice,* page 10.)

Because each individual state can regulate the legal boundaries for advanced practice of nursing, it's imperative that you be knowledgeable about the current scope of practice in the state where you work and where you live. Additionally, before posing a scope of practice question, you need to find out the source of the rule in question. (See *Who makes the rules?* page 11.)

In those instances in which state legislation doesn't meticulously define advanced practice nursing, the court may influence limits on the scope of practice. For example, in New Jersey, the board of medical examiners reviewed the complaints of two patients who charged two NPs in a *health maintenance organization* with prescribing drugs and making a medical diagnosis. The ANA supported the nurses, stating that they were acting well within the nurse practice act. Although the parties settled out of court, the board cited the complaints as the basis for issuing stricter definitions of physicians' and NPs' responsibilities.

Similarly, in a Missouri case, *Sermchief v. Gonzalez* (1983), physicians on the board of registration of healing arts accused two NPs who provided family planning services of practicing medicine. Two consulting physicians were accused of contributing to the nurses'

(Text continues on page 9.)

State nurses' associations

This chart lists the name, address, telephone number, and e-mail address (when available) of nurses' associations in the United States and its territories. The state nurses' associations have a Web site with links to each state's Web site at *www.nursingworld.org/snaaddr.htm*.

Alabama State Nurses' Association
360 N. Hull St.
Montgomery, AL 36104-3658
(334) 262-8321
E-mail: *alabamasna@mindspring.com*

Alaska Nurses' Association
237 E. Third Ave., Suite 3
Anchorage, AK 99501-2523
(907) 274-0827
E-mail: *aknurse@Alaska.com*

Arizona Nurses' Association
1850 E. Southern Ave., Suite 1
Tempe, AZ 85282-5832
(480) 831-0404
E-mail: *azna@aol.com*

Arkansas Nurses' Association
804 N. University
Little Rock, AR 72205
(501) 664-5853
E-mail: *arna@prodigy.net*

California Nurses' Association
2000 Franklin St.
Oakland, CA 94612
(510) 273-2200
E-mail: *execoffice@calnurses.org*

Colorado Nurses' Association
950 S. Cherry, Suite 508
Denver, CO 80246
(303) 757-7483
E-mail: *cna@nurses-co.org*

Connecticut Nurses' Association
Meritech Business Park
377 Research Pkwy., Suite 2D
Meriden, CT 06450
(203) 238-1207
E-mail: *ct_nurses_assoc@compuserve.com*

Delaware Nurses' Association
2644 Capitol Trail, Suite 330
Newark, DE 19711
(302) 368-2333
E-mail: *delnurse@erols.com*

Dist. of Columbia Nurses' Association
5100 Wisconsin Ave., N.W., Suite 306
Washington, DC 20016
(202) 244-2705
E-mail: *dcnal@cs.com*

Florida Nurses' Association
P.O. Box 536985
Orlando, FL 32853-6985
(407) 896-3261
E-mail: *theflnurse@aol.com*

Georgia Nurses' Association
1362 W. Peachtree St., N.W.
Atlanta, GA 30309
(404) 876-4624
E-mail: *gna@mindspring.com*

Guam Nurses' Association
P.O. Box CG
Hagatna, Guam 96932
011 (671) 477-6877
E-mail: *guamnurs@ite.net*

Hawaii Nurses' Association
677 Ala Moana Blvd., Suite 301
Honolulu, HI 96813
(808) 531-1628
E-mail: nancy@*hawaiinurses.org*

Idaho Nurses' Association
200 N. Fourth St., Suite 20
Boise, ID 83702-6001
(208) 345-0500
E-mail: *idanurse@rmci.net*

Illinois Nurses' Association
105 W. Adams St., Suite 2101
Chicago, IL 60603
(312) 419-2900, ext. 231
E-mail: *jbundley@illinoisnurse.com*

Indiana State Nurses' Association
2915 N. High School Rd.
Indianapolis, IN 46224-2969
(317) 299-4575
E-mail: *isnarn@prodigy.net*

State nurses' associations *(continued)*

Iowa Nurses' Association
1501 42nd St., Suite 471
West Des Moines, IA 50266
(515) 255-0495
E-mail: *iowanurses@aol.com*

Kansas State Nurses' Association
1208 S.W. Tyler
Topeka, KS 66612-1735
(785) 233-8638
E-mail: *troberts@echo.sound.net*

Kentucky Nurses' Association
1400 S. First St.
P.O. Box 2616
Louisville, KY 40201
(502) 637-2546/47
E-mail: *Kentucky.nurses@prodigy.net*

Louisiana State Nurses' Association
5700 Florida Blvd., Suite 720
Baton Rouge, LA 70806
(225) 201-0993;
(800) 457-6378
E-mail: *lsna@lsna.org*

Maine State Nurses' Association
295 Water St.
P.O. Box 2240
Augusta, ME 04338-2240
(207) 622-1057
E-mail: *Mainenurse@aol.com*

Maryland Nurses' Association
849 International Dr.
Airport Square 21, Suite 255
Linthicum, MD 21090
(410) 859-3000
E-mail: *marylandnursesassociation@erols.com*

Massachusetts Nurses' Association
340 Turnpike St.
Canton, MA 02021
(781) 821-4625
E-mail: *massnurses@mnarn.org*

Michigan Nurses' Association
2310 Jolly Oak Rd.
Okemos, MI 48864-4599
(517) 349-5640
E-mail: *tom.renkes@minurses.org*

Minnesota Nurses' Association
1295 Bandana Blvd. N., Suite 140
St. Paul, MN 55108-5115
(651) 646-4807;
(800) 536-4662
E-mail: *mnnurses@mnnurses.org*

Mississippi Nurses' Association
31 Woodgreen Pl.
Madison, MS 39110
(601) 898-0670
E-mail: *mna@msnurses.org*

Missouri Nurses' Association
1904 Bubba Ln., Box 105228
Jefferson City, MO 65110
(888) 662-MONA
(573) 636-4623
E-mail: *belinda@monursesassociation.org*

Montana Nurses' Association
104 Broadway, Suite G-2
Helena, MT 59601
(406) 442-6710
E-mail: *info@mtnurses.org*

Nebraska Nurses' Association
715 S. 14th St.
Lincoln, NE 68508
(402) 475-3859
E-mail: *ne.nurses@prodigy.net*

Nevada Nurses' Association
P.O. Box 530399
Henderson, NV 89053-0399
(702) 260-7886
E-mail: *nvnurses@aol.com*

New Hampshire Nurses' Association
48 West St.
Concord, NH 03301-3595
(603) 225-3783
E-mail: *nh_nurses@compuserve.com*

New Jersey State Nurses' Association
1479 Pennington Rd.
Trenton, NJ 08618-2661
(609) 883-5335, ext. 10
E-mail: *andrea@njsna.org*

(continued)

State nurses' associations *(continued)*

New Mexico Nurses' Association
P.O. Box 80300
Albuquerque, NM 87198
(505) 268-7744
E-mail: *nmna@aol.com*

New York State Nurses' Association
11 Cornell Rd.
Latham, NY 12110
(518) 782-9400, ext. 201
E-mail: *martha.orr@nysna.org*

North Carolina Nurses' Association
103 Enterprise St.
Box 12025
Raleigh, NC 27605
(919) 821-4250
E-mail: *ncnurses@aol.com*

North Dakota Nurses' Association
549 Airport Rd.
Bismarck, ND 58504-6107
(701) 223-1385
E-mail: *ndna@prodigy.net*

Ohio Nurses' Association
4000 E. Main St.
Columbus, OH 43213-2983
(614) 237-5414, ext. 1020
E-mail: *gharsheymeade@ohnurses.org*

Oklahoma Nurses' Association
6414 N. Santa Fe, Suite A
Oklahoma City, OK 73116
(405) 840-3476
E-mail: *audra@oknurses.com*

Oregon Nurses' Association
9600 S.W. Oak, Suite 550
Portland, OR 97223
(503) 293-0011
E-mail: *ona@oregonrn.org*

Pennsylvania Nurses' Association
P.O. Box 68525
Harrisburg, PA 17106-8525
(717) 657-1222;
(888) 707-7762
E-mail: *psna@psna.org*

Rhode Island State Nurses' Association
550 S. Water St., Unit 540B
Providence, RI 02903-4344
(401) 421-9703
E-mail: *risna@prodigy.net*

South Carolina Nurses' Association
1821 Gadsden St.
Columbia, SC 29201
(803) 252-4781
E-mail: *scna@prodigy.net*

South Dakota Nurses' Association
818 E. 41st St.
Sioux Falls, SD 57105
(605) 338-1401
E-mail: *southdakota.nurses@prodigy.net*

Tennessee Nurses' Association
545 Mainstream Dr., Suite 405
Nashville, TN 37228-1201
(615) 254-0350
E-mail: *tna@tnaonline.org*

Texas Nurses' Association
7600 Burnet Rd., Suite 440
Austin, TX 78757-1292
(512) 452-0645
E-mail: *memberinfo@texasnurses.org*

Utah Nurses' Association
3761 S. 700 E., #201
Salt Lake City, UT 84106
(801) 293-8351
E-mail: *una@xmission.com*

Vermont State Nurses' Association
1 Main St., #26 Champlain Mill
Winooski, VT 05404-2230
(802) 775-3583
E-mail: *vtnurse@prodigy.net*

Virgin Islands Nurses' Association
P.O. Box 583
Christiansted, St. Croix, VI 00821-0583
(809) 773-1261
E-mail: *vcgvina@viaccess.net*

Virginia Nurses' Association
7113 Three Chopt Rd., Suite 204
Richmond, VA 23226
(804) 282-1808/2373
E-mail: *vnajmj@aol.com*

State nurses' associations *(continued)*

Washington State Nurses' Association
575 Andover Park W., Suite 101
Seattle, WA 98188-3321
(206) 575-7979
E-mail: *jhunting@wsna.org*

West Virginia Nurses' Association
119 Summers St.
Charleston, WV 25301
(304) 342-1169;
(800) 400-1226
E-mail: *centraloffice@wvnurses.org*

Wisconsin Nurses' Association
6117 Monona Dr.
Madison, WI 53716
(608) 221-0383
E-mail: *wna@execpc.com*

Wyoming Nurses' Association
Majestic Bldg., Room 305
1603 Capitol Ave.
Cheyenne, WY 82001
(307) 635-3955
E-mail: *wyonurse@aol.com*

alleged illegal practice by delegating medical tasks to them. The tasks included performing pelvic examinations and Papanicolaou smears, treating vaginitis, counseling, providing contraceptives, and inserting intrauterine devices. The NPs claimed that their tasks were valid under protocols they developed jointly with their supervising physicians. However, the Missouri Nurse Practice Act defined professional nursing in more general terms, according to specialized education, judgment, and skills. The Act didn't require NPs to have direct physician supervision. In finding that the nurses were practicing within the scope of nursing and not medicine, the court noted that the NPs had the education and skills required to perform their actions and that they were practicing nursing as the Missouri legislature had intended when it enacted its nurse practice act.

STATE BOARDS OF NURSING. Another determining factor in NP practice is the state board of nursing. A state board of nursing derives its authority from the state's nurse practice act and sets policy regarding licensure in that state. The nurse practice act creates the state board of nursing and authorizes this board to administer and enforce rules and regulations concerning the nurs-

ing profession and specifies the make-up of the board — the number of members as well as their educational and professional requirements. In addition, other regulatory boards may have rules and regulations that impact on NP practice. State boards of nursing also establish requirements for obtaining an advanced practice nursing license. The board may require an APN to have national certification or a master's degree in a clinical specialty. For example, Delaware's Nurse Practice Act defines an APN as "an individual whose education and certification meet criteria established by the Board of Nursing, who is currently licensed as a registered nurse, and who has a master's degree or a post–basic program certificate in a clinical nursing specialty with national certification."

Knowingly violating your scope of practice as defined by the nurse practice act or any official ruling of the board of nursing (sometimes called the state board of nurse examiners) carries the potential for disciplinary action. In Texas, for example, the board of nurse examiners is responsible for the initial approval and renewal of an NP to prescribe medications. The rules state that in order to prescribe medication, the NP shall, at a minimum:

Defining the boundaries of NP practice

You may characterize your state's nurse practice act as traditional, transitional, or modern, depending on how it defines the boundaries of nurse practitioner (NP) practice.

Traditional

Traditional nurse practice acts allow only conventional nursing activities. They limit the nurse's responsibilities to traditional patient care, disease prevention, and health maintenance. These nurse practice acts don't allow registered nurses (RNs) to participate in such expanded nursing activities as diagnosis, prescription, and treatment. Only a few states continue to have such limited practice acts.

Transitional

Transitional nurse practice acts have broader boundaries, and may include a "laundry list" of permitted nursing functions. For example, Maine's act lists six specific RN activities:
- traditional patient care
- collaboration with other health professionals in planning care

- diagnosis and prescription delegated by physicians
- delegation of tasks to licensed practical nurses, licensed vocational nurses, and nurses' aides
- supervision and teaching
- carrying out physicians' orders.

Because it allows expanded duties such as diagnosis and prescription, Maine is edging toward a modern type of nurse practice act.

Other states with transitional acts, such as Massachusetts, broaden the nurses' role by including a separate definition of NPs. This wording allows NPs to diagnose and treat patients.

Modern

States with modern nurse practice acts — New York, for example — allow RNs to diagnose and treat health problems as well as to provide traditional nursing care. New York's definition of registered nursing is so broad that it encompasses not only current nursing activities, but also much of what nurses are likely to do in the future.

- complete a course in pharmacology and related pathology
- complete continuing education in clinical pharmacology and related pathology
- complete continuing education as otherwise required by the board of nurse examiners
- apply to the board of nurse examiners for a prescription authorization number.

To avoid risking your license, you may need to check with your board of nursing for answers to your scope of practice questions or to formally request an expansion of scope of practice. (See *State boards of nursing,* pages 12 to 15.)

If you want to find out the board's stand on an issue, you can start with an informal query, which may simply involve a phone call to the executive director. To handle the volume of calls, some nursing boards refer queries to practice consultants or a practice committee or council.

If you learn that the board has made a ruling that permits NPs to take on the task in question (for example, inserting a chest tube), determine what conditions you must meet to be in compliance with the ruling. Do you need to meet specific educational or credentialing criteria? Can you perform the task only in certain settings (the trauma unit) or under certain conditions (with

(Text continues on page 15.)

Who makes the rules?

To take ownership of your NP practice, you must understand how your scope of practice is defined and where to go when you have questions.

SOURCE OF PRACTICE RULES	EXAMPLES OF ISSUES COVERED	WHERE RULES ARE DOCUMENTED	HOW TO INITIATE CHANGE
Federal legislation	• Medicare or Medicaid provisions related to reimbursement for nursing services	• Federal statutes	• Review documents. • Draft desired legislative changes. • Obtain support of colleagues, nursing organizations, other health care providers, and the public, if appropriate. • Obtain support and sponsorship from a U.S. congressman or senator, who will introduce the bill. • Lobby for the bill's passage.
State legislation	• Scope of practice for registered nurses, licensed practical nurses, and advanced practice nurses • Nursing educational requirements • Composition and disciplinary authority of board of nursing	• Nurse practice act • Medical practice act • Other statutes	• Review documents. • Draft desired legislative changes. • Obtain support of colleagues, nursing organizations, other health care providers, and the public, if appropriate. • Obtain support and sponsorship from a state legislator, who will introduce the bill. • Lobby for the bill's passage.
Board of nursing	• Delegation • Medication administration • Unprofessional conduct • Licensing	• Rules and regulations • Position statements • Declaratory rulings (as found in meeting minutes or newsletters), which may be specific to a particular setting or institution	• Review documents. • Initiate a formal query to the licensing board. • Obtain board support for change. • The board may issue a position statement or declaratory ruling or hold a formal public hearing before voting to promulgate new rules or change existing ones.
Health care facility	• Clinical practice guidelines • Policies specific to the institution, specialty, or practice setting • Personnel and employment policies	• Office-based policies • Institutional policies • Institutional credentialing policies	• Review institutional policies. • Follow institutional policies or the chain of command to make inquiries or propose change.

Adapted from Laskowski-Jones, L. "Reaching Beyond the Rules: understanding — and Influencing — Your Scope of Practice," *Nursing98*, September 1998, with permission of the publisher.

State boards of nursing

The following list includes boards of nursing for all U.S. states and territories.

Alabama Board of Nursing
RSA Plaza, Suite 250
770 Washington Ave.
Montgomery, AL 36130-3900
Phone: (334) 242-4060
Web site: *www.abn.state.al.us*

Alaska Board of Nursing
Dept. of Community and Economic
Development
Div. of Occupational Licensing
3601 C St., Suite 722
Anchorage, AK 99503
Phone: (907) 269-8161
Web site: *dced.state.ak.us/occ/pnur.htm*

American Samoa Health Services
Regulatory Board
LBJ Tropical Medical Center
Pago Pago, AS 96799
Phone: (684) 633-1222

Arizona State Board of Nursing
1651 E. Morten Ave., Suite 210
Phoenix, AZ 85020
Phone: (602) 331-8111
Web site: *www.azboardofnursing.org*

Arkansas State Board of Nursing
University Tower Bldg.
1123 S. University, Suite 800
Little Rock, AR 72204
Phone: (501) 686-2700
Web site: *www.state.ar.us/nurse*

California Board of Registered Nursing
400 R St., Suite 4030
Sacramento, CA 95814-6239
Phone: (916) 322-3350
Web site: *www.rn.ca.gov*

Colorado Board of Nursing
1560 Broadway, Suite 880
Denver, CO 80202
Phone: (303) 894-2430
Web site: *www.dora.state.co.us/nursing*

**Connecticut Board of Examiners
for Nursing**
Division of Health Systems Regulation
410 Capitol Ave., MS# 12HSR
P.O. Box 340308
Hartford, CT 06134-0328
Phone: (860) 509-7624
Web site: *www.state.ct.us/dph*

Delaware Board of Nursing
861 Silverlake Blvd.
Cannon Bldg., Suite 203
Dover, DE 19904
Phone: (302) 739-4522

District of Columbia Board of Nursing
Department of Health
825 N. Capital St., N.E., 2nd Floor,
Room 2224
Washington, DC 20002
Phone: (202) 442-4778

Florida Board of Nursing
4080 Woodcock Dr., Suite 202
Jacksonville, FL 32207
Phone: (904) 858-6940
Web site: *www.doh.state.fl.us/mqa/
nursing/rnhome.htm*

Georgia Board of Nursing
237 Coliseum Dr.
Macon, GA 31217-3858
Phone: (912) 207-1640
Web site: *www.sos.state.ga.us/ebd-rn/*

Guam Board of Nurse Examiners
P.O. Box 2816
Barrgada, GU 96910
Phone: 011 (671) 475-0251

Hawaii Board of Nursing
Professional and Vocational Licensing
Division
P.O. Box 3469
Honolulu, HI 96801
Phone: (808) 586-3000
Web site: *mano.icsd.hawaii.gov/doh/
index.html*

State boards of nursing *(continued)*

Idaho Board of Nursing
280 N. 8th St., Suite 210
P.O. Box 83720
Boise, ID 83720
Phone: (208) 334-3110
Web site: *www.state.id.us/ibn/ibnhome.htm*

Illinois Department of Professional Regulation
James R. Thompson Center
100 West Randolph St., Suite 9-300
Chicago, IL 60601
Phone: (312) 814-2715
Web site: *www.dpr.state.il.us/*

Indiana State Board of Nursing
Health Professions Bureau
402 W. Washington St., Room W041
Indianapolis, IN 46204
Phone: (317) 232-2960
Web site: *www.ai.org/hpb*

Iowa Board of Nursing
RiverPoint Business Park
400 S.W. 8th St., Suite B
Des Moines, IA 50309-4685
Phone: (515) 281-3255
Web site: *www.state.ia.us/government/ nursing/*

Kansas State Board of Nursing
Landon State Office Bldg.
900 S.W. Jackson, Suite 551-S
Topeka, KS 66612
Phone: (785) 296-4929
Web site: *www.ksbn.org*

Kentucky Board of Nursing
312 Whittington Pkwy., Suite 300
Louisville, KY 40222
Phone: (502) 329-7000
Web site: *www.kbn.state.ky.us/*

Louisiana State Board of Nursing
3510 N. Causeway Blvd., Suite 501
Metairie, LA 70002
Phone: (504) 838-5332
Web site: *www.lsbn.state.la.us/*

Maine State Board of Nursing
158 State House Station
Augusta, ME 04333
Phone: (207) 287-1133
Web site: *www.state.me.us/nursingbd/*

Maryland Board of Nursing
4140 Patterson Ave.
Baltimore, MD 21215
Phone: (410) 585-1900
Web site: *//dhmh1d.dhmh.state.md.us/ mbn/*

Massachusetts Board of Registration in Nursing
239 Causeway St.
Boston, MA 02114
Phone: (617) 727-9961
Web site: *www.state.ma.us/reg/boards/rn/*

State of Michigan
Department of Consumer and Industry Services
Bureau of Health Services
611 W. Ottawa St., 4th Floor
Lansing, MI 48933
Phone: (517) 373-9102
Web site: *www.cis.state.mi.us/bhser/ genover.htm*

Minnesota Board of Nursing
2829 University Ave. S.E., Suite 500
Minneapolis, MN 55414
Phone: (612) 617-2270
Web site: *www.nursingboard.state.mn.us/*

Mississippi Board of Nursing
1935 Lakeland Dr., Suite B
Jackson, MS 39216
Phone: (601) 987-4188
Web site: *www.msbn.state.ms.us/*

Missouri State Board of Nursing
3605 Missouri Blvd.
P.O. Box 656
Jefferson City, MO 65102-0656
Phone: (573) 751-0681
Web site: *www.ecodev.state.mo.us/pr/nursing*

(continued)

State boards of nursing *(continued)*

Montana State Board of Nursing
301 South Park
P.O. Box 200513
Helena, MT 59620-0513
Phone: (406) 444-2071
Web site: *www.com.state.mt.us/
license/pol/index.htm*

**Nebraska Health and Human
Services System**
301 Centennial Mall S.
P.O. Box 94986
Lincoln, NE 68509-4986
Phone: (402) 471-4376
Web site: *www.hhs.state.ne.us/crl/nns.htm*

Nevada State Board of Nursing
1755 E. Plumb Ln., Suite 260
Reno, NV 89502
Phone: (888) 590-NSBN,
in Las Vegas (775) 688-2620
Web site: *www.nursingboard.state.nv.us/*

New Hampshire Board of Nursing
78 Regional Dr., Bldg. B
P.O. Box 3898
Concord, NH 03302
Phone: (603) 271-6605
Web site: *www.state.nh.us/nursing/*

New Jersey Board of Nursing
124 Halsey St., 6th Floor
P.O. Box 45010
Newark, NJ 07101
Phone: (973) 504-6586
Web site: *www.state.nj.us/lps/ca/medical.htm*

New Mexico Board of Nursing
4206 Louisiana Blvd., N.E., Suite A
Albuquerque, NM 87109
Phone: (505) 841-8340
Web site: *www.state.nm.us/clients/nursing/*

New York State Board of Nursing
State Education Department
Cultural Education Center, Room 3023
Albany, NY 12230
Phone: (518) 474-3845
Web site: *www.op.nysed.gov/prof/nurse.htm*

North Carolina Board of Nursing
3724 National Dr., Suite 201
Raleigh, NC 27612
Phone: (919) 782-3211
Web site: *www.ncbon.com*

North Dakota Board of Nursing
919 S. 7th St., Suite 504
Bismarck, ND 58504
Phone: (701) 328-9777
Web site: *www.ndbon.org/*

Ohio Board of Nursing
17 S. High St., Suite 400
Columbus, OH 43215-3413
Phone: (614) 466-3947
Web site: *www.state.oh.us/nur/*

Oklahoma Board of Nursing
2915 N. Classen Blvd., Suite 524
Oklahoma City, OK 73106
Phone: (405) 962-1800

Oregon State Board of Nursing
800 N.E. Oregon St., Box 25, Suite 465
Portland, OR 97232
Phone: (503) 731-4745
Web site: *www.osbn.state.or.us/*

Pennsylvania State Board of Nursing
124 Pine St.
P.O. Box 2649
Harrisburg, PA 17101
Phone: (717) 783-7142
Web site: *www.dos.state.pa.us/bpoa/
nurbd/mainpage.htm*

**Commonwealth of Puerto Rico
Board of Nurse Examiners**
800 Roberto H. Todd Ave.
Room 202, Stop 18
Santurce, PR 00908
Phone: (787) 725-8161

Rhode Island Board of Nurse Registration and Nursing Education
105 Cannon Bldg.
Three Capitol Hill
Providence, RI 02908
Phone: (401) 222-5700
Web site: *www.health.state.ri.us*

State boards of nursing *(continued)*

South Carolina State Board of Nursing
110 Centerview Dr., Suite 202
Columbia, SC 29210
Phone: (803) 896-4550
Web site: *www.llr.state.sc.us/bon.htm*

South Dakota Board of Nursing
4300 S. Louise Ave., Suite C-1
Sioux Falls, SD 57106-3124
Phone: (605) 362-2760
Web site: *www.state.sd.us/dcr/nursing/*

Tennessee State Board of Nursing
426 5th Ave. N.
1st Floor–Cordell Hull Bldg.
Nashville, TN 37247
Phone: (615) 532-5166
Web site: *170.142.76.180/bmf-bin/BMFproflist.pl*

Texas Board of Nurse Examiners
333 Guadalupe St., Suite 3-460
Austin, TX 78701
Phone: (512) 305-7400
Web site: *www.bne.state.tx.us/*

Utah State Board of Nursing
Heber M. Wells Bldg., 4th Floor
160 E. 300 South
Salt Lake City, UT 84111
Phone: (801) 530-6628
Web site: *www.commerce.state.ut.us/dopl/dopl1.htm*

Vermont State Board of Nursing
109 State St.
Montpelier, VT 05609-1106
Phone: (802) 828-2396
Web site: *//vtprofessionals.org/nurses/*

Virgin Islands Board of Nurse Licensure
Veterans Drive Station
St. Thomas, VI 00803
Phone: (340) 776-7397

Virginia Board of Nursing
6606 W. Broad St., 4th Floor
Richmond, VA 23230
Phone: (804) 662-9909
Web site: *www.dhp.state.va.us/levelone/nurse.htm*

Washington State Nursing Care Quality Assurance Commission
Department of Health
1300 Quince St. S.E.
Olympia, WA 98504-7864
Phone: (360) 236-4740
Web site: *www.doh.wa.gov/nursing/*

West Virginia Board of Examiners for Registered Professional Nurses
101 Dee Dr.
Charleston, WV 25311
Phone: (304) 558-3596
Web site: *www.state.wv.us/nurses/rn/*

Wisconsin Department of Regulation and Licensing
1400 E. Washington Ave.
P.O. Box 8935
Madison, WI 53708
Phone: (608) 266-0145
Web site: *//badger.state.wi.us/agencies/drl*

Wyoming State Board of Nursing
2020 Carey Ave., Suite 110
Cheyenne, WY 82002
Phone: (307) 777-7601
Web site: *//nursing.state.wy.us/*

a physician's collaboration)? Your next step may involve obtaining the appropriate credentials to legally and safely expand your practice.

If the board has made no decisions or rulings on the issue, however, the executive director or practice consul-tant won't be able to give you an answer. Your next step would be to send a formal written query to the board of nursing.

Some boards of nursing have stopped providing rulings on scope of practice issues because the task can be overwhelming in this era of rapidly changing technology. The trend is to provide a decision-making algorithm so you can answer the question based upon applicable laws and regulations.

Of course, the board might opt not to consider your query at all. In general, practice issues the board agrees to explore are applicable to a wide range of nurses. The board is unlikely to tackle narrow issues that are unique to a specific provider or institution. The board also avoids violating the employer-employee relationship and will steer clear of queries that seem to reflect an underlying dispute between an NP and her employer.

Expanding your scope of practice

Expanding the limits of your scope of practice can be an opportunity for professional growth. Let's say you want a state board of nursing decision that will expand some aspect of your scope of practice. To start, search Internet resources or make a telephone call to the executive director or practice consultant of the board to ask about previous rulings on the issue. If the issue hasn't been addressed — or if the board has previously taken a position against expanding the scope of practice in your area of interest — consider formally presenting your case to the board.

Contact the board office and ask them for information on the proper procedure to follow. Because some regulatory boards adhere to very specific administrative procedures, make sure you comply with all instructions outlining how you should interact with the board. Although not a substitute for valid content, a presentation that is organized and concise but comprehensive makes it easier for board members to understand your request and follow your thinking to a logical conclusion.

Although each regulatory board handles requests differently, follow these general guidelines when submitting a request for expansion of scope of practice:

● Obtain permission allowing you to type your letter to the board using your facility's letterhead. The letter should concisely state your request for an expansion of your scope of practice and ask for permission to make a formal presentation at a scheduled board meeting. Because board members are reluctant to become involved in employer-employee relationships, it's important to establish that you have your facility's support for the change in scope of practice that you propose.

● Put together a packet of information that describes the health care setting, the proposed educational and training requirements, the plan for competency evaluation, and the qualifications of NPs who will be eligible for the expansion in scope of practice. Include verification of administrative support, medical direction or oversight, and any pertinent facility policies, procedures, or protocols.

● Provide a review of current literature and professional standards that support your position.

● Provide reference information about nurse practice acts, rules and regulations, position statements, and declaratory rulings from other jurisdictions that support your position.

After your request is on the board's agenda, recruit key people to help you with the presentation, as allowed by the board. For example, the administrative executive accountable for your particular practice setting can verify that you have your facility's support. If medical direction is involved, bring along a physician from your practice setting who will be able to answer any questions about protocols, supervision, performance standards, and quality review. In addition, consider offering periodic status reports to the board outlining the progress of the project when appropriate.

Most regulatory boards include laypersons, who represent the public, as well as licensed nurses. For this reason, you'll need to design a presentation in terms that everyone can understand. Audiovisual aids can help board members understand key presentation concepts or the chain of logic behind the request.

It's important to exhibit a professional demeanor. Answer questions in a calm and helpful manner. Avoid becoming defensive or confrontational if you must answer difficult questions. Keep in mind that the board's primary responsibility is to protect the public, so board members must scrutinize issues until they're confident that the change you propose is safe.

After your presentation, one of three outcomes is possible. The board may approve or disapprove the expansion in scope of practice. Alternatively, they may defer a decision until a more in-depth review has been completed. In-depth review may include interaction with a practice committee, consultants, legal council, or other regulatory boards.

STANDARDS OF NP PRACTICE

Standards of care set minimum criteria for your competency on the job, enabling you and others to judge the quality of care that you and your NP colleagues provide. States typically include standards of care in the nurse practice act. Standards are also developed by professional organizations, agency policy and procedures, court cases, job descriptions, and professional journals and books.

Evolution of NP standards

As early as the 1890s, nursing leaders fought for and stressed the importance of having recognized standards for all nurses. In 1950, the ANA adopted its first *Code of Ethics for Nursing* and began the tradition of written nursing standards of care.

In 1973, the ANA Congress for Nursing Practice established the first generic standards for the profession — standards that could be applied to all nurses in all settings. Some states have incorporated the ANA standards into their nurse practice acts. (See *ANA's standards of clinical nursing practice,* pages 18 to 20.)

By 1974, each of the ANA divisions of nursing practice (such as community health, geriatrics, maternal-child, mental health, and medical-surgical) had established distinct standards for its specialty. The ANA Congress called these **specialty standards.** State nursing associations also helped develop specialty nursing standards. In 1996, the ANA published a standard for APNs entitled *Scope and Standards of Advanced Practice Registered Nursing.*

Other organizations have contributed to the development of nursing standards. The **Joint Commission on Accreditation of Healthcare Organizations (JCAHO),** a private, nongovernmental agency that establishes guidelines for the operation of hospitals and health care facilities, also has developed nursing standards to be used in hospital audit systems. In some states, JCAHO standards have been incorporated into law, resulting in broadly applicable standards of patient care. In addition, state nursing associations and specialty nursing organizations actively work with hospital nursing administrators for adoption of standards.

Federal regulations for staffing **Medicare** and **Medicaid** services have influenced the development of standards, especially nursing home standards. By suggesting ethical approaches to nursing practice, ethics codes written by the ANA and the **International Council of Nurses** also influence how care standards are developed.

(Text continues on page 20.)

ANA's standards of clinical nursing practice

The American Nurses Association (ANA) developed the following standards of clinical nursing practice to provide guidelines for determining quality nursing care. These standards may be used by courts, hospitals, nurses, and patients. The standards of clinical nursing practice are divided into the "standards of care," which identify the care that is provided to recipients of nursing services, and the "standards of professional performance," which explain the level of behavior expected in professional role activities. Each standard is followed by measurement criteria that give key indicators of competent practice for that standard.

Standards of Care

Standard I: Assessment
The nurse collects patient health data.
MEASUREMENT CRITERIA
1. Data collection involves the patient, partners, and health care providers when appropriate.
2. The priority of data collection activities is determined by the patient's immediate condition or needs.
3. Pertinent data are collected using appropriate assessment techniques and instruments.
4. Relevant data are documented in a retrievable form.
5. The data collection process is systematic and ongoing.

Standard II: Diagnosis
The nurse analyzes the assessment data in determining diagnosis.
MEASUREMENT CRITERIA
1. Diagnoses are derived from the assessment data.
2. Diagnoses are validated with the patient, partners, and health care providers, when possible.
3. Diagnoses are documented in a manner that facilitates the determination of expected outcomes and plan of care.

Standard III: Outcome Identification
The nurse identifies expected outcomes individual to the patient.
MEASUREMENT CRITERIA
1. Outcomes are derived from the diagnoses.
2. Outcomes are mutually formulated with the patient and health care providers, when possible.
3. Outcomes are culturally appropriate and realistic in relation to the patient's present and potential capabilities.
4. Outcomes are attainable in relation to resources available to the patient.
5. Outcomes include a time estimate for attainment.
6. Outcomes provide direction for continuity of care.
7. Outcomes are documented as measurable goals.

Standard IV: Planning
The nurse develops a plan of care that prescribes interventions to attain expected outcomes.
MEASUREMENT CRITERIA
1. The plan is individualized to the patient's condition or needs.
2. The plan is developed with the patient, partners, and health care providers.
3. The plan reflects current nursing practice.
4. The plan provides for continuity of care.
5. Priorities for care are established.
6. The plan is documented.

Standard V: Implementation
The nurse implements the interventions identified in the plan of care.
MEASUREMENT CRITERIA
1. Interventions are consistent with the established plan of care.
2. Interventions are implemented in a safe, timely, and appropriate manner.
3. Interventions are documented.

Standard VI: Evaluation
The nurse evaluates the patient's progress toward attainment of outcomes.

ANA's standards of clinical nursing practice *(continued)*

MEASUREMENT CRITERIA
1. Evaluation is systematic, ongoing, and criteria-based.
2. The patient, partners, and health care providers are involved in the evaluation process when appropriate.
3. Ongoing assessment data are used to revise diagnoses, outcomes, and the plan of care as needed.
4. Revisions in diagnoses, outcomes, and the plan of care are documented.
5. The effectiveness of interventions is evaluated in relation to the outcomes.
6. The patient's responses to interventions are documented.

Standards of Professional Performance

Standard I: Quality of Care
The nurse systematically evaluates the quality and effectiveness of nursing practice.
MEASUREMENT CRITERIA
1. The nurse participates in quality of care activities as appropriate to the nurse's education and position. Such activities may include:
● identifying aspects of care important for quality monitoring
● identifying indicators used to monitor quality and effectiveness of nursing care
● collecting data to monitor quality and effectiveness of nursing care
● analyzing quality data to identify opportunities for improving care
● formulating recommendations to improve nursing practice or patient outcomes
● implementing activities to enhance the quality of nursing practice
● participating on interdisciplinary teams that evaluate clinical practice or health services
● developing policies, procedures, and practice guidelines to improve quality of care.
2. The nurse uses the results of quality of care activities to initiate changes in practice.
3. The nurse uses the results of quality of care activities to initiate changes through-

out the health care delivery system as appropriate.

Standard II: Performance Appraisal
The nurse evaluates her own nursing practice in relation to professional practice standards and relevant statutes and regulations.
MEASUREMENT CRITERIA
1. The nurse engages in performance appraisal on a regular basis, identifying areas of strength as well as areas where professional development would be beneficial.
2. The nurse seeks constructive feedback regarding her own practice.
3. The nurse takes action to achieve goals identified during performance appraisal.
4. The nurse participates in peer review as appropriate.
5. The nurse's practice reflects knowledge of current professional practice standards, laws, and regulations.

Standard III: Education
The nurse acquires and maintains current knowledge and competency in nursing practice.
MEASUREMENT CRITERIA
1. The nurse participates in ongoing educational activities related to clinical knowledge and professional issues.
2. The nurse seeks experiences that reflect current clinical practice in order to maintain current clinical skills and competency.
3. The nurse seeks knowledge and skills appropriate to the practice setting.

Standard IV: Collegiality
The nurse interacts with, and contributes to the professional development of, peers, health care providers, and others as colleagues.
MEASUREMENT CRITERIA
1. The nurse shares knowledge and skills with colleagues and others.
2. The nurse provides peers with constructive feedback regarding their practice.
3. The nurse interacts with colleagues to enhance her own professional practice.

(continued)

ANA's standards of clinical nursing practice *(continued)*

4. The nurse contributes to an environment that is conducive to clinical education of nursing students and other health care students as appropriate.
5. The nurse contributes to a supportive and healthy work environment.

Standard V: Ethics
The nurse's decisions and actions on behalf of patients are determined in an ethical manner.
MEASUREMENT CRITERIA
1. The nurse's practice is guided by the Code for Nurses.
2. The nurse maintains patient confidentiality.
3. The nurse acts as a patient advocate and assists patients in developing skills so they can advocate for themselves.
4. The nurse delivers care in a nonjudgmental and nondiscriminatory manner that is sensitive to patient diversity.
5. The nurse delivers care in a manner that preserves and protects patient autonomy, dignity, and rights.
6. The nurse seeks available resources to help formulate ethical decisions.

Standard VI: Collaboration
The nurse collaborates with the patient, partners, and health care providers in providing patient care.
MEASUREMENT CRITERIA
1. The nurse communicates with the patient, partners, and health care providers regarding patient care and nursing's role in the provision of care.
2. The nurse collaborates with the patient, family, and health care providers in the formulation of overall goals and the plan of care, and in decisions related to care and the delivery of services.
3. The nurse consults with health care providers for patient care as needed.
4. The nurse makes referrals, including provisions for continuity of care as needed.

Standard VII: Research
The nurse uses research findings in her practice.
MEASUREMENT CRITERIA
1. The nurse uses interventions substantiated by research as appropriate to the individual's position, education, and practice.
2. The nurse participates in research activities as appropriate to her position and education. Such activities may include:
● identifying clinical problems suitable for nursing research
● participating in data collection
● participating in a unit, organization, or community research committee or program
● sharing research findings with others
● conducting research
● critiquing research for application to practice
● using research findings in the development of policies, procedures, and guidelines for patient care.

Standard VIII: Resource Utilization
The nurse considers factors related to safety, effectiveness, and cost in planning and delivering patient care.
MEASUREMENT CRITERIA
The nurse evaluates factors related to safety, effectiveness, and cost when two or more practice options would result in the same expected patient outcome.

Reprinted with permission from American Nurses Association, *Standards of Clinical Nursing Practice 2nd edition*, © 1998 American Nurses Publishing, American Nurses Foundation/American Nurses Association, Washington, D.C.

LOCAL OR NATIONAL STANDARDS. The courts once used local standards — reflecting a community's accepted, common nursing practices — to judge the quality of a nurse's care. This practice has been eroded in recognition of national standards applied by accreditation agencies. NPs and other health care professionals are more often held to a national standard.

Legal significance of standards

Standards have important legal significance. The allegation that an NP failed to meet appropriate standards of care and that breach of these standards caused harm (proximate cause) to the patient is the basic premise of every health care professional's malpractice lawsuit.

During a malpractice trial, the court will measure the ***defendant***-NP's action against the answer it obtains to the following question: What would a ***reasonably prudent NP,*** with similar education and experience, do under these circumstances?

To answer this question, the ***plaintiff***-patient, through his attorney, has the burden to show that certain standards of care exist and that the defendant-NP failed to meet those standards in her treatment of the patient. The plaintiff-patient must also show the appropriateness of those standards, how the NP failed to meet them, and how that failure caused injury.

When the standard of care is at issue, the plaintiff-patient is usually required to present expert witness testimony to support his claims. The defendant-NP and her attorney will also produce expert witness testimony to support the claim that her actions didn't fall below accepted standards of care and that she acted in a reasonable and prudent manner.

The court may consider written standards when considering the standards of care involved in a NP's malpractice lawsuit. The court seeks information about the national standards applicable to the defendant-NP's actions. The court also may seek applicable information about the policies of the defendant-NP's employer.

Because of two trends — uniform NP educational requirements and standardized clinical practice treatment regimens — national standards are now the recognized standard in court cases. As a result, the ANA's standards have become more influential than local standards of other organizations. For example, in the case of *Planned Parenthood of Northwest Indiana v. Vines* (1980), an NP who inserted an intrauterine device was held to the minimum standard of care that was uniform throughout the U.S.

As the role of NPs expands across the U.S., so do standards of care. NPs who perform the same medical services as physicians are subject to the same standard of care and liability. *Pommier v. ABC Insurance Company,* 715 So.2d 1270, 1297 (La. App. 3d Cir. 1998).

HOW STANDARDS ARE APPLIED IN COURT. Few cases involving NP standards of care have settled; here's an example of a case involving an RN and standards of care. NP standards of care would be applied in a similar manner if the case involved an NP.

In a 1987 Louisiana case, *Story v. St. Mary Parish Service District*, a 66-year-old man was admitted to the hospital complaining of abdominal distention and pain, nausea, and vomiting. Throughout the next 2 days, he complained several times to the nurses and attendants about shortness of breath and severe pain in his elbows and chest.

One evening, the staff nurse (a new graduate who had only recently taken her nursing boards) wrote in her nurses' notes, "Complains of both elbows hurting severely, denied pain anywhere else. Slightly irritable and confused. Assisted back to bed. Admits to arthritis. Slight shortness of breath noted. Abdominal distention in moderation noted; soft to touch. Blood pressure 150/98; pulse 88. Will have medicated." She didn't indicate any consultation with the charge nurse. The patient died at 11:45 p.m. and the subsequent *autopsy* revealed a myocardial infarction.

Pretrial testimony revealed that the patient had stated that the nurses didn't listen to his reports of pain. In the pretrial memorandum, the plaintiff's attorney cited a variety of nursing practice standards, including:
● the Louisiana Nurse Practice Act, which describes the nurse's responsibility for performing patient assessment and intervening as appropriate
● a board of nursing rule stating that graduate nurses must have RN supervision when they provide care
● nursing care standards established by JCAHO.

Although this case was settled out of court, it provides a good example of how practice standards can be used extensively as evidence in a lawsuit.

Consider, too, the case of a nurse who was found negligent for not recognizing and reporting inconsistent intentions of the attending physician and the first-year resident. (As in the previous example, lacking a similar case involving NP negligence, an RN case is reviewed here to illustrate the point.)

In *St. Germain v. Pfeifer,* 637 N.E.2d 848 (Mass. 1994), a first-year orthopedic resident ordered a plaintiff, who underwent a midlumbar osteotomy, out of bed on the 2nd day postoperatively, whereas the attending orthopedic surgeon's postoperative plan was for the plaintiff to be confined to bed for 4 or 5 days following surgery. The charge nurse noted the resident's order without question and without considering the plaintiff's care plan of which she should have been aware. Therefore, she should have known and reported the inconsistent intentions of both physicians regarding the movement of the plaintiff. As a result, the

plaintiff got out of bed, and as he moved, he heard a loud snapping sound in the back of his neck and fell backward screaming in pain. The hooks and rods in his back snapped out of position and he was severely injured. The nurse's motion to *dismiss* the case against her was granted, but the grant was overturned because there was expert opinion that her acts fell below the standard of care.

As a nurse, you're accustomed to being part of an organized system of checks and balances. In advanced practice, it's vital to remember that there is often no other health care professional double-checking your orders on a day-to-day basis. Thus, it's important not only to perform the appropriate evaluation and give the appropriate information, but also to verify the patient's understanding and perform a timely follow-up evaluation.

Resolving possible violations

Your nursing license entitles you to practice as a professionally qualified NP. However, like most privileges, your nursing license imposes certain responsibilities. You're responsible for providing quality care to your patients. To meet this responsibility and to protect your right to practice, you need to understand the professional and legal significance of your license. Because a state board of nursing approves an NP's right to practice in a state, it can also suspend or revoke an NP's license.

DISCIPLINARY ACTION
The state board of nursing can take disciplinary action against an NP for any violation of the state's nurse practice act. In all states, an NP faces discipline if she endangers a patient's health, safety, or welfare. Depending on the severity of the violation, a state board

may formally reprimand the nurse (by suspending or revoking her license) or place her on probation. Other types of disciplinary action include imposing a probationary period, imposing a fine, and restricting her scope of practice. Some boards may require an NP to take courses in the legal aspects of nursing.

The list of punishable violations varies from state to state. The most common are:

● *incompetence* because of negligence or because of physical or psychological impairments

● habitual use of or addiction to drugs or alcohol

● unprofessional conduct, including (but not limited to) falsifying, inaccurately recording, or improperly altering patient records; negligently prescribing medications or treatments; performing beyond the limits of the state's nurse practice act; failing to take appropriate action to safeguard the patient from incompetent health care; violating the patient's *confidentiality;* violating the patient's dignity and human rights by basing care on prejudice; abandoning a patient; and abusing a patient verbally or physically.

ADMINISTRATIVE REVIEW PROCESS

When an NP is accused of professional misconduct, the state board of nursing usually investigates, then conducts an administrative review if warranted.

Usually, the board's actions are "complaint driven," meaning that the board investigates complaints about licensees rather than actively looking for infractions of the nurse practice act to prosecute.

As an administrative body, the state board of nursing wields broad *discretionary powers* and can issue a decision or ruling. As a result, court proceedings, and possibly legal penalties, may result from the board's adminis-

trative review findings. You have the right to appeal through the court system for reversal of the nursing board's decision. (See *Disciplinary proceedings for misconduct,* page 24.)

Steps in administrative review

In most states, the nurse practice act specifies the steps the board of nursing must follow during an administrative review. In some states, a general administrative procedure act (separate from the nurse practice act) specifies the steps; in still other states, the board of nursing determines protocol.

An administrative review begins when a person, a health care facility, or a professional organization files a signed *complaint* against an NP with the state board of nursing or when the board itself initiates such action.

The board reviews the complaint to decide if the NP's action appears to violate the state's nurse practice act. The NP receives a letter informing her that she's being investigated by the board and asking her to contact the board to arrange a meeting. At the meeting, an investigator shares the records or evidence of questionable care given by the NP. The NP has the opportunity to respond and explain the reasons for her actions and also has the right to be represented at the meeting by her attorney. The investigator then gathers additional information from other sources, such as colleagues, patients, administrators, and auditors. After he has obtained all pertinent information, the investigator recommends to the board either that the investigation be dropped or that it progress to a hearing.

If the board prepares for a formal hearing, it will *subpoena* witnesses. When these preparations begin, the accused nurse's *due process rights* include the right to receive timely notice of both the charge against her and the hearing date.

Disciplinary proceedings for misconduct

The flowchart below shows what happens when the state board of nursing takes disciplinary action against a nurse practitioner (NP) for violation of the state's nurse practice act.

Sworn complaint filed

A sworn complaint is brought before a state board by:
- a health care agency
- a professional organization
- an individual.

▼

If the board finds sufficient evidence, a formal review is conducted.

▼

State board of nursing review

The board:
- reviews the evidence
- calls witnesses
- determines if there is evidence of NP misconduct.

▼

If the board finds NP misconduct, it can take disciplinary action.

▼

Disciplinary action

The board can:
- issue a reprimand
- place the NP on probation
- refuse to renew her license
- suspend her license
- revoke her license.

▼

If the NP wants to challenge the board's decision or disciplinary action, she can file an appeal in court.

▼

Court review

At trial, the court will examine the board's decision and decide if the board acted appropriately. Depending on the jurisdiction, the case is filed in the lowest state court or in a special court that handles appeals from the state agencies.

▼

If the NP wants to challenge the court's ruling, she can appeal to a higher court. If the board wants to challenge the court's ruling, it, too, can appeal to a higher court.

▼

Appellate review

The NP or the board can appeal for a reversal of the lower court's ruling.

At the hearing, the NP has the due process rights:
- to have an attorney represent her
- to present evidence and ***cross-examine*** witnesses
- to appeal the board's decision to a court.

At the formal hearing, an impartial attorney may act as a hearing officer (in lieu of a judge), or the board itself may hear the case. A court reporter documents the entire proceeding, or it may be taped. Members of the board act as the plaintiffs bringing the claim against the defendant-NP. Witnesses — including coworkers — testify for the board and the NP.

It's imperative that every NP have a medical insurance liability policy to cover legal expenses.

JUDICIAL REVIEW PROCESS

In every state, NPs have the right to challenge the board's disciplinary decisions by the process of appeal through the courts. This basic right can't be revoked by any means; in many states, this right is spelled out in the nurse practice act.

Each state and court jurisdiction sets its own rules on how to file this type of appeal. In some jurisdictions, the NP, through her attorney, must appeal to a special court that handles only cases from state agencies. In other states, she must appeal to the lowest level court.

In an appeal, the court reviews the legality of the state board's original decision against the NP — not the NP's allegedly improper conduct. The court attempts only to determine if the board of nursing exceeded its legal powers or conducted the hearing improperly. It decides if the state board's decision is unlawful, arbitrary, or unreasonable according to law, or if it constitutes "abuse of discretion" (meaning the board didn't have enough evidence to determine unpro-

fessional conduct and made a decision without proper foundation). The court may also review the original evidence before deciding whether to sustain or reverse the board's decision.

The court may also allow a ***trial de novo,*** in which the court hears the board's complete case against the NP as though the administrative review had never happened. New evidence, if it exists, may be introduced by the plaintiff (the board) or by the defendant-NP, through her attorney. The court hears the case and then either sustains or reverses the board's original decision.

If the defendant-NP loses this appeal, she may — depending on the jurisdiction — appeal to a higher court. (If the NP wins, the board of nursing can also appeal to a higher court.) To begin a new appeal, the NP's attorney must file it with the lower court that ruled against the NP; this court will send the trial transcript and the appeal to the higher court. All states have rules and regulations governing appeals, and abiding by them is an attorney's legal responsibility.

The higher court decides whether to hear the appeal, based on its merits. The appeal usually must establish that the lower court made an error of law. The higher court won't hear the case a second time or reconsider facts, but the defendant-NP and her attorney may continue to appeal through all higher courts up to the state's highest court. Exceptional cases may reach the U.S. Supreme Court.

LICENSE REINSTATEMENT

License revocation, if sustained despite all appeal efforts, usually is permanent. Check to see whether your state's nurse practice act provides for revoked-license reinstatement.

If your license is suspended, you may petition for reinstatement. Every nurse practice act contains a provision allowing reinstatement of a suspended license, and some license suspension orders specify a date when the NP may apply. In most states, after a suspension has been in effect for more than a year, the board of nursing will consider a reinstatement.

Your first step would probably be to petition the board for reinstatement. Then the board would have to decide whether you're qualified to practice nursing again. In some states, you have the right to another hearing before the board makes this decision.

The board usually bases its decision on current evidence of the NP's fitness to practice. For example, in a drug violation case, the board may consider whether an NP has successfully completed a drug rehabilitation program.

Distinguishing NP practice from medical practice

How the practice of an NP and a physician relate to each other primarily depends on how each state's nurse practice act and medical practice act distinguish the differences between nursing and medicine. The relevant statutes commonly lack specific detail, however, and there is a great deal of overlap between nurse and medical practice acts, especially in defining the roles of NPs.

The NP's expanded role offers you exciting new challenges. Be aware, however, that not knowing exactly where your practice begins and ends can create legal risks. This is especially problematic for NPs who regularly perform functions that formerly were physicians' exclusive responsibilities.

Some states have solved the problem of overlap between the nursing and medical professions by passing laws making some functions common to both. New York's law, for example, allows both NPs and physicians to diagnose and treat patients, with the proviso that a ***nursing diagnosis*** shouldn't alter a patient's medical regimen. Almost all states permit you to perform patient care that a physician requests, as long as a written or oral order exists and the requested action is reasonable and safe.

The key to limiting liability and disciplinary action is to know your state's nurse practice act inside and out so that you fully recognize where nursing practice stops and where medical practice begins.

DEFINING MEDICAL PRACTICE

Medical practice acts may be divided into two types: those that define medical practice and those that don't. Both types forbid the practice of medicine by nonphysicians.

When a state's medical practice act includes a definition, it usually defines medicine as any act of diagnosis, prescription, surgery, or treatment. Not every definition includes all four elements, and some states' definitions add other elements.

Some state medical practice acts also limit physicians' rights to delegate tasks. For example, Texas's medical practice act permits physicians to delegate tasks only to "any qualified and properly trained person or persons," only if doing so is "reasonable and prudent," and then only if the delegating doesn't violate any other state laws. Most state courts would probably interpret their state medical practice acts similarly, even if this restriction isn't written into the acts. It's crucial to be aware of all statutory and administrative laws (including medical practice acts and pharmacists practice acts) that may affect your practice. The bottom line is that you're responsible for ensuring that you meet pertinent criteria as mandated by all statutory and administrative laws.

COURT CASES

In NP practice, the courts are regularly called on to decide if a specific action constitutes medical practice.

Consider the following examples of overlapping medical practices and expanded nursing roles. In *Fein v. Permanente Medical Group* (1985), the court recognized the overlapping functions between physicians and NPs, and considered whether the standard of care for an NP is the same as for a physician or a surgeon. After a series of appeals, the court finally said that the standard of care for an NP is that of a reasonably prudent NP in conducting an examination and prescribing treatment, and that a NP's conduct isn't to be measured against a physician's standard of care. Rather, the NP must meet the standards for NPs as established by the board of registered nursing.

Berdyck v. Shinde (1993) similarly held that NPs must employ that degree of care and skill that an NP using ordinary care, skill, and diligence would employ in like circumstances. This case addressed overlaps in clinical practice between physicians and NPs. The court said that although nurses are prohibited from practicing medicine, the fact that a particular act is within the duty of care owed to a patient by an attending physician doesn't necessarily exclude it from the duty of care owed to the patient by an APN.

In *Louisiana State Medical Society v. The Louisiana State Board of Nursing* (1986), the medical society tried, without success, to stop the practice of NPs, declaring that NPs were **practicing medicine without a license.** A number of cases discuss "the healing arts" and whether NPs fall within the definition of a practitioner of "healing arts". In an Oregon case, *Cook dba Gresham Health Center NP Clinic v. Workers' Compensation Board* (1988), an NP argued successfully that NPs were eligible to act as "attending physicians," defined under Workers' Compensation Law as a "physician or physician duly licensed" to practice one or more of the "healing arts" in the state.

In a recent Kansas case, *The State Board of Nursing and State of Kansas ex rel. State Board of Healing Arts v. E. Michelle Ruebke* (1996), the state boards of nursing and medicine were united in trying to stop a **lay-midwife** from offering prenatal, labor, and delivery services to pregnant women in Kansas. The boards alleged that the lay-midwife was improperly functioning as either a professional nurse or a practitioner of the healing arts. The trial court held for the midwife saying that the provisions of both the medical and the nurse practice act were unconstitutionally vague, and that the midwife's practice fell within exceptions to both acts even if the acts applied and were constitutional.

On appeal, the court upheld the constitutionality of the medical and nurse practice acts, yet still found for the midwife, ruling that assistance with the normal processes of birth isn't the exclusive domain of either nurses or physicians.

Issues currently facing legislative or judicial review

Prescriptive authority and scope of practice remain at the forefront as legislative issues. However, other issues are also receiving attention, such as independent reimbursement and vicarious liability.

INDEPENDENT REIMBURSEMENT

Approximately 38 million Americans receive health insurance through Medicare. Medicare guarantees insurance to individuals over age 65, to individuals with kidney disease, and to individuals with disabilities. Medicare Part A covers hospitalization, skilled nursing facilities, hospice, and home health care and is paid for by federal payroll tax. Medicare Part B covers physician and other provider services and is paid for by voluntary supplemental insurance through Medicare beneficiary premiums. Services provided by nurses in hospitals are covered by Medicare Part A. Physicians bill Medicare Part B for services provided in all settings, including hospitals.

Since the 1960s, efforts to obtain direct Medicare reimbursement for NPs have led to incremental changes in Medicare law. Legislation in the Balanced Budget Act of 1997 (BBA) now provides direct reimbursement for NPs regardless of geographic setting at 85% of the prevailing physician rate. As of January 1998, NPs can bill Medicare directly for services provided under Medicare Part B as long as their services aren't already covered by Medicare Part A payment to hospitals.

Prior to the new legislation, NPs could only bill for Medicare Part B services in rural areas, skilled nursing facilities, or when services were provided "incident to" physician services. "Incident to" reimbursement was paid at 100% of the prevailing physician rate, but created barriers to practice and impinged on nursing autonomy because it required that the physician be present in the office or suite in which the service was provided. Such a restriction implied the need for direct supervision of the NP even though state practice regulations may not have required such a provision.

Although the new legislation pays 15% less per service, it has the advantage of increasing access to community-based care for Medicare beneficiaries. It also enhances NPs' ability to bill for outpatient services when the collaborating physician is off-site. The new legislation also brings payment for NP services into mainstream payment systems, which provides greater NP visibility.

If you're billing for Medicare Part B services it's important that you aren't already receiving payment from Medicare Part A. Medicare Part A covers nursing services in hospitals and some outpatient settings. If your salary comes from Medicare Part A, then you're precluded from also billing Medicare Part B. Understanding these billing issues is crucial to avoid legal and financial penalties under federal law.

As a means of preventing double billing, you're now required to submit your own billing number for all services furnished in facilities or other provider settings. This requirement doesn't apply when you're performing facility services and your costs are included in the intermediary payment to the facility.

So, if you must bill Medicare Part B, obtain a Unique Provider Identification Number (UPIN). UPIN numbers are currently available and are now necessary to bill Medicare, even in cases where the NP is an employee and the employer had previously billed for their services using the employer's UPIN number with a modifier. Modifiers are now only applicable when submitting "assistant to surgery" claims.

In April 1998, the U.S. HCFA issued a Program Memorandum for carriers implementing the direct Medicare reimbursement provisions of the BBA. The Memorandum was issued to clarify a number of ambiguous issues in the new law and attempts to ensure that carriers resolve reimbursement issues in a uniform manner. Despite the release of the Memorandum, many issues of importance remain unresolved. The issuance of the document, however, enables carriers to process claims in a more orderly and efficient manner and will increase your familiarity with the new law and billing procedures.

In 1989, the federal government established direct Medicaid payment for pediatric and family NPs to increase access to health care services for children. As a federally mandated program, states have discretion in how Medicaid funds are allocated. As a result, some states interpret language regarding NP payment broadly and provide direct Medicaid payment to all NPs in their state. Because there is so much disparity in how various regions disseminate Medicaid funds, you need to research variations in Medicaid structures in your area.

VICARIOUS LIABILITY

Because you'll be providing health-care services in conjunction with other co-providers, you should be aware of the legal accountability of co-providers involved with your practice. In the past, collaborating and supervising physicians have, at times, been held legally responsible for the NP's actions.

Vicarious liability arises when liability for another person's actions is imposed due to the existence of a certain relationship. It's important to emphasize that an NP is always directly responsible for her own actions. Whether additional liability is imposed because of an NP's negligence depends on the legal relationships between the NP and the co-provider.

A common example of vicarious liability is the employer-employee relationship. The doctrine of **respondeat superior** governs the application of vicarious liability. The employer is liable when an employee causes harm to an individual in the course and scope of the employee's employment. Thus, a medical group, a hospital, or an individual physician may be held liable for any negligent acts committed by the NP. Under *respondeat superior,* the employer is held vicariously liable for the

employee's negligent acts. The employer is liable even though the employer had no contact with the patient and had evaluated the employee's credentials satisfactorily.

The employer can avoid liability if the NP's actions were beyond her scope of employment or were in violation of the employee's responsibilities as established by the employer's policies and procedures.

Vicarious liability may also be applied in the absence of an employer-employee relationship. Under the doctrine of apparent agency, if a patient reasonably believes, as a result of the NP's actions or representations, that the NP is an agent or employee of another, the employer may be held vicariously liable for the NP's negligent acts.

For vicarious liability to apply in a supervisory relationship, the supervisor should have direct and absolute control of another's actions. Physicians who supervise an NP may fear being held liable for the NP's actions. Most often, however, the physician isn't supervising the NP. Instead, the physician is a consultant to the NP or is functioning in a collaborative role and doesn't control the NP's actions. A vicarious liability claim wouldn't apply unless the physician had direct control over the NP's actions.

Selected references

American Academy of Nurse Practitioners. Position statement: Scope of Practice, 1998.

American Academy of Nurse Practitioners. Position statement: Standards of Practice, 1998.

American Health Information Management Association: *www.ahima.org*

American Hospital Association: *www.aha.org*

Brown, S.J. "A Framework for Advanced Practice Nursing," *Journal of Professional Nursing* 14(3):157-64, May-June 1998.

Goolsby, M.J. "Understanding Nurse Practitioner Preparation," *Journal of the Ameri-*

can *Academy of Nurse Practitioners* 12(2):43-8, February 2000.

Hickey, J.V., et al. *Advanced Practice Nursing: Changing Roles and Clinical Applications,* 2nd ed. Philadelphia: Lippincott Williams & Wilkins, 2000.

Lewis, C.K., and Carson, W.Y. "Nurse Practitioner Certification: Benefits and Drawbacks," *Advanced Practice Nursing Quarterly* 4(3):72-77, Winter 1998.

Office of the Law Revision Counsel: *uscode.house.gov*

Peters, S. "Nurse Practitioner Education in the New Century," *Advance for Nurse Practitioners* 8(3):47-48, March 2000.

Pryor, C. "Balanced Budget Act Enhances Value of Physician Assistants, Nurse Practitioners," *Health Care Strategic Management* 17(8):12-13, August 1999.

U.S. Department of Health and Human Services, Office of the Inspector General: *www.dhhs.gov/progorg/oig*

Washburn University School of Law: *www.washlaw.edu/uslaw/statelaw.html*

Washington State Register: *slc.leg.wa.gov/wsr*

Chapter Two

LEGAL RISKS AND RESPONSIBILITIES ON THE JOB

THE U.S. HEALTH CARE SYSTEM is currently undergoing a restructuring process that is establishing professional autonomy for **nurse practitioners (NPs)**. **Advanced practice nurses (APNs)** may work independently, in a collaborative relationship with a physician; in a private practice, in an employee relationship with a facility; or dependently under the orders of a physician. The legal risks and responsibilities of the NP on the job primarily depend on the **nurse practice act** of the state where she works.

As an NP, you may face complex legal dilemmas in your daily practice. As the nursing profession grows and you take on greater responsibilities, you'll inevitably face increased legal vulnerability. Almost no aspect of NP practice is untouched by legal risk.

Reading this chapter will enable you to identify the legal responsibilities and risks of your profession. You'll find information on the legal consequences of violating your health care facility's policies and suggestions to help you cope with conflicts that may arise with a collaborating physician. You'll read about your responsibilities for prescribing medication and maintaining patient safety as well as such issues as risk management and reimbursement. You'll also learn about your responsibility under the law when you encounter victims of **child abuse**, are forced to make a decision on whether to use restraints on a psychologically disturbed patient, or are asked by police to turn over a patient's belongings or blood samples for evidence. Throughout the chapter, you'll discover the special legal risks incurred when working in an emergency department (ED), in an acute care facility, and in independent practice.

Basic standards

As an NP, you're legally accountable for your nursing actions. In any practice setting, your care must meet baseline legal **standards.** Your care should also:
● reflect the scope of your state's nurse practice act
● meet established practice standards
● consistently protect your patient.

Upholding these standards should be the basis for sound legal practice no matter where you practice as an NP.

Practicing medicine

On the job, NPs have the responsibility to define and clarify their role with physicians and other members of the health care team. For instance, in the state of Washington, the law states that a person is practicing medicine if he:
● offers or undertakes to diagnose, cure, advise, or prescribe for any human disease, ailment, injury, infirmity, deformity, pain, or other condition, physical or mental, real or imaginary by any means or instrumentality
● administers or prescribes drugs or medicinal preparations to be used by any other persons
● severs or penetrates the tissue of human beings.

This definition of practicing medicine describes the usual employment responsibilities of an NP. Therefore, collaborating providers must clarify their distinctive and overlapping roles through the use of written practice agreements, which describe the responsibilities of the NP working together with the physician and other health care team members. Agreements provide legal protection regarding scope of practice issues and establish an interdisciplinary practice consensus. A major legal issue is the permissible **scope of practice** for NPs in both independent and employee-employer job situations.

Law and legislation

Congressional and state legislators are supporting legislation that, if passed, will give NPs the right to fully utilize their knowledge and skills. Judicial decisions are also holding that NPs have a right to practice within the limits of their education and expertise. Along with the benefits of increased autonomy for NPs, the NP on the job must also assume the legal liability that comes with this independent practice.

The courts have held that individuals who represent themselves to an employer or to patients in an independent practice as an APN (in this case as an NP) will be responsible and held to an expanded standard of care. **Standards of care** set minimum criteria for your proficiency on the job, enabling you and others to judge the quality of care you and your colleagues provide. They're guidelines, not laws, based on the care that a reasonable and prudent NP would provide in particular circumstances. Every NP's actions are measured against these standards of care. The NP on the job must also fully understand the scope of her practice so she can recognize when standards aren't met or are exceeded. For example, conducting physician-delegated responsibilities or failing to refer to a physician when appropriate is a legal risk because the NP is violating her scope of practice.

Prescriptive authority

To prescribe medication, NPs must be granted prescriptive authority through their state legislature. The scope of prescriptive authority for NPs differs from state to state. Every NP must understand the scope and limitations of prescriptive authority granted by her state medical, pharmacy, or nurse practice acts as well as the rules and regulations that further define these acts.

The political climate which favors health care reform also encourages competition among health care team members. When NPs first began to gain prescriptive authority, many other health care providers wanted the same privilege. For example, pharmacists argued that they're better qualified for prescriptive authority than NPs, due to their extensive educational preparation in pharmaceuticals and their accessibility to patients in rural

Understanding controlled substance schedules

Controlled substances are depressants, stimulants, narcotics, and hallucinogenic drugs covered by the Controlled Substances Act of 1970. There are five controlled substance schedules:

● Schedule I (C-I): High abuse potential and no accepted medical use — for example, heroin, marijuana, and LSD.

● Schedule II (C-II): High abuse potential with severe dependence liability — for example, narcotics, amphetamines, dronabinol, and some barbiturates.

● Schedule III (C-III): Less abuse potential than schedule II drugs and moderate dependence liability — for example, nonbarbiturate sedatives, nonamphetamine stimulants, anabolic steroids, and limited amounts of certain narcotics.

● Schedule IV (C-IV): Less abuse potential than schedule III drugs and limited dependence liability — for example, some sedatives, antianxiety agents, and nonnarcotic analgesics.

● Schedule V (C-V): Limited abuse potential. Primarily small amounts of narcotics, such as codeine, used as antitussives or antidiarrheals. Under federal law, limited quantities of certain C-V drugs may be purchased without a prescription directly from a pharmacist if allowed under specific state statutes. The purchaser must be at least age 18 and must furnish suitable identification. The dispensing pharmacist must record all such transactions.

areas. They also claimed that they're highly qualified for counseling patients regarding medications.

Most prescriptive authority acts require that a physician cooperate with an NP through a collaborative or supervisory agreement in order for the NP to prescribe medications. Some NPs like the idea that physicians are working in partnership with them because they feel this will help them to avoid or minimize errors. Regardless of the existence of a collaborative agreement, prescriptive authority increases accountability and may increase lawsuits and liability insurance rates if the NP fails to follow protocols and safe practice standards.

The laws that allow you to prescribe and dispense medications also specifically identify which schedules you're authorized to prescribe. Therefore, you must understand the prescriptive authority laws within the state where you practice. (See *Understanding controlled substance schedules*.) In recent years,

attempts have been made to have the federal government pass laws that govern prescriptive authority throughout the country. It's unlikely that this will occur in the near future. States' rights for licensing and regulating professionals are still retained as an honored tradition.

DRUG-CONTROL LAWS

A drug may be described as a substance that affects the structure or function of the body and is commonly used to diagnosis, cure, treat, or prevent disease. Legally, a drug is any substance listed in an official state, jurisdictional, or national formulary.

A *prescription drug* is any drug restricted from regular commercial purchase and sale. For these drugs, a state, jurisdictional, or national government has determined they are, or might be, unsafe unless used under a qualified medical practitioner's supervision.

Federal laws

Two important federal laws governing the use of drugs in the United States are the Comprehensive Drug Abuse Prevention and Control Act, and the Food, Drug, and Cosmetic Act. The Comprehensive Drug Abuse Prevention and Control Act (incorporating the Controlled Substances Act) seeks to categorize drugs by how dangerous they are and regulates drugs thought to be most subject to abuse. The Food, Drug, and Cosmetic Act restricts interstate shipment of drugs not approved for human use and outlines the process for testing and approving new drugs.

State laws

At the state and jurisdictional level, pharmacy practice acts that mirror federal laws are the main laws affecting the distribution of drugs. Criminal penalties can attach under state or jurisdictional law for various violations. These laws give pharmacists the sole legal authority to prepare, compound, preserve, and dispense drugs. *Dispense* refers to taking a drug from the pharmacy supply and giving or selling it to another person. This is different from administering drugs — actually getting the drug into the patient. Your nurse practice act is the law that most directly affects how you prescribe drugs and also identifies which schedules of drugs you may prescribe.

Most nursing, medical, and pharmacy practice acts include a definition of the tasks that belong uniquely to the profession and a statement that anyone who performs such tasks without being a licensed or registered member of the defined profession is breaking the law. In some states and jurisdictions, certain tasks overlap.

If, for example, the NP goes into the pharmacy or drug supply cabinet and measures out doses of a drug, or prepares a drug, such as putting powder into capsules, she's ***practicing pharmacy without a license.*** For this ac-

tion, she can be prosecuted or lose her license, even if no harm results. In most states, to practice a licensed profession without a license is, at the very least, a ***misdemeanor.***

Policies

Under special circumstances, such as in emergency situations, some hospitals and extended care facilities have written policies that permit a nurse without prescriptive authority to go into the pharmacy and dispense an emergency drug dose. Frequently, physicians in the ED write emergency orders for one to three doses — just enough to hold the patient until the prescription can be filled by a pharmacist. If there is no pharmacist on duty, facility policy may allow the nurse without prescriptive authority to obtain the required drug, bottle it, and label it.

Regardless of whether your employer has such a policy, if you're dispensing drugs, you're doing so unlawfully unless your state's pharmacy practice act specifically authorizes these actions. If an error in dispensing the drug is made and the patient later sues, the fact that you were practicing as an unlicensed pharmacist can be used as evidence against you. If your facility or agency policy requires you to dispense emergency medications, and it's in clear violation of your state's nurse practice act, consider taking steps to have your facility or agency policy changed so it meets the requirements of state law. Start by approaching your employer with a copy of the nurse practice act and relevant policies. Point out the inconsistencies and the professional risk you're taking. Offer to accompany your supervisor when she approaches the administrators or the policy and procedure committee. In this scenario, administrators may designate an ED pharmacist, hire additional pharmacy staff, or prevail upon pharmacists on staff to take greater responsibility for the distribution of ED medications.

Although many of the prescriptive authority provisions suggest that NPs may dispense certain medications, the *American Nurses Association (ANA),* in suggesting legislation on prescriptive authority, has urged NPs to take great caution in the area of dispensing. The legislation suggested by the ANA recommends that NPs have limited dispensing authority of no more than the dose of medication necessary until a patient can obtain a full prescription from a pharmacist.

GUIDELINES FOR PRESCRIBING

The requirements for granting prescriptive authority lie within the power of the state legislature. NPs are granted the right to prescribe drugs through their state laws. The rules and regulations that define the scope of the prescriptive practice allowed by NPs are usually defined in the rules and regulations promulgated by state boards of nursing in most states. In some states, however, the medical board oversees the rules and regulations related to NP's prescriptive authority. Commonly, medical and nursing boards work in combination to develop regulations that authorize certified registered NPs to prescribe and sometimes dispense drugs. (See *Prescriptive authority state by state,* page 36.)

REQUIREMENTS FOR PRESCRIPTIVE AUTHORITY

The prescriptive authority laws as well as the rules and regulations that authorize NPs to prescribe medications require successful completion of a formal course in pharmacology before an NP can prescribe medications. State boards of nursing in collaboration with the educators of NPs set minimum standards for course hours required and supervised education the NP must receive before being granted prescriptive authority. Most state rules and reg-

ulations also specify that continuing education in pharmacology be required of all NPs licensed to prescribe and dispense medications.

LEGAL RISKS WHEN PRESCRIBING

Prescribing drugs to patients continues to be one of the most important and one of the most legally risky tasks an NP performs. Legally and ethically, the NP has a responsibility to the patient to prescribe with caution and precision. The NP must always remember that medications are powerful chemicals and, as such, when an NP exercises prescriptive authority, she has the responsibility to determine the correct diagnosis of a patient as well as to select the medication that is best for the patient. Lawsuits related to medication errors prescribed by physicians are numerous. NPs can expect to share in this liability as prescriptive authority has offered both the benefits and the burdens of autonomous practice. (See *Prescribing peril,* page 37.)

DECREASING LEGAL RISKS

An NP can take some steps to help decrease legal risks related to prescriptive authority.

Use medication samples wisely

Pharmaceutical suppliers will often provide samples of medications for you to give to your patients. Only when the drug is the "drug of choice" should these samples be used in place of a prescription. Patients may be grateful for the free medications but it isn't worth the risk of giving an inappropriate or ineffective drug to maintain good patient relations. Your professional judgment of which medications are indicated to obtain the best results for your patient should override your decision to choose free medications.

Prescriptive authority state by state*

This table provides a state-by-state analysis of the degree of independence for the prescriptive authority aspect of NP scope of practice.

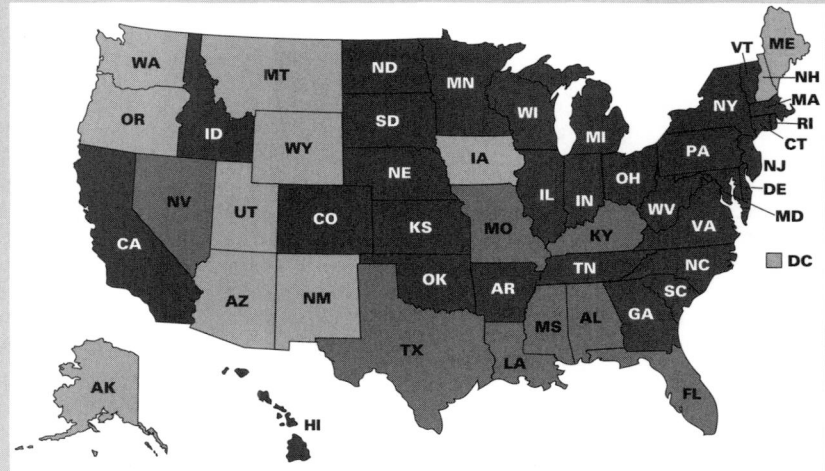

□ States where nurse practitioners† (NPs) can prescribe (including controlled substances) independent of any required physician involvement in prescriptive authority: **AK, AZ, DC, IA, ME, MT, NH, NM, OR, UT‡, WA, WY**

■ States where NPs† can prescribe (including controlled substances) with some degree of physician involvement or delegation of prescription writing: **AR, CA, CO, CT, DE, GA§, HI, ID, IL, IN, KS, MA, MD, MI, MN, NC, ND, NE, NJ, NY, OH, OK, PA, RI, SC‡, SD, TN, VA, VT, WI, WV**

■ States where NPs† can prescribe (excluding controlled substances) with some degree of physician involvement or delegation of prescription writing: **AL, FL, KY, LA, MO, MS, NV, TX**

□ States where NPs† have no statutory or regulatory prescribing authority: (None)

[Washington, D.C. is included as a state in this table.]

* In ALL states, NPs† have the authority to receive and/or dispense drug samples according to the authorized scope of practice, statute, or rules and regulations.
† The information may apply to other advanced practice nurses (clinical nurse specialists, nurse midwives, and nurse anesthetists).
‡ Schedule IV and/or V controlled substances only.
§ State doesn't have written prescribing or dispensing authority; falls under delegated medical authority.

Adapted with permission from *The Nurse Practitioner* 26(1):13, January 2001.

COURT CASE

Prescribing peril

Although the case described involves a physician, and the court failed to establish its case, it aptly illustrates the disruption and problems that can ensue when rules and regulations aren't followed.

In a 1981 Alabama case, the United States sued a physician for violation of the Federal Food, Drug, and Cosmetic Act. 21 U.S.C.§ 301(k). The issue was whether the physician followed the "adequate directions for use" as required by the Act. The physician had a clinic specializing in the treatment of chronic degenerative diseases. A central part of the physician's approach to treatment was his use of "chemo-endarterectomy therapy" for relief of poor circulation caused by hardening of the arteries. Calcium EDTA, the medication that the physician prescribed for this therapy, bonds with heavy metals, allowing them to pass out of the body through the kidneys. However, the physician used this medication to remove calcium from the blood vessels and prescribed a dosage not approved by the Food and Drug Administration (FDA). The government claimed the drug was not FDA-approved for this purpose and sued the physician. In this case, the final outcome favored the physician. The court concluded that the government failed to establish its case against the physician, and the physician was allowed to continue prescribing the drug for an unapproved use and in an unapproved dose, as long as it wasn't contraindicated for the patient.

What the NP can learn

Nurse practitioners should only prescribe medications for conditions for which the medication was approved, using approved dosages. Medications prescribed for nonapproved application or in dosages that differ from the FDA-approved dosages could be grounds for a potential lawsuit. *United States v. Evers*, 643 F.2d 1043 (5th Cir. 1981).

Write legibly

Benjamin Franklin said it best, "An ounce of prevention is worth a pound of cure." Misunderstandings regarding the medication that is being ordered by the NP can be avoided by such preventive measures as writing the prescription legibly, including tablet and syrup strength, using generic names, and noting the purpose of the medication. The current focus on medication errors has brought attention to the commonalties between many drugs that have very different uses but can be dispensed in error due to a prescription communication error. It's important to clarify with your patient what you are prescribing and for what purposes in order to allow the patient to be actively involved in his own safety.

Know your patient

In order to ensure that medications are prescribed and dispensed appropriately, you must understand the medical history of the patient before making prescription decisions. Always ask the patient to bring a list of all medications, including over-the-counter and homeopathic herbal products, vitamins, and minerals they're taking. Inquire about the dosage, the times the patient is taking the dose, and any adverse effects, reactions, or allergies they experienced from previous medications. This information will help you avoid prescribing medications that will cause adverse drug reactions and those that may result in adverse interactions with other medications the patient is currently taking.

Make the correct diagnosis

To prevent legal problems when prescribing medications, the NP must learn as much about the disease or condition for which the medication is being prescribed. Collaborate with physicians and pharmacists to learn everything possible about the medications you're considering prescribing. Always repeat the instructions that you have given to a patient regarding the symptoms of adverse reactions. Resolve any misunderstandings about the medication's effects, possible adverse reactions and interactions, and allow the patient sufficient time to ask questions about the diagnosis and treatment. Encourage your patients to consistently use the same pharmacy for all of their medication needs to serve as a safeguard in preventing adverse drug interactions from medications your patients may have forgotten to tell you about.

Teach the patient

NPs can minimize personal liability by encouraging patients to serve as their own advocates when taking medications. Teach the patient the drug's purpose, dosage, and adverse reactions. Explain the need to carefully read the label and visually identify the drug. Review how long medication should be taken. By understanding their medications and the desired results, patients can identify and bring dispensing errors to their pharmacist's or NP's attention before taking medications that are incorrectly prescribed or dispensed.

PRESCRIPTIONS. Encourage patients to double-check the labels of medications they receive from the pharmacist to ensure that they're receiving the medication you have prescribed. Patients should always read the label carefully and check the medication before taking the first dose. If there is any difference in the appearance or shape of the medication between refills, encourage the patient to bring this to the attention of the pharmacist. Remind patients that many medications have similar names and look alike. Also, be sure to clarify when a medication must be taken until exhausted and when medication should only be taken until symptoms subside.

Good communication between you and your patient will also minimize liability. Encourage your patients to read the directions on the prescription labels; if any information seems to contradict what you've told them, have them call you immediately. Caution patients to always:
● keep medications in the original container
● store medications out of the reach of children
● check the expiration dates on all medications and throw away out-dated products
● reread the label before each dose and never take medications without glasses if needed for reading
● never take medications in the dark.

Many patients take several medications, so the risk of over-medication exists. Warn your patient to get medical attention immediately if he experiences itching, swelling, or difficulty breathing or swallowing. Also alert your patient about all adverse effects so he can communicate with you in a timely manner before problems become severe. In addition, remind your patient to take medications exactly as you've prescribed them. In some cases, medications can be stopped when symptoms improve; however, in other cases the total prescribed amount of medication must be completed for therapy to be effective. Discuss these issues in order to maximize the effectiveness and the helpfulness of the medication. For example, the complete dosage of an antibiotic must often be taken in order for the treatment to be effective. On the other hand, an antihistamine that is taken beyond the point when symptoms require usage may be harmful.

PAMPHLETS. Always include patient teaching, such as pamphlets or brochures, when prescribing or providing drugs. Send this information with the patient for future reference, and document that the pamphlet and patient instructions were given. Pamphlets can increase the patient's understanding of the medications they're taking and the patient will perceive this as a quality practice procedure.

MEDICATION LOG. To avoid common miscommunication errors related to the prescriptions you've prescribed, encourage your patients to keep a medication log (or medication diary). Request that they keep this record to discuss at future appointments. This type of log will also help patients who are taking several medications to clarify and verify that they're taking the appropriate medication in the correct dosages at the appropriate times. If the patient doesn't seem capable of communicating all of the information you need to know to evaluate if your prescribed drugs are having the intended outcome, encourage the patient to bring a family member with them who is familiar with the patient's daily medication practices.

Know all prescribers
Many patients are being encouraged to receive second opinions if diagnosed with a serious disorder. It isn't uncommon for patients to see several practitioners who may be prescribing medications without the knowledge that the patient is being treated by another practitioner. Keep communication open and encourage the patient to let you know if he's seeing another NP or physician who may also be prescribing medications for him. In order to provide safe care, you must be fully informed about all of the treatments and medications your patient is receiving.

Document precisely
The NP must thoroughly document all conversations with the patient about medication decisions. If there are "like" options and the patient specifies the drug he wishes to have prescribed, note the conversation in the patient's record. In order to obtain informed consent, the NP must also validate through discussion that the known risks and benefits (including adverse reactions) of the medication are understood by the patient. By having the patient repeat significant information, the NP can document the patient's understanding of the information provided. If an elderly patient or a child is being treated, involve a family member to ensure that the patient understands the necessary protocol. Again, documentation of the interaction with the patient and his family is always important. Documentation of informed consent can be done quickly. After the notation detailing the prescribed medication, write "ICG" (for "informed consent given") and circle it. Although not absolute proof, this documentation signifies you that were cognizant of the need to review the aspects of informed consent in relation to the prescribed medication and that you documented the patient's agreement to the treatment at that time.

NEGATIVE OUTCOMES. If an error is made in prescribing a drug or if your patient reacts negatively to a properly prescribed drug, immediately document the incident thoroughly. Include information on the patient's reaction and any interventions taken or instructions given to the patient.

In the event of error, you should also file an incident report. Identify what happened, the names and functions of all personnel involved, and what actions were taken to protect the patient after the error was discovered. (See *Filing an incident report: Chain of events.*)

DRUG EXPERIMENTATION

At times, you may participate in prescribing and administering medication pursuant to experimental protocols. Your legal duties don't change in this situation. If you have any questions, you'll get your answers from the experimental protocol, not your usual sources, such as books and package inserts. Also, an institutional review board (IRB) probably reviewed and accepted the protocol before it was instituted. The IRB is another resource for the NP to access, especially if ethical concerns regarding the treatment develop. You'll also need to make sure no drug is given to a patient who hasn't consented to participate. (If it's a federally funded experiment, consent should be in writing.)

Informed consent given

Any use of experimental drugs or involvement in experimental protocols requires written informed consent from the patient. However, implied consent can be obtained in most situations where the NP explains the options to the patient, including the substantial risks and benefits of the proposed treatments, and the patient indicates which of the options he prefers. The patient must have the capacity to consent, which usually includes being over age 18 and having the mental competence to understand the implications of the decision they're making.

Health care facilities

Every health care facility — whether it's a physician's office, a clinic, an acute care facility or long-term care facility, or your independent practice setting — has policies, a set of general principles by which it manages its affairs. As an NP, you're obligated to know those policies and follow the established procedures that flow from them.

Never do this blindly. As an NP, you're also obligated to maintain your professional standards, and these standards may sometimes conflict with your facility's policies and procedures. At times, you may be forced to make decisions and take actions that risk violating those policies and procedures. You must always do what is best for the patient. If it's unsafe to follow the policy, then don't; just make sure that you document the reasons you didn't.

At times like these, you need help balancing your duty to the patient with your responsibility to your employer and your professional standards. Your best help is a department policy manual that states relevant, clear guidelines based on up-to-date standards of care that are generally accepted by your profession.

FACILITY POLICIES

A policy manual that states relevant, clear guidelines based on up-to-date standards of care is the mark of a successful facility — one whose first concern is delivering high quality patient care. If policies need to be changed in order to meet the standard of care needed to protect the patient's rights, take the time to become involved on the committees that set policies. Bring needed changes to the attention of the

Filing an incident report: Chain of events

The flowchart below provides a comprehensive overview of incident report routing in most facilities.

Patient incident

▼

Record significant facts in patient's chart.

▼

Write incident report close to the time that the incident took place or is discovered.

▼

Give incident report to the office manager or supervisor. In the event there is none, maintain a separate file for incident reports.

▼

Office manager or supervisor forwards the report to the appropriate administrator within 24 hours.

▼

Administrator reviews the report.

▼

Administrator forwards pertinent information from the report to the appropriate department for follow-up action.

▼

Incident reports are collected and summarized to detect patterns and trends and highlight trouble spots.

▼

Administrator reviews patterns and trends, using this information in continuous quality improvement projects for a single nursing unit or a multidisciplinary committee.

▼ ▼

Refer information to existing quality improvement teams.

Use information as the basis for establishing new quality improvement projects.

administration and the board of directors as well as the committee that specifically has been designated to review policy and procedures. Policies and procedures should be reviewed and updated at least every 2 years to stay current with the changing health care environment. Always document the changes you've brought to the attention of the facility and follow through if needed changes aren't made immediately.

When your facility policies and your nurse practice act conflict, you must bring this to the attention of those who set policies for the facility. Your nurse practice act is the legal guideline that describes your scope of practice. Your facility shouldn't require you to perform any task that the nurse practice act in your jurisdiction doesn't allow — if a certain task is required by that facility, and performing it means you work outside the scope of your nursing license, you could be accused of practicing medicine.

You must be your own advocate as well as the advocate of the patient in bringing about change in policies that require you to practice outside of your NP license. Any time you provide care that falls short of current legal and NP standards, you become a target for a malpractice suit.

Whenever a question regarding policies and procedures arises, you do need to start the change process but the immediate action you take should be based on your first duty, which is to protect your patient. If your judgment says that your patient's condition warrants collaboration with a physician, don't hesitate to call, even in the middle of the night. Most NPs have protocols that define when consultation with a physician is required. For your own protection, carefully record all contacts with the physician, including the date, time, and the substance of the communication.

How facility policies affect your job

Facility administrators write policies to guide employees in daily operations. These policies stem from the philosophy and objectives that are part of the facility's planning process. They directly affect your role as an NP.

If you're considering employment at a facility, ask to see its policies. Study these policies carefully; if they're well defined, they may give you an indication of how satisfied and secure you can expect to be in your job. Also make sure that your NP specialty is clearly defined and in compliance with your jurisdictional nurse practice act and within the standards recommended by accrediting agencies and professional medical and nursing associations.

In addition to policies, the general principles that guide a facility's management can be found in the facility's *rules.* These rules describe the actions that employees should or shouldn't take in specific situations. "No smoking in the patient's room," for example, is a rule that should be enforced without exception. If NP and physician protocols are discussed, these rules must be followed when working for this agency.

If you feel reasonably comfortable with the facility's philosophy, objectives, policies, rules, and quality of care, you'll probably feel comfortable on the job. If, on the other hand, the facility's policies call for procedures that conflict with your personal nursing standards or *ethics,* then you should consider looking elsewhere for employment.

How laws affect facility policies

Many facility policies and procedures are mandated by state or jurisdictional licensing laws or by federal regulations as the conditions for participation in *Medicare.*

In the United States, for instance, the Patient's Self-Determination Act is a federal law that requires hospitals, nursing homes, home health care agencies, and *health maintenance organizations (HMOs)* that are Medicare providers to inform patients about their rights to execute living wills. The Freedom of Information Act requires facilities to give patients access to certain data previously considered privileged. In addition, the Department of Health and Human Services regulations require that facilities observe strict guidelines when using patients in research studies.

When facility policy and your nurse practice act conflict

You must refuse to follow facility policy when it conflicts with your nurse practice act. Any willful violation of rulings passed by the board of nursing, even with your agency's knowledge and encouragement, could result in suspension or revocation of your license. The case of *O'Neill v. Montefiore Hospital* (N.Y. 1960) illustrates the dilemma a nurse faced when she had to choose between hospital policy and her professional standards. Although this wasn't an APN, this same situation could likely occur with an NP in a hospital setting. In this case, the nurse, who followed the hospital policy, refused to admit a patient because he belonged to an insurance plan her hospital didn't accept. The man returned home and died. Although the trial court ruled in favor of the nurse, the New York Supreme Court reversed the decision and ruled the hospital nurse negligent for refusing to admit the patient.

How facility policies affect court decisions

Policies aren't *laws,* but courts use policy violations as evidence that a facility's standard of care wasn't met. In general, a court won't rule against an NP solely because she violated a policy unless the policy reflects a legal requirement. Courts have also held facilities *liable* for poorly formulated, or poorly implemented, policies. The NP's legal duties are described in nurse practice acts, licensing board regulations, state and federal laws, case law, and professional organization standards. Legally, if you're employed by a facility and you practice within the scope of your *job description* and are sued for malpractice, the facility may have to assume secondary responsibility. Whether you've acted properly is ordinarily determined in court by the standard of care reasonably expected in your community.

In addition, if you're practicing independently as an NP, these same sources will be used in evaluating the reasonableness of your practice. The standard of care is defined as care that a *reasonably prudent NP* would have provided under similar circumstances. Although the facility policies and procedures set the standard of care for the facility, these policies and procedures must be in compliance with the applicable sources of law. If a lawsuit develops, the policies and procedures of the facility will be examined for compliance with the standard of care expected of an NP. If the policy is within the law, then the NP will be held to the standard set forth by the facility policy.

Changing facility policy

If it becomes evident that your facility policy doesn't comply with your nurse practice act, make sure you protect yourself. Document your efforts to change facility policy. You can involve your health care team colleagues by discussing policy problems at committee meetings, conferences, and interdepartmental meetings. Many health care facilities require policy implementation to follow the chain of command.

Your supervisor or collaborating physician can give you direction on where to start on a particular issue. Alternatively, you can communicate directly with the administration through the **grievance procedure,** feedback questionnaires, or formal and informal management committees.

PROVIDER'S OBLIGATION TO TREAT

Like physicians, NPs enter into a non-written contract when they provide care to a patient; in general, NPs also aren't obligated to agree to treat every patient that presents to them. Under common law, a private health care facility is also under no duty to accept a given patient. This was true for all patients, even those requiring hospital treatment, until legal precedents began to change this view and Congress passed the Emergency Medical Treatment and Active Labor Act (EMTALA).

Legal precedents

The origins of the common law that allowed facilities to choose patients were based on the rights of businesses to make a profit. Forcing a private facility to accept every patient could force it to close. Unfortunately, when private health care facilities could choose the patients they wanted to treat based on non–health-related issues, such as ability to pay, some patients suffered debilitating effects, even death. This common law rule began to change with the Delaware Supreme Court ruling in the case of *Wilmington General Hospital v. Manlove* (1961). The court in this case held that if a seriously injured patient presents at the ED of a private facility for care and the denial of care would result in the worsening of the patient's condition because of the time lost in the attempt to obtain medical care at another facility, this refusal could easily be viewed as negligence. The court stated that the facility's of-

fering of an ED constituted an invitation to those in need of assistance. In *Stansbury v. Sipes* (1969), the court held that the inability to pay was an inappropriate reason to refuse care to a patient. Finally, in *Guerrero v. Copper Queen Hospital* (1976), a patient came to the ED with severe frostbite of his feet. The hospital refused to treat the patient because he was a nonresident alien. The patient's condition was worsened by the delay in receiving treatment. Based on evidence that this was the only hospital in the local area and the only center with emergency medical services, the Arizona Supreme Court ruled that nonresident aliens of the U.S. are among those who can obtain care in an ED.

EMTALA

In 1986, Congress amended the Social Security Act to prevent hospitals from turning away uninsured or indigent patients. Called patient antidumping legislation, these **amendments** require all hospitals that participate in Medicare and have an ED to provide appropriate medical screening and stabilizing treatment for anyone who presents with an emergency condition or any pregnant patient in labor. Amendments also set guidelines for transferring patients to other health care facilities and for discharging patients from the facility.

INTERFACILITY TRANSFER. EMTALA tries to ensure that the decision to transfer a patient to another facility is made in the best interests of the patient. This means that if the ED doesn't provide the services needed to best treat the patient's condition, a valid cause exists to transfer the patient. The decision should never be based on the patient's ability to pay. EMTALA also requires that the patient be stabilized before transfer. For example, even when maternity services aren't provided by a facility, a pregnant woman who enters the ED in the late stages of active labor must be stabilized before a transfer can take place. Documentation and certification that the patient is stable is necessary. If the transfer of a patient is necessary, it's important to choose the most appropriate means of transportation. If the patient is to be transferred a great distance or if time is of the essence, a medical helicopter may be the best means of transportation. EMTALA provides specific guidelines for transfers.

Facilities are required to adopt a written policy that reflects EMTALA's language and guidelines. The guidelines also require that each transfer from the ED be reviewed to determine compliance. Failure to comply with EMTALA's guidelines for transfers can lead to fines, loss of Medicare provider status, or both. This statute specifically authorizes civil suits for damages, access to federal courts, and a 2-year statute of limitations within which legal action can be taken.

THE NP'S ROLE IN TRANSFERRING PATIENTS. If, in your professional judgment, the patient has a condition requiring transfer, you must stabilize the patient's condition, then admit him, or appropriately transfer him to another facility.

Potential problems with medical screening or stabilization of the patient before transfer result when misdiagnosis of the seriousness of the patient's condition occurs. As appropriate, consult with the medical staff to certify that the patient's condition is stable before transferring him to another facility.

EMTALA AND MANAGED CARE ORGANIZATIONS. Organizations, such as HMOs, *managed care organizations (MCOs),* or *preferred provider organizations (PPOs),* may be impacted by EMTALA

when the decision to cover emergency care becomes a profit-motivated decision. Managed care programs have been charged with controlling costs by withholding appropriate diagnostic procedures and treatments, delaying or even denying necessary treatments altogether, or electing the least expensive approach, even when a more costly approach might save a patient undue suffering and death. Administrative risks and the liability associated with stabilizing patients before discharging or transferring may shift from the individual provider, who may be a physician or an NP, to the MCO and the individual provider if the EMTALA rules and regulations are ignored by the MCO. If you're employed by an MCO that has a written policy in contradiction to EMTALA, you and the MCO are at risk for legal action under EMTALA. Even if you consider yourself an independent contractor, you may, for legal purposes, be considered an employee of the MCO if the MCO has the right to control your time and the manner or method by which you execute your work as stated in your contract. Some court cases have found that even if the employer has control over an NP's time or salary — without control over the manner and method of the NP's practice — the employer may still be held liable for the NP's actions.

On-call practitioners
The NP who is on call in the ED may be impacted by the legal theories of agency and *vicarious liability.* The case of *Sloan v. Metropolitan Health Council* considered an HMO's liability. The appellate court found that the employment contract between the staff physicians and the HMO were evidence that the staff physicians were under the control of the HMO's medical director and therefore an employee-employer relationship existed. This relationship established vicari-

ous liability for the HMO due to the *malpractice* of the employee physicians. Other factors that courts include in their analysis of an employee-employer relationship are the skill of the worker, the method of payment, and the custom of the industry.

Independent contractors
Another legal theory under which a facility may be liable for an NP's negligence, when the NP is an *independent contractor,* is apparent or ostensible agency. If the facility represents to the public that the NP is its agent and the patient that justifiably relies on their representation is harmed, the facility may be liable for the independent practitioner's actions. Although the current cases discuss the negligence of a physician, the same legal theories can be applied to NPs. A 1989 case held an MCO vicariously liable for the negligence of a physician who was a consultant to one of the MCO's physicians. Even though he wasn't an employee of the MCO, the court found apparent agency based on the fact that the consulting physician didn't act on his own initiative nor independently of the MCO facility, but was making recommendations directly to the MCO physician. The court found that the MCO had the ability to control the consulting physician because he was performing services that fell within the scope of the MCO's regular business.

HOSPITAL PRIVILEGES
The right to prescribe medications and receive third-party reimbursement made it possible for NPs to practice independently. Independent practice made NPs aware of their need to have hospital admitting privileges, the right to care for patients after admission, and the right to function as hospitalists.

Obtaining hospital privileges
The ability to admit patients to hospitals and independently care for them was only recently considered a possibility for NPs. Such political factors as the support of medical associations, the growing percentage of consumers on state nursing and medical boards, and the presence of an NP committee on these boards have positively affected the granting of hospital privileges to NPs. Commonly, the hospital has different levels of privileges that are designated by title. Common titles used in hospitals to designate level of privileges include associate, affiliate, independent, full, active, or complimentary.

NPs who have any level of admitting privileges need backup consultants. Most commonly these consultants are physicians but they may be other NPs. Nurse practice acts often require NPs to get a written consultation agreement with a physician, but don't require the NP to work under the direct supervision of a physician. However, many NPs welcome a consulting agreement with a physician to whom they can refer the patient when they have exhausted their resources.

To obtain hospital privileges, the NP must undergo the credentialing process. Each hospital has its own policies and procedures for credentialing care providers.

THE PROCESS. The application process should be clearly outlined by the hospital's policies and procedures, including the qualifications for each category of applicant and the expense of applying.

Generally, the credentialing process involves gathering information about the practitioner who has applied for admitting and staff privileges. (See *Agency credentialing: What information is required.*) The information is first verified and then used to evaluate the applicant (in this case the NP) against the hospital's preestablished criteria. Based on how well the applicant's credentials meet the hospital's criteria, the decision is then made to grant or refuse the requested privileges. HMOs, PPOs, and *independent provider organizations* follow a similar credentialing process before granting health care provider status.

THE RATIONALE. The credentialing process exists to protect the safety of patients as well as to meet the credentialing organization's legal responsibility to insure that proper licensure requirements of their staff are met. Accrediting bodies such as the *Joint Commission on the Accreditation of Healthcare Organizations (JCAHO)* and the *National Committee for Quality Assurance (NCQA)* oversee the credentialing process by requiring that the credentialing process meet certain minimum standards. A hospital may limit the number of staff they desire and other credentialing agencies such as HMOs and PPOs may limit the number of health care providers.

If the NP has a past record of poor patient outcomes, privileges may be denied in order to avoid the hospital or organization being named as a responsible party in future incidents.

If privileges are denied, recourse is generally through an appeal process. Pursuant to the hospital's bylaws, it may have the duty to provide a "fair hearing" to an NP who hasn't yet established privileges on the hospital's medical staff or managed care panel.

THE APPLICATION. The applicant has the right to receive the credentialing criteria in written form before making her application. To fill out the application, you'll need proof of your state NP licensure, Drug Enforcement Agency (DEA) number, and professional liabili-

---

Agency credentialing: What information is required

A nurse practitioner's credentialing file usually consists of specific documentation as determined by the facility. It may include:

- evidence of graduation from an approved nursing school
- evidence of advanced education or a degree in a specialty
- evidence of specialized training or experience in procedures not included in her educational preparation
- experience
- references
- specialty certification
- licensure information
- Drug Enforcement Agency license number
- evidence of continuing education
- teaching appointments and references
- professional association memberships
- professional liability insurance information
- any liability history, judgements, settlements, or disciplinary actions.

---

ty insurance information. These are usually the baseline requirements in order to be sent an application. Other information commonly requested includes personal demographics; work history; education; board certification, if applicable; malpractice history; criminal record information; and professional liability status, including the amounts of coverage. Information regarding any suspensions, limitations, revocations, or denials of licensure certification (DEA certificate), *Medicaid* and Medicare status, and affiliations with managed care entities may also be requested.

The specific clinical privileges being requested may be asked for on the application. If privileges are granted, a temporary status may be required in order to allow the hospital to actually observe the skills of the practitioner through a proctoring process. The NP's sponsoring or collaborating physician may serve as the proctor in this situation.

THE LAW. The hospital's bylaws describing the credentialing process must incorporate the protections offered through the Health Care Quality Improvement Act of 1986, including attention to the need for due process, which are spelled out in Title 42, sections 111.01 to 111.15 of the U.S. Code Annotated. Passed in an effort to promote professional review activities, the act requires that the credentialing process be undertaken in furtherance of quality health care. Reasonable efforts are made to obtain and review all facts in order to provide due process to the practitioner applicant. Proponents of "any willing provider laws" seek to avoid exclusion of any practitioner based on discriminatory actions. After a class of providers has received privileges at a hospital or other agency, future applicants in the same provider group must receive a fair review. Hospitals do have the right to determine the number of certain specialists needed to accomplish the facility's mission. A written plan should identify these parameters of need. If a hospital has chosen not to use the services of certain categories of practitioners, applications for admitting and care privileges may not be available to this category of provider. Therefore, credentialing criteria must be objective and consistently applied by the hospital or MCO. Quality of care and economic goals should be consistent with state and federal requirements. The requirements of the accrediting or certifica-

tion body such as JCAHO or NCQA must also be met.

CASE LAW. Case law appropriate to the credentialing and privileging process includes the *Darling v. Charleston Community Memorial Hospital* case, which represents the hospital's obligation to oversee the quality of patient services provided by the practitioners they credential. The *McClellan v. Health Maintenance Organization of Pennsylvania* and *Harrell v. Total Health Care, Inc.*, (Pa. 1989) cases held that HMOs have a duty to select only competent primary care physicians. Although these cases dealt with credentialing of physicians, the same principles could be applied to the practice of NPs.

Hospitalists
Inpatient specialists, or hospitalists, generally assume complete responsibility for the hospital care of patients that are admitted by their primary care physicians. Following discharge, the responsibility of the patient care reverts back to the primary care provider. Many hospitalists are also known as general internists, internal medicine sub-specialists, and family physicians or pediatricians. NPs and ***physician assistants*** are also serving as hospitalists in growing numbers, and the demand for acute care NPs to serve in a hospitalist capacity is rising. Today, more than 3,000 hospitalists are practicing according to the National Association of In-Patient Physicians. In some regions of the U.S., the majority of in-hospital care is being provided by hospitalists. The number of hospitalists could reach 20,000 in the near future. The role of the hospitalist developed in an attempt to relieve the time demands of primary care practitioners and to allow them to attend to patients in their offices. The higher acuity of patients in the hospital also encouraged utilization of hospitalists. Use of

hospitalists enables primary care providers who don't have admitting privileges at a hospital to refer patients to a hospital that uses hospitalists. Some MCOs, such as Kaiser, recommend the use of hospitalists to reduce costs while maintaining a high quality of care for their patients. A major advantage of a hospitalist is that they're more likely to be available to coordinate all of the patient care needs in a more timely fashion.

More importantly, the hospitalist is very familiar with the hospital's policies and personnel. Studies have shown that utilization of hospitalists can decrease the length of stay of patients anywhere from 10% to 25%. For example, one hospital employs a team of hospitalists consisting of three NPs who collaborate with four physicians; the NPs admit and care for in-hospital patients. The physicians are able to return to their practices following morning rounds while the NPs handle the day-to-day hospital responsibilities, including discharging patients and admitting new patients sent to the hospital by the physicians. The NP hospitalist can order diagnostic tests and respond to onsite complications. They perform emergency procedures and collaborate with the physician team members. Surgeons and other specialists also utilize NP hospitalists to provide consultation including preoperative clearances, family interventions, postdischarge rehabilitation, hospice care, and grief counseling.

The role of hospitalist allows the NP to be effective even without hospital admitting privileges, but the NP still must be credentialed or employed by the hospital. If there is a collaborating physician who can admit the patient, the NP hospitalist can provide the direct care. However, a growing number of NPs are beginning to gain hospital admitting privileges. New York and Oregon promote that NPs have hospital privileges.

Quality care

Regardless of where you provide care for your patients, your main goals are to provide quality care that meets established standards and to make decisions based on the best options available for your patients. Quality care involves following the best proven practices to achieve the optimal outcome of care. Because your legal risks and responsibilities as an NP are increased by your advanced level of expertise, your liability increases if you perform below the standards of care as laid out in your state's nurse practice act. To reduce your risks, various review organizations including JCAHO and NCQA recommend that you follow clinical practice guidelines or protocols and participate in quality improvement programs. It's also important that you continuously update your knowledge and skills through continuing education to help you provide the highest quality care to your patients in your daily practice. (See *Organizations that ensure quality patient care,* page 50.)

CONTINUING EDUCATION
You have a legal duty to your patients not only to make a diagnosis but also to take the appropriate action to meet all existing health care needs. Doing so helps protect your patient from harm and you from malpractice charges. To do this, you must maintain current knowledge of latest practices and research. Read professional journals, attend clinical and continuing education programs, and seek advice from specialists as needed. If your facility doesn't offer continuing education programs, suggest that they do so. Remember, ignorance of new techniques and medical information is no excuse for substandard care. If you're

Organizations that ensure quality patient care

National Committee for Quality Assurance (NCQA)

NCQA is a consumer oriented, nonprofit organization founded in 1990. It accredits health maintenance organizations and other health plans. NCQA has developed a set of clinical performance measures called the Health Plan Employer Data and Information Set (HEDIS). The 75 HEDIS performance indicators (generally directed toward prevention and early detection) are used to evaluate health care providers and health plans. The criteria define and measure quality and that information is then shared with purchasers and the public.

Joint Commission on Accreditation of Healthcare Organizations (JCAHO)

JCAHO, which traditionally evaluated only inpatient organizations, has expanded its scope to include the evaluation of health plans, preferred provider organizations, and integrated systems. In 1997, JCAHO introduced its Oryx system, which made performance measurement an integral part of evaluations.

Agency for Health Care Research and Quality (AHCRQ)

AHCRQ is a government agency that studies and evaluates which health care practices work best. Panels of experts have developed clinical practice guidelines and standards of care that can be accessed through the Internet and utilized in agencies and private practices.

sued for malpractice, your patient care will be judged by current APN standards, regardless of whether your facility or hospital has offered you the necessary continuing education. Knowing the most current information is your responsibility.

PRACTICE GUIDELINES

Development or use of research-based clinical practice guidelines is one way to ensure that your standard of care is adequate.

Research-based clinical practice guidelines were developed to promote quality patient care outcomes. If the facility for which you work has established a policy that mandates the use of practice guidelines, you must follow these guidelines. Most facilities regularly update practice guidelines. However, if the practice guidelines need to be updated because they don't reflect evidence based research or current best practice or if new research findings require treatment changes, bring this fact to the policy-making committee's attention. (See *Understanding evidence-based care.*) This is important to ensure that your patient receives the best possible care and to protect yourself. Clinical practice guidelines are the standard of care by which the NP will be measured. If the NP practices outside of the clinical practice guidelines and patient injury occurs, the NP will be held liable.

Justifying deviations

Clinical practice guidelines may become the facility's — and perhaps the community's — identified standard of care for treatment of certain diseases. If, in your professional judgment, a clinical practice guideline doesn't describe what appears to be the best treatment for an individual patient and you deviate from the practice guideline, you must document the justification for the deviation. It's also highly recommended that you act in consultation with other NPs and physicians whenever you feel that deviations from practice guidelines are necessary. Otherwise, you may appear to be working below the facility's or agency's own self-set standards of care. If the practice guidelines that you're requested to follow are mere guidelines and not formal policy, you can override the guidelines if you believe the patient's individuals needs aren't met by the guidelines' recommendations. Still, it's important that you document why you deviated from the guidelines. Facilities that use practice guidelines will often provide feedback to NPs on the frequency with which they didn't follow guidelines compared with their peers, and they'll also provide summaries of the outcomes of patients treated within and outside the guidelines.

Quality outcomes

The NP's performance may also be measured by the facility and MCOs for whom they work. Performance measurements may include the number of patients served as well as the quality of the outcomes achieved. NPs would be wise to familiarize themselves with the performance measurements used by the facility or agency for whom they work. (See *Specific performance measures,* pages 52 and 53.) One of the greatest criticism of MCOs is that they're focused on service to a greater number of enrollees at a reduced cost and with less expensive treatments. Critics of MCOs are focusing on quality outcomes in demand for a balance between cost and quality of care for the patient. In 1994, a lawsuit was filed in Massachusetts charging that, over a 5-year period, the medical care providers at an HMO negligently failed to address a lump that appeared in the plaintiff's navel. She was passed from one nonphysician practitioner within the HMO to the next. Only on one occasion was she actually seen for a 15-minute visit by her assigned physician. The other times she was seen by an NP. Four years after the initial identification of the lump, a physician ordered diagnostic tests that revealed a metastatic ovarian-type cancer. Six weeks before the case was scheduled to go to trial, the parties settled for $1.5 million.

Understanding evidence-based care

Evidence-based care is the conscientious and prudent use of the current best available evidence in making decisions about the care of individual patients. The practice of evidence-based care means integrating individual clinical expertise with the best available external clinical evidence from research. Individual clinical expertise includes the proficiency and judgment that individual clinicians acquire through experience and practice. The best available external clinical evidence includes clinically relevant research, often from the basic sciences of medicine, but also from patient-centered clinical research into the accuracy and precision of diagnostic tests and the efficacy and safety of therapeutic, rehabilitative, and preventive regimens. External clinical evidence invalidates previously accepted diagnostic tests and treatments and replaces them with new ones that are more powerful, more accurate, more efficacious, and safer.

Specific performance measures

The National Committee for Quality Assurance (NCQA) has defined specific performance measures of care to audit so that it can quantify data. These benchmarks are research-proven practices (for example, performing annual dilated retinal examinations in diabetic patients diagnosed for more than 5 years) that increase the level of health in a given population. Knowing what these benchmarks are and what specific items the NCQA will audit lets you demonstrate the quality of care you provide. Specific sections of Health Plan Employer Data and Information Set (HEDIS) under the nurse practitioner's (NP's) control include:

- adult cancer screening
- post-myocardial infarction (MI) care with beta-adrenergic blockers
- cholesterol management
- depression pharmacotherapy
- chronic illness management
- diabetic retinal eye examination
- elderly health maintenance
- immunization
- mental illness follow-up
- perinatal care
- smoking cessation.

Below you'll find information on HEDIS performance measures and data sources that you can use to help provide the highest level of care.

Adult cancer screening

Performance measures for adult cancer screening focus on a mammogram in the past 2 years for women ages 52 to 69 and a Papanicolaou (Pap) test in the past 3 years for those ages 21 to 64. For various reasons, many patients neglect to act on these referrals. Follow-up contact by an NP's office reinforces the need for the tests and boosts compliance rates. Health plans collect data on cancer screening from CPT codes on bills and medical record audits. Simply referring a patient for screening isn't enough because only completed mammographies and Pap tests are tallied.

Post-MI care with beta-adrenergic blockers

The performance measure in post-MI care with beta-adrenergic blockers applies to patients diagnosed with acute MI. Specifically, auditors look for the prescription of beta-adrenergic blockers within 7 days of discharge. Patients are excluded if they have an allergy or contraindication to beta-adrenergic blockers, were readmitted to a hospital within 7 days of discharge, or were transferred to a subacute care facility.

Cholesterol management

Cholesterol management selects patients who have had an acute cardiovascular event within the past year. The performance measure criteria is a low-density lipoprotein (LDL) screening within the past year. Starting in 2000, auditors began checking for an LDL level below 130 mg/dl in patients who had an acute cardiovascular event in the previous year.

Depression pharmacotherapy

The performance measure for depression pharmacotherapy selects records of patients treated with antidepressants. The three elements audited are three follow-up office visits during the 12-week period after a new episode, at least 12 weeks of antidepressant medication, and completion of a 6-month treatment course.

Chronic illness management

HEDIS measures focus on six chronic conditions: MI or acute cardiovascular event, diabetes, schizophrenia, manic-depressive illness, paranoia, and depression. The performance measures address specific aspects of these illnesses.

Diabetic retinal eye examination

Auditors use administrative data to locate entries with the ICD-9 code for diabetes and then eliminate patients under age 31. They then review patient charts and check for

Specific performance measures *(continued)*

the eye examination CPT billing code within the past year.

Elderly health maintenance

The first performance measure for elderly health maintenance is influenza immunization within the past year in older adults (auditors exclude those who have a history of egg allergy or Guillain-Barré syndrome, are residents in hospice care, or are insured commercially or through Medicaid). The second criterion uses a patient survey form that measures functional status and allows the compilation of data on each patient over several years. Using a five-point scale, patients answer the following four questions:

- How would you rate your own health?
- In the past month, have emotional problems interfered with your daily activities?
- In the past month, has your physical health interfered with your daily activities?
- In the past month, has pain interfered with your normal daily activities?

Immunization

The performance measure for immunization checks the immunization status at ages 2 and 13. Specific criteria for 2-year-olds are four shots of diphtheria and tetanus toxoid and pertussis vaccine, three polio vaccines, one dose of measles-mumps-rubella vaccine (MMR), one varicella vaccine, a minimum of two haemophilus b conjugate vaccines, and two hepatitis B vaccines. By age 13, each child should have received a sec-

ond dose of MMR, a third hepatitis B vaccine, and a tetanus-diphtheria booster.

Mental illness follow-up

The performance measure for mental illness follow-up audits records of patients who were hospitalized for manic-depressive illness, paranoia, or schizophrenia. The criterion is an outpatient visit to a mental health provider within 30 days of discharge. Patients under age 6, those transferred to a subacute care facility, and those readmitted within 30 days of discharge are excluded.

Perinatal care

Auditors look at two aspects of primary care during pregnancy: a visit in the first trimester and a postpartum checkup within 6 weeks of delivery. Specifically, they look for CPT codes or evidence of obstetric screening tests within the appropriate date ranges for patients who have given birth. Although the performance measures define a timeframe for the visits, they don't specify the type of practitioner; the patient may see a physician's assistant, an NP, a family physician, a nurse-midwife, or an obstetrician.

Smoking-cessation advice

NCQA audits for smoking-cessation advice randomly select patient surveys for adults who report they're current smokers or have recently quit. The auditor then asks these patients if they have received smoking-cessation advice from a practitioner.

Risk management strategy

Risk management involves following sound practices to avoid problems later. You face certain risks associated with your practice, including the risk of making a clinical error. You can reduce your risk of liability by forming a positive relationship with your patient through the use of effective communication skills. To do this, actively listen to patients' concerns, share your chain of reasoning, and develop an appropriate treatment plan that includes diagnostic testing and documentation.

LISTENING TO PATIENTS

Patients who become agitated after an extended wait in your office to receive care are more likely to become your adversary if problems develop later. It's good practice to have your office staff communicate with your patients to explain why there is a wait and to give them the expected waiting time. This type of common courtesy is a good risk management tool.

Develop a positive working relationship with your patient, including addressing him by name, maintaining eye contact, and showing interest in his concerns. It's a good practice to sit down beside your patient rather than stand. When you're speaking with the patient, practice active listening as he states his problems. This will encourage the patient to give detailed information that will help you make an accurate diagnosis and give the patient the message that you truly care about his well-being. As you make your diagnosis and treatment plan, always try to determine your patient's priorities and, when appropriate, treat what he perceives to be the problem. In other words, make the current patient's needs your highest priority. Patients who feel they're receiving your full attention will be more confident in the decisions you make regarding their care.

Always review the patient's record before entering the examination room to refresh your memory regarding his medical history and conversations you've had on previous visits. The patient's confidence will be shaken if you begin your intervention with him by confusing him with another patient. Finally, it's always a good idea to end your conversation by inquiring if there is anything else that the patient would like to discuss or if there is anything you haven't asked about or haven't mentioned. Also, ask if your suggested treatment plan sounds acceptable. Patient compliance will be improved if your patient feels a part of the decision-making process. By asking if there is anything else you can do, the patient will feel as though you aren't hurrying to complete your time with him, but rather that you're interested in his total well-being. In addition, encourage your patients to contact you with any questions or concerns; reiterate that you're available 24 hours a day, 7 days a week.

SHARING YOUR REASONING

Sharing with your patient the chain of reasoning that guided your professional judgment is another method of reducing risk. You should always develop a differential diagnosis list as well as a working diagnosis to provide direction as the patient's condition progresses. Share your impressions with the patient. For example, statements such as "from what you're telling me, it sounds like (specify your working diagnosis). If so, you should start to feel better in (specify an expected resolution date). However, things that would make me reconsider are (danger signs and symptoms) and I would like you to contact the office if they occur. I also want you to contact me or the office if your symptoms persist, change, or worsen; if new symptoms develop; or if you feel anxious or have questions." By sharing your reasoning with the patient, you'll have the opportunity to clarify that your working diagnosis and treatment plan seem to meet the patient's needs.

DEVELOPING A TREATMENT PLAN

Your treatment should be specific to the patient's needs and always include diagnostic testing and documentation.

Using judgment

Don't make your final diagnosis by therapeutic trial. For example, cardiac pain can respond to muscle relaxants or analgesics and calculi can shift coincidentally after an antacid is given. Electrocardiogram changes may not show at the time of presentation, and cardiac markers aren't 100% error-free. When your differential diagnosis list contains potentially life-threatening disorders or those that can progress rapidly if missed, you should err on the side of caution when deciding follow-up evaluation time frames. For instance, if you've ruled out myocardial infarction or meningitis, those patients should be contacted for follow-up evaluation within 12 to 24 hours.

Documenting your plan and reasoning

Documentation is sometimes your only means of retaining what you've said and done for your patient. Always remember to note the differential diagnosis list or evaluations and testing that demonstrate you considered appropriate differentials. Document that you discussed the treatment plan with the patient. As with informed consent documentation, be sure to include the possible adverse affects and the potential outcomes that you discussed. If the patient has rejected any of your suggested plans, such as admission to a substance abuse program or routine screening tests, include this information in your documentation as well. Also be sure to document the significant risks that you discussed with the patient.

Additionally, when you're reviewing the notes from other health care team members, acknowledge the note and indicate that you've considered the information they've shared. This type of interteam documentation and communication encourages the team approach and allows integration of the findings when team members are working with the same patient.

MINIMIZING YOUR RISKS AFTER AN INCIDENT

Can you minimize the chances that a patient will sue after an incident? Can you protect yourself and your facility in case he does? In everyday practice, regardless of the patient and the environment, the best way to protect yourself is to follow the "three Rs" of risk management strategy: rapport, record, and report.

Maintaining rapport with the patient

Answer his questions honestly. Don't offer any explanation if you weren't personally involved in the incident; instead, refer the patient to someone who can supply answers. If you try to answer his questions without direct knowledge of the incident, inconsistencies could arise and the patient could interpret these as a cover-up.

If you feel uncomfortable talking to the patient or family, ask your collaborating physician or an administrator for advice on how to answer questions, or ask them to participate and help you provide answers. Remember, patients usually respond favorably if they know you're being honest and show that you care about their well-being.

Don't blame anyone for the incident. If an incident changes the patient's plan of care (such as a prescribed medication), tell the patient about it and clearly explain the reasons for the change.

Recording the incident

Be sure to note the facts of the incident in the patient's medical record. Avoid opinions that cast blame. Remember, truthfulness is your best protection against lawsuits. If you try to cover up or play down an incident, you could end up in far more serious legal trouble than if you had reported it objectively. Never write in the patient's medical record that an incident report has been completed. An incident report isn't clinical information but rather an administrative risk management tool still not discoverable in many jurisdictions. However, it can be admitted as evidence if you refer to it in the medical record.

Reporting every incident

Some NPs think incident reports are more trouble than they're worth, and, furthermore, that they're a dangerous admission of guilt. That is false. Here's why incident reports are important:

● Incident reports jog our memories. The medical record is patient-focused, and facts pertinent to the incident — but not the patient — may be left out. Much time may pass between an incident and when it comes to court. We simply can't trust our memories — but we can trust a properly completed incident report.

● Incident reports help administrators to act quickly to change the policy or procedure that seems to be responsible for the incident. An administrator can also act quickly to talk with families and offer assistance, explanation, or other appropriate support. Sometimes, helpful communication with an injured patient and his family can be the balm that soothes the family's anger and prevents a lawsuit.

Patient teaching

Both ***statutory law*** and common law support the patient's right to have information about his condition and treatment. In fact, when patients are admitted to a facility, they may be handed a ***patient's bill of rights*** that clearly outlines all their rights including their right to teaching. The doctrine of informed consent further supports the patient's right to know.

Despite the NP's deep involvement in patient teaching, the courts have rarely addressed the NP's liability in this area of patient care. This issue typically arises in litigation when a patient sues and the defendant-NP attempts to prove patient responsibility for the poor outcome. For example, a patient is seen in the ED for an infection, is prescribed an antibiotic, told to follow up with a specialist, and discharged. The patient doesn't follow the instructions and gets worse. To rebut his own negligence, the patient will argue that he wasn't told the risks if he didn't follow the NP's advice. Some legal experts believe that as NPs take on greater patient-teaching responsibilities, they'll increasingly become the target of lawsuits dealing with the patient's right to information.

A court faced with a question involving an NP's responsibility for patient teaching will probably examine the question under the general category of a patient's right to know. Because health care requires the patient's participation and cooperation, the right to know is an inherent part of successful treatment. When the right to know becomes critical to the patient's health, a court is likely to view patient teaching as a practitioner's legal duty.

Suppose you're sued for malpractice, and your alleged wrongful act involves patient teaching. The court will consider whether patient teaching was your legal duty to the patient and whether you met or breached it. (See *Patient education.*)

PATIENT TEACHING AND THE LAW

Anytime you give a patient information about his care or treatment, you're involved in patient teaching — a professional nursing responsibility and a potential source of liability.

Patient teaching has taken on increased significance due to decreased lengths of stay in hospitals and an increased amount of care provided at home. Patients and their families need more understanding of patients' illnesses and how to manage them at home.

Patient education

COURT CASE

The court in *Kyslinger v. United States* (1975) addressed the nurse's liability for patient teaching. In this case, a Veteran's Administration (VA) hospital sent a hemodialysis patient home with a dialysis unit. He eventually died (apparently while on the machine), and his wife sued the federal government — because a VA hospital was involved — alleging that the hospital and its staff had failed to teach either her or her late husband how to properly use and maintain a home hemodialysis unit.

After examining the evidence, the court ruled against the patient's wife, as follows:

"During those 10 months that plaintiff's decedent underwent biweekly hemodialysis treatment on the unit (at the VA hospital), both plaintiff and decedent were instructed as to the operation, maintenance, and supervision of said treatment. The Court can find no basis to conclude that the plaintiff or plaintiff's decedent weren't properly informed on the use of the hemodialysis unit."

What the NP can learn

Although teaching in detail to both the patient and family is important, documenting your teaching in detail is crucial. It's helpful to have written materials and videotapes of procedures and key concepts that reinforce teaching. After teaching sessions, you should have the patient and caregivers sign a form that outlines what teaching took place.

Patient teaching may be formal or informal. You teach *formally* when, for example, you prepare instructions on stoma care for a colostomy patient. When giving the patient this detailed information, you should follow these steps:

● assess what the patient wants and needs to know
● identify goals that you and the patient want to reach
● choose teaching strategies that will help reach the goals
● evaluate how well you have reached the goals.

You teach *informally* when, for example, you calm a patient's fears by explaining an upcoming diagnostic test.

For best results, patient teaching should include the family and others involved in the patient's care. If family members understand the reason for a patient's treatment, they will be more willing to provide emotional support.

If the patient doesn't want to be taught

Suppose you begin teaching a patient about the medications he's taking, only to hear him say, "Oh, just tell my wife; she gives me all my pills." When something like this happens, be sure to document the incident. Include the patient's exact words; then describe what you taught his wife, and how.

PATIENT-TEACHING STANDARDS

Most nurse practice acts in the U.S. contain wording about promoting patient health and preventing disease or injury; however, they don't specify a nurse's responsibility for patient teaching. NPs can find this information in the practice standards developed by professional organizations and in statements about nursing practice from national commissions.

JCAHO requires that the "patient and his or her family be provided with appropriate education and training to increase the knowledge of the patient's illness and treatment needs and to learn skills and behaviors that promote recovery and improve function." In addition, JCAHO requires that patient teaching be done in an interdisciplinary manner, considering the patient's ability to learn and any cultural or emotional factors or any cognitive or physical limitations that would impact his ability to learn.

Patient teaching should be a dynamic process that changes to meet the patient's and the family's needs. It should include instruction about how to adapt to the illness as well as how to prevent future problems.

COOPERATING WITH COLLEAGUES

Physicians, nurses, and other health team members sometimes disagree about how patient teaching should be done and who should do it. To avoid conflict, always consult physicians and other appropriate health team members when you're preparing routine patient-teaching protocols. A team approach to patient teaching not only decreases conflicts, but also ensures continuity in teaching — and a better-educated patient.

You can also avoid conflicts by listening to the instructions that physicians, respiratory therapists, dietitians, and others give the patient. Then you'll know exactly what has already been said to him, and you can structure your teaching accordingly.

Candor and diplomacy, of course, also help reduce conflict. Everyone profits when health team members share their patient-teaching approaches and work together to achieve patient-teaching goals.

Caring for a minor

A minor is any person under the age of majority, which is usually 18 or 21, depending on state law. When you care for a minor, you should keep in mind the way minors' legal rights are structured. What legal rights a minor has depends largely on his age. He may also have special legal status.

MINOR'S RIGHTS

A minor's rights fall into three categories:
- *Personal rights that belong to everyone from birth.* Examples include the right to **privacy** and the right to protection against crimes.
- *Rights that can be exercised as a minor matures.* These fall into two groups. The first includes the right to drive a car, to work at a paying job, and to have sexual relations — as long as both partners are of legal age. These rights are granted at certain ages, according to state laws, whether or not the minor is mature enough to exercise the right intelligently.

The second group includes rights granted by the courts rather than by statutory law. These are given to any minor who shows the mental and emotional ability to handle them.
- *Rights that belong to adults and can be exercised only by* **adults** *and by* **emancipated minors.** Examples include many financial and contractual rights such as the right to consent to medical treatment.

The law provides special protection for minors so that they may exercise certain rights after reaching the **age of majority.** For example, because a minor can't sue in court, most states give minors a **grace period** after they reach the age of majority to bring any lawsuit relating to when they were minors. This includes suing people their parents could have sued earlier on the minors' behalf but chose not to. Because this can include a lawsuit for medical malpractice, the law generally requires that hospitals keep the records of pediatric patients longer than the records of adults.

MATURE MINOR

A mature minor is a nonemancipated minor in his middle to late teens who shows clear signs of intellectual and emotional maturity. A mature minor may be able to exercise certain adult rights, depending on the laws in his state.

BECOMING EMANCIPATED

Emancipation is the legal process whereby children may obtain freedom from the custody, care, and control of their parents before the age of majority. Under most state statutes, an emancipated minor loses his right to financial support from his parents in exchange for the ability to govern his own affairs. Emancipation may also enable a minor to enter into binding contracts and to sue and be sued in his own name. Some statutes also give an emancipated minor the ability to consent to medical, dental, or psychiatric care without parental consent.

Depending on the jurisdiction, emancipation may be addressed by common law or statutory law. Most state statutes require a hearing in emancipation cases.

Standards for emancipation

Standards for emancipation may include:
- *best interests of the minor.* (Many state statutes contain a provision allowing judges to use the best interests of the child as a standard for emancipation.)
- *ability to manage financial affairs.* (Many state statutes have a provision requiring that a minor demonstrate the ability to manage financial affairs before becoming emancipated.)
- *living separate and apart from parents.* (Many state statutes require that minors who wish to be emancipated live separate and apart from their parents. Some require parental consent for separate living arrangements.)
- *parental consent.* (Many states require parental consent for an emancipation petition; others ignore this requirement altogether.)
- *age.* (Most states require that children be at least age 16 before initiating emancipation proceedings. A few states don't have an age requirement.)

Under most circumstances, you should treat an emancipated minor as if he were an adult.

Restrictions on rights

Note that even an emancipated minor may not exercise some rights. If he's 18 and the drinking age in his state is 21, he still can't legally buy or drink alcoholic beverages. Some states set a minimum age for making a will (usually the age of majority). In those states, even if the minor is married or has a child, any will he draws up won't be valid.

GUARDIANS *AD LITEM*

A *guardian ad litem* is a person appointed by the court to protect the interest of a minor in a legal proceeding. The court may appoint a guardian *ad litem* when these two conditions coexist:
- a decision is needed for the minor
- a "diversion of interest" exists; that is, the court possesses evidence that the interest of the minor's parents or **legal guardians** probably doesn't coincide with the minor's welfare.

The court may appoint a guardian *ad litem* even if one or both parents are still living and interested in the minor's welfare or if the minor already has a guardian.

OBTAINING CONSENT

By far, the most common problem with minors is properly obtaining **informed consent** for their medical care. Here are 11 different situations you may face in helping to obtain a minor's consent.

Nonemancipated minor

If the minor isn't emancipated, his mother, father, or legal guardian has the right to refuse or consent to treatment for him. Whenever possible, consent should be obtained from both parents or both guardians when joint guardians have custody of the minor.

If the parents are divorced or separated, the policy is to obtain consent from the parent who has custody. If the minor's parents are incompetent or dead and he has no legal guardian, the court will usually appoint a legal guardian for him. The guardian can consent or refuse, just as if he were a parent.

Mature, nonemancipated minor

In the U.S., nonemancipated but mature minors' rights aren't as broad. In some jurisdictions, however, parental consent is no longer necessary for various types of medical and psychiatric care. In California, for example, nonemancipated minors age 15 and older, who live separate from their parents and manage their own finances, may consent to their own medical care. Ask your attorney to check your state's statutes in this area.

In its rulings on abortion and contraception, the U.S. Supreme Court has indicated that mature minors have certain rights of consent and privacy.

Emancipated minor

An emancipated minor can usually refuse or consent to treatment himself. But if he's unable to do so (for example, he's unconscious after an accident), you have to try to find someone who can give consent for him. Talk to your attorney to determine if there are laws in your state

that designate surrogate decision makers when the patient becomes incompetent. Possibilities, in descending order of preference, include his spouse, parents or guardians, and nearest living relative. You may waive this requirement for consent only in an emergency situation, when your failure to treat a minor immediately could result in further injury or death.

When parents or joint guardians disagree

Problems can arise when parents (whether married, divorced, or separated) or joint guardians disagree about consenting to treatment for a nonemancipated minor. Your only recourse may be to go to court, where a judge either makes the decision himself or assigns responsibility to one parent or guardian. You may find yourself caught in a situation in which a minor's parents or guardians can't agree on consenting to his treatment. When this happens, if the minor is in a hospital, tell the administrators immediately so they can talk to the parents or guardians and, if necessary, alert the hospital's attorney. If the minor is in your office, collaborate with the other NPs and physicians in your group and alert your attorney.

When a minor needs emergency care

The legal rule to follow when a minor needs emergency care is the same as that for adults: Treat first and get consent later. Some courts have held that any mature minor, emancipated or not, may give valid and binding consent to emergency treatment. For example, in *Younts v. St. Francis Hospital and School of Nursing* (1970), a nonemancipated but mature 17-year-old was held able to consent to surgical repair of a severed fingertip.

When a minor requests an abortion

Recent U.S. Supreme Court rulings, including *Ohio v. Akron Center for Reproductive Health* (1990) and *Hodgson v. Minnesota* (1990), indicate that state laws can't prevent a minor from seeking and obtaining a *legal abortion;* however, states can impose conditions on consent. The law in some states may require a minor seeking an abortion to notify her parents or to bypass this consent requirement by going before a judge, a procedure called *judicial bypass.*

For the rules your state requires you to follow when verifying consent for a minor's abortion, check with your attorney.

When a minor asks for a contraceptive

In *Carey v. Population Services International* (1977), the U.S. Supreme Court ruled unconstitutional a state law prohibiting the sale of contraceptives to anyone under age 16. The court held that the decision to bear a child is a fundamental right and that state interference can only be justified if it protects a compelling state interest. As a result, a minor can obtain contraceptives without parental consent.

Again, consult your attorney if you have questions regarding restrictions on distributing contraceptives to minors. For example, your state may require you to notify a parent or guardian about the matter.

When a minor needs treatment for a communicable disease

Most states have laws that permit minors to consent to treatment for serious communicable diseases, including sexually transmitted diseases, without parental approval.

If you must deal with a minor who is refusing diagnosis or treatment for a communicable disease, check your state's laws. Most states permit public health authorities to deal with a nonconsenting minor as an adult, including deciding whether he should be quarantined.

When a minor needs treatment for drug abuse

State and federal laws generally permit minors to consent to take part in *drug abuse* treatment and rehabilitation programs as though they were adults. Like adults, minor patients in drug treatment programs are entitled to have their records kept confidential.

When religious beliefs conflict with a minor's treatment

If your patient or his parents or guardians are Jehovah's Witnesses or Christian Scientists, you may have special problems getting consent to treatment.

Although competent adults or emancipated minors may refuse treatment for religious reasons, nonemancipated minors may not. In most states in which the question has come before the courts, judges have ruled that parents and guardians can't stop a facility from treating their child solely on religious grounds if a reasonable chance exists that the treatment will help the patient.

Note, however, that in this situation a court will have to appoint a guardian *ad litem* for the sick minor. This may take some time; to avoid delaying the minor's treatment unnecessarily, notify your facility administration as quickly as possible.

When a minor seeks or receives mental health care

Minors, like adults, may be treated at private and state-run mental health facilities. When the minor and his parents agree to seek such treatment for the minor, the facility will follow its normal medical guidelines and procedures in deciding whether to admit him. This usually involves informing the patient and his parents or guardian of their rights and then obtaining their informed consent for admission.

The U.S. Supreme Court, in *Parham v. J.R.* (1979) and in *Secretary of Public Welfare v. Institutionalized Juveniles* (1979), held that nonconsenting minors can be admitted to state-run mental health facilities at the request of either or both parents. Such minors, however, always have the right to have a psychiatrist or other trained fact finder review the request at or before admission and periodically thereafter. The fact finder may be the facility's regular admissions officer.

In many states, however, the rules controlling admission of minors to **inpatient** mental health facilities are more rigorous. The rules may call for a full-scale hearing, with attorneys present, within a set time after admission (if not concurrent with admission).

Caring for an abused patient

In the course of your career, you're likely to encounter both adult and child victims of abuse. Sometimes abuse is physical battering such as when a son regularly beats his aging father. At other times, abuse involves a verbal, a sexual, or an emotional attack, or neglect and abandonment.

PROFILE OF THE ABUSER

People who abuse others come from all socioeconomic levels and all ethnic groups. No specific psychiatric diagnosis encompasses the abuser's personality and behavior. However, many abusers have a history of being abused themselves when young or of having witnessed abuse of parents or siblings.

(Such childhood experiences are usually profound and can influence a person's behavior throughout his adult life.) In many cases, abusive people lack self-esteem and the security of being loved — qualities that help nonabusive people cope with stress.

In times of crisis, abusers resort to the behavior learned in childhood. They abuse just as they were abused — all in an attempt to restore their own feelings of self-control and self-esteem. After all, if abuse was an acceptable behavior for their parents, why can't it be the same for them now?

Abusers are usually unable to tolerate personal failure or disapproval from spouses, children, or friends. When an abuser's self-esteem is low, he expects rejection and will act in ways that cause others to reject him. Rejection, in turn, provokes the abuser to commit further verbal or emotional abuse.

Abusers commonly have unrealistic expectations of the people they abuse. When an individual fails to live up to these expectations, the abuser feels a stronger compulsion to control, mortify, reject, and, if necessary, physically injure that individual.

Cycle of abuse

Low self-esteem may prompt an abuser to choose a partner much like himself. Each will then feed into the other's form of abuse. If the couple has children, in many cases they become targets of their parents' abusive behavior. What the children witness, and suffer, begins another cycle of abused child to child abuser.

CHILD ABUSE

Children who are abused are most likely to die before age 4. According to recent studies, 76% of maltreatment fatalities occur before age 4, and 84% occur before age 5. (See *Responding to suspected child abuse.*) Children with

Responding to suspected child abuse

Suppose you're on duty in the emergency department when Mrs. Firth comes in with her son Billy, age 4. She tells you, "Billy was riding in a friend's car and they had an accident. I didn't think he was hurt at first, but later on his knee swelled up. I decided I'd better have a doctor look at it."

You examine Billy closely for head and neck injuries. You don't find any, but you do notice some bruises on his left arm and on his legs that look several weeks old. You question Mrs. Firth about the accident, but she offers few details. Then, when you ask her about Billy's injuries, she gets defensive. Although his injuries look painful, Billy sits quietly while you examine him.

How to respond

You suspect Billy has been abused. What should you do next? Follow these guidelines:

- Order a total-body X-ray. Also, inform your supervisor of the situation.
- If you suspect the child has been forced to ingest drugs or alcohol, order toxicology studies of the child's blood and urine.
- If the child is severely bruised, order a blood coagulation profile.
- If X-rays or other studies suggest that the child has been abused, confront the parents.
- If a parent admits to abusing the child and appears to want help, give the address and telephone number of a local group, such as a local chapter of Parents Anonymous, and encourage the parent to call.
- Whether the parent admits to abusing the child, report all suspected abuse to the state-designated agency empowered to investigate the situation. Keep in mind that in many states failure to report suspected abuse is a crime.

behavior problems are particularly vulnerable to abuse, as are malformed or developmentally disabled children and those born prematurely or born to unmarried parents. From the abusive parent's perspective, such a child represents an unplanned disruption or a stress-producing crisis. If the child has mental or physical defects, the parent may see this as reaffirming his own inadequacy and weakness. If the child has severe defects, the parent may be unable to accept that the child is his and he may pour on abuse in an effort to be rid of the child.

Parents may also view children as extensions of people they hate. Sometimes this results from similarities in physical appearance or similarities in behavior. If a child resembles a spouse who deserted the family, he may be blamed for the spouse's failures and abused accordingly.

ADULT ABUSE

Spouses, disabled people, and elderly parents or relatives are the most common victims of adult abuse.

In many cases, the abused spouse suffers from lack of self-esteem. An abused spouse's parents may have abused each other, or one parent may have abused the other. Having witnessed these attacks as a child, the present-day abused spouse accepts that she, too, will be abused. By behaving passively, spouses make it easy for their partners to abuse them repeatedly without fear of retaliation.

Like children, adults can abuse victims if they're viewed as too dependent, too sickly, or too much like a hated person. Many ill or elderly people who make financial, emotional, or personal demands become injured when the stress they create becomes intolerable for their abusers. (See *Elder abuse.*)

Among abusers of adults, men who abuse women predominate, but sometimes the opposite happens. Abused men, married or not, typically show the same low self-esteem and passivity as abused women. Sometimes an abused man is the less aggressive and more subservient member of the relationship and accepts a certain level of abuse in the hope that it won't get worse. At other times, he may be so ashamed by his inability to provide adequately that he invites abuse to give himself a feeling of atonement.

Also be aware that abuse occurs in same-sex relationships but the abused person may fail to report it out of fear of homophobia.

ABUSE AND THE LAW
In 1874, grossly battered "Mary Ellen," age 9, was found chained to her bed in a New York City tenement. Etta Wheeler, a church worker, tried to find help for Mary Ellen, but she quickly discovered that New York had no laws to protect children. Her only recourse was the American Society for the Prevention of Cruelty to Animals, which agreed to intervene on Mary Ellen's behalf.

A year after Mary Ellen's case reached the courts, New York state adopted the country's first child-protection legislation. This gave child-protection agencies a legal base and proved a breakthrough for other disadvantaged groups as well.

Since then, child abuse has gained increasing attention from the public, legislators, and concerned health care professionals. In 1946, for example, radiologists reported that subdural hematomas and abnormal X-ray findings in the long bones were commonly associated with early childhood traumatic injuries. In 1961, an American Academy of Pediatrics symposium on child abuse introduced the term "battered child."

The first statutes requiring mandatory reporting of child abuse resulted from a 1963 report by the Children's Bureau of the U.S. Department of Health, Education, and Welfare (now the Department of Health and Human Services). Most states, using the model in the report, developed protective legislation by the early 1970s. Unfortunately, the diversity of these laws makes uniform interpretation impossible.

To help remedy this, Congress passed the Child Abuse Prevention and Treatment Act in 1973. This act requires states to meet certain uniform standards in order to be eligible for federal assistance in setting up programs to identify, prevent, and treat the problems caused by child abuse. The act also established a national center on child abuse and *child neglect.*

The act was amended in 1984 in response to "Baby Doe" cases. These cases involved parents who refused life-saving treatment for mentally and physically handicapped infants. The amendments require the states to respond to reports of a child's medical neglect. States must respond to reports that medically indicated treatment (including appropriate nutrition, hydration, and medication) has been withheld from an infant. The law allows three exceptions under which treatment may be withheld:
● when the infant is chronically ill and irreversibly comatose
● when treatment would only prolong dying
● when treatment itself would be inhumane and futile in terms of survival.

According to interpretive guidelines to the regulations (which don't have the force of law), even when one of these exceptions is present, the infant must still receive appropriate nutrition, hydration, and medication.

Elder abuse

Elder abuse has reached alarming proportions, having increased 150% between 1986 and 1996. Estimates range from 700,000 to 2 million annual cases of mistreatment in the United States alone. A study by the Administration on Aging and the Administration for Children and Families estimates that more than 500,000 older people in domestic settings were abused or neglected during 1996 and that for every reported incident, about five went unreported.

The greater an elderly person's disabilities, the more vulnerable he is to abuse or neglect by caregivers — usually his relatives. Family members provide about 80% of all care given to older people; about 85% of all reported abuse involves a family member's behavior.

Defining abuse and neglect

Nearly every state has laws mandating that suspected elder abuse be reported to the authorities. Not all states define elder abuse; instead, they leave its diagnosis to health care professionals. Sample definitions of abuse and neglect are as follows:
- Elder abuse is destructive behavior directed at an older adult, carried out in a context or relationship of trust, and occurring intensely or frequently enough to produce harmful physical, psychological, social, or financial suffering and a decreased quality of life.
- Elder neglect is harm caused by failure to provide prudently adequate and reasonable assistance to meet the elderly person's basic physical, psychological, social, and financial needs.

Detecting abuse

As a nurse practitioner — especially if you're in a primary care or emergency department setting — you may be the first to notice or suspect mistreatment of an elderly patient. If you suspect elder abuse, report it to the appropriate authorities.

Signs and symptoms

Detecting abuse in a frail, elderly person with multiple health problems can challenge your assessment skills. A situation or condition that suggests mistreatment may actually represent the progression of disease. For example, you may suspect that an elderly woman covered with bruises is battered when in fact she has a coagulation disorder caused by the medication she takes for heart disease.

The following signs and symptoms, although not definitive for abuse, call for further investigation and reporting:
- unexplained bruises, fractures, or burns
- poor hygiene or nutritional status
- pressure sores or other evidence of skin breakdown or infection
- dehydration
- fear of a family member or caregiver
- indications of overmedication or undermedication, such as grogginess or decreased level of consciousness
- unusual listlessness or withdrawal
- signs and symptoms of sexually transmitted disease.

State law

Two common features characterize most state child abuse legislation:
- empowering of a social welfare or law enforcement bureau to receive and investigate reports of actual or suspected abuse
- granting of legal *immunity from liability,* for defamation or invasion of privacy, to any person reporting an incident of actual or suspected abuse.

Laws protecting abused spouses are still being written. Although many domestic relations laws exist, additional legislation is required to help protect victims of domestic violence.

YOUR LEGAL DUTY TO REPORT ABUSE

As an NP, you play a crucial role in recognizing and reporting incidents of suspected abuse. While caring for patients, you can readily note evidence of apparent abuse. When you do, you must pass the information along to the appropriate authorities. In many states, failure to report actual or suspected abuse constitutes a crime.

Protection from liability

If you have ever hesitated to file an abuse report because you fear repercussions, remember that the Child Abuse Prevention and Treatment Act protects you against liability. If your report is bona fide (that is, if you file it in good faith), the law will protect you from any suit filed by an alleged abuser.

FILING A REPORT

Make your report as complete and accurate as possible. Be careful not to let your personal feelings affect either the way you make out a report or your decision to file the report.

Abuse cases can raise many difficult emotional issues. Remember, however, that not filing a report can have more serious consequences than filing one that contains an unintentional error. It's better to risk error than to risk breaching the child abuse reporting laws — and, in effect, perpetuating the abuse.

RECOGNIZING ABUSE

Learn to recognize the events that trigger abuse and the signs and symptoms that mark the abused and the abuser. Early in your relationship with an abused patient, you'll need to be adept in order to spot the subtle behavioral

and interactional clues that signal an abusive situation.

Examine the patient's relationship with the suspected abuser. For example, abused people tend to be passive and fearful. An abused child usually fails to protest if his parent is asked to leave the examining area. An abused adult, on the other hand, usually wants his abuser to stay with him.

Abused people may react to needed clinical procedures by crying helplessly and incessantly. They tend to be wary of physical contacts, including physical examinations.

. Many health care facilities have a policy, procedure, or protocol that establishes criteria to help NPs, nurses, and other health care practitioners make observations that will help identify possible victims of abuse. Learning these criteria will make spotting victims of abuse more objective and prevent cases from going unrecognized.

Assessing the abuser

Sometimes the abuser will appear overly agitated when dealing with hospital personnel; for example, he'll get impatient if they don't carry out procedures instantly. At other times, he may exhibit the opposite behavior: a total lack of interest in the patient's problems.

Patient history

When you take an abuse victim's history, he may be vague about how he was injured and tell different stories to different people. When you ask directly about specific injuries, he may answer evasively or not at all. Sometimes, he'll minimize or try to hide his injuries.

Physical examination

Look for characteristic signs of abuse. In most cases of abuse, you'll find old bruises, scars, or deformities the patient can't or won't explain. X-ray examinations may show the presence of many old fractures.

Documenting abuse

Always document your findings objectively; try to keep your emotions out of your charting. One way to do this is to use the **SOAP** technique, which calls for these steps:

● In the subjective (S) part of the note, record information in the patient's own words.
● In the objective (O) part, record your personal observations.
● Under assessment (A), record your evaluations and conclusions.
● Under plan (P), list sources of hospital and community support available to the patient after discharge.

OFFERING SUPPORT SERVICES

Many support services have become available for both abusers and their victims. For example, if a female victim is afraid to return to the scene of her abuse, she may find temporary housing in a women's shelter. If no such shelter is available, she may be able to stay with a friend or family member.

Social workers or community liaison workers may also be able to offer suggestions for shelter. Another possibility is a church, synagogue, or mosque, which may have members willing to take the patient in. If no shelter can be found, the patient may have to stay at the health care facility for her safety.

Alert the patient to state, county, or city agencies that can offer protection. The police department should be called to collect evidence if the patient wants to press charges against the abuser. If the patient is a child, the law will probably require filing a report with a government family-service agency.

Help for the abused and the abuser

These organizations offer support and counseling for the abuse victim and the abuser. Also check the "Guide to Human Services" section of your telephone directory under "Abuse" and "Child & Youth" for local or state agencies.

Child Help USA/I.O.F.
(800) 4-A-CHILD
Web site: *www.childhelpusa.org*

National Clearinghouse on Marital and Date Rape
(510) 524-1582
Web site: *www.ncmdr.org*

National Coalition Against Sexual Assault
(717) 728-9764
Web site: *www.ncasa.org*

National Committee for Prevention of Child Abuse
(312) 663-3520
Web site: *casanet.org*

Help for the abuser

You need to evaluate the abuser's ability to handle stress. He'll probably pose a continued threat to others until he gets help in understanding his behavior and how to change it. In such a situation, you may attempt to refer him to an appropriate local or state agency that can offer help.

For abusive fathers or mothers, a local chapter of **Parents Anonymous (PA)** may be helpful. (See *Help for the abused and the abuser.*) PA, a self-help group made up of former abusers, attempts to help abusive parents by teaching them how to deal with their anger.

In addition to helping short-circuit abusive behavior, a self-help group takes abusive parents out of their isolation and introduces them to individuals who are capable of understanding their feelings. It also provides help in a crisis, when members may be able to prevent an abusive incident.

Telephone hot lines to crisis intervention services also give abusers someone to talk with in times of stress and crisis and may help prevent abuse. Commonly staffed by volunteers, telephone hot lines provide a link between those who seek help and trained counselors.

These and other kinds of help are also available through family-service agencies and hospitals. By becoming familiar with national and local resources, you'll be able to respond quickly and authoritatively when an abuser or his victim needs your help.

TEACHING THE PUBLIC

In addition to your duty to report abuse, you also have the opportunity to teach the public about abuse. The Child Abuse Prevention and Treatment Act encourages health care institutions to develop programs to identify, report, and ultimately prevent abuse. You can help reduce the incidence of abuse by teaching people about its signs and symptoms, diagnosis, and treatment, not just in the workplace, but in health fairs, at school presentations, or other interactions with the public.

Caring for a mentally ill or developmentally disabled patient

Despite his usually dependent condition, a mentally ill or developmentally disabled patient has most of the same rights as other members of society. In fact, the law typically covers such a patient's rights in extra detail to ensure that he receives proper care and treatment. If you violate these rights, even unwittingly, you could face serious legal complications.

Much of today's concern for the rights of the mentally ill and developmentally disabled stems from attempts to correct past abuses. Under the U.S. Constitution, a person's rights can't be limited or denied merely because of his mental status. Many health care professionals still don't realize that the courts have generally interpreted the Constitution to mean that mentally ill and developmentally disabled people have a right to fair and humane treatment, including during hospitalization. Under most circumstances, such a patient can't be kept in a hospital against his will, for example, nor can he be denied the right to refuse treatment or to receive information so he can give informed consent to proposed surgery.

GOVERNMENT ACTION

State governments have tried to assure the rights of this special population by enacting legislation specifically addressing the problems of the mentally ill and developmentally disabled. This legislation describes and authorizes specific services and provides the necessary funding.

The federal government also provides for the mentally ill and developmentally disabled. The Rehabilitation Act of 1973, for example, earmarked funds specifically for rehabilitative programs. It provides cash assistance for people who, because of their disabilities, aren't able to provide adequately for themselves or their families. The Act also outlines 14 patient rights to ensure high standards of health care. Facilities that participate in Medicare must comply with these 14 rights and make sure that the patient, his guardian, **next of kin,** or sponsoring agency knows about them, too.

The Americans with Disabilities Act of 1990 (P.L. 101-336) further ensures a disabled citizen's rights by providing a "national mandate for the elimination of discrimination against individuals with disabilities." This act addresses discrimination in employment, public accommodations, and public services, programs, and activities.

ESTABLISHING LEGAL RESPONSIBILITY

When a mentally ill or developmentally disabled child is admitted to a hospital, legal responsibility for him must be established immediately. If a parent accompanies the patient, usually the parent will be legally responsible.

If the child has been institutionalized before entering the hospital, the institution may have responsibility. However, this is true only if the parents have waived responsibility and the institution has written evidence to prove it.

If the courts have found the parents unfit or unable to care for the child, a legal guardian will have been appointed. This person has the legal right to assume responsibility for the child.

When no guardian has been appointed for the child, the state may act as a guardian under the doctrine of *parens patriae.* This doctrine also applies to mentally ill or developmentally disabled adults, who must have guardians.

Adult guardianship

If your mentally ill or developmentally disabled patient is an adult, check his medical record to see if he requires a legal guardian and to establish who it is. It may be a parent. If the patient is married, it may be the patient's spouse.

Sometimes an adult patient and his guardian will seriously disagree about the patient's care. When this happens, get clarification by going through the proper hospital channels.

Remember, you have no right to control the life of a mentally ill or developmentally disabled patient. Restricting his liberty for any reason is almost never legally permissible, except when he may otherwise harm himself or others. You must analyze each situation carefully to determine at what point the patient needs help in making health care decisions.

OBTAINING INFORMED CONSENT

When consent is required from a patient who is mentally ill or developmentally disabled, consider the following three questions:

● Can consent for treatment or a special procedure be obtained the same way it is from any other patient?
● Does the patient fully understand the procedure that he's to undergo, including the risks and alternatives?
● Does the patient have the authority to give his own consent, or must someone else give it?

The answers to these questions will vary with each patient. Clearly, if the patient is of unsound mind and can't understand the nature, purpose, alternatives, and risks of the proposed treatment, he can't legally consent. In such a case, consent must be obtained from the patient's legal guardian.

If the legal guardian is unavailable, a court that is authorized to handle such matters may authorize treatment.

Questioning a patient's ability to give consent

Sometimes a physician or an NP may doubt a patient's capacity to consent, even though he hasn't been judged incompetent. This commonly happens during an illness that causes temporary *mental incompetence.* In such a situation, you must follow your state laws to determine who can make health care decisions for the patient. Typically, the nearest relative's consent is commonly obtained or, if none can be found, the court must authorize treatment.

In the New York case of *Collins v. Davis* (1964), a hospital administrator sought a court order to permit surgery on an irrational adult whose life was considered to be in danger. The patient's wife had previously refused to give consent, allegedly for reasons she felt served the patient's best interest. The court, after considering the entire situation — especially the patient's prognosis if surgery wasn't performed — agreed that the hospital and the physician had only two choices: either let the patient die, or perform the operation against his wife's wishes. The court overruled the wife's refusal, holding that the patient had sought medical attention and that treatment normally given to a patient with a similar condition should be provided.

NP role

You can best protect the mentally ill or developmentally disabled patient's legal rights to informed consent by providing him or his guardian with information. Find out if the patient's and guardian's questions have been answered to their satisfaction.

Unless your absence would place the patient in danger, you should refuse to perform, or assist with, procedures on a patient whose informed consent hasn't been obtained. If you do participate, you can be held liable.

FORCED HOSPITALIZATION AND USE OF RESTRAINTS

Mentally ill or developmentally disabled people may be involuntarily kept in hospitals or other institutions if they're at risk of taking their own lives or if they pose a threat to other peoples' property or lives. However, mental illness alone isn't a sufficient legal basis for detaining a patient. The U.S. Supreme Court, in *O'Connor v. Donaldson* (1975), held that a state can't constitutionally confine a patient, without treatment or without rehabilitation necessary to reintegrate him into society, "who is capable of surviving safely in freedom by himself or with the help of willing and responsible family members or friends."

Similar restrictions apply to physical restraint of patients. Most states require a written order. The restraint order should be in the patient's medical record before restraints can be applied.

Restraint (or seclusion) may be used only in an emergency, when there is eminent risk that a patient may physically harm himself or others — and only when nonphysical interventions aren't effective or viable. Whenever possible, use minimal restraint — only that amount necessary to protect the patient and safeguard the staff and others. Restraint should never be used for punishment, for the convenience of staff, or as a substitute for treatment programs. Use of restraints is limited to a specific time. (See *Restraints or seclusion.*)

If you make the decision to apply restraints to a patient, you should immediately write the order. If the patient has consented to have his family kept informed of his care, contact the family to inform them of the use of restraints or seclusion. In an emergency — such as a violent outburst with actual or potential harm to self or others — a facility may authorize qualified **registered nurses (RNs)** or other trained staff members to apply restraints to the patient. Write an order for the restraint as soon as possible and document the incident carefully, including:

● circumstances that led to the use of restraints or seclusion

Restraints or seclusion

Before you write orders for a patient to be placed in restraints or in seclusion, you must be certain such measures are justifiable. The 2000 Joint Commission on Accreditation of Healthcare Organizations (JCAHO) standards are specific regarding restraint and seclusion.

Authorization

JCAHO requires that before restraints or seclusion are used:
- documentation shows that such interventions are clinically justified
- less restrictive interventions have been attempted
- the patient's current condition is considered.

Orders are to be time limited and written for a specific episode, with start and end times, rather than for an unspecified time in the future. Orders for restraint and seclusion are limited to:
- 4 hours for patients age 18 or older
- 2 hours for patients age 9 to 17
- 1 hour for children under age 9.

If restraint or seclusion is warranted beyond the specified time limit, the patient must be reevaluated in person and a new order written.

In an emergency, specially trained staff may initiate the use of restraints or seclusion and obtain an order within a specified time (as soon as possible, but no longer than 1 hour).

Care requirements

When caring for a patient in restraints or seclusion, periodic monitoring and observation are essential (specific protocols are generally established by your facility's policy).

For patients who require frequent or prolonged restraint or seclusion, the treatment team should meet to consider alternatives and changes in the plan of care. In addition, clinical leadership must be notified about any patient who remains in restraints or seclusion for more than 12 hours or who experiences more than two separate episodes of restraint or seclusion within 12 hours. If either condition continues, leadership must be notified every 24 hours.

Write orders to ensure the patient is clearly monitored and that his needs are met, and document that you're evaluating the patient's hydration, feeding, toileting, range of motion, and skin integrity.

- failure of nonphysical interventions
- rationale for the type of restraint selected
- notification of the patient's family
- behavior criteria for discontinuing the restraint (and patient notification of the criteria)
- reevaluation of the patient.

Potential liability

As an NP, you may be held liable in a lawsuit if you can't verify that — in your judgment — a patient needed to be restrained, and that he was restrained only as long as necessary. If you write orders to restrain or seclude

a patient simply for shouting obscenities, for example, you risk a lawsuit for *false imprisonment.*

You should also make sure you understand how to use restraining devices safely and effectively. You may be held liable if the restraints you ordered don't prove effective and the patient is injured as a result. (See *Use of restraints and liability,* page 72.)

If a competent patient makes an informed decision to refuse restraint, the hospital may require the patient to sign a release that would absolve the hospital of liability should injury result

Use of restraints and liability

Improperly restraining a patient can leave the practitioner vulnerable to a host of legal charges, such as negligence, professional malpractice, false imprisonment, or battery. The case discussed below provides an example of health care professionals who failed to use restraints effectively.

The patient who escaped
In *Rohde v. Lawrence General Hospital* (1987), the patient was brought into the hospital at 1 a.m. by police, following an auto accident. The patient assaulted a clinician in the emergency department (ED) and was diagnosed as having an "acute psychotic episode." The physician ordered application of leather restraints.

Around 6 a.m., the patient escaped from four-point restraints, went into the parking lot, found a car that had been left running,

and drove off. He crashed the car and was seriously injured.

The patient sued the hospital, the ED physician, and two nurses for medical malpractice, claiming that the staff didn't supervise him properly and that his restraints weren't securely fastened.

What the nurse practitioner can learn
The use of restraints isn't a replacement for supervision. When writing orders for the use of restraints or seclusion, you should order frequent patient checks by staff to verify the patient isn't getting free or in need of attention. When you have cause to believe a patient is at risk for harming himself or others, you should institute one-on-one observation until a psychiatric specialist states that it isn't needed.

---

from the patient's refusal to be restrained.

When to apply restraints
If you must apply restraints, follow these guidelines:
● Restraint is a form of imprisonment, so it should only be used as a last resort. Before restraining a patient, consider alternatives, such as constant observation or walking with the patient.
● Take care to avoid undue force; otherwise, you may invite a lawsuit for *battery.* Even threatening to use force may be sufficient cause for legal action.

Which types of restraints to use
You're responsible for seeing that restraints and seclusion are used only to the extent necessary to prevent injury. Follow these guidelines:

● Most states follow the *least restrictive principle,* which holds that no more restraint should be used than necessary. For example, a restraining vest shouldn't be used when simple wrist restraints will suffice.
● To avoid allegations of false imprisonment, document carefully and the decision-making process that led to the use of restraints, and review the continuing need for restraints on a regular basis.
● Tranquilizing drugs may provide an alternative to restraints. However, prescribe them sparingly and with caution. The patient's right to the least restrictive treatment or to an open-door policy that allows patients to move about "freely" means little if accompanied by indiscriminate drug use as a substitute for restraints.

RIGHT TO PRIVACY

The law has tried to protect all citizens from unwarranted intrusion into their private lives. Unfortunately, mentally ill and developmentally disabled patients' rights to privacy are easily violated. A good definition of privacy, first presented at the International Commission of Justice in 1970, reads: "Privacy is the ability to lead one's life without anyone:

● interfering with family or home life
● interfering with physical or mental integrity or moral and intellectual freedom
● attacking honor and reputation
● placing one in a false light
● censoring or restricting communication and correspondence, written or oral
● disclosing irrelevant or embarrassing information
● disclosing information given or received in circumstances of professional confidence."

Keep this definition in mind as you work with all types of patients, and do all you can to protect their right to privacy.

RIGHT TO WRIT OF HABEAS CORPUS

Institutionalization may, at times, breach a patient's rights, giving him cause to petition for a **writ of habeas corpus.** This writ seeks to ensure the timely release of any person who claims that he's being detained illegally and deprived of his liberty.

RIGHT TO TREATMENT

In *Wyatt v. Stickney* (1972), the court upheld the legal right of a mentally ill person hospitalized in a public institution to receive adequate psychiatric treatment. This decision suggests that when a patient is involuntarily committed because he needs treatment, his rights are violated if he doesn't receive proper care. Furthermore, if the underlying reason for a patient's **commitment** is that he's dangerous to himself or others, treatment must be provided to make him less so.

In the *Wyatt* decision, the court outlined a complete bill of rights for the mentally ill patient. Among the key points, the court said treatment should be given:

● by adequate staff
● in the least restrictive setting
● in privacy
● in a facility that ensures the patient a comfortable bed, adequate diet, and recreational facilities
● with the patient's informed consent
● with payment for work done in the institution, outside of program activities
● according to an individual treatment plan.

If possible, you must ensure that any mentally ill or developmentally disabled patient knows what treatment he needs and how he'll get it. You must know what his major problems are and what he can do for himself — or what others must do for him — to help him get ready for discharge. You should also involve him in formulating his treatment plan, unless you have a documented reason why he can't or won't be involved.

SEXUAL RIGHTS

Many questions remain regarding the sexual rights of mentally ill and developmentally disabled patients. For example, should developmentally disabled people be given sex education? Should they be allowed to reproduce, practice contraception, or undergo voluntary sterilization? Although the general inclination is to let guardians make these decisions, the issue of the individual's right to make his own decisions won't go away. If good care can be given to the developmentally disabled and their offspring, who's to say that they should be denied the opportunity to enjoy the same satisfactions others do?

The U.S. Supreme Court has upheld the rights of mentally ill or developmentally disabled patients:
● to marry
● to have children
● to employ contraception, abortion, or sterilization, if desired
● to follow a lifestyle of their own choosing.

Several cases, such as *Sengstack v. Sengstack* (1958), *Wyatt v. Stickney* (1972), and *O'Connor v. Donaldson* (1975), have used the U.S. Supreme Court decisions as a basis for their rulings.

Involuntary sterilization

Involuntary sterilization of developmentally disabled patients isn't employed today as in the past. Although the U.S. Supreme Court upheld the constitutionality of involuntary sterilization in *Buck v. Bell* (1927), if a similar case were to come before the Supreme Court today, the precedent would likely be overturned.

In *Buck v. Bell*, the court held that the state has the right to sterilize a developmentally disabled or mentally ill person provided that:
● the sterilization isn't prescribed as punishment
● the policy is applied equally to all
● a potential child's interest is sufficient to warrant the sterilization.

Courts will authorize such a procedure only within specific guidelines or not at all. Generally, it must be shown that sterilization is the only workable means of contraception. In some cases, the court orders a separate, independent presterilization review of the case. (In New York state, for example, an independent medical review board must review and approve every planned involuntary sterilization before it can be performed.) Even though the patient's guardian has

requested sterilization, if the patient refuses to submit to surgery, the court may call for use of a less permanent birth control method.

PARTICIPATION IN RESEARCH

Another troublesome area involves using mentally ill and developmentally disabled people as subjects for medical or other research — especially if risks are involved. Guidelines for consent to experimentation and drastic, questionable, or extreme forms of treatment are complicated and raise many unresolved questions. The so-called *Willowbrook* decision, *N.Y. State Association for Retarded Children, Inc. v. Care* (1977), however, decreed that both voluntary and involuntary residents of an institution have the constitutional right to be protected from harm. The proper authority (usually an IRB) should allow the patient to participate in the research only if it's relevant to his needs and the needs of others like him and its potential benefits outweigh its potential risks. For example, a depressed patient shouldn't be asked to participate in research involving anxiety and schizophrenia.

Strict federal regulations guide how experimental treatment can be carried out. Such treatment must be given with extreme caution to mentally ill or developmentally disabled patients.

RESPONDING TO PATIENT REQUESTS

"Ordinary" requests made by mentally ill or developmentally disabled patients may require special consideration.

For example, a patient may demand to smoke a cigarette now. If the patient should smoke only under supervision because of the danger of fire, you may decide to stay with him while he does so or write an order to have the staff stay with him. If you have a duty to be elsewhere, you should refuse his request, explaining why and telling him when he'll be able to smoke. Or, if you know a refusal will agitate and anger him, you can ask a nurse to supervise the patient while he smokes.

Perhaps the patient is well aware that he's violating the health care facility's no-smoking policy and his request is really a challenge to authority. If so, you may decide to refuse the request, explaining the need to follow the hospital's social and safety policies.

If the patient's behavior is part of a pattern that includes, for example, refusing to shower, refusing to go to bed by a certain time, and demanding to make an immediate phone call, then you need to refer the situation to the treatment team for a well-thought-out decision — one that serves the best interests of the patient and the hospital. After it's made, ask all the health team members to enforce this decision consistently.

Caring for a suspected criminal

Suppose you're asked to care for an injured suspect who's accompanied by police. Because the police need evidence, they ask you to give them the patient's belongings and also a sample of his blood. Should you comply? The answer to this question isn't simple. If you're ignorant of the law and fail to follow proper protocol, the evidence you turn over to police may not be admissible in court. Worse still, later on, the patient may be able to sue you for invasion of privacy.

CONSTITUTIONAL RIGHTS

The Fourth Amendment to the U.S. Constitution provides that "the right of the people to be secure in their persons, houses, papers, and effects, against unreasonable searches and seizures shall not be violated, and no warrants shall issue, but upon probable cause." This means that every individual, even a suspected criminal, has a right to privacy, including a right to be free from intrusions that are made without search warrants. However, the Fourth Amendment doesn't absolutely prohibit all searches and seizures, only unreasonable ones.

Further, under constitutional law, when a magistrate issues a warrant authorizing a police officer to conduct a search, the warrant must be specific about the places to be searched and the items to be seized.

The ***exclusionary rule*** is probably the most common rule affecting NPs in relation to suspected criminals and their victims. This rule stems from the Fourth Amendment's prohibition of unreasonable searches and seizures. In the landmark case of *Mapp v. Ohio* (1961), the U.S. Supreme Court held that evidence obtained through an unreasonable or unlawful search can't be used against the person whose rights the search violated.

Searches without a warrant

Under certain circumstances, a police officer may lawfully conduct a search and obtain evidence without a warrant:

● If an accused person consents to a search, any evidence found is considered admissible in court (*Schneckloth v. Bustamonte* [1973]).

● A search incidental to an arrest may be conducted without a warrant. Usually, such a search shouldn't extend beyond the accused person's body or the immediate area where he could reach for a weapon. However, in *Maryland v. Buie* (1990), the U.S. Supreme Court ruled that a search incidental to an arrest could extend to adjoining rooms and closets of a private residence from which an accomplice could attack. Police may even conduct a sweep of an entire area if they have reason to think they may be in danger. Although this Supreme Court case dealt with searches in a private home, the ruling could apply to searches conducted in a hospital.

● In *Horton v. California* (1990), the U.S. Supreme Court ruled that police could seize any evidence in plain view, as long as they're lawfully in a position to see the object. Thus, when looking for people who pose a danger, police can seize incriminating items in plain view.

● Police may search an area, even out of arms reach, to recover a weapon that could pose a threat to their safety (*New York v. Class* [1985]).

● Police may enter a private area and seize any items in plain view if they're in "hot pursuit" of a criminal suspect (*Warden v. Hayden* [1967]).

Evidence obtained as part of a blood test

Opinions differ as to whether a blood test, such as a blood alcohol test, is admissible in court if the person refused consent for the test. In *Schmerber v. California* (1966), the U.S. Supreme Court said that a blood extraction obtained without a warrant, incidental to a lawful arrest, isn't an unconstitutional search and seizure and is admissible evidence. Many courts have held this to mean that a blood sample must be drawn after the arrest to be admissible.

Further, the blood sample must be drawn in a medically reasonable manner. In *People v. Kraft* (1970), a suspect was pinned to the floor by two police officers while a physician drew a blood sample. In *State v. Riggins* (1977), a suspect's broken arm was twisted while a policeman sat on him to force consent to a blood test. In both cases, the courts ruled the test results inadmissible. The courts have also ruled as inadmissible — and as violative of *due process rights* — evidence gained by the forcible and unconsented insertion

of a nasogastric tube into a suspect to remove stomach contents (*Rochin v. California* [1952]).

Courts have admitted blood tests as evidence when the tests weren't drawn at police request but for medically necessary purposes, such as blood typing (*Commonwealth v. Gordon* [1968]). Some courts have also allowed blood work to be admitted as evidence when it was drawn for nontherapeutic reasons and voluntarily turned over to police.

Be careful, though. A physician, an NP, or a nurse who does blood work without the patient's consent may be liable for committing battery, even if the patient is a suspected criminal and the blood work is medically necessary.

Blood alcohol tests and drunk driving arrests

Many states have enacted so-called implied consent laws as part of their motor vehicle laws. These laws hold that by applying for a driver's license, a person implies his consent to submit to a blood alcohol test if he's arrested for drunken driving. Many of these laws state specifically that if an individual refuses to submit to the chemical test, it may not be given, but the driver then forfeits his license. Check to see whether such laws exist in your state.

Evidence obtained during a surgical procedure

A Massachusetts case, *Commonwealth v. Storella* (1978), involved a bullet that a physician removed during a medically necessary operation. After the operation, the physician turned the bullet over to the police. The court allowed the bullet to be admitted as evidence because the physician was acting according to good medical practice, and not as a state agent, in removing the bullet.

In 1985, the U.S. Supreme Court ruled that the constitutionality of court-ordered surgery to acquire evidence must be decided on a case-by-case basis. The interest in individual privacy and security must be weighed against the societal interest in collecting evidence. Therefore, you should be wary if asked to assist in a highly invasive procedure to help the state obtain evidence if the suspect doesn't consent. If necessary, consult an attorney.

Swallowed contraband
Drug couriers have been known to carry contraband by swallowing it in small balloons, which can be recovered during elimination. As an NP, you may become involved in efforts to detect and recover swallowed contraband. In *United States v. Montoya de Hernandez* (1985), the U.S. Supreme Court ruled that the police could lawfully detain drug couriers until swallowed items could be recovered and seized.

Searches by a private party
In *Burdreau v. McDowell* (1921), the U.S. Supreme Court said that the Fourth Amendment protections applied only to governmental (such as police) action and not to searches conducted by private parties. Although several courts have criticized this rule, it has been repeatedly upheld.

In *State v. Perea* (1981), a nurse took a suspect's shirt for safekeeping, then turned it over to the police even though they hadn't requested it. A New Mexico court allowed the shirt to be admitted as evidence. The reason: Because no governmental intrusion was involved, the suspect's Fourth Amendment right wasn't violated.

The case of *United States v. Winbush* (1970) produced a similar result. In this case, the court ruled that evidence found during a routine search of an unconscious patient's pockets was admissible because the purpose of the search was to obtain necessary identification and medical information.

Evidence in plain view
As an NP, if you find a gun, knife, drug, or other item that the suspect could use to harm himself or others, you have the right to remove it. You should, however, notify the facility's administration immediately and maintain control over the evidence until you can give it to an administrator or law enforcement official.

When the suspect may sue
In general, searches that occur as part of medical care don't violate a suspect's rights. But searches made for the sole purpose of gathering evidence — especially if done at police request — very well may. Several courts have said that a suspect subjected to an illegal private search has a right to seek remedy against the unlawful searcher in a civil lawsuit. One such case was *Stone v. Commonwealth* (1967). (See *Conducting a drug search,* page 78.)

A word of caution
The laws of search and seizure are complex and subject to change by new legal decisions. Consult with your facility's administration or an attorney before complying with a police request to turn over a patient's personal property. Some state laws require that police obtain a warrant before they're legally entitled to this evidence.

DOCUMENTING YOUR ACTIONS
Be careful and precise in documenting all medical and nursing procedures when you care for a suspected criminal. Note any blood work done, and list all treatments and the patient's response to them.

If you turn anything over to the police or administration, record what it was and the name of the person you gave it to. Record a suspect's state-

Conducting a drug search

Drug abuse is now prevalent in many practice settings. You may be faced with patients hiding drugs not only in emergency departments (EDs), medical-surgical units, and school settings, but also in rehabilitation centers, skilled nursing facilities, and retirement facilities. If you suspect your patient is abusing drugs or alcohol, you have a duty to do something about it. If such a patient harms himself or anyone else, resulting in a lawsuit, the court may hold you liable for his actions.

When you know about drug abuse

Suppose you know for certain that a patient is abusing drugs — if you're practicing in an ED, you may find drugs hidden on the patient as you complete your examination. Your facility's policy may obligate you to confiscate the drugs and take steps to see that the patient doesn't acquire more.

When you suspect drug abuse

When a patient's erratic or threatening behavior makes you suspect he's abusing drugs or alcohol, your facility's policy may require that you conduct a search. Is your search legal? As a rule of thumb, if you strongly believe the patient poses a threat to himself or others, and you can document your reasons for searching his possessions, your actions are legally justified.

Guidelines for searches

Before you conduct a search, review your facility's guidelines on the matter; then, follow these guidelines carefully. Contact your office manager or supervisor and explain you have legitimate cause for a search. If available, ask a security guard to accompany you. In addition to protecting you, he'll serve as a witness if you do find drugs. When you're ready, confront the patient, tell him you intend to conduct a search, and tell him why.

Depending on your facility's guidelines, you can search a patient's belongings as well as his room. If you find illegal drugs during your search, confiscate them. Remember, possession of illegal drugs is a felony. Depending on your facility's guidelines, you may be obligated to report the patient to the police.

If you find alcoholic beverages during your search, facility guidelines may require you to take them from the patient. Explain to the patient that you'll return them when he leaves or turn them over to family members.

Maintaining written records

After you've completed your search, record your findings in your notes and in an incident report. Your written records will be an important part of your defense (and your facility's) if the patient decides to sue.

ments that are directly related to his care. If a suspect says, "I shot a cop in the arm tonight," that isn't related to his care. But if he says, "I think I was shot in the leg by a cop," that relates directly to his medical care.

SAFEGUARDING EVIDENCE

Before any evidence can be admissible in court, the court must have some guarantee of where, and how, it was gathered. Someone must account for the evidence from the moment you collect it until it appears in court: a continuum known as the *chain of custody.* You can't leave evidence unattended where it might be tampered with.

If you discover evidence, use your facility's chain-of-custody form. First used when evidence is taken from the patient, this form should remain with the evidence until the trial. It documents the identity of each person handling the evidence as well as the date and times it was in their possession. In effect, the form should serve as an uninterrupted log of the evidence's whereabouts.

If your facility doesn't have a chain-of-custody form, keep a careful note as to exactly what was taken, by whom, and when. Give this information to the hospital administrator when you deliver the evidence. Until such time as the evidence can be turned over, it should be kept in a locked area.

When a suspect dies, most states provide that the **coroner** can claim the body. Police are free to gather any evidence that won't mutilate the body. A dead body has no constitutional rights, so no rights are violated by a search.

NPs WORKING BEHIND BARS

Even after conviction, an individual doesn't forfeit all constitutional rights. Among those retained is the Eighth Amendment's proscription against cruel and unusual punishment. This implies that prison officials and health care workers must not deliberately ignore a prisoner's medical needs.

The U.S. Supreme Court, in *Estelle v. Gamble* (1976), stated that the Eighth Amendment prohibits more than physically barbarous punishment. The amendment embodies "broad and idealistic concepts of dignity, civilized standards, humanity, and decency against which we must evaluate penal measures."

Right to medical care

The state has an obligation to provide medical care for those it imprisons. The Supreme Court has concluded that "deliberate indifference to serious medical needs of prisoners constitutes the unnecessary and wanton infliction of pain proscribed by the Eighth Amendment. This is true whether the indifference is manifested by prison physicians in response to a prisoner's

needs or by prison personnel in intentionally denying or delaying access to medical care or intentionally interfering with the treatment once prescribed."

In *Ramos v. Lamm* (1980), the court outlined several ways in which prison officials show deliberate indifference to prisoners' medical needs:
● preventing an inmate from receiving recommended treatment
● denying access to medical personnel capable of evaluating the need for treatment
● allowing repeated acts of negligence that disclose a pattern of conduct by prison health staff
● allowing such severe deficiencies in staffing, facilities, equipment, or procedures to exist that inmates are effectively denied access to adequate medical care.

Providing care

Working daily with prisoners is difficult and demanding, both professionally and emotionally. Along with exhibiting a host of other unpleasant behaviors, prisoners can be abusive, manipulative, and angry. In spite of this, health care professionals can't forget their ethical and legal duty to provide quality care.

NPs working in a prison setting should be aware that the doctrine of **respondeat superior** doesn't apply to prison cases when the prisoner sues for violations of his constitutional rights. Neither you nor the facility can be held responsible for accusations of "cruel and unusual punishment" unless you've personally acted to deprive the prisoner of medical care (*Vinnedge v. Gibbs* [1977]). The prison or facility can be sued if they had knowledge of a pattern and practice of abuse by the NP that eventually was sanctioned.

When a prisoner refuses treatment

Several courts have stated that individuals have a constitutional right to privacy based on a high regard for human dignity and self-determination. That means any competent adult may refuse medical care, even lifesaving treatments. For instance, in *Lane v. Candura* (1978), an appellate court upheld the right of a competent adult to refuse a leg amputation that would have saved her life.

A suspected criminal may refuse unwarranted bodily invasions. However, an arrested suspect or convicted criminal doesn't have the same right to refuse lifesaving measures. In *Commissioner of Correction v. Myers* (1979), a prisoner with renal failure refused hemodialysis unless he was moved to a minimum security prison. The court disagreed, saying that although the defendant's imprisonment didn't divest him of his right to privacy or his interest in maintaining his bodily integrity, it did impose limitations on those constitutional rights. As a practical matter, any time a patient refuses lifesaving treatments, inform your facility's administration. In the case of a suspect or prisoner, notify law enforcement authorities as well.

Reimbursement issues and liability

Differences between third-party payers arise partly because they follow regulations by state laws both where the third-party payer originates and where the service is performed in addition to region-specific and employer-specific regulations. Medicare, however, remains the gold standard as far as reimbursement guidelines in health care are concerned. Most insurance companies start with the Medicare

guidelines and then expand on them. Thus, an understanding of Medicare requirements creates a strong foundation of the concepts needed to practice, document, and bill appropriately for reimbursement in health care.

BILLING MEDICARE

Federal laws and regulations, plus rules by the Department of Health and Human Service's HCFA, establish the credentials, scope of practice, and collaborative relationships necessary for the NP and the clinical nurse specialist practicing in an extended role. The rules detail how an NP may provide and bill for services as a participating provider of the Medicare program. Failure to comply with these many program-specific requirements may result in civil, criminal, and administrative sanctions. These sanctions, imposed by HCFA or the Department of Health and Human Services' Office of Inspector General (OIG), negatively impact the relationships, reputation, and resources of the NP as well as the NP's employer and collaborating practitioners.

Medicare requirements

Direct billing for medical services provided by the NP is allowed and encouraged by the federal government. Since 1990, some medical services provided by NPs in nursing facilities were reimbursed by the Medicare program on a reasonable charge basis. In 1991, this coverage was expanded to NPs practicing in any setting located in areas that qualified under federal law as rural areas.

Effective January 1, 1998, the restriction on settings for services provided by NPs was removed as a result of the Balanced Budget Act of 1997 (BBA). NPs are now eligible for Medicare reimbursement, regardless of the setting in which their services are provided, but only if no other facility or provider charges are paid in connection with these services. Payment is equal to 80% of the actual charge, or 85% of the physician fee schedule, whichever is lower. Payment is made directly to the NP, or to a third party such as the NP's employer or billing company, in accordance with the reassignment requirements established by the Medicare program in the Medicare Carrier Manual.

NPs who don't already bill for covered services under the Medicare program are required to complete an HCFA Form 855 and submit it to HCFA in order to receive a unique personal identifying number, commonly referred to as a UPIN. To receive a HCFA Form 855, you should contact your local Medicare carrier. Additional information regarding this application procedure is available on HCFA's Web site.

Medicare will pay for medical services provided by NPs as long as the NP is legally authorized to perform the service and does so in accordance with state laws and regulations of the state in which she practices. In general, the provision of medical services by the NP is covered by the Medicare program if the following requirements are met. First, the services must be of the type considered to be physicians' services if furnished by a doctor of medicine or osteopathy (collectively referred to as a "physician"). Second, the services must be performed by an NP who satisfies Medicare's definition of an NP, which includes the following criteria:
● being a registered professional nurse with a master's degree in nursing, who is currently licensed to practice in the state in which the services are furnished
● satisfying the applicable requirements for qualifications as an NP in the state in which the services are pro-

vided and meeting at least one of the following requirements:
– current certification as a primary care NP by the ANA or by the National Board of Pediatric Nurse Practitioners and Associates
– successful completion of a formal education program, which includes at least 1 academic year that prepares RNs to perform an expanded role in the delivery of primary care, plus at least 4 months of classroom instructions, plus the award of a degree or diploma
– successful completion of a formal education program that otherwise doesn't qualify under the previous criteria but prepares RNs to perform an expanded role in the delivery of primary care. In order to qualify, the APN must have performed the expanded role for at least 12 months during the 18-month period immediately preceding February 8, 1978.

In addition, the NP must be legally authorized to perform the services in the state in which they're performed, the services must be performed in collaboration with a physician, and the services must not be precluded from coverage because of a statutory exclusion.

HCFA has published a proposed rule that would change the credentialing requirements for NPs who wish to bill the Medicare program. The proposed rule would require that after January 1, 2001, an NP applying for a Medicare billing number for the first time must be a registered professional nurse who is authorized by the state in which the services are furnished to practice as an NP plus be certified as an NP by a recognized national certifying body that has established standards for NPs. The proposed rule also requires that after January 1, 2003, an NP applying for a Medicare billing number for the first time must also possess a master's degree in nursing.

For purposes of these Medicare requirements, the term **collaboration** is defined as the process in which the NP works with one or more physicians to deliver health care services within the scope of the professional expertise of the NP. Collaboration must be performed with medical direction and supervision must be provided by the collaborating physician as defined in jointly developed guidelines. Collaborative practice must follow the laws and regulations of the state in which the services are provided. Federal programs don't require the collaborating physician to be present when the NP provides services, or to make an independent evaluation of a particular patient seen by the NP. This direct supervision isn't required as part of the initial visit or as part of an established treatment plan. Further, NPs may establish collaborative relationships with several physicians, either as an employee of a group practice, a member of a facility's medical staff, or as a result of one or more **collaborative practice agreements** entered into by the NP and the collaborating physicians. (See *Collaborative agreements.*)

Because rules and regulations vary widely from one area to another, be sure to consult with your licensing body and Medicare carrier to determine which requirements govern your jurisdiction.

"Incident to" billing
Under Medicare's current requirements, the NP, in addition to other nonphysician practitioners, may also provide certain "incident to" services under the direct personal supervision of a physician, for which the physician may receive reimbursement under the physician's billing number.

To qualify as "incident to" services under the Medicare program, the services must be:

● provided routinely in a physician's office or clinic
● delegated by the physician as an integral part of the physician's professional service
● provided by an individual who qualifies as an employee of the physician (this designation includes independent contractors)
● provided under the physician's direct personal supervision.

"Direct personal supervision" doesn't mean that the physician must be present in the same room when the "incident to" services are being provided. However, the physician must be present in the office suite or building and readily available to provide assistance and direction throughout the time the NP is performing the "incident to" services.

"Incident to" billing doesn't require contact between the physician and patient on each occasion of service. A service could be considered to be "incident to" when furnished as part of a course of treatment meeting each of the following criteria:
● the physician performs an initial service
● the physician evaluates a new patient or an existing patient with a new problem
● the physician is actively involved in managing the course of treatment for the new patient or problem (for example, the physician sees the patient on at least every third office visit).

Under the current Medicare rules, the physician bills for all "incident to" services provided in the office or clinic setting and receives payment representing 100% of the physician fee schedule.

FRAUD AND ABUSE VIOLATIONS
Federal regulations specify what constitutes fraud and abuse in billing Medicare. Medicare fraud is the intentional violation of Medicare rules,

Collaborative agreements

Typically, a collaborative practice agreement includes the following minimum elements:
● Complete names, home and business addresses, zip codes, pager numbers, and all personal, business, car, and cellular telephone numbers of the collaborating physician and the advanced practice nurse (APN)
● A description (and listing as appropriate) of all professional licenses, Drug Enforcement Agency registrations, hospital credentials, specialty or board certifications of the physician and the APN
● A description of the specific manner in which the physician and APN will cooperate, collaborate, and control the delivery of services under the arrangement, which includes in some form a description of the following:
– work schedules
– practice settings
– supervision requirements and expectations
– peer review requirements and expectations
– any specific situations that require direct supervision

– coverage requirements and expectations during absence, incapacity, infirmity, or emergency by the physician and APN
– in the event the APN is to prescribe medications pursuant to the collaborative practice arrangement, a description of what limitation, if any, the physician has placed on the APN's prescriptive authority
– a description of the time and manner of the physician's review of the APN's provision of medical services (such as the group's peer review practices) and, in particular, prescribing practices (such as at least 5% of prescriptions reviewed weekly)
– a list of all other written practice agreements between the physician and the APN
– the duration or term of the agreement between the physician and APN, and any methods by which the parties may terminate the agreement
– a list of all usual procedure codes (CPT/HCPCS) in code and narrative format that the physician has agreed to collaborate with the APN
– signature of both physician and APN
– all amendments to be filed with the agreement.

deliberate deception, or the misrepresentation of facts for unlawful gain.

Medicare abuse is a lesser offense. It refers to incidents and practices that directly or indirectly cause financial losses to the Medicare program, Medicare beneficiaries, or the families of Medicare beneficiaries. Practices inconsistent with accepted and sound medical or business habits may constitute Medicare abuse. Examples of Medicare abuse are:
● excessive or unnecessary charges to the Medicare program
● improper billing practices
● accepting payment for services that don't meet recognized standards of care

● accepting payment for medically unnecessary services.

Federal statutes, acts, and laws

From a fraud and abuse standpoint, NPs who provide health services for which reimbursement is sought through Medicare, Medicaid, or other federal and state health care programs are called providers. Providers are subject to fraud and abuse laws, regulations and requirements, including:
● the Anti-Kickback Statute
● the *False Claims Act*
● the Ethics in Physician Referrals Act, also known as the Stark act, to the extent that physicians are involved
● the Civil Monetary Penalties Act

● the many manuals, advisory opinions, fraud alerts, and other compliance directives published by HCFA and the Department of Health and Human Services' OIG, all of which set forth specific requirements governing the organization, service delivery, and reimbursement of various types of health care providers participating in the Medicare, Medicaid, and other government programs.

ANTI-KICKBACK STATUTE. The Anti-Kickback Statute (also called the Statute) was originally enacted in 1972 and has been amended several times since then. In general terms, the Statute prohibits the knowing payment of anything of value to influence the referral of federal health care program business. Medicare and Medicaid are both programs covered by this statute.

The Statute prohibits the offering or giving of **remuneration** to induce the referral of a Medicare or Medicaid patient to receive one's services. Similarly, it prohibits inducing a person to purchase, arrange for, or recommend an item or service that will be paid in any part with funds from the Medicare or Medicaid programs.

Violations of the Statute are punishable by up to 5 years in prison, criminal fines up to $25,000, administrative civil monetary penalties up to $50,000, and exclusion from participation in federal health care programs.

Because the Statute can be interpreted to cover a wide variety of actions, concerns arose among practitioners that the Statute prohibits many types of existing commercial arrangements. In 1987, Congress responded to these concerns by authorizing the OIG to issue regulations designating specific "safe harbors" for various payments and business practices that, while potentially prohibited by law, wouldn't be prosecuted.

In addition to several exceptions set forth in the Statute, the OIG has published 21 regulatory safe harbors under the Statute that establish minimum requirements. If these requirements are met, certain practices are protected from the Statute's harsh prohibition, including:
● certain types of ownership investments
● space and equipment rentals
● employees, personal services, and management contracts
● the sale of a practice
● referral services
● discounts
● the waiver of beneficiary coinsurance payments.

Recognizing the special needs of rural, underserved areas, the safe harbors regulations provide more lenient guidelines governing practices performed in these areas. Specifics addressed include:
● joint ventures (having a financial investment in a business concern that patients are referred to)
● practitioner recruitment
● the sale of physician practices
● subsidies for obstetrical malpractice insurance (having the NP pay $1,000 towards the collaborating physician's malpractice insurance).

The penalties for violating the Anti-Kickback Statute are harsh. However, the Statute requires that in order to prove a violation, a specific intent to disobey the law must be evident. As a criminal statute, the government must prove beyond a reasonable doubt that there is specific intent to violate the Statute in order to obtain a conviction.

CASE LAW. Most of the courts that have considered the standard for intent under the Anti-Kickback Statute have held that "knowingly and willfully" means that if even one purpose of a business arrangement is to induce referrals, the Statute is violated. This "one purpose" test of intent was established in *United States v. Greber*, U.S. (1985) and affirmed in *United States v. Kats*, U.S. (1989).

Under the *Greber* "one purpose" test, the government can prove the necessary intent even if other beneficial and legal reasons also exist. However, in *Hanlester Network v. Shalala*, U.S. (1995), the U.S. Court of Appeals for the Ninth Circuit established a different standard of intent that is much more difficult for the government to prove and more favorable to providers. In that case, the court held that the "knowingly and willfully" language requires the government to prove two things in order to prove a violation of the Statute. First, it must be proven that the provider knows the Statute prohibits offering or paying remuneration to induce referrals. Second, it must be proven that the provider engaged in prohibited conduct with the specific intent to disobey the law.

However, the *Hanlester* decision doesn't apply in all cases. It's binding only in the Ninth Circuit, which governs the states of Alaska, Hawaii, Arizona, California, Nevada, Oregon, Washington, Idaho, and Montana. Moreover, the view of the OIG is that *Hanlester* was wrongly decided and the OIG has indicated it will continue to follow the "one purpose" test for proof of intent.

FALSE CLAIMS ACT. The False Claims Act is the federal government's primary litigative tool for combating fraud. In addition, the Act empowers private persons, known as **whistle-blowers** or "relators", to institute civil actions known as **qui tam actions** to enforce the Act. In *qui tam*, an action is brought by a relator (on behalf of himself and the commonwealth), and con-sequently he receives a portion of the penalties, fines, and awards collected.

The Act is violated when a provider knowingly presents a false claim for payment or approval to an employee of the U.S. government or armed forces, or conspires to defraud the government by getting a false claim approved or paid. Such violations require either that a false claim was submitted for payment, or that a false statement related to an underlying service or provider was submitted in order to get the claim paid. In either case, false claims and statements are submitted "knowingly." This means the provider had actual knowledge the statements made were false or acted with deliberate ignorance or reckless disregard as to their veracity.

Examples of false claims include:
● overbilling
● billing for services that weren't rendered
● billing for services that weren't medically necessary
● unbundling one service into several claims
● upcoding services for a higher reimbursement
● providing inferior or poor quality services
● falsifying claims or medical records to certify patients for benefits
● billing for services provided by non-qualified practitioners or personnel.

PENALTIES. If the government or the relator prevails on the merits, the government is awarded, under the Act, treble damages plus a $5,000 to $10,000 penalty for each false claim submitted. The Act also contains "voluntary disclosure" provisions. With voluntary disclosure, a person's exposure to liability is arguably limited to double the government's damages and civil penalties.

If an NP chooses to seek reimbursement through Medicare, Medicaid, or other federal and state health care programs, she should be fully aware of the sanctions that can be imposed. Providers of medical and other designated health services are subject to numerous criminal, civil, and administrative sanctions if convicted of fraudulent and abusive behavior. The False Claims Act and the Civil Monetary Penalties Act, which address the reduction or limitation of health care services to entitled individuals of federal health care programs, provide for penalties related to submission of claims for payment.

A penalty of $2,000 may be imposed on a facility for each Medicare or Medicaid patient for which such a payment is made as well as upon any physician who knowingly accepts such a payment. A civil monetary penalty of up to $10,000, plus an amount equal to three times the amount claimed, may be fined for each claim submitted for items or services that the provider knows, or should know, weren't provided as claimed. The provider may also be excluded from the Medicare, Medicaid, or other health benefits program as a result of this misconduct.

PREVENTIVE MEASURES. Given the significant risks under the Act, the NP should adopt the following safeguards to avoid a future investigation or enforcement action:
● Document all evaluation and management (E&M) services in accordance with the E&M documentation guidelines currently acceptable to HCFA and your Medicare carrier.
● Participate in internal audits within your practice to check the adequacy and accuracy of your services, the related documentation, and the resulting claims submitted for payment.
● Encourage all members of your practice, in addition to your staff and patients, to come forward with their

questions, concerns, or billing problems so that they may be promptly resolved without the need for a complaint to an external agency.

Such measures will enable you to remain proficient in the delivery of services as well as the many clinical, record-keeping and claims standards imposed by, among other third-party payers, the Medicare program.

STARK II. The Ethics in Patient Referrals Act is more commonly known as Stark (named after its founder, Congressman Pete Stark); Stark II represents the final version passed into law. The Stark law prohibits a physician (or an immediate family member of the physician) who has a financial relationship with an entity from making referrals to the entity for designated health services covered by either the Medicare or Medicaid programs.

Under Stark, a financial relationship is defined as an ownership or investment interest in the entity, or a compensation arrangement between the physician (or immediate family member) and the entity. Ownership interests can arise through debt, equity, or other means. Ownership includes an investment in an entity (or parent organization) that holds an investment interest in any entity providing the designated service. Compensation arrangements are defined to include any arrangement involving any remuneration between a physician and an entity. In this case, the term remuneration has been defined to include any type of exchange of something of value. This includes payment that is either direct or indirect, overt or covert, in cash or in kind.

The original prohibitions on physician referrals ("Stark I"), applied only to referrals for clinical laboratory services that were covered by Medicare.

These prohibitions have been extended in Stark II to include a range of other designated health services covered by Medicare or Medicaid, including:

- physical therapy services
- occupational therapy services
- radiology services (except screening mammography and invasive radiology procedures)
- radiation therapy services and supplies
- durable medical equipment and supplies
- parenteral and enteral nutrients, equipment, and supplies
- prosthetics, orthotics, and prosthetic devices, and supplies
- home health services
- outpatient prescription drugs
- inpatient and outpatient hospital services.

Stark broadly defines the term referral as the request by a physician for a particular item or service. This includes the request by a physician for a consultation with another physician, and any test or procedure ordered by, or to be performed by that other physician (or someone under the physician's supervision). Additionally, the request or establishment of a plan of care by a physician that includes the provision of designated health services constitutes a referral. Thus, the physician need not actually refer the patient to an entity or recommend that the patient obtain services from an entity in order to commit the prohibited referral. Instead, the physician need only order the service and the patient ultimately receive the service from an entity with which the physician has a financial relationship.

Moreover, the HCFA states in the preamble to the final Stark I regulations that any time a physician orders anything, it's "pursuant to a plan of care" on the physician's part, even if not officially called that. As a result of Stark's broad definition of the term *referral,* a physician's order for a designated health service that doesn't direct a patient to a particular entity can still constitute a referral under the statute.

Therefore, collaborating practitioners could inadvertently act in a prohibited manner. For example, an NP, working independently but under the supervision of a collaborating physician, could order a designated health care service. The patient could take the prescription to an area health care provider (Department of Human Services [DHS] Provider). A problem could arise if the collaborating physician has a financial investment in the company the patient chose. This referral is prohibited even though the physician isn't aware it was ordered, the NP is unaware of the physician's investment or the patient's choice of provider, and the patient chose the provider independently.

STARK VS. ANTI-KICKBACK. One of the biggest differences between the two laws is that Stark is "fact-based" rather than "intent-based." What this means is that, under Stark, it doesn't matter what the provider intended to do — if the provider is in violation, there is civil liability, even if it's an innocent mistake.

PENALTIES. Sanctions against the offender under Stark are significant. First, Medicare will deny payment for services rendered in violation of Stark. Secondly, if a provider collects on a bill for a service that was in violation of Stark, then the provider must refund the money within 60 days. More importantly, any provider presenting a claim or bill for a service that the provider knows, or should have known, is a violation of Stark can be subject to a civil money penalty of up to $15,000 for each service in question. An assessment of up to three times the total penalty, plus exclusion from the Medicare and Medicaid programs, becomes an important reason for the NP to carefully evaluate the other NPs and collaborative physicians involvement in any financial relationships involving a third-party DHS Provider.

PREVENTIVE MEASURES. It's important, therefore, to be aware of ownership interests or compensation arrangements that may exist between all practitioners and collaborating physicians and the particular DHS Provider. Before designating a health care service that involves a DHS Provider with whom the NP or collaborating physician has a financial interest, make sure it complies with at least one of the applicable Stark exceptions, which are comparable in many ways to the Statute's safe harbors. (See *Two Stark exceptions.*)

CIVIL MONETARY PENALTIES ACT. The Civil Monetary Penalties (CMP) Act also provides for civil monetary penalties against any person or entity that is responsible for misconduct as defined by the statute. The misconduct includes actions such as the submission of "upcoded" claims or claims for medically unnecessary services, the submission of false statements and certifications, and the offer or transfer of remuneration (such as free or discounted services or a waiver of coinsurance) to a Medicare or Medicaid patient that is likely to induce the patient to receive or order services from the particular provider.

The current regulations have increased the CMP maximum amount from $2,000 to $10,000 for each false item or service or prohibited practice, and raised the amount of authorized penalties from double to triple the amount claimed.

HCFA AND OIG PUBLICATIONS. In recent years, Congress has expanded the authority of HCFA and the OIG, among other agencies, to combat fraudulent activities in federal health care programs. Accordingly, these agencies have released a multitude of manuals, advisory opinions, fraud alerts, and other directives that describe and further explain those actions which are illegal under the various federal health care programs.

For example, HCFA's Medicare Carriers Manual (MCM) contains instructions for various medical services provided by physicians and other nonphysician practitioners. The MCM's instructions also govern providers of clinical laboratory services who must follow the manual's instructions in order to receive payment for Medicare or Medicaid services.

CONGRESSIONAL ACTION. Congress, by way of the Health Insurance Portability and Accessibility Act and the BBA, also required the Department of Health and Human Services to give health care providers some guidance on the application of the various fraud and abuse laws discussed above. In addition to the Statute's "safe harbors" and Stark's exceptions, the OIG was authorized to issue advisory opinions on potential issues under the Statute. HCFA was similarly authorized to issue advisory opinions on these same types of arrangements under Stark. Over the course of the last 3 years, the OIG has issued many advisory opinions under the Anti-Kickback Statute, all of which are available on the OIG's Web site. HCFA has also issued several advisory opinions under the Ethics in Physician Referrals Act, all of which are available on HCFA's Web site.

Two Stark exceptions

Stark II defines a "compensation arrangement" as an arrangement involving remuneration between a physician (or immediate family member) and an entity. Remuneration includes anything given directly or indirectly, overtly or covertly, in cash or in kind. However, there are exceptions to the prohibited compensation arrangement, such as those described below.

Fair market value exception
The "fair market value exception" protects any compensation arrangement between a physician and an entity if the arrangement satisfies specific conditions. An example is a facility providing free parking for a physician while the physician makes patient rounds. While a physician is making rounds, the free parking benefits the facility and its patients rather than personally benefiting the physician; therefore, it isn't regarded as a compensation arrangement under Stark.

De minimis exception
This rule includes an exception for *de minimis* remuneration. *De minimis* is defined as something that is so minuscule that the law won't consider it. Examples of this would be a physician receiving training sessions that aren't considered part of the legal agreement, or *de minimis* items, such as free pens or note pads. There are limitations here as well, including a $50 per gift or a $300 per year limit, and compensation can't be based in any way on the volume or value of the physician's referrals.

Minimizing damages
Of course, it's in the best interest of the NP and the collaborating physicians to comply with the above laws, regulations, and other applicable requirements governing the organization, delivery, and reimbursement of high quality and medically necessary health care services. But is it enough for the NP, or the NP's organization, to establish policies that simply demand compliance with these many laws, regulations, and requirements?

CORPORATE COMPLIANCE PLAN. The fact is that federal and state enforcement agencies are placing greater emphasis and resources on investigating and prosecuting violations of such requirements. This is of particular interest when the requirements relate to quality of care, medical necessity, qualified personnel, documentation, and claims processing. Thus, there is an essential need for an effective corporate compliance program that incorporates these standards into day-to-day operations and practices. (See *An effective corporate compliance program,* page 90 and 91.)

An effective corporate compliance program must properly evaluate, and bring into compliance where necessary, the facility's many clinical and business practices and relationships. An ideal place to start is with practices and relationships related to the delivery of covered services under Medicare, Medicaid, and other government-sponsored programs. The establishment of this type of program creates a culture of compliance at the "grass roots" level that is intended to prevent violations from occurring, and to promptly correct such action if it does occur.

An effective corporate compliance program

Through an effective corporate compliance program (CCP), a facility actively polices itself. The government takes into account the existence of an effective CCP when establishing culpability and penalties. Federal sentencing guidelines state that civil and criminal penalties are lessened "if the offense occurred despite an effective program to prevent and detect violations of law."

The following seven elements are stated in the U.S. Sentencing Guidelines for Organizations as a minimum for developing an effective CCP:

Standards and procedures

The organization must have established compliance standards and procedures to be followed by its employees and other agents that are reasonably capable of reducing the prospect of criminal conduct.

It's important that all employees and independent contractors involved are aware of and agree to abide by the established standards and procedures. There must be specific measures listed and utilized to convince employees that top management is committed to the program.

Compliance oversight

Specific individuals within high-level personnel of the organization must have been assigned overall responsibility to oversee compliance with such standards and procedures.

There must be adequate staffing to investigate, analyze, and report violations. The corporate compliance officer reports to top management — this will attest to the active and full support of top management. The corporate compliance officer's duties include:

● taking reports of problems or violations and correcting them
● overseeing a periodic compliance audit and monitoring compliance
● training employees in compliance matters.

Due diligence

The organization must have used due care not to delegate substantial discretionary authority to individuals whom the organization knew, or should have known, through the exercise of due diligence, had a propensity to engage in illegal activities.

This is one reason background checks are performed on employees, particularly those in areas where fraud and abuse potential is high.

Employee training

The organization must have taken steps to communicate effectively its standards and procedures to all employees and other agents, such as requiring participation in training programs or disseminating publications that explain in a practical manner what is required.

There must be a plan with specific measures for informing all employees of the program. This includes information about proper standards and procedures, but also about the CCP, mechanisms for reporting problems, and safeguards to protect the employee from reprisal.

Auditing and monitoring compliance

The organization must have taken reasonable steps to achieve compliance with its standards, such as utilizing monitoring and auditing systems reasonably designed to detect criminal conduct by its employees and other agents and by having in place and publicizing a reporting system whereby employees and other agents could report criminal conduct by others within the organization without fear of retribution.

This involves self-auditing and self-analysis of charting, documentation, and billing within the organization to ensure adherence to the established standards and procedures. This also calls for a mechanism that employees may use to report potential or actual problems.

An effective corporate compliance program *(continued)*

Discipline policies

The standards must have been consistently enforced through appropriate disciplinary mechanisms, including, as appropriate, discipline of individuals responsible for the failure to detect an offense. Adequate discipline of individuals responsible for an offense is a necessary component of enforcement; however, the form of discipline that will be appropriate will be case-specific.

This refers to the consequences imposed by the organization for not adhering to the established standards and procedures. The consequences must be the same for all organizational members.

Prevention

After an offense has been detected, the organization must have taken all reasonable steps to respond appropriately to the offense and to prevent further similar offenses — including any necessary modifications to its program to prevent and detect violations of law.

This involves quality improvement and acceptance of corporate responsibility. After a problem has been identified, an action plan must be developed and implemented, then evaluated and further refined as needed. It's important to contact experienced legal counsel to determine if and when to report violations.

Some common steps used to prevent offenses and meet the CCP requirements are:
- ombudsmen or mediators
- review boards
- internal audits
- written standards of conduct
- ethics training programs
- anonymous hotlines or drop boxes
- newsletters.

An effective compliance program greatly reduces the risk of enforcement actions, including the *qui tam* actions brought under the Act that usually involve disgruntled employees, angry competitors, or dissatisfied patients, and therefore also reduces potential civil or even criminal liability of the facility and its staff. Finally, a corporate compliance program that is committed to preventing and detecting criminal or other noncompliant conduct by an organization's employees, contractors, and agents will serve as a mitigating factor. In the event criminal or civil penalties are imposed as a result of an enforcement action, an effective corporate compliance plan can significantly decrease associated financial penalties.

In short, implementation of a corporate compliance program is a proactive step that must be instituted in order to safeguard the provider's resources, relationships, and reputation.

Selected references

Closs, S.J., and Cheater, F.M. "Evidence for Nursing Practice: A Clarification of the Issues," *Journal of Advanced Nursing* 30(1):10-17, July 1999.

Hardy, T., et al. "The Evolution of Hospitalist Programs," *Healthcare Financial Management* 54(9):63-68, September 2000.

Health Care Financing Administration: *www.hcfa.gov*

HEDIS 3.0 Health Plan Employer Data and Information Set, Technical Specifications, Vol. 2. National Committee for Quality Assurance: Washington, D.C., 2001.

Huff, C. "Hospital Heavies: Venture Capital Bulks Up Companies That Outsource Medicine's Newest Specialty, Inpatient Only Care," *Hospitals and Health Network* 72(15/16):44-46, August 5-20, 1998.

Lardner, J. "For Nurses a Barrier Broken,"
U.S. News & World Report 125(4):58-61,
July 27, 1998.

Price, D.M. "Evaluating Managed Care,"
Journal of Nursing Law 5(3):47-50, 1998.

Sox, H.C. "Independent Primary Care Practice by Nurse Practitioners," *JAMA: Journal of the American Medical Association*
283(1):106-108, January 5, 2000.

Tashakkori, Z., and Aghajanian, A. "Reimbursement Issues in Advanced Practice
Nursing: An Overview," *Medsurg Nursing*
9(2):93-96, April 2000.

U.S. Dept. of Health & Human Services Office of Inspector General:
www.dhhs.gov/progorg/oig

Wing, K.R. *The Law and the Public's Health,*
5th ed. Chicago: Health Administration
Press, 1999.

Withrow, S.C. *Managing Healthcare Compliance.* Chicago: Health Administration
Press, 1999.

Chapter Three

LEGAL ISSUES ON THE JOB

The structure of professional relationships in health care delivery has changed significantly over the last two decades. *Nurse practitioners (NPs)* have emerged as important providers of health care who practice in a wide range of environments, including ambulatory care settings, *health maintenance organizations (HMOs),* private physicians' offices, and their own private practices. Becoming knowledgeable about conditions of employment and related laws is one of the best measures that NPs can take to protect themselves from employment disputes and costly litigation due to violation of state and federal laws. Moreover, knowing one's rights as an employee is essential to achieve optimal working conditions, financial security, and job satisfaction and, most importantly, to provide optimal patient care.

This chapter explores legal issues associated with being employed as an NP, such as collaborative practice agreements with physicians and how you can negotiate your autonomy, based on your state's requirements. It reviews sources of legal conflicts in the workplace and ways to prevent those conflicts through the use of contracts. You'll also learn about the process of successful contract negotiation. Finally, the chapter covers several important employee issues, such as protection of *whistle-blowers,* working within the managed care system, and collective bargaining.

Collaborative practice

Once you're certified as an NP, you may be able to practice independently or in a collaborative arrangement with a physician. Most NPs choose to be employed by others rather than start their own practice.

If entering into a collaborative arrangement, you and the physician must reach an agreement about the level of independence that you'll exercise in clinical and business matters. Although this may change over time, the basic components should be outlined in your contract. Most states require some level of physician involvement.

Expanded roles for nurses are still evolving, and state legislators are addressing questions about the NP's *scope of practice* and collaborative arrangements. Nursing boards and NPs have thus far fought successfully to overcome the attempts of some organized medical groups to subjugate NP practice. Joining an NP organization is an effective way to stay informed about current issues facing NPs in your specialty or your region and about the frequently changing laws and policies that affect your practice. (See *Nurse practitioner organizations,* pages 95 to 98.)

FEDERAL DEFINITION OF COLLABORATION

Until 1998, the federal government's definition of *collaboration* was "mandated supervision by a physician." This changed with passage of the Medicare Reform Act of 1997; effective January 1, 1998, collaborative practice referred to collaboration as defined by state *nurse practice acts,* rather than the earlier, more restrictive, language of the federal government.

STATE DEFINITION OF COLLABORATION

The definition of collaboration varies from state to state. *Collaborative practice* may be defined as a mutually agreed upon plan with one or more physicians that designates the scope of collaboration necessary to manage patient care. Collaboration provides medical direction to the NP. As an NP, you'll maintain primary responsibility for a patient's care, but you may need to seek the advice or opinion of a physician or another member of the health care team, as necessary, to ensure that services are provided in conformance with accepted standards of medical and nursing practice and with the statutes and regulations governing the practice of medicine, nursing, and the prescribing of drugs.

If you practice in a state requiring collaboration with a physician, you'll usually need to have a collaborative practice agreement in writing. De-

pending on your state's law, a written collaborative practice agreement may include provisions for referral and consultation, coverage for emergency absences of either the NP or the physician, mechanisms for resolving disagreements about patient care, and procedures by which patient records will be reviewed.

Your state may also require that you and your collaborating physician develop clinical practice protocols, which involve the joint formulation and joint approval of orders or guidelines for NP practice. Again, requirements vary from state to state, but typically your collaborating physician will periodically review your orders and documentation to ensure that services are provided in accordance with accepted standards of medical and NP practice.

You may be required to submit a copy of your practice agreement and practice protocols to state health authorities. In addition, your state may require that your collaborating physician's name be posted along with your own in your practice setting.

Collaborative practice agreement

When drafting the collaborative practice agreement, make sure that the roles of the physician and the NP are clearly defined. NPs have indicated that a key factor enhancing the negotiations of their roles has been their willingness to acknowledge their own limitations. Typically, NPs have been more effective in negotiating their roles in smaller organizations. It's sometimes difficult to negotiate roles in large bureaucratic settings.

A *collaborative practice agreement* outlines the level of support and supervision between the collaborating physician and the NP. The first step in developing a collaborative practice agreement is to review your state law regarding your scope of practice. If

(Text continues on page 98.)

Nurse practitioner organizations

Most nurse practitioner (NP) organizations were formed with the intention of promoting high standards of health care delivery by NPs, advocating for patients and NPs, and assisting NPs in staying informed about education and legislation issues. Some organizations are involved with certification, but not all. Here's a list of national and state organizations.

National organizations

American Academy of Nurse Practitioners
Capitol Station LBJ Bldg.
P.O. Box 12846
Austin, TX 78711
(512) 442-4262

American Association of Colleges of Nursing
One Dupont Circle N.W., Suite 530
Washington, DC 20036
(202) 463-6930

American Association of Occupational Health Nurses, Inc.
50 Lenox Pointe
Atlanta, GA 30324-3176
(404) 262-1162

American College of Nurse Midwives
818 Connecticut Ave., N.W., Suite 900
Washington, DC 20006
(206) 728-9860

American College of Nurse Practitioners
2401 Pennsylvania Ave. N.W., Suite 350
Washington, DC 20037-1718
(202) 466-4825

American Nurses Association
600 Maryland Ave. S.W., Suite 100 W.
Washington, DC 20024-2571
(202) 651-7001 or
(800) 274-4262

Association of Women's Health, Obstetric, and Neonatal Nurses (AWHONN)
700 14th St. N.W., Suite 600
Washington, DC 20005
(202) 662-1600

National Alliance of Nurse Practitioners
325 Pennsylvania Ave. S.E.
Washington, DC 20003
(202) 675-6350

National Association of Neonatal Nurses
1304 South Point Blvd., Suite 280
Petaluma, CA 94954-6859
(800) 451-3795

National Association of Nurse Practitioners in Reproductive Health
2401 Pennsylvania Ave. N.W., #350
Washington, DC 20037-1718
(202) 466-4825

National Association of Pediatric Nurse Associates & Practitioners (NAPNAP)
1101 Kings Hwy. N., #206
Cherry Hill, NJ 08034-1912
(609) 667-1773

National Association of School Nurses
P.O. Box 1300
Scarborough, ME 04070-1300
(207) 883-2117

National Conference of Gerontological Nurse Practitioners
P.O. Box 270101
Fort Collins, CO 80527-0101
(970) 493-7793

National Organization of Nurse Practitioner Faculties
One Dupont Circle N.W., Suite 530
Washington, DC 20036
(202) 452-1405

Nurse Practitioner Associates for Continuing Education (NPACE)
5 Militia Dr.
Lexington, MA 02173
(617) 861-0270

Uniformed Nurse Practitioner Association
1153 Evergreen Pkwy., M-181
Evergreen, CO 80439
(800) 759-2881

(continued)

Nurse practitioner organizations *(continued)*

State organizations

Alaska Nurse Practitioner Association
237 E. 3rd Ave.
Anchorage, AK 99501
(907) 274-0870

Arizona Nurse Practitioner Council
1850 E. Southern Ave., Suite 1
Tempe, AZ 85282-5832
(602) 831-0404

Arkansas Certified Nurse Midwives
Attn: Joni Yarnell
University of Arkansas Medical Sciences
Dept. Ob/Gyn - Mail Slot 518
4301 W. Markham
Little Rock, AR 72205
(501) 686-7161

Arkansas Department of Health NP Group (ADH)
Cherise Cornett
200 S. University, Suite 310
Little Rock, AR 72204
(501) 663-6080

Arkansas-Missouri Association of Nurse Practitioners (AMANP)
HC80 Box 127
Melbourne, AR 72556
(501) 368-1911

Arkansas Nurses Association (ArNA) Council for Advanced Practice Nursing
117 S. Cedar
Little Rock, AR 72205
(501) 664-5853 (501) 686-9628

Arkansas State Chapter National Association of Pediatric Nurse Associates & Practitioners (NAPNAP)
Kristie James, President
c/o University Hospital
4301 W. Markham
Little Rock, AR 72205
(501) 686-7585

Northwest Arkansas Alliance of Nurse Practitioners
546 Vinson
Fayetteville, AR 72701
(501) 442-3884 (p.m. only)

California Alliance of Advanced Practice Nurses
9852 Katella Ave., Suite 407
Anaheim, CA 92804
(310) 598-9767

Colorado Society of Nurse Practitioners
6340 S. Oak Way
Littleton, CO 80127
(303) 890-8464 (pager)

Connecticut Nurse Practitioner Group, Inc.
c/o CNA
377 Research Pkwy., Suite 2D
Meriden, CT 06450
(203) 238-1207

Nurse Practitioner Association of the District of Columbia
4227 37th St. N.W.
Washington, DC 20008-3148
(202) 686-5514

Georgia Nurse Practitioner Council
Attn: Patricia Yeargin
1362 W. Peachtree St. N.W.
Atlanta, GA 30309
(404) 876-4624

Iowa Association of Nurse Practitioners
c/o Pat Clinton
College of Nursing
University of Iowa
Iowa City, IA 52245
(319) 335-7055

Kansas Alliance of Advanced Nurse Practitioners
c/o Stephen Brotton
4421 E. Kellogg, Suite 1
Wichita, KS 67218
(316) 682-5770

Nurse practitioner organizations *(continued)*

Kentucky Coalition of Nurse Practitioners and Nurse Midwives
3988 Forest Green Dr.
Lexington, KY 40517
(606) 271-0942

Louisiana Association of Nurse Practitioners
606 Good News
Belle Chasse, LA 70037
(504) 826-2094

Maine Nurse Practitioner Association
Student Health Services
c/o Carrie Nix Kivela
University of Southern Maine
96 Falmouth St.
Portland, ME 04103
(207) 780-4650

Nurse Practitioner Association of Maryland, Inc.
110 West St.
Annapolis, MD 21401-2802
(410) 269-6970

Massachusetts Coalition of Nurse Practitioners
2465 Massachusetts Ave.
Cambridge, MA 02140
(617) 575-1565

Ob/Gyn NP Interest Group, AW/HONN Chapter/Minnesota Nurses' Association Affiliate
c/o Dawn Bowker
1675 Beam Ave., Suite 210
Maplewood, MN 55109
(612) 770-3320

Nevada Nurses' Association NP Group
3929 Briar Crest Ct.
Las Vegas, NV 89120
(702) 825-3555

New Hampshire NP Association
P.O. Box 833
Concord, NH 03302-0833
(603) 648-2233

Forum for Nurses in Advanced Practice (New Jersey)
320 W. State St.
Trenton, NJ 08618
(609) 392-4884

New Mexico Nurse Practitioner Council
909 Virginia N.E., #101
Albuquerque, NM 87108
(505) 268-7744

New York State Coalition of Nurse Practitioners, Inc.
48 Howard St.
Albany, NY 12207-1608
(518) 445-2667

Association of Oklahoma Nurse Practitioners
c/o Pamela Rollins
6108 N. Meridian, #801
Oklahoma City, OK 73112
(405) 271-4471

Oklahoma Nurses' Association
6414 N. Santa Fe, Suite A
Oklahoma City, OK 73116-9114
(405) 840-3476

Nurse Practitioners of Oregon
9600 S.W. Oak St., Suite 550
Portland, OR 97223
(503) 293-0011

Pennsylvania Coalition of Nurse Practitioners
893 Stone Jug Rd.
Biglerville, PA 17307
(717) 677-6400

Texas Nurse Practitioners
P.O. Box 3407
Austin, TX 78764

Vermont Nurse Practitioners, Inc.
c/o Iris McDonald
80 Central Ave.
S. Burlington, VT 05403
(802) 862-8151 (home)
(802) 656-2345 (work)

(continued)

Nurse practitioner organizations *(continued)*

Virginia Council of Nurse Practitioners
c/o Virginia Nurses' Association
7113 Three Chopt Rd., Suite 204
Richmond, VA 23226
(804) 282-1808

ARNPs United (Washington)
c/o Robert Smithing
ARNP
Nurse Practitioner Support Services
220 Railroad Ave. N.
Kent, WA 98032

Metro Milwaukee Nurse Practitioners (Wisconsin)
1257 N. 24th St.
Milwaukee, WI 53205-2421

Wisconsin Nurse Practitioners in Reproductive Health
c/o Deborah Kuklinski
W290N8268
Florencetta Heights
Hartland, WI 53029
(414) 538-1304

Wisconsin Nurses Association NP Council
6117 Monona Dr.
Madison, WI 53716
(608) 221-0383

your state law mandates that the board of nursing (or, possibly, both the board of nursing and the board of medicine) must approve your collaborative practice agreement, obtain a copy of the required components. Many states have sample collaborative practice agreements that they'll furnish on request. Ensure that you and the physician both meet the necessary requirements. For instance, the physician may be exceeding the number of simultaneous collaborative practice agreements allowable by law.

The collaborative practice agreement should outline the level of independence that you'll exercise. It should specify the services you can provide (based on your education, experience, and certification); for example, it may state that you can:
● diagnose and develop a treatment plan for common acute problems and chronic stable problems.
● perform procedures, such as cryotherapy or fracture immobilization.

● order and interpret diagnostic tests, including laboratory tests, ECGs, and X-rays.
● make rounds for hospitalized, nursing-home, or homebound patients.
● prescribe medications and controlled substances.
● refer to the collaborating physician or a medical specialist.

Likewise, the agreement should specify the services that the collaborating physician will provide, such as:
● assist in the establishment and review of drug policies and clinical practice guidelines at least annually.
● review and discuss the diagnosis and treatment plan for selected patients at least monthly.
● be available for consultation with the NP as needed, and arrange for another physician to accept this responsibility when the primary collaborating physician isn't available.

CONSULTATION
A collaborating physician generally must also be available by telephone for

consultation about medical problems, complications, emergencies, and patient referrals, but he need not be on-site during the hours you see patients. Your state may have rules regarding how frequently your collaborating physician must be on-site. In addition, some states limit the number of collaborative practice agreements that may be entered into by any one physician.

A SUCCESSFUL COLLABORATIVE PRACTICE

To establish a successful collaborative practice, the NP and the physician should have mutual respect for the other's skills, strengths, and professional autonomy. If you're in a collaborative practice relationship with a physician, you'll want him to be able to provide skillful, reliable, and prompt consultations while respecting your independent judgment and promoting your professional development.

NPs have been praised by patients for spending ample time with them during office visits, for exploring patient concerns, and for educating patients regarding health care issues. A physician who appreciates the value of these attributes will make an excellent collaborative partner.

EMPLOYMENT RELATIONSHIP

As an NP, you have the option to work either as an **independent contractor** or as an employee.

Independent contractor

As an independent contractor, you would be responsible for paying taxes, obtaining professional and personal insurance, and possibly even providing the necessary tools, supplies, and work area. The independent contractor isn't eligible for **worker's compensation** if injured while working. In addition, an independent contractor may be terminated without cause at any time unless otherwise specified through a contract.

Employee or independent contractor?

The following questions may help in determining if a worker is an employee or an independent contractor.

● According to the agreement, how much control does the employer exercise over the details of the work? For example, who sets the hours, days of the week, and schedule?

● Is the worker engaged in a distinct occupation or business?

● Is the work usually done under the direction of the employer, or is the worker a specialist who works without supervision?

● Does the work require unique skills?

● Does the employer or the worker supply the workplace and the tools the worker uses?

● For what length of time is the worker employed?

● Is the worker paid by the job or for hours spent working?

● Is the work a part of the regular business of the employer?

● Does either party believe they are creating an employer-employer relationship?

● Is the worker in business for himself?

Adapted from *Nurse Practitioner's Clinical Companion*, Springhouse, Pa.: Springhouse Corporation, 2000.

Although being an independent contractor has certain advantages for both the collaborating physician and the NP, the federal government (including the Internal Revenue Service and the Workers' Compensation Commission) examines these situations closely. For this reason, you should consult an attorney specializing in health care contracts to assist you in developing an independent contractor's agreement. (See *Employee or independent contractor?*)

Components of a legal contract

To be legal, a contract must include these four components:

A promise
Two or more legally competent parties must promise each other to do or not to do something.

Mutual understanding
The parties involved must clearly understand the terms and obligations that the contract imposes on them.

A lawful purpose
The parties must agree that their actions will be lawful. Any contract involving illegal acts or fraud is not enforceable.

Compensation
The parties involved must agree that, to fulfill the contract, the lawful actions will be performed in exchange for something of value.

Employee

If you choose to work as an employee, your employer would be responsible for withholding your federal, state, and local taxes, as well as Medicare, Social Security, and unemployment benefits. As an employee, you would be eligible for worker's compensation for injuries sustained at work. In addition, you may be entitled to health care benefits. The employee is also protected from termination on the basis of age, gender, race, or disability.

Your employer could be held responsible for your actions and therefore is likely to purchase professional liability insurance or demand that you have individual coverage.

Contracts

In recent years, it has become standard practice for NPs to enter into written employment contracts. The contracts, which are often complex and detailed, contain legally binding clauses that require careful analysis and complete understanding before they're executed.

DEFINITION OF A CONTRACT
In general, a contract is a promise, or a set of promises, for breach of which the law gives a remedy and the performance of which the law in some way recognizes as a duty. In all contracts, there is mutual consent and a willingness by both parties that certain acts will be performed. (See *Components of a legal contract.*)

Employment contracts are based on these general principles:
● A contract is legally binding.
● The law provides a remedy if a legal contract is breached.
● The nature of the employment relationship is expressly defined.
● Both expressed and implied terms are included.
● If the contract is employment-at-will, it's generally terminable by the employer or the employee without notice and for any reason.
● The contract should contain procedures for handling work-related disputes.
● The contract may be incorporated into employee handbooks.

In the United States, contracts contain an implied covenant of good faith and fair dealing. The implied covenant includes a contractual limitation on an employer's right to terminate an employee at will. It thus prohibits an employer from discharging an employee in "bad faith." Breaches of the implied covenant of *good faith* and fair dealing arise from terminations that have the effect of depriving a party of future compensation for past services (that is, for services already rendered), termination for failure to commit perjury (which is a violation of public policy), wrongful discharge for doing what the law requires (for example, for serving on a jury), wrongful discharge for refusing to commit an unlawful act (for example, refusing to commit perjury), and taking disciplinary action for exercising a legal right (for instance, filing a workers' compensation claim).

What constitutes public policy is a question of law for a trial judge to determine; whether a termination violates public policy is generally determined by a jury. Examples of wrongful termination include cooperating with police investigations and whistle-blowing to expose situations that seriously compromise patient care. (See *Legitimate grievances,* page 102.)

EMPLOYMENT CONTRACTS

Employment contracts are by nature legally binding unless they are illegal, in violation of public policy, made under undue influence, or entered into when one party to the agreement lacks the capacity to enter into the contract. For this reason, you must understand the basic principles and key points of contract and employment law.

All applications for employment should clearly define the nature of the employment relationship. An employment contract can be either expressed or implied. Expressed contracts are formed by oral or written language. Implied contracts are formed by manifestations of assent — that is, by the parties' conduct — rather than by oral or written language. When a lawsuit is brought in which one party seeks to enforce a contract or to obtain damages for breach of contract, a court must first decide whether there was, in fact, a contract.

EMPLOYEE-AT-WILL AGREEMENT

In nonunion or noncollective bargaining settings, unless an employment contract cites specific dates of employment, the applicant has entered an *employee-at-will agreement.* As a general rule, an at-will employee has no definite period of employment; the employment is terminable by either employer or employee without notice and for any or no reason. NPs hired as at-will employees should be aware that they're subject to dismissal or discipline without notice or cause at the employer's discretion. Similarly, an at-will employee can terminate the employment at any time. Moreover, in an at-will employment relationship, the employer may clearly state that it reserves the right to unilaterally abolish or modify any personnel policy without prior notice to the employee.

Certain restrictions exist, however, on an employer's ability to discharge an at-will employee. For example, an employer may be liable for wrongful termination if a discharge is found to be in violation of public policy, a breach of good faith and fair dealing, an invasion of privacy, or an instance of discrimination.

BREACH OF CONTRACT

Unjustified failure to perform all or part of a contractual duty is a *breach of contract.* Substantial breaches are never lawful. Either the employee or the employer may be accused of breaching a contract. If the breach is substantial, the courts may rule that the contract has been broken, and legal damages could result. If only a portion of the contract is breached, the portion not in question may remain in effect, and both parties may want to continue the relationship, with some clarifications made. Breaches can be avoided if both parties carefully consider the

Legitimate grievances

Not all complaints against an employer meet the definition of a legitimate grievance. If your complaint fits into one of the following categories, chances are that it's a legitimate grievance that can undergo external review and, possibly, arbitration.

Contract violations

Your employment contract is binding between you and your employer. If your employer violates it, you have a valid grievance. The following examples describe violations that would likely be prohibited in an employment contract:
- You've had to work undesirable shifts or be on call more often than other providers.
- Your employer doesn't post time schedules in advance.
- Your employer fires you without just cause.

Federal and state law violations

Any action by your employer that violates a federal or state law would be the basis of a grievance, even if the employment contract permits the action. For example:
- You receive less pay for performing the same work because of your gender.
- You're paid by the hour and don't receive the overtime pay you're entitled to.
- Your employer doesn't promote you because of your race.

Past practice violations

A past practice — one that has been accepted by both parties for an extended time but that is suddenly discontinued by the employer without notification — may be the basis for a grievance. The past practice needn't be specified in the contract. If the practice violates the contract, either party can demand that the contract be enforced. If the practice is unsafe, an arbitrator may simply abolish it. Examples of past practice violations might include the following:
- Your employer charges you for breaking equipment when others haven't been charged.
- Your employer revokes productivity bonuses.
- Your employer eliminates a rotation system for being on call on nights or weekends.

Health and safety violations

These grievances usually involve working conditions for which the employer is responsible. Legitimate grievances may be recognized even if the contract doesn't address the specific complaint. For example:
- You're required to reuse single-use items that may be contaminated.
- There are no hand-washing facilities near examination rooms.

Employer policy violations

Employers have the right to establish *reasonable* work rules and policies. These rules and policies aren't usually specified in the employment contract. Your employer can't violate its own rules without being guilty of a grievance (note, however, that an employer can change rules unilaterally). For example:
- You haven't received a performance evaluation in 2 years, although your employee handbook states that such evaluations will be done annually.
- Your employer assigns you a vacation period without your consent, contrary to personnel policies.

terms and conditions of the contract and know what they're promising each other. (See *Breach of contract claims,* page 104.)

Rationale for contracts

To achieve the compensation and working conditions you deserve, you need to understand your rights as an employee and the relationship between you and your employer. An ***employee contract*** will help minimize misunderstandings and protect both you and your employer. In our rapidly changing health care environment, even experienced NPs who have practiced in the same setting for many years are likely to consider negotiating a contract.

AVOIDING MISUNDERSTANDINGS

A contract serves as effective protection for you and your employer when legal questions arise in everyday practice. For example, how should an NP respond to requests for narcotics from another provider's patient? Is an NP expected to follow a primary care provider's plan of care and automatically write a prescription based on the history listed in the patient's chart? Who among the office staff is permitted to triage patients over the phone, in person, or both? To avoid misunderstandings that could result in misguided care, it's best to seek an employee contract that addresses such issues.

Work environment

A contract allows you and the employer to agree in advance on issues that are important to both parties, including the overall work environment, benefits, and compensation. In the contract, detail what the support staff will do for you (such as make appointments) and what you'll do for the support staff (such as respond quickly when summoned for emergencies). Determine the chain of command so that communication is appropriately directed and effective for both clinical and business issues. Be aware that clinical issues such as concerns about a treatment plan may be directed to a physician, whereas business issues, such as supplies or a patient's lack of insurance coverage, may be directed to an office manager or administrator.

Work expectations

Your employee contract should also specify the employer's expectations of you, including the extent of the services to be performed and the number of office hours you're expected to work each week. The contract should state how often you'll be on call, including at night, days off, and weekends. On-call expectations should list for whom you'll cover (for example, just the providers within that practice or a wider base of local medical practices) and whether you'll be answering calls outside your specialty area (for example, if you're an adult care NP and you receive calls from a family practice). In addition, the contract should state if the employer expects you to bring your own patients or be responsible for adding a minimum number of patients to the practice. It also may indicate whether you're expected to see patients of other providers in the practice when the other provider is over-booked.

PROTECTION FOR EMPLOYER

The employer can reduce his risk of liability by stating in the contract certain requirements that the NP must meet to retain employment. Examples include maintaining required certification, completing continuing education activities, preserving patient confidentiality, and following established disease-management protocols.

If the employer chooses, he can also include a drug-testing policy in the contract, as well as designate the office as a drug- and alcohol-free workplace.

PROTECTION FOR EMPLOYEE

Contracts also protect the employee. They specify the duration of employment, how the agreement can be altered or updated, salary and benefits, and reasons for termination. Job security is one significant protection. Employee contracts and agreements also

Breach of contract claims

Listed below are the primary types of breach of contract claims, along with an example of each. Note that some of the examples may prompt an attorney to plead more than one cause of action.

CLAIM TYPE	EXAMPLE
Breach of contract: Failure to perform a promise or obligation made within a contract without legal justification	Failure to pay an employee for services rendered
Negligent misrepresentation: Failure to provide significant information, usually with the intent to deceive or be unfair	Withholding of information about a practice's or an NP's level of reimbursement, with the effect of decreasing the NP's contracted bonus compensation
Negligent infliction of emotional distress: Failure to act appropriately, causing emotional distress to another	Failure to uphold an NP's right to renegotiate a contract, or a mandate that the NP must choose between quality care and state board of nursing regulations
Intentional infliction of emotional distress: Action that causes emotional distress to another	Knowingly allowing an NP's professional reputation to be maligned; telling falsehoods about the NP's skill and practice outcomes
Intentional interference with contractual or advantageous business relations: Words or actions designed to cause loss of opportunity to another	A current or former employer providing false information to a prospective employer
Misrepresentation, fraud, or deceit: Action designed to mislead or deceive	Promising one employee that all weekend hours are divided equally among all providers, then promising another employee all weekends off
Unfair and deceptive business practices: A practice that offends established public policy and that is immoral, unethical, oppressive, unscrupulous, or substantially injurious to another	Misappropriating funds from the practice's gross income
Defamation or slander: Words calculated to disparage another in any office, profession, calling, trade, or business	Discussing a person's confidential affairs with another person who has no legal justification for having the information

provide a source for the policies and procedures that a practice will follow.

Job security

A contract provides job security in that it limits the conditions under which termination may occur. An employer's reasons for termination may be totally unrelated to the NP's performance. Although this may seem an unlikely situation, it could happen if, for example, a practice suddenly lost a large portion of its patient base, or if less-qualified but less-costly practitioners were available. In these situations, the NP without a contract is more vulnerable to abrupt termination.

Setting practice policies and protocols

An employee contract is the place to establish practice policies and procedures for dealing with difficult issues. For instance, the contract may describe in detail how narcotics will be ordered and dispensed within the facility and may establish a policy whereby no provider prescribes controlled substances for another provider's patients. In such instances, office staff would be instructed to defer appointments strictly for pain medication until the primary care provider returns or to refer patients to the emergency department. In urgent situations, small amounts of medication may be prescribed but limited to the need to sustain the patient until his primary care provider is available.

The contract can also identify the source of the practice guidelines or protocols that you're expected to use as guidance in maintaining the current standard of care. This is valuable information for you and your employer and can improve the quality of care for all patients in the practice.

Contract structure

Labor attorneys are your first resource for helping you to draft a contract. If you feel comfortable drafting your own contract, you may still want an attorney to look it over before you sign it. Remember, clarity is the most important factor in drafting a contract. Avoid legal and technical terminology that may be vague or open to interpretation. Use definitions to explain key terms and a numbering system with well-organized headings to make it easier to find essential information. The form or structure of a contract should simplify and clarify the agreement.

BASIC COMPONENTS

A contract begins with a title describing the instrument (for example, "Nurse Practitioner Agreement"). After the title, the caption identifies the names of the parties and the legal action taken, along with the transition phrase, which contains words signifying that the parties have entered into an agreement. Then, the contract includes the recitals, which are best explained as the "whereas" clauses. These clauses aren't intended to have legal significance but may become relevant to resolve inconsistencies in the body of the contract or if the drafter inappropriately includes substantive provisions in them. The use of the word *whereas* is merely tradition and has little legal significance.

The next part of the contract may contain definitions of all key contract terms, followed by the contract's operative language, which includes the substantive health-related provisions that define the responsibilities and obligations of each party, representations and warranties, and declarations. The last section of the contract, the closing or testimonium, reflects the assent of the parties by their signatures. Sometimes, the drafters of a provider contract decide to have the signature page on the first page for administrative simplicity. (See *Sample nurse practitioner agreement,* pages 107 to 112.)

Provisions within contracts

Issues that may be addressed within the contract include dispute-resolution procedures and **remuneration.** These issues frequently cause concern for NPs.

The contract should specify precise methods of dealing with work-related disputes. It may detail the chain of command or provide for formal investigations and the presence of an attorney. If your contract doesn't include procedures to resolve disputes, have your attorney add them to the agreement.

Remuneration details how you'll be compensated for your services. You may be paid by a set salary, a percentage of the practice's profits, a base salary plus a percentage of the practice's profits, or an hourly wage. It's important to identify your patient population, the individual who controls the way the practice is administered, and the effect this is likely to have on your compensation in relation to the payment method.

SALARY. If you're paid a salary, you'll receive the same amount of money on a set time schedule, regardless of the hours you work or the funds generated.

PERCENTAGE OF PROFIT. If you're paid by percentage, the amount you receive is a percentage of the net profits. This is determined by taking the payments received then subtracting the costs of overhead and physician consultation.

SALARY PLUS PERCENTAGE. This is a combination of the two previous methods of payment. If you generate income over a predetermined amount, you'll receive additional compensation.

HOURLY SALARY. In this arrangement, you're paid a set hourly wage.

EXHIBITS AND APPENDICES

Frequently, contracts incorporate references and other documents, some of which will be appended to the agreement as attachments or exhibits. Ensure that you have copies of all attachments and exhibits and that you fully understand their meaning before signing the contract. Exhibits and appendices are frequently used by organizations to promote efficiency in administering many provider contracts. From an administrative view, there are advantages to this. First, it eases the burden and expense of redrafting and revising contracts. Second, if an exhibit or appendix needs to be amended, the rest of the contract doesn't automatically need to be renegotiated. Third, when a contract is under consideration for renewal and the main issue is an item listed separately in the appendix, a provider is less likely to suggest amending other provisions of the contract.

IMPORTANT CLAUSES

Informal employment agreements may be easier in the short term, but contracts force the employer and employee to consider and discuss issues before they arise. It's wise to be aware of potential areas of concern so rebuttal arguments or alternative suggestions may be formulated. Three important clauses commonly found in employment agreements for NPs are noncompetition clauses (also known as restrictive covenants), bonus formulas, and termination clauses.

(Text continues on page 112.)

Sample nurse practitioner agreement

Nurse Practitioner Agreement
EMPLOYMENT AGREEMENT BETWEEN _____

Date

AND
Nurse Practitioner _____

Date

THIS EMPLOYMENT AGREEMENT, made and entered into on the date set forth on the signature page hereto, by and between Inc., a corporation (hereinafter referred to as "XYZ"), which is organized and operated as a professional corporation under the laws of the State of ___, and the individual nurse practitioner identified on the signature page hereto (hereinafter referred to as "Nurse Practitioner").
WITNESSETH:
WHEREAS, XYZ desires to employ Nurse Practitioner to provide clinical, professional, and administrative services as an employee of XYZ, and Nurse Practitioner desires to be employed by XYZ to provide such services within her areas of professional competence and expertise, and on the terms and conditions provided herein;
WHEREAS, Nurse Practitioner is a duly licensed Nurse Practitioner (or if Primary Care Nurse Practitioner is a legal entity, the members of such entity are duly licensed Nurse Practitioners) in the State of ___ ; whose license is without limitation or restriction to practice in the advanced nursing role; and on the terms and conditions provided herein;
WHEREAS, XYZ and Nurse Practitioner mutually desire to enter into an Agreement whereby the Nurse Practitioner shall provide and coordinate the health care services to Members of XYZ.
NOW, THEREFORE, in consideration of the mutual promises and covenants herein contained, the parties agree as follows:

1. Duties and Obligations of the Nurse Practitioner

1.1 Duties. During the term of this Agreement, the Nurse Practitioner shall perform such clinical and non-clinical duties as may be assigned to the Nurse Practitioner by XYZ from time to time including, but not limited to, those duties described below. The Nurse Practitioner shall, as part of her duties, perform clinical services including, but not limited to ____. The Nurse Practitioner may also perform _____. The Nurse Practitioner shall perform such duties under the supervision and direction of the Medical Director and other XYZ physicians who may be assigned by the Medical Director.

1.2 Time Commitment and Best Efforts. Beginning (date of hire), the Nurse Practitioner shall devote at least 40 hours per week to providing services as an employee of XYZ pursuant to this Agreement. The Nurse Practitioner shall provide such services at times to be set by XYZ. It is currently anticipated that XYZ will schedule her to work five 8-hour days each week (with adjustments for weeks containing holidays). It is currently anticipated that during the time the Nurse Practitioner is working as a full-time employee of XYZ, XYZ will schedule her to work her scheduled hours between Monday and Friday from 8 or 9 or 10 a.m. to 4 or 5 or 6 p.m., with possible evening hours once a week at the discretion of the Medical Director. The Nurse Practitioner warrants that she will make her best efforts to perform all work in a quality manner and on a timely basis.

1.3 Qualifications. The Nurse Practitioner shall at all times during the term of this Agreement: (a) maintain an unrestricted license to practice as a Nurse Practitioner in the State of ___ ; (b) maintain a current and valid certificate from the Drug Enforcement Administration to prescribe controlled substances in the State of ___; (c) be and remain a member in good standing on the medical staff of any hospital to which she is assigned to work, with such

(continued)

Sample nurse practitioner agreement *(continued)*

clinical privileges as are required to enable her to perform the services that she is engaged to perform hereunder; and (d) be and remain a participating provider with any governmental or other third-party payer or insurer with which XYZ is now or hereafter has a relationship. This Agreement is not and should not be construed as any form of guarantee or assurance that the Nurse Practitioner will receive necessary medical staff membership or privileges at any hospital for purposes of discharging her responsibilities hereunder, and application, appointment, reappointment and granting of privileges at any hospital shall be governed solely by the applicable medical staff and hospital bylaws of such hospital then in effect. The Nurse Practitioner represents and warrants that she possesses the professional skills and training necessary to perform the services she is to perform hereunder.

1.4 Standards. The Nurse Practitioner shall provide services under this Agreement in accordance with the accepted standards of care of her profession and specialty including, but not limited to, the American Medical Association, the American Association of [type of nursing specialty] Nurses, and the American College of [type of specialty] Medicine, and in compliance with all applicable statutes, regulations, rules and directives of federal, state, and other governmental and regulatory bodies having jurisdiction; the by-laws, rules, and regulations of XYZ; and all applicable rules, regulations, policies, by-laws, and protocols of any hospital at which the Nurse Practitioner works under the terms of this Agreement and its Medical Staff.

1.5 Assignment. The Nurse Practitioner hereby assigns and grants to XYZ the right to bill and collect for all professional services rendered by the Nurse Practitioner pursuant to this Agreement, and all accounts receivable and the proceeds thereof arising out of such services. The Nurse Practitioner shall maintain the necessary identification numbers to permit XYZ to bill third-party payers for clinical services that the Nurse Practitioner renders pursuant to this Agreement. Upon termination of this Agreement for any reason whatsoever, all such accounts receivable then outstanding shall be the sole and exclusive property of XYZ and not subject to any claim by the Nurse Practitioner.

1.6 Records and Reports. The Nurse Practitioner shall complete medical records in a timely and legible fashion as required by applicable laws and in keeping with generally accepted standards of records keeping and documentation, including a clear notation of all treatments and procedures, and shall maintain and furnish XYZ with such records, reports, and documentation evidencing the performance of the Nurse Practitioner's duties hereunder as may be requested by XYZ or required by applicable law. Should XYZ so request, the Nurse Practitioner shall dictate medical reports for transcription and edit the transcribed drafts for final printing.

1.7 Conduct Upon Termination. The Nurse Practitioner agrees as a condition of her employment that during the term of this Agreement and for a period of three years after the termination or expiration of this Agreement (including extensions, renewals, or successors of this Agreement), the Nurse Practitioner shall refrain from soliciting business with, negotiating with, or providing clinical or administrative services to any client of XYZ (whether or not there is a formal written contract between XYZ and the client) without the prior written consent of the Medical Director of XYZ. This clause merely prohibits the Nurse Practitioner from soliciting business with, negotiating with, or providing services to XYZ clients without written consent; it does not restrict the Nurse Practitioner from practicing or working in any geographic area or location. The Nurse Practitioner acknowledges that any violation of this provision on the part of the Nurse Practitioner would cause irreparable harm to XYZ and agrees that, should she violate or breach this provision, XYZ shall be entitled to damages and attorneys' fees, as well as other remedies provided by law, and shall be entitled to obtain preliminary and permanent injunctive relief against any such breach.

1.8 Medical Staff Privileges. The Nurse Practitioner acknowledges that absent an extension, or successor agreement between the parties, termination or expiration of this Agreement for any reason may immediately and automatically cause to terminate the medical staff mem-

Sample nurse practitioner agreement *(continued)*

bership and clinical privileges of the Nurse Practitioner at any hospital or medical facility at which the Nurse Practitioner works for XYZ if such termination is provided for under a contract then in place between XYZ or an affiliate of XYZ and such hospital or medical facility. The expiration of medical staff membership and clinical privileges described in this Section 1.8 shall occur without the Nurse Practitioner having any right to notice, hearing, appellate review, or any of the other procedures described in any hospital or medical staff by-laws.

2. Obligations of XYZ

2.1 Compensation. XYZ shall pay the Nurse Practitioner an annual salary of $ _____ dollars a year for services rendered pursuant to this Agreement. The Nurse Practitioner's salary, less amounts withheld by law, shall be payable by XYZ in 26 equal biweekly installments on the first or second Wednesday, and the third or fourth Wednesday, of each month. (The precise day of the week on which salaries will be paid is subject to change without notice at the sole discretion of XYZ.)

2.2 Fringe Benefits. XYZ shall, from time to time, adopt a fringe benefit plan (the "Benefit Plan") for its physician extender employees (i.e., Nurse Practitioners or Physician Assistants). XYZ hereby agrees to provide the Nurse Practitioner with benefits consistent with the Benefit Plan as in effect during her employment. Any such Benefit Plan may be modified prospectively at any time and will remain in effect until such time as a subsequent Benefit Plan is adopted by XYZ. The current Benefit Plan is described in Schedule 2.2, which is attached hereto and incorporated herein by reference. A part of any such Benefit Plan shall be reimbursement to the Nurse Practitioner of the full cost of professional liability insurance coverage against liabilities arising from services rendered by the Nurse Practitioner under this Agreement in the amount of at least $1,000,000 of each occurrence with a per annum aggregate limit of at least $3,000,000 (if such limits are available to Nurse Practitioners practicing in the State of ____). The Nurse Practitioner shall be responsible for obtaining and maintaining in full force and effect a valid professional liability policy generally required for Nurse Practitioners specializing in [insert type of nursing practice here] with coverage limits of at least $3,000,000 (if such limits are available to Nurse Practitioners practicing in the State of ____). The policy required under this Section 2.2 shall be with the Medical Professional Mutual Insurance Company (also known as ABC) unless the Nurse Practitioner obtains written permission from the Medical Director to substitute a policy from another insurance company or carrier.

2.3 Facilities and Services. XYZ will provide or arrange for the provision of office space, secretarial assistance, clinical assistance, supplies, and equipment suitable to the performance of the Nurse Practitioner's duties under this Agreement.

2.4 Right to Bill and Set Charges. XYZ shall have the exclusive right and responsibility to bill and collect from all patients and third-party payers for all services rendered by the Nurse Practitioner under this Agreement and shall have the authority to determine the charges to be established for such services. The Nurse Practitioner shall not bill any patient or third-party payer for any services rendered by the Nurse Practitioner under this Agreement.

3. Term and Termination

3.1 Term. This Agreement shall commence on [insert date] and shall have an initial term of 13 months, ending on [insert date], unless terminated earlier pursuant to Section 3. This Agreement shall be automatically renewed for successive 1-year terms upon expiration of the initial term unless either party notifies the other party at least 120 days prior to the expiration of the then-current term that it does not wish to renew the Agreement for an additional term.

(continued)

Sample nurse practitioner agreement *(continued)*

3.2 Termination for Cause. XYZ shall have the right to terminate this Agreement for cause by giving at least 30 days prior written notice to the Nurse Practitioner, which notice shall state the cause and specify the effective date of such termination; provided, however, that the Nurse Practitioner shall have the right within 20 days of receipt of such notice to cure the alleged default to the satisfaction of XYZ. The Nurse Practitioner shall have the right to terminate this Agreement for cause by giving at least 60 days prior written notice to XYZ, which notice shall state the cause and reason and specify the effective date of such termination; provided, however, that XYZ shall have the right within 45 days of receipt of such notice to cure the alleged default to the satisfaction of the Nurse Practitioner.

a. XYZ. For XYZ, cause shall include without limitation (i) a material breach by the Nurse Practitioner of any of her obligations hereunder; or (ii) other good cause relating to patient care, the existence of which shall be a matter for the final judgment of XYZ upon recommendation of its Medical Director.

b. The Nurse Practitioner. For the Nurse Practitioner, cause shall include without limitation a material breach by XYZ of any of its obligations hereunder.

3.3 Immediate Termination by XYZ. XYZ may terminate this Agreement for cause, such termination to be effective immediately upon provision of notice thereof to the Nurse Practitioner, if the Nurse Practitioner ceases to meet the qualifications set forth in Section 1.3 or if the Nurse Practitioner's license to practice nursing in the [State of ____] is revoked, suspended, terminated, or restricted.

4. Notices

Any notices permitted or required to be given hereunder shall be deemed properly given when sent by registered or certified mail, postage pre-paid, return-receipt requested, as follows:

If to XYZ, to:
[insert name], M.D.
Medical Director
XYZ Corporation
Street Address, Suite #
City, State Zip Code
If to the Nurse Practitioner, to:
[insert name], N.P.
Street Address
City, State Zip Code
or such other person or address as any party may designate by notice duly given.

5. Assignment

Assignment by either party of any rights or obligations under this Agreement is expressly prohibited.

6. Severability

Should any provision of this Agreement or application thereof be held invalid or unenforceable, the remainder of this Agreement shall not be affected and shall continue to be valid and enforceable to the fullest extent permitted by law unless to do so would defeat the purpose of this Agreement.

Sample nurse practitioner agreement *(continued)*

7. Waiver
The failure by a party at any time to require performance of any provision of this agreement shall not constitute a waiver of such provision and shall not affect the right of such party to require performance at a later time.

8. Confidentiality
The parties agree to hold confidential the terms contained herein except to the extent that such terms need to be disclosed to effectuate the terms of this Agreement to close business advisors (such as accountants and attorneys) with whom it is essential to do so. Any such disclosures shall be subject to the same confidentiality requirement.

9. Amendment
This Agreement represents the entire agreement and understanding between the parties with respect to the subject matter hereof and may not be amended except by the written agreement of the parties.

10. Governing Law
This Agreement shall be governed by and construed in accordance with the laws of [State of ___].

11. Counterparts
This Agreement may be executed in two or more counterparts, each of which shall be deemed an original but all of which shall constitute one and the same instrument.

IN WITNESS WHEREOF, the parties hereunto set their hands to this Agreement as of the day and year first written above.
XYZ, INC.
By:

_____
Name of Medical Director or Agent Thereof

_____
Name of Nurse Practitioner

Schedule 2.2
FRINGE BENEFITS FOR PHYSICIAN EXTENDERS

1. Vacation
Employees of XYZ who are full-time Physician Extenders (i.e., Nurse Practitioners or Physician Assistants) shall be entitled to 4 weeks of paid vacation per calendar year, which paid vacation time shall accrue based on actual time worked, with 1 week of vacation accruing for each 4 months worked. For Physician Extenders employed by XYZ on less than a full-time basis, but at least a half-time basis (i.e., at least 20 hours a week), vacation shall accrue on a prorated basis rounded to the nearest 4-hour period such that a Nurse Practitioner working at 80% of full-time would accrue vacation at 80% of the accrual rate for a full-time Nurse Practitioner. Vacation time must be taken during the year in which it is accrued unless XYZ agrees in writing to some alternative arrangement. Vacation time, however, may be taken by the Physician Extender as financial compensation. The Nurse Practitioner shall notify XYZ at least 2 months in advance of the desire to take vacation time, and shall

(continued)

Sample nurse practitioner agreement *(continued)*

not take more than two consecutive vacation weeks unless such longer vacation period is approved by XYZ. XYZ reserves the right to approve or assign which weeks will be taken as vacation time; however, XYZ will make a reasonable effort to accommodate specific times and requests.

2. XYZ Leave
Full-time physician extenders shall be entitled to 1 week of paid leave for continuing education related to the practice each year. The Nurse Practitioner shall notify XYZ at least 2 months in advance of a desire to take such leave. XYZ reserves the right to approve or assign which weeks will be taken as education leave; however, XYZ will make reasonable effort to accommodate specific times and requests.

3. Sick Leave
Full-time physician extenders shall be entitled to up to 5 days of paid sick leave each year. Unused sick leave shall accumulate and may be taken as compensation at a time and one-half rate or as scheduled vacation time. Scheduling of such vacation time must be approved in advance by XYZ.

4. Holidays
Full-time physician extenders shall be entitled to 10 paid holiday days per year. These shall include New Year's Day, Columbus Day, Thanksgiving Day, Christmas Day, and two personal days to be mutually agreed upon by the Nurse Practitioner and XYZ.

5. Health Insurance
Full-time employees of XYZ who are Physician Extenders shall be entitled to participate in the current XYZ group health insurance plan. XYZ will pay 60% of the insurance premiums for a family plan, or 80% of the insurance premiums for an individual plan.
Nursing and Medical Malpractice Insurance. Full-time Physician Extenders shall be entitled to paid medical malpractice insurance as described in their individual contracts.

Noncompetition clause
A typical noncompetition clause will provide that an employee, after termination of the contract, may not compete with his employer for a stated period of time in a particular territory. A territory range varies and can be as narrow as a one- or two-block radius or as broad as worldwide.

A second type of noncompetition clause is related to either the employer's former or current client base, or both. This type of restrictive covenant typically restrains the employee from contracting, soliciting, or otherwise doing business with a client of the employer. In Massachusetts, the recent trend has been for courts to enforce employee noncompetition agreements as narrowly as possible. The standard the courts look to is the "reasonableness" of certain provisions within the contract. In many states, noncompetition agreements aren't legally enforceable against physician providers in clinical practice. With respect to NPs, while the law is less well-defined at this time, depending on the state, it would be reasonable to expect the courts to apply similar standards when interpreting noncompetition agreements.

Bonus formulas

Bonus formulas specify conditions under which an NP is rewarded for good performance. Types of bonus formulas include those associated with productivity (based on the number of patient visits within a specified time), profit (based on gross or net profits), and quality (based on meeting or exceeding certain standards). Some bonus formulas, such as those rewarding health care providers for not ordering expensive tests, have been outlawed in a number of states.

PRODUCTIVITY-BASED. Productivity-based bonuses reward the NP for completing a large number of visits. This formula benefits the NP working in a practice that sees at least half fee-for-service patients and a limited number of managed care patients.

PROFIT-BASED. The profit-based formula is a profit-sharing method. Essentially, the more money the practice makes, the more money the NP makes. Be aware, however, that more than one accounting method can be used to determine profit; for example, will the profit be determined by gross earnings or net earnings? Because this is an area of frequent dispute, the NP who is considering this formula should include a clause granting a process for dispute resolution as well as the right for an independent financial audit.

OUTCOME-BASED. Outcome-based formulas, also called quality-based formulas, reward the NP on the basis of meeting predetermined outcome-based criteria. Examples of outcome-based criteria are those used in ***Health Plan Employer Data Information Sets (HEDIS),*** including having all children immunized appropriately, seeing all new mothers within 6 weeks of delivery, and having post-myocardial infarction patients on beta-adrenergic block-

ers. This method of calculating bonuses is most beneficial when a large percentage of patients are members of a managed care plan.

Whichever type of bonus formula is used, NPs should understand how the formula works and ensure that it promotes acceptable patient care services. Like all provisions of a contract, the bonus formula should be written in clear, concise, and unambiguous terms. Measurement tools should be well planned out and in conformance with all state and federal laws to avoid moral or ethical problems.

Termination clause

Termination clauses provide the guidelines for termination. These clauses can be "for cause" or "without cause." Conditions constituting grounds for ***termination*** typically include:
● disability that prevents the NP from performing her agreed-upon duties
● loss of professional licensure or certification
● restriction of the NP's ability to perform by a governmental authority (for example, the passing of legislation that prohibits the NP from prescribing medication or performing independent evaluation and treatment).

"Without cause" termination clauses provide that an employer can terminate an employee at any time, without cause, and may or may not give a time frame of notice.

Successful negotiation

As health care professionals, NPs are in a position to earn competitive wages, secure excellent benefit packages, and work under optimal conditions. The way to secure these valuable options is to negotiate for them. Developing ***negotiation*** skills and becoming comfortable using them can be learned through education and practice. For NPs, this starts with developing an awareness of what you want and then negotiating to get it.

IDENTIFYING ISSUES

The art of negotiation involves a process of communication between two or more parties to reach an agreement. Specifically, it involves a series of trade-offs. Negotiating strategy is determined by the objectives and relative negotiating strength of each party. Thus, in order to be an effective negotiator, a party must have some ability to influence the other side. Unless the relative negotiating strength is so one-sided that one party can dictate the terms to the other party, prior to entering into any type of negotiation, both parties must identify the negotiable issues, their initial position on the issues, and the degree to which they're willing to compromise. For example, suppose salary is your prime consideration and you're at the top of the pay scale for your position within your health care facility; if you otherwise love the facility and don't want to leave, you may need to reconsider the situation and other available options, such as seeking a better-paying position within your facility.

During negotiations, first consider who you're negotiating with. What is that person's relative negotiating power? At the same time, you need to consider your own negotiating power, based on what you've accomplished professionally. It may help to write a detailed description of what you want to achieve and give it to someone else to read to see if it makes sense. A related issue to consider is what the other party wants to achieve. If you don't know the answer, it may be helpful to ask. Also consider your own motives. Why do you want what you're asking for?

NEGOTIATING A CONTRACT

If you're currently working without a contract and preparing to negotiate one, you need to research the practice and your value to it. Outline how you see yourself as an asset to the practice. Do this by identifying the number of patient visits, billable services, and monies received in the past year. List your other contributions to the practice, including patient education classes and administrative duties such as preparing the office for a certification agency's site visit (such as the National Committee for Quality Assurance or *Joint Commission on Accreditation of Healthcare Organizations [JCAHO]*). If possible, compare your contributions and compensation to those of the other providers within the practice.

Determine the practice's income over the previous year as well as which third-party payers reimburse for NP services and how much they reimburse. Identify which CPT codes are billed most frequently in the practice and the amount received for those services.

Determine what percentage of your income covers practice expenses. For practices with few providers, office expenses are typically between 40% and 50%. In contrast, practices with more than 10 providers spend about 25% on office expenses. Subtract this amount from gross income. Then, deduct the collaborating physician's consultation fee (generally 10% to 15% for an experienced NP versus 25% for a new graduate). From the remainder, deduct an additional 10% to 15% as net profit that goes to the managing physician.

NEGOTIATING TACTICS AND GUIDELINES

When beginning negotiations, allow the employer to talk, which gives you the opportunity to learn what his initial offer is without revealing your position or expectations.

The process of negotiating

As this flowchart shows, the art of negotiating involves a process of communication — a series of trade-offs — between two or more parties that is designed to reach an agreement.

> Be prepared.
> Identify your issues and how much you're willing to compromise.
> Identify your prospective employer's issues by researching the practice or organization. If possible, identify the person you'll be negotiating with and any issues he has expressed in the past.

> At the onset, focus on the other side's issues.
> Focus on areas of agreement first.

> Move to areas of disagreement later.
> Never give something for nothing.

> Put tough issues aside until the end of the day.
> Be aware of the effect of silence and time pressure.
> Consider the 80/20 rule: 80% of agreement is reached in the last 20% of the allotted time.

> Always be prepared to walk away from negotiations.

During negotiations, focus on areas of agreement first and then move to areas of disagreement. If the employer extends an offer that you find inadequate, show reluctance and present a counter-offer. Then allow the employer to talk. Keep in mind that skilled negotiators generally never give up something for nothing.

Set aside tough issues and likely areas of disagreement until the end of negotiations. By discussing easier issues first, it sets the stage with a warm-up phase. Be aware of the effect of silence and time pressure on negotiations and the 80/20% rule — 80% of concessions take place within the last 20% of the time allotted to negotiate.

More importantly, be prepared to walk away from negotiations if you can't reach an agreement that's compatible with your personal and professional goals. (See *The process of negotiating*.)

BEFORE SIGNING

Once you and the employer have agreed on terms and the contract appears settled, it needs a final review. First, read the proposed contract carefully and get clarification of any areas that seem vague or unclear. Remember, every point is negotiable and the contract can be easily amended at this stage.

Final attorney review

After you're satisfied with the contract, hire an attorney to perform a final review. If possible, select an attorney who has experience with NP contracts.

The next best choice would be an attorney familiar with physician contracts. You should pay a flat fee for review of the contract; expect to pay approximately $400.

Employee rights

Employee rights have been significantly affected by ongoing changes in the health care industry. Privatization of public health facilities and the conversion of not-for-profit health care facilities and insurers to for-profit facilities has occurred through sales, mergers, and other means. Business decisions reflecting the for-profit management style have raised awareness of issues related to business and health care, such as fraud and remuneration.

As an NP, you may face difficult situations that may make you question your legal and ethical duties. It's reassuring to know that state and federal laws exist to protect you if you decide to confront issues that may elicit negative outcomes. Suppose, for example, that you cooperate with the billing practices of your facility; you later learn that a practice is fraudulent, and management refuses to address or correct the problem. What can you do?

Will managed care and for-profit health care facilities and organizations place their duty to stockholders over their duty to stakeholders? What do you do if you're asked to participate in an incentive arrangement that calls for you to put 10% of your salary "at risk" and share in the positive or negative results of the health care facility or organization, but the standards to be measured or the criteria by which profits would be shared aren't specified?

How might your health care facility's or organization's business decisions affect your employment? What can you do to prepare for these contingencies? What can you and your colleagues do, individually and collectively, to maintain professional integrity when dealing with such conflicts of interests?

LEGAL PROTECTION

In most states, if an employee discloses wrongdoing or safety hazards or refuses to perform certain kinds of unsafe work, they're protected by laws forbidding discharge or retaliatory action. In some states, such as Massachusetts, employees may sue for three times lost wages.

In the health care industry, whistle-blowers have become more prominent primarily due to the vigilance of the federal government in monitoring Medicare fraud and issues related to overbilling. In 1986, Congress passed the *False Claims Act* to help combat fraud against the federal government; within a short time, the number of lawsuits involving whistle-blowing dramatically increased by over 1,500%. (See *Whistle-blower.*)

Increasingly, states are enacting laws to protect the health care provider who reports dangerous patient-care situations to federal, state, or local agencies. New York is the latest in a number of states to specifically protect health care workers in this area of the law.

Federal statutes

Federal statutes also protect employees from wrongful termination or retaliatory action for disclosing unsafe conditions in the workplace. These statutes include the Clean Air Act, the Water Pollution Act, the Economic Energy Act, the Railroad Safety Act, and various antitrust laws.

For health and safety issues in the workplace, the Occupational Safety and Health Act of 1970 placed safety and health enforcement under a federal agency, the *Occupational Safety and Health Administration (OSHA)*. OSHA was given broad authority to establish comprehensive safety and health standards, inspect workplaces without advance notice, assess substantial fines, and order employers to eliminate safety hazards from the workplace. This law gives employees the right to work in a safe environment and encourages employees to learn and understand issues about air quality, noise levels, and chemicals that they may be exposed to in the work environment. Any private employee can file a complaint with OSHA, even if they aren't personally exposed to a dangerous condition. Public sector employees aren't covered by OSHA. (See *Whistle-blower protections*, page 118.)

MANAGED CARE

NPs in managed care situations are encountering legal issues similar to those faced by their physician coworkers. Both have become victims of downsizing due to the high cost of patient care in a capitated environment. Consider the following situations:
● A staff-model HMO loses a large state-employee contract, thus losing thousands of patients overnight and leaving the HMO with more primary care physicians and NPs than it needs.
● A primary care group mismanages its specialist networks and, as a result, finds itself in serious financial straits.
● A hospital desiring to expand buys more primary care practices than it can afford.

Any one of the above situations could result in downsizing and layoffs for the physicians, NPs, and others working at the facilities. In any of these situations, collective bargaining may improve the outcome for the employees involved. If the providers in the above examples are members of unions, for instance, their contract may address issues affecting job security and may call for up to a year's salary as severance pay.

Whistle-blower COURT CASE

In *Poulton v. Anesthesia Associates of Burlington, Inc.*, an anesthesiologist who was the new president of a 25-member physician group in Burlington, Vt., blew the whistle on some of the group's billing charges, which he considered to be patently illegal. He was particularly concerned about double billing for critical care services, consulting services, and after-the-fact interpretations of a resident's work by attending physicians. After failing to meet satisfactorily with senior staff, he filed suit against his own medical group and affiliating institutions, charging them with filing false claims to the Medicare program. The case was settled in the fall of 1999 after the health care system agreed to pay the government $3,000,000 and the medical group agreed to pay $200,000. The anesthesiologist received between $480,000 and $800,000 for his role as a whistle-blower.

COLLECTIVE BARGAINING

What effect do incentive arrangements have on the ethical values of the nursing profession, such as patient advocacy, loyalty, the patient-nurse relationship, and independent professional judgment? Is there a plan to measure the effect of the incentives on patients and a plan to discontinue the practice if it's found to be detrimental to patient outcomes? How can you choose not to participate in such an arrangement? These are just a few of the reasons why NPs may seek to form a *collective bargaining* unit in the workplace.

As an employee, you have the right to organize on the job whether you're seeking one particular improvement or organizing a union. Section 7 of the National Labor Relations Act (NLRA),

Whistle-blower protections

In most states, public employees are protected by laws forbidding discharge or retaliatory action because an employee discloses wrongdoing or safety hazards or refuses certain kinds of unsafe work. In addition, the federal government has passed laws to protect employees from wrongful termination or retaliatory action for reporting unsafe conditions in the workplace.

● The False Claims Act empowers individuals to bring civil actions on behalf of the U.S. government for false claims made to the federal government. It generally covers fraud for all federally funded programs. These actions frequently involve fraud by nursing homes, hospitals, computer companies, and defense contractors.

● The Clean Air Act, enforced by the Environmental Protection Agency, sets limits on how much of a given pollutant can be in the air anywhere in the United States. Similarly, the Clean Water Act strives to restore and maintain the chemical, physical, and biological integrity of the nation's water. The act sets up a system of water quality standards and discharge limitations.

● Antitrust laws promote the public welfare by preserving competition. They promote creative innovation and flexibility by encouraging health care providers to distinguish themselves in ways that will attract patients. An example of innovation and flexibility are call-in hours when patients can call and speak directly to a physician, nurse practitioner, or physician assistant. Developing and following clinical practice guidelines are other methods of providing the best services at reasonable prices. Antitrust laws prohibit providers from conspiring to fix prices, decreasing services, or limiting the options available to patients. They also prohibit mergers or acquisitions that would lessen competition or create monopolies.

● The Occupational Safety and Health Act of 1970 provides for protection of employees in the workplace. It requires employers to educate employees on actual and potential hazards in the workplace, to record and report occupational injuries and illnesses to the federal government, and to provide safety controls and protective equipment.

● Health care whistle-blower protection acts, in a few states, give additional remedies to health care providers who report dangerous patient care situations to federal, state, or local agencies.

which applies to private sector employment, states: "Employees shall have the right to self-organization, to form, join, or assist labor organizations, to bargain collectively through representatives of their own choosing, and to engage in other concerted activities for the purpose of collective bargaining or other mutual aid or protection." Early studies of collective bargaining by nurses revealed that union members view certain professional issues as important. Historically, collective bargaining issues for nurses generally focused on wages, benefits, hours, and conditions related to work. In addition, collective bargaining for professional employees in health care settings has involved issues of professional development and issues related to patient care. (See *The National Labor Relations Board: Protecting your right to organize a union.*)

Legal protection in collective bargaining extends only to concerted activities (actions taken by two or more employees to improve conditions or actions taken by an individual on behalf of other employees). Workers have a collective right to discuss salaries or other issues involving the workplace during a break or outside of work; to object to personnel decisions, such as the firing or transfer of a coworker; to

The National Labor Relations Board: Protecting your right to organize a union

If your facility punishes you solely because you're involved in union-organizing activities, the federal government, in the form of the National Labor Relations Board (NLRB), will protect you. This board enforces the National Labor Relations Act, which explicitly sets forth your rights to form and join a union.

An example

Suppose you're working as a hospital pediatric nurse practitioner, and you support unionization of the hospital's nurses. Union organizers ask you to distribute pro-union pamphlets to your colleagues. You begin giving out pamphlets in the staff lounge, but a hospital administrator orders you to stop. He says the hospital solicitation policy prohibits anyone from distributing literature inside the hospital. You remind him that the hospital has allowed staff members to dis-

tribute other information, such as literature to solicit volunteers for the local cancer society. You ignore the administrator's order and resume handing out pamphlets. You're suspended or intimidated by management staff.

You file an unfair labor practice charge with the NLRB. After a hearing, the board concludes that the hospital can't prevent you from distributing the pamphlets on your own time in a nonwork area. The board also concludes that the hospital was discriminatory in applying the non-solicitation policy.

A likely ruling

In this situation, the board would order the hospital to reinstate you, pay your back wages, and refrain from punishing you or any other nurse who was active in the union drive.

make demands for improved wages and working conditions; and to organize a union.

Subjects that must be addressed through collective bargaining at the request of either party during union contract negotiations are called "mandatory subjects." These include:
- automation and new technology
- bonuses
- Christmas bonus
- consolidations
- definition of bargain unit work
- discipline and discharge
- drug testing of employees
- evaluation systems
- grievance procedures
- holidays
- layoff procedures
- leaves of absence
- life insurance
- management rights clause
- medical insurance
- merit increases
- no discrimination clause
- overtime pay
- pension plans
- profit-sharing plans
- promotions within the bargaining unit
- rest periods
- safety and health
- sanitation
- seniority
- severance pay
- sick leave
- stock purchase plans
- subcontracting
- union security
- vacations
- wage rates
- work assignments
- work requirements
- work schedules.

Recognizing unfair labor practices

If eligible, you have a legal right to participate in union activities. Though you may be ineligible to join the union, you still have some protection under Section 7 regarding the organization of a union in your institution and management's practice regarding the National Labor Relations Act. If your employer infringes on that right — through interference, domination, discrimination, or refusal to bargain — you can charge your employer with unfair labor practices.

Interference

Employers may interfere with a union election by unilaterally improving wages or benefits to encourage votes against the union. This is considered an unfair labor practice. Other unfair labor practices include:
- helping employees withdraw from union membership
- making coercive statements about participation in union activities
- libeling or slandering union officials
- threatening to close down the facility
- questioning employees about union activities or organizers
- spying on — or implying the possibility of spying on — union meetings
- creating an atmosphere of fear.

Domination

The National Labor Relations Board (NLRB) doesn't allow management to dominate a union by paying a union's expenses, giving union leaders special benefits, or taking an active part in organizing a union.

Discrimination

This unfair labor practice may involve discharging, disciplining, or threatening an employee for joining a union or for encouraging others to join. Other types of discrimination include:
- refusing to hire anyone who belongs to a union
- refusing to reinstate or promote an employee because she testified at an NLRB hearing
- enforcing rules unequally between employees who are involved in union activities and those who aren't.

Refusal to bargain

To weaken union participation, management may not refuse to take part in collective bargaining. It's an unfair labor practice to take unilateral action to alter employment conditions that either are covered in an existing contract or are included among legally mandated areas of bargaining. Other unfair labor practices include:
- refusing to meet with a union representative
- refusing to negotiate a mandatory issue
- demanding to negotiate a voluntary issue.

Topics that the employer or union may refuse to discuss are called "permissive subjects" and include:
- corporate structure
- decision to close all or part of a business (if based on reasons other than labor costs)
- definition of the bargaining unit
- drug testing of job applicants
- general business practices
- selection of supervisors

- settlement of unfair labor practice charges.

Employers may not interfere with efforts to organize a union or punish employees who take part in organizing. Employers must recognize unions chosen by a majority of employees. Moreover, employers must bargain in good faith with unions about wages, hours, and working conditions. Violations of the NLRA are unfair labor practices that may result in a hearing with orders directed at employers to reinstate discharged employees, reimburse employees who lose their pay or other benefits, and bargain in good faith with unions. (See *Recognizing unfair labor practices.*)

You and your colleagues must remain aware of the complex issues currently facing the health care industry and your own facility or organization. Before a crisis arises, develop a plan, individually and collectively, that allows you to maintain professional integrity while dealing with dilemmas that affect both patients and providers.

Selected references

American College of Nurse Practitioners: *www.nurse.org/acnp.*

Aquilino, M.L., et al. "Primary Care Physician Perceptions of the Nurse Practitioner in the 1990s," *Archives of Family Medicine* 8(3):224-7, May-June 1999.

Blumenreich, G.A. "Nurse Anesthetists in the Middle: Covenants Not to Compete," *AANA Journal* 66(6):541-4, December 1998.

Blumenreich, G.A. "The Overlap Between the Practice of Medicine and the Practice of Nursing," *AANA Journal* 66(1):11-5, February 1998.

Buckner, F. "Arbitration Clauses in Contracts Between Providers and Patients," *Journal of Medical Practice Management* 14(2):98-101, September-October 1998.

Buppert, C. "HEDIS for the Primary Care Provider: Getting an 'A' on the Managed Care Report Card," *Nurse Practitioner* 24(1):84-6, 88-9, 92-4 passim, January 1999.

Herman, J. "Documenting Acute Care Nurse Practitioner Practice Characteristics," *AACN Clinical Issues* 9(2):277-82, May 1998.

Landis, N.T. "Patient Outcomes Comparable for Primary Care Physicians, Independent Nurse Practitioners," *American Journal of Health-System Pharmacy* 57(5):424, 426, March 1, 2000.

O'Connor, S. "At-Will Employment Status," *Michigan Health and Hospitals* 34(4):58, July-August 1998.

Pulcini, J., et al. "NPACE Nurse Practitioner Practice Characteristics, Salary, and Benefits Survey," *Clinical Excellence for Nurse Practitioners* 2(5):300-6, September 1998.

Selph, A.K. "Negotiating an Acute Care Nurse Practitioner Position," *AACN Clinical Issues* 9(2):269-76, May 1998.

Shell, G.R. *Bargaining for Advantage.* New York: Viking, 1999.

Taylor, M. "Chicago Hospitals Targeted. Federal Government Joins Whistle-blower Suit Alleging Upcoding," *Modern Healthcare* 29(12):12-3, March 1999.

Chapter Four

LEGAL RISKS WHILE OFF DUTY

When you're on duty, numerous guidelines define the legal limits of your practice and your legal risks. They include facility *policies, standards* issued by nursing organizations, and state nurse practice acts. Federal and state statutory law and *common law* provide additional direction. When you're off duty, however, you have few specific guidelines. Your legal responsibilities aren't as clear-cut.

For example, you probably wouldn't hesitate to perform the abdominal thrust maneuver to save a choking victim. But what if you panic, make a mistake, and injure the patient? Can you be sued by the victim or his estate? Can your nursing license be suspended or revoked? Does the law protect you because of your good intentions?

Fortunately, thus far, lawsuits resulting from off-duty nursing actions have been extremely rare. However, whether you frequently provide off-duty care or whether you just give free advice occasionally to your neighbor, it's important to act on sound legal footing.

This chapter discusses legal issues related to off-duty situations. You'll find information on:

- *acting as a **Good Samaritan*** — your liability when you give emergency care at an accident scene or in a disaster
- *giving free health care advice* — legal ramifications of giving advice to family members and friends
- *donating your services* — protecting yourself legally when you volunteer your skills
- *acting during disasters* — legal aspects of providing **nurse practitioner (NP)** services during emergencies and declared disasters.

You'll learn to distinguish between what the law requires and what the law allows. You'll also find out how your **nurse practice act** and other state laws apply to off-duty actions. (Incidentally, you may discover that, except for **Good Samaritan acts,** the law has relatively little to say about off-duty nursing.)

Legal protection for Good Samaritans

Imagine yourself driving in heavy traffic. Not far ahead, you see an automobile accident and a bloodied motorist gesturing for help. Nearby, another victim lies sprawled at curbside. What should you do? Your conscience and compassion prompt you to help the victim in any health care emergency. Your common sense prompts you to ask if helping out means courting legal trouble.

YOUR OPTIONS

In the situation described above, you have three options. You can:
● help the accident victim at the scene
● leave the scene, stop at the nearest phone, and call for an ambulance or other rescue service
● pass the scene and make no attempt to call for help.

In almost every state, you have the legal right to choose any of these options. In most cases, off-duty nurses in the United States have no legal duty to rescue anyone.

Obligation to rescue

In general, the only people with a legal duty to rescue others are individuals who perform rescues as part of their jobs — fire fighters, police officers, emergency medical technicians, and a few others, such as public transportation workers. In a few states, such as Vermont, Minnesota, and Wisconsin, *duty-to-rescue laws* may apply to nurses. Unless you're covered by a duty-to-rescue law, your decision to help remains voluntary and personal.

Common and statutory law

If you choose to help the accident victim, two kinds of laws protect you: common law and statutory law (specifically, Good Samaritan acts).

Common law is the cumulative result of court decisions over the years. These decisions may provide guidelines for acting in an accident situation.

Good Samaritan acts grew out of *health care professionals'* concerns that common law didn't sufficiently

protect their actions. Legislation was needed to encourage medical personnel to stop and render appropriate medical care at an emergency site without unnecessary fear of incurring criminal charges or civil liability.

PROVING MALPRACTICE

To bring a malpractice suit to a jury trial, the patient must establish the following:
● you owed a *duty,* based on an NP-patient relationship
● you breached that duty by deviating from the acceptable standard of nursing practice for the NP
● the patient was harmed
● your *breach of duty* caused the harm.

Consider these points as they apply to the auto accident.

Your legal duty

As long as you pass the accident scene — whether or not you stop down the road to call for help — you owe the victim no legal duty (unless you're in a state where a person is required to stop). He isn't your patient, and he has no legal claim to your professional services. (Remember, ethical questions aren't at issue here.)

Just by stopping your car at the scene, however, you may incur a legal duty. Once you provide care at the scene, the NP-patient relationship is established. From that point on, you can't leave the victim until he's being cared for by another health care professional with at least as much training as you have or until the police order you from the scene.

When you stop your car at the scene, you give the appearance to other potential rescuers that you'll take care of the victim. At that point, you establish an NP-patient relationship for that particular emergency. You owe the victim the normal duty you owe any patient — treatment that meets the *standard of care* of a reasonably prudent NP in a similar situation.

Breach of duty

Once you've stopped to help, you can avoid breaching your duty by using the same good judgment that you use every day on the job. But what if you do breach your duty in this unusual situation?

If your performance falls below the standard of care, the court will decide whether your act worsened the victim's condition. In most states, your action or inaction has to be grossly negligent for there to be a cause of action. If your act didn't make the victim measurably worse, the court may find that the harm committed doesn't warrant damages. Your act must cause measurable harm for the court to consider you legally responsible.

Determining causation

Some states acknowledge that proving causation can be difficult and will allow an "increased risk of harm standard." That is, your action or inaction increased the risk of harm and was a substantial factor in causing the patient's damages. Because the typical victim has already suffered injuries from the accident, however, he's likely to have a hard time proving that your error caused or worsened his injuries.

In making it more difficult for the accident victim to prove your negligence in an emergency situation, the courts balance the victim's right to justice against society's need to encourage trained professionals to assist in emergencies.

GOOD SAMARITAN LAWS

Good Samaritan acts limit your liability for any service you render at an accident or emergency scene. To win a malpractice suit against you under a Good Samaritan law, a patient must prove that you intentionally caused his injury or were grossly negligent in your care. In effect, Good Samaritan acts offer you *immunity from suit* as long as you don't intentionally or recklessly cause the accident victim harm.

Determining gross negligence

No law can protect you if you commit an act of *gross negligence* — an extremely careless act or omission that seriously violates the applicable standard of care.

In court, jury members decide whether your negligent error constitutes "ordinary" or "gross" negligence. To make this distinction, your error is measured against a standard, as established by an expert witness who is an *advanced practice nurse (APN);* the court determines whether your conduct is in conformity with the applicable standard of care for an APN in the same or a similar situation. From this, the acceptable standard of nursing practice will be determined in accordance with a local or national standard, depending on the jurisdiction in which the case applies.

Additionally, the court considers your training and experience to decide whether you've breached the standard of care and, if so, to what degree. This means that the court holds APNs — even as Good Samaritans — to a higher standard than it holds *registered nurses (RNs).* Further, where the APN possesses special knowledge, skills, and competence in particular areas of practice, that NP must maintain those standards of care as well. (See *Care tips for Good Samaritans.*)

Legal discrepancies

Good Samaritan protection varies. For example, some acts specifically include nurses, whereas other acts, such as those in Florida and Alaska, protect any person who offers help to a victim. Some acts protect out-of-state nurses only if they're trained in cardiopul-

Care tips for Good Samaritans

When you stop at an emergency scene to offer assistance, always observe professional standards of nursing care, regardless of the setting. To reduce your malpractice risk, follow these guidelines:

- Ask the injured person (or family member, if available) for permission to help.
- Care for the victim in the vehicle or at the exact site, if you can do so safely.
- Assess the possibility of fractures.
- Move the victim if he's in danger and if conditions permit. Avoid moving him needlessly, and don't try to straighten his arms and legs.
- Let him lie or sit quietly. Don't carry him or force him to walk.

- Keep his airway open.
- Stop his bleeding.
- Keep the victim warm.
- Determine his level of consciousness.
- Ask the victim where he feels pain.
- Avoid speculating about who or what caused the accident.
- Allow only skilled personnel to attend or treat the victim.
- Stay at the accident site until skilled personnel arrive to assume care of the victim.
- Provide a complete picture of the care given.
- Guard the injured person's personal property. Release it to the police or members of his family.

monary resuscitation. In some jurisdictions, Good Samaritan acts include only "practitioners of the healing arts." The courts usually interpret this terminology to mean physicians and dentists. (See *Understanding Good Samaritan acts*, page 126.)

Compensated care vs. gratuitous care

Keep in mind that most Good Samaritan acts apply only to uncompensated rescues. If you charge or accept money for your services, the law usually says that you forfeit the special protections afforded by such acts.

INVOKING GOOD SAMARITAN LAW

Regardless of the kind of Good Samaritan act your state or jurisdiction has, accident victims rarely sue "Good Samaritans." In addition, although nurses have been sued occasionally, no nurse has ever been found responsible when the Good Samaritan defense has been raised. This doesn't grant you immunity from litigation,

however. (See *Good Samaritan*, page 127.)

In some states, physicians have invoked a Good Samaritan act as a defense against malpractice suits, claiming that the act protects them from liability for emergency services they provided in a hospital. In Illinois, a physician responded to an in-hospital emergency where both parties (mother and fetus) later died, and the estate brought suit. The physician successfully invoked, as part of his defense, the Illinois Good Samaritan Act. The ***appellate court*** found that the Act protected the physician from liability for a true hospital emergency where the service was provided in good faith and without fee. Using this argument in California, physicians have met with mixed results. The same argument hasn't held for nurses in California because the Good Samaritan act covers nurses only during emergencies "outside both the place and course" of employment.

Understanding Good Samaritan acts

Am I covered by a Good Samaritan act if I respond to an emergency outside work while I'm officially on duty?

That depends on two things: the wording of the act in your state and court decisions, if any, interpreting that act. All Good Samaritan laws cover aid at the scene of an emergency, an accident, or a disaster. If an emergency occurs just outside the facility and you provide care while on duty, most likely this would be considered providing care in an emergency setting and, therefore, would be covered under Good Samaritan law. Note that some states' Good Samaritan statutes specifically cover emergencies outside of the hospital, medical office, and other places that have medical equipment.

I live and work in Kansas. Every year, I go skiing in a different state. What if I help an accident victim while I'm vacationing? Does the Good Samaritan act of the state I'm in apply to me?

It does if that state's act says it applies to "any person." It may not, however, if the act specifically states that it applies only to "nurses." The designation "nurses" in a law or act may mean an advanced practice nurse, a registered nurse, a licensed practical nurse, or a licensed vocational nurse in that state.

Does the Good Samaritan act apply if I accept money from the person I've helped?

Not usually. By accepting money in such a situation, you establish a professional relationship with the person you've helped. State statutes often include the language "gratuitous only" to clarify this situation.

For how long am I responsible to the person I've helped?

Statutory law doesn't address this subject, but common law does. The courts say your responsibility ends:

- when the emergency ends (when you're certain that the victim is no longer in danger)
- when an authorized rescue or other qualified medical service takes over for you
- when the victim is pronounced dead
- when you're physically unable to continue.

If a physician and I respond to the same emergency, does the Good Samaritan act cover us equally?

Not necessarily. In some states, the Good Samaritan act for nurses differs completely from the Good Samaritan act for physicians. Contact your state nursing board to find out what is true for your state.

DUTY TO RESCUE

Four states have taken the Good Samaritan principle a step further by requiring potential rescuers to help a victim. Vermont's law, the first of its type in the United States, defines a *rescuer* as any person who knows that another is exposed to grave physical harm. The Vermont law requires anyone (Vermont resident or not) who can help a victim to do so, provided he won't be endangering himself or interfering with important duties he owes to others. Minnesota has a similar law, as do Wisconsin (which has a "duty to rescue crime victims" law) and

Wyoming (where the duty-to-rescue law applies only to physicians).

The Vermont statute provides for criminal penalties for failure to render assistance as required under the law. Minnesota makes the failure to render "reasonable assistance at the scene of an emergency" a petty **misdemeanor.**

However, in states with a duty-to-rescue law, how this would apply to NPs remains uncertain. For example, if you pass an accident scene on the way to your dentist, the duty-to-rescue law requires you to stop and try to help. What if you're on your way to your job? Would your work be considered an im-

Good Samaritan

This 1997 Rhode Island case was brought by the spouse of a man who died of anaphylactic shock during a music festival; the man apparently ate some Cajun gumbo that contained fish to which he was allergic. After receiving notice that there was a man having problems, the volunteer physician of the festival's first aid crew rendered emergency assistance. The volunteer festival nurse stayed behind to staff the first aid center. On discovering the nature of the problem, the physician sent crew members to the first aid tent to retrieve an adrenaline injector and to call an ambulance. The physician administered the adrenaline injection, and the patient said he couldn't catch his breath and lost consciousness. There was no additional adrenaline on the scene to administer and efforts to revive him were unsuccessful. The man's estate sued for negligence, eventually charging that the nurse and physician were "unprepared." The court determined that the nurse and physician weren't guilty of negligence.

What the NP can learn

Good Samaritan statutes generally state that no one is liable for rendering emergency medical assistance voluntarily and without charge, unless there is a showing of gross, willful, or wanton negligence. *Boccasile v. Cajun Music Ltd.*, 694 A. 2d 686 (R.I., 1997).

portant duty owed to others? What if you're the only practitioner scheduled to staff the emergency room? What if you're scheduled to make rounds on patients and discharge or clear them for surgery? What if you work in a primary care office or clinic and you're the only person scheduled to evaluate patients that day? What if you work in primary care but aren't the only person scheduled to see patients that day? The answers to these questions will eventually come from the courts.

Giving free health care advice

Most likely, friends and family members may look to you for advice on health matters. Respond cautiously, even though this may seem unnatural when speaking with individuals you know well. Keep in mind that you can be sued for giving inappropriate advice. If you decide not to give advice at all, be reassured: The law doesn't require it.

If you choose to offer advice, be aware of positions on the issue taken by your nurse practice act, the common law, and professional organizations. (See *Minimizing legal risks when giving advice,* page 128.)

FREE ADVICE AND THE LAW

In a work setting, giving health care advice may be construed to be a part of patient teaching, a recognized nursing function. Outside of the work setting, giving advice may subject you to liability if, in providing the advice, your actions aren't reasonably prudent.

The person suing you for harm caused by inappropriate advice must prove that you owed him a specific duty, that you breached that duty, that he was harmed, and that the harm was a result of the breach of duty.

Establishing breach of duty

For a duty to exist, you must have a professional relationship with the person asking for your advice. This rarely occurs in everyday, short-lived conver-

Minimizing legal risks when giving advice

Here are some steps you can take to minimize your risk when giving health care advice to friends or family.

What to do
● Be sure that your advice reflects accepted professional, community, and national standards.
● Check whether your professional liability insurance covers such off-the-job activities as giving advice.
● Remember that Good Samaritan acts exclude gratuitous actions not associated with an emergency.
● Know what — if anything — your state's nurse practice act says about giving advice to friends.
● Give advice only within the confines of your nurse practice act, education, and experience.

● Make sure that the advice you give is up-to-date. You'll be judged on current standards if your advice results in a lawsuit.

What not to do
● Don't charge a fee or accept money for your advice.
● Avoid speculating about your friends' illnesses or ailments.
● Never suggest that friends change or ignore their physician's orders.
● Steer clear of offering advice outside your scope of practice.
● Avoid giving any directions that, if wrong or misinterpreted, could result in serious or permanent injury.

sations with other people. Suppose, for example, that you're a guest at a party. Another guest finds out that you're an NP and bombards you with questions about his health. If you decide to answer, you have a duty to answer as correctly as any *reasonably prudent NP* would, but you have no duty to follow up after the party is over and no duty to monitor the outcome of your advice. The person who's asking your advice hasn't established, or indicated that he intends to establish, an ongoing NP-patient relationship with you.

Following through on potential or established duties
The situation may be different if you decide to give advice to a neighbor. For instance, imagine that your neighbor calls across the yard and asks you about her child's fretfulness. You observe honestly that the child's activity doesn't appear to warrant a call to the primary care provider. A day later, you see the mother and child together outdoors, and the child appears particularly listless. If you discover that the child has a fever or other signs and symptoms of illness, you're legally and professionally responsible for telling the mother to take the child to her primary care provider as soon as possible. This holds true regardless of your original advice.

You must respond to the mother's potential reliance on you for further advice, even though your original intention wasn't to form a professional relationship with her and her child.

Again, if you realize that your neighbor now relies on you for further advice, you have an obligation — a legal and professional duty — to keep your advice current as the situation changes. At this point, you may opt to take formal steps to break off the rela-

Neighborly advice: Some legal safeguards

My best friend Sara and I have babies the same age. Sara isn't a nurse, and I know she relies on my judgment a lot. How should I answer her when she asks questions? For instance, yesterday she asked, "If your Richie had a rash like Tommy's, would you take him to the physician?"

If your answer is yes, no harm will result from your advice, and you'll be on safe legal ground. If you answer no, and if following your advice results in harm to the child, you may be liable. In such situations — best friend or not — conservative advice is legally safer, especially if you have any doubts.

I seem to be the neighborhood ear-piercer. Of course, with children I require a parent's permission, and I warn everyone about the risks of infection and how to reduce them. Still, I'm worried: If someone got an infection and sued me, would this verbal warning protect me from malpractice liability?

Some states have legislation or regulations governing ear piercing, so check with your state licensing board. If your state doesn't have regulations on ear piercing, your warn-

ings about possible infection protect you only if infection results from piercing done according to accepted standards. The warning doesn't protect you if the infection results from your negligence.

One of my neighbors comes to see me whenever one of her family members gets sick or enters the hospital. She's a good friend and I'm glad to help, but I think she's making a habit of asking my advice. I feel especially uncomfortable when she asks me to explain everything the physician tells her. Once she said, "The physician says my husband might have adhesions from a previous operation. What does that mean? Is that common?" How can I answer her questions and protect myself, too? Should I say, "I can only tell you what I know from my own experience?"

You'd be better off saying, "I can tell you what those terms usually mean, but not what they mean in your husband's case." You can best serve your neighbor, though, by encouraging her to ask the physician to explain anything she doesn't understand.

---

tionship by telling the mother to look elsewhere for help.

Keep in mind that the principles that apply to your on-duty work also apply to off-duty advice. The help and advice you give your patient Monday morning may have to be changed by Tuesday afternoon. In addition, if a patient's questions reveal that his problem may be beyond your scope of practice, you have a clear duty to refer. (See *Neighborly advice: Some legal safeguards.*)

PROFESSIONAL STANDARDS
Whenever you establish a professional relationship with an individual seeking advice, you must give an answer as

good as any reasonably prudent NP would give in similar circumstances.

Do this by applying the same standards that you're expected to apply in your regular work. If you feel confident that you know the answer — and your education and experience support you — you're legally authorized to give it. Naturally, you must be sure that your answer is correct and that giving it falls within your scope of nursing practice.

To protect yourself, you might say something like, "I think your problem sounds like arthritis, but it could be something more serious, and I'm not sure. You should ask your ***primary care provider.***"

Remember, you're always legally protected if you refer the questioner to a person with the proper credentials or background. However, the law doesn't require you to make that suggestion if you're honestly convinced that it isn't necessary and that a reasonably prudent NP wouldn't make it either.

Guard against the temptation to say, "Don't worry," when family members or friends ask for advice. Reassure them only if you're certain that nothing is seriously wrong. The law requires you to apply this standard: If I were at work and if one of my patients asked the same question, what would I tell him? Try to imagine that an inquiring family member or friend is a complete stranger. Then give your best professionally considered answer.

Donating NP services

Many health care professionals, including NPs, donate their professional services to community organizations or activities.

Usually, when you volunteer your nursing services, no pay is involved. At times, you may "volunteer" services for pay by providing nursing care outside of your usual paid work. In such situations, you're volunteering your personal time while being paid for your services.

You might donate your services to family members, friends, or such community organizations and activities as:
● a community ambulance service
● a bloodmobile or hypertension outreach program
● a home and school association panel discussion on child health issues.

Your responsibilities to patients don't change when you donate your NP services. However, your legal status does. It becomes less defined than when you're paid. In most states, nurse practice acts specify only the legal limits of paid nursing practice.

DONATED SERVICES AND THE LAW

Being exempt from your state's nurse practice act if you donate nursing services doesn't mean you'll be exempt from a lawsuit. In such a situation, the court can use the provisions of your state nurse practice act — together with *expert witness* testimony and applicable standards of nursing care — to determine if you acted as a prudent NP would have acted in similar patient care circumstances. If the court finds that your care didn't conform to the requirements of your state's nurse practice act, you may be facing a malpractice suit. (See *Minimizing legal risks when volunteering*, page 132.)

Even if no lawsuit results, you may be subject to discipline by your state nursing board if the board finds that your services fell below the accepted standard of care. In such a situation, the board may suspend or even revoke your license.

VOLUNTEERING OUT OF STATE

If you travel to a state in which you aren't licensed to practice, you aren't prohibited from donating your nursing services as long as that state's nurse practice act covers only paid nursing care. But if you're sued, the court will probably evaluate your actions and their consequences against whatever standard of nursing care would apply in that state rather than in your home state.

GOOD SAMARITAN ACTS

Good Samaritan laws won't cover you in day-to-day situations in which you donate nursing services. These acts apply only to accidents or other emergencies. In addition, not all state Good Samaritan acts extend coverage to all nurses.

Acting during a disaster

A tornado levels a part of your community. Spring floods take life and property at the south end of town. A freight train derails, blanketing the community with toxic vapor. The brakes fail on an airplane carrying 137 passengers; the craft careens off the runway. Any of these disastrous events can overload local medical and nursing resources. In situations such as these, nurses have special responsibilities and legal rights.

CONTRACT DUTIES

When you give nursing care during a disaster, professional, ethical, and legal concerns figure heavily in every decision you make. In general, with the exception of **declared emergencies,** an NP's responsibilities in a disaster don't differ legally from everyday responsibilities. You may have specific duties to perform in specific kinds of disasters, and you may be legally bound to perform those duties, but that's likely to be based on your employment contract and not on laws or precedent-setting legal cases.

If you work in a city hospital, for example, your employment contract may contain a provision that you can be called to work whenever a government official declares a **state of emergency.** If you refuse to come in, you can be disciplined, suspended, or fired. This rule applies even if the work you're assigned to do isn't normally part of your job description.

If you're already on the job when a disaster occurs, the same contractual provisions may be invoked to keep you from going home at the end of your shift. The same penalties apply if you refuse to cooperate.

Similarly, if you're an unpaid volunteer for a community service, such as the **Red Cross** or an ambulance unit, you may be expected to report for duty in any local disaster as long as your re-

porting doesn't conflict with your regular employment. If you refuse, the service can drop you from its roster; if you're a paid, part-time worker for such an organization, you can be dismissed. These duties apply even if your work arrangements are unwritten but are part of an oral agreement.

CONTRACT DEFENSES

Because reporting for work in an emergency, including a disaster, is usually a contract matter, specific **contract defenses** apply if you're disciplined for failing to fulfill your duties. One such contract defense is that of **impossibility.** If reporting is impossible for you, and you can prove it — even if you're contractually required to do so and would be paid for the work — you can't be disciplined or prosecuted. For example, if a blizzard absolutely prohibits travel from your home to the hospital, or disastrous flooding causes the governor to ban all travel in your area, what your contract says doesn't matter much. And if you're disciplined, you have a legal defense. Watch for exceptions to travel bans, however; for example, a ban may be announced for all but "required personnel" or "persons with medical or nursing training." In those situations, obviously you must report for duty.

VOLUNTEERING DURING A DISASTER

No law prevents you from voluntarily donating your services, and specific statutory or common laws may provide protection. If you want to volunteer your help in a disaster, do it, whether or not anyone in authority has asked you. (See *Minimizing legal risks during a disaster,* page 132.)

Suppose you're working in a facility that doesn't have a policy mandating that health care personnel report to work when a disaster occurs. You can still volunteer to stay for extra shifts or

Minimizing legal risks during a disaster

By taking a few precautions, you can help ensure protection from liability when working under disaster conditions.

Be prepared
Don't wait for a disaster to happen before you ask what you'll be required to do during a disaster. Keep any equipment you're likely to need available and in proper working condition.

Follow instructions
In any disaster, public officials and other authorities — such as medical personnel, public health workers, or municipal staff — will probably issue orders. Even if these people aren't normally your superiors, follow their directions as much as possible. Offer advice only when you think necessary.

Know your limits
Don't work beyond the point of effectiveness. If you're so tired that you can't make correct decisions, no one will benefit from your care. Describe your fatigue to the person in charge, and ask for a break.

to perform services outside your normal scope of employment. The facility will almost certainly accept your offer, if they haven't already asked for help. That is especially likely if emergency conditions prevent other staff from reporting to work.

Volunteering in another state
Nurse practice acts don't legally restrict you from volunteering during a disaster in an out-of-state location. For instance, suppose you're licensed in California and, while you're on vacation in Oregon, a disaster occurs. You can give your nursing services during the disaster without concern that you're breaching California's or Oregon's nurse practice act. That is because most nurse practice acts have a special exemption for care given in emergencies that usually includes disasters.

Right to refuse
If you don't want to volunteer, and your facility's policy or contract doesn't require it — or if you don't have a contract — in most states you have the right to refuse. Most nurse practice acts don't require you to provide emergency care in disasters, any more than they require you to perform any care. They only permit such care. Similarly, Good Samaritan acts provide some legal immunity for giving emergency care but don't require you to provide that care — except in states with duty-to-rescue laws.

Civil defense laws, also known as disaster relief laws, don't apply in most states to nurses who aren't already involved in civil defense work, although in a declared national emergency, nurses (like anyone else) can be drafted. Alternatively, martial law may be imposed, which makes all citizens subject to public authority. Many civil defense laws authorize state or federal governing bodies to enforce special regulations dealing with the duties of medical and nursing personnel in a declared emergency. Some states already have such plans ready for use in a sufficiently serious disaster.

Deciding whether to volunteer
When deciding whether to help out in a disaster, assess your actual ability to help. Caring for the disaster victims may require particular skills — for example, knowledge of a special area such as toxicology. Alternatively, the

skill required may be as simple as rowing a boat in a flood.

Also consider whether you can get to the disaster site or to the place where care will be provided. If an airliner crashes, for example, and emergency departments throughout the city are treating victims, your ability to get to your facility or hospital quickly may figure in whether you decide to volunteer. For example, what if the disaster involves a riot occurring during a total blackout in your city, and the mayor decrees, "Don't travel to work unless you're within walking distance"? If you try to drive into the city from your suburban home, you'll only complicate driving conditions — and you probably won't get to your hospital in time to be helpful.

You may also consider whether volunteering in the disaster will keep you from working and earning your regular salary. Find out, too, whether your **professional liability insurance** covers off-the-job activities.

WORKING OUTSIDE YOUR SCOPE OF PRACTICE

In a disaster, you may find yourself performing duties outside your usual scope of practice. If you're an APN, you may be asked to perform duties that ordinarily would be restricted to physicians. Conversely, an APN or a physician may be asked to do work that a nursing assistant would normally do. Provided you have the knowledge and skill to meet minimum safety requirements, you're permitted to give such substitute care in disasters based on the same exemption in nurse practice acts that lets an out-of-state nurse volunteer her services in a disaster. This exemption may be construed as letting you expand the scope of your practice in a disaster. Even if it can't be construed this way, statutory or common laws usually permit regulatory authorities to place the public welfare above strict enforcement of the letter of the law.

Selected references

Brown, S.M. "Good Samaritan Laws: Protections and Limits," *RN* 62(11):65-8, November 1999.

Burns, L. "Don't Volunteer for Trouble," *Michigan Health and Hospitals* 35(3):38-9, May-June 1999.

Daniels, S. "Good Samaritan Acts," *Emergency Medicine Clinics of North America* 17(2):491-504, xiii, May 1999.

Gross, C.P., et al. "The Physician as Ambivalent Samaritan: Will Internists Resuscitate Victims of Out-of-Hospital Emergencies?" *Journal of General Internal Medicine* 13(7): 491-4, July 1998.

Johnson, L.J. "Do Good Samaritan Laws Cover In-Hospital Emergencies?" *Medical Economics* 75(12):113, June 29, 1998.

'Lectric Law Library: *www.lectlaw.com*.

Medi-Smart: *www.medi-smart.com/law.htm*.

Vernaglia, L.W. "The Good Samaritan Physician," *Medicine and Health, Rhode Island* 82(8):304-6, August 1999.

Chapter Five

MALPRACTICE LIABILITY

Nurse practitioners (NPs) currently practice in a variety of health care settings, including acute care facilities, community health agencies, health clinics, long-term care facilities, **managed care organizations,** physician offices, schools, and private practice. As NPs have attained greater roles and responsibilities, they've also assumed greater liability. Courts and state professional boards hold NPs accountable to a high standard of patient care. For this reason, NPs must be aware of the ongoing changes in health care and in the legal system.

No legal issue sparks as much anxiety among NPs as **malpractice** liability. That is because malpractice litigation can be emotionally harrowing and financially devastating. Unfortunately, NPs are beginning to bear the same burden as their physician coworkers — facing as much legal liability. Several reasons exist for this phenomenon:

● Patients are increasingly knowledgeable about health care, and their expectations are higher than in the past.

● The health care system is increasingly reliant on NPs and providers other than physicians to help contain costs.

● NPs are continuously advancing in their profession and expanding their **scope of practice** (for example, some NPs now specialize in trauma).

● NPs are increasingly autonomous in their practice.

● The courts are expanding the limits of **liability,** holding all types of professionals to higher standards of accountability than ever before.

● Increasing numbers of NPs are assuming positions of greater responsibility in health care research, including active roles in development, implementation, and evaluation.

As NPs have assumed higher levels of responsibility for patient care and safety, they are held to higher standards of responsibility by the courts and face correspondingly higher exposure to legal liability.

Losing a malpractice lawsuit can jeopardize your career. Prospective employers and insurance companies will inquire if you've been found liable for malpractice, or if you've ever been a **defendant** in a malpractice suit. (See *National Practitioner Data Bank.*) If you've been named a defendant but not found guilty, you may still find job

134

National Practitioner Data Bank

In 1990, the National Practitioner Data Bank (NPDB) began operation. As a result, physicians, dentists, nurses, and other licensed health care professionals who are forced to pay malpractice judgments have a much harder time concealing their professional histories from potential employers. Nurse practitioners (NPs) are among those health care professionals whose data are being stored in the NPDB. The data bank, which stores malpractice data on a nationwide scale, was created under the Health Care Quality Improvement Act of 1986 and the Medicare and Medicaid Patient and Program Protection Act of 1987.

Reporting requirements

The NPDB collects information about health care professionals who have paid judgments, entered into settlements, or had adverse action on their license or privileges to practice. All hospitals and health care facilities, professional health care societies, state licensure boards, and insurance companies are now required to report the following information about NPs to the data bank:

● malpractice payments made by an NP (including judgments, arbitration decisions, and out-of-court settlements)
● actions taken against an NP's clinical privileges
● adverse licensure actions, including revocations, suspensions, reprimands, censure, or probation.

Failure to report an NP's malpractice payment of any amount — no matter how small — carries a $10,000 fine. However, the fact that a suit has been filed isn't, by itself, reportable; only the making of a payment is. Adverse clinical privilege actions against NPs are to be reported by the reviewing health care agency.

Federal agencies

Under the law, federal agencies aren't required to report to the NPDB. However, the Department of Defense, the Drug Enforcement Administration (DEA), and the Department of Health and Human Services have voluntarily agreed to observe the regulations.

NPs who hold DEA numbers to prescribe controlled substances need to remember that they are governed by the DEA's regulations. If judgments are brought against the NP in this area, the data may be available to the data bank.

Availability of information

The information in the data bank isn't available to the general public nor is it available to attorneys except in a very specific context. If an NP is sued and it's determined that the employer didn't check the data bank, the attorney can send verification that the employing institution didn't check, along with the charges currently pending. If a similar case is in the data bank, notification will be sent. State licensing boards, hospitals, professional societies, and health care facilities involved in peer review may access the data bank. Individual NPs have access to their own records.

Facilities aren't required to query the NPDB about an NP unless she's been granted clinical privileges or is employed by the medical staff. However, if an NP obtains clinical privileges, the facility must check the data bank and request information on the NP every 2 years. The courts will presume that the facility is aware of any information the data bank contains on any NP or other health care professional in its employ. If the information contained in the data bank, if known, would have resulted in denial of clinical privileges, the facility could be held vicariously liable in a malpractice lawsuit for actions performed by the NP and for negligence in hiring the NP.

Information in the data bank

Reports made to the NPDB include:
● the NP's full name, home address, date of birth, professional schools attended and graduation dates, place of employment, Social Security number, and license number and state

(continued)

National Practitioner Data Bank *(continued)*

- name, title, and phone number of the official submitting the report
- relationship of reporting person to practitioner
- dates of judgment or settlement or amount paid
- description of judgment, settlement, or action.

Disputing a report
If a report about you is submitted to the data bank, you'll receive a copy for your review. If you believe the report is in error, ask the official submitting the report to correct it. The official making the report must submit corrections to the NPDB.

If you fail to get satisfaction from the reporting official, you'll have to follow a detailed procedure for disputing the report. This must be done within 60 days of the initial processing of the report. Ultimately, you may request review by the Secretary of Health and Human Services.

---

hunting more difficult. You'll also pay a higher premium for *professional liability insurance*, and some insurance companies may refuse to insure you.

Fortunately, you can limit your vulnerability to malpractice litigation. The most important strategy is to give your patients the best possible care, according to the highest professional *standards*. Standards of care consist of the minimum care required as defined by your state's nurse practice act, your education and experience, policies and procedures established by the health care facility where you work, standards adapted by the *American Nurses Association (ANA)*, and standards of clinical specialty organizations. Familiarity with the *nurse practice act* in your state and other standards applicable to your practice is your best legal protection.

You can further protect yourself by becoming familiar with malpractice law. This chapter describes malpractice issues, defines key legal terms, and explains legal doctrines that may be used as a defense during a malpractice lawsuit. You'll find extensive information on steps to take to avoid malpractice suits and advice on how to shop for professional liability insurance.

Understanding malpractice law

Our legal system's view of malpractice evolved from the premise that everyone is responsible, or *liable*, for the consequences of his own actions. Malpractice law deals with a professional's liability for negligent acts, omissions, and intentional harms. (See *Understanding tort law*, pages 137 and 138.)

NP LIABILITY
After World War II, educational and licensing requirements increased for nurses. Nursing tasks became more complex, leading to specialization. These changes meant that nurses made independent judgments. Although this increased responsibility provides a more rewarding working environment, it also makes NPs more liable for errors and increases their likelihood of being sued. As the profession increases its scope of practice and clinical expertise, liability also increases.

Causes of lawsuits against NPs
As the NP's scope of practice has widened, court decisions, federal laws, and guidelines have recognized the overlapping functions of NPs and

Understanding tort law

Most lawsuits against nurse practitioners fall into the tort category. If you're ever a defendant in a lawsuit, understanding the distinctions in this broad category may prove especially important.

A **tort** is a civil wrong or injury resulting from a breach of a legal duty that exists either by virtue of society's expectations regarding interpersonal conduct or by the assumption of a duty inherent in a professional relationship (as opposed to a legal duty that exists by virtue of a contractual relationship). More generally, you may define a tort as "any action or omission that harms somebody." *Malpractice* refers to any tort committed by a professional acting in his professional capacity.

Unintentional vs. intentional torts

The law broadly divides torts into two categories — unintentional and intentional. An *unintentional tort* is a civil wrong resulting from the defendant's negligence. If someone sues you for negligence, he must prove four things in order to win:
● You owed him a specific duty. (In nursing malpractice cases, this duty is equivalent to the standard of care.)
● You breached this duty.
● The plaintiff was harmed. (The harm can be physical, mental, emotional, or financial.)
● Your breach of duty caused the harm.

An *intentional tort* is a deliberate invasion of someone's legal right. In a malpractice case involving an intentional tort, the plaintiff doesn't need to prove that you owed him a duty. The duty at issue (for example, not to touch people without their permission) is defined by law, and you're presumed to owe him this duty. The plaintiff must still prove that you breached this duty. These lawsuits are usually based on a theory of lack of informed consent.

TORT CLAIM	ACTIONS THAT LEAD TO CLAIMS
Unintentional tort Negligence	● Leaving foreign objects inside a patient after surgery or a procedure ● Failing to observe a patient and evaluate the plan of care according to standards of care ● Failing to obtain informed consent before performing a treatment or procedure ● Failing to intervene in a change in a patient's condition or following up on symptoms to ensure they're responsive to your treatment plan ● Failing to report a colleague's negligence that you witnessed ● Failing to provide for a patient's safety, such as including in your differential diagnoses a list of serious and common disorders that also cause the presenting symptoms ● Failing to provide the patient with appropriate teaching before ending the visit, such as educating the patient about serious medication adverse effects or potential interactions with other currently prescribed medications
Intentional torts Assault	● Threatening a patient
Battery	● Assisting in nonemergency procedures performed without the patient's consent ● Forcing a patient to ambulate against his wishes ● Forcing a patient to submit to unwanted treatments ● Striking a patient

(continued)

Understanding tort law *(continued)*

TORT CLAIM	ACTIONS THAT LEAD TO CLAIMS
Intentional torts (continued) False imprisonment	● Confining a patient in a psychiatric unit without a clinical professional's order or evaluation ● Refusing to let a patient return home if deemed physiologically and psychologically stable
Invasion of privacy	● Releasing private information about a patient to third parties ● Allowing unauthorized persons to read a patient's medical records ● Allowing unauthorized persons to observe a procedure ● Taking photographs or videotape of the patient without his consent, including procedures performed on the patient
Defamation	● Making false statements about a patient to a third person that damage the patient's reputation

physicians. With increasing autonomy, NPs have displayed the ability to provide many of the health care services that were once considered the private domain of the medical profession.

NPs are legally accountable for their own actions and are responsible for exercising independent and rational judgments based on assessments of their patients when rendering care. Problems that could prompt a lawsuit against the NP include:
● delayed initial evaluation due to waiting for a preauthorization call from a third-party payer
● inadequate documentation, such as:
– failure to document functional and sensory deficits that were evident before a procedure or treatment
– failure to document significant differential diagnoses that were considered
– missing event information (for example, omitting the time that the NP performed an assessment or procedure)
– missing patient information (for instance, omitting history and allergy information)

● lack of thorough patient education, such as:
– failure to include risks of nonadherence with the recommended treatment plan on the patient instruction sheet
– failure to include signs and symptoms that the patient should report or a time frame by which he should report them
● delayed patient notification of diagnostic test results
● misdiagnosis or delayed diagnosis
● delayed initiation of treatment (such as prompt initiation of thrombolytic therapy), which may negatively affect the outcome
● informed consent disputes (See *Providing an interpreter.*)
● managed care issues, such as premature discharge and emergency care treatment
● inadequate assessments or failure to review assessments or testing performed by other health care professionals, such as paramedics, consultants, or nursing staff

COURT CASE

Providing an interpreter

In this 1997 Washington case, the court determined that a hospital must provide reasonable accommodation for a patient's sensory disability and that the hearing-impaired patient could sue the hospital for being denied timely access to an American Sign Language interpreter. The hearing-impaired patient was first seen in the emergency department of a rural hospital but was transferred and admitted to a suburban hospital for pneumonia and possible sepsis. The mentally confused patient's hands — her primary means of communication — were restrained. An outside interpreting agency was called but was told that there was no emergency and that an interpreter was needed the next day. Over the course of the patient's hospital stay, interpreters weren't scheduled to coincide with physician visits.

The court found the hospital at fault for failing to place an emergency call to the interpreting agency on the patient's admission and for failing to coordinate the interpreter's visit with the physician's visit.

What the NP can learn

Each patient with a disability has the right to a reasonable accommodation, most fundamentally the right to communicate with health care providers. *Negron v. Snoqualmie Valley Hospital,* 936 P. 2d 55 (Wash. App., 1997).

● performance of procedures for which the NP lacks credentials (See *Qualifying guidelines,* page 140.)
● lack of appropriate follow-up of patient care or interventions (for example, not reminding the patient to have an annual gynecologic examination)
● lack of appropriate referral to a specialist or collaborating physician
● initiating or implementing patient care services or procedures outside the scope of the NP's practice.

In addition, NPs who work in special practice areas may be especially vulnerable to lawsuits. (See *Liability in special practice settings,* pages 141 to 143.)

Negligence vs. malpractice

The court's view of nursing liability has changed significantly. As the NP's professional practice has grown and the number of malpractice cases has increased, the courts have expanded the depth and breadth of their opinions. All health care professionals have become possible defendants, including NPs. (See *NP liability,* page 144.)

Negligence is the failure to exercise the degree of care that a person of ordinary prudence would exercise under the same circumstances. A claim of negligence requires that there be a ***duty*** owed by one person to another, that the duty be breached, and that injury and damages result. Malpractice is negligence as it relates to a professional; it's generally defined as a violation of professional duty or a failure either to meet a standard of care or to use the skills and knowledge of other professionals in similar circumstances. Malpractice also requires that duty, ***breach of duty,*** injury, and damages be shown.

The distinction shows that courts recognize nursing as a legitimate profession. This professional status may affect the ***statute of limitation*** applicable in a particular case. These statutes define the time period during which a suit may be filed. Many states have statutes of limitation for medical malpractice claims that are shorter than those for ordinary negligence actions.

As an NP, you must keep abreast of the scope of practice and limitations in

Qualifying guidelines

Although you're permitted to perform a procedure that you didn't learn in your nurse practitioner program, you must be able to document what qualifies you, or prepares you, to perform it. It's helpful to keep a file documenting all your continuing education activities, such as:

● taking an online continuing education course
● attending a seminar or workshop
● receiving verbal instruction from an experienced professional
● observing a technique being done three times (document the dates)
● performing a procedure with supervision for a specified number of times (document the dates)
● developing or reviewing the protocol for a procedure.

the state where you practice. If you relocate to another state to work, you're responsible for knowing the expectations and limitations of that state's licensure laws and nurse practice act.

Criminal negligence

Whereas malpractice is generally a civil matter, courts may consider criminal charges against nurses for negligence when their acts or omissions are grossly negligent or indicate wanton disregard of a patient's well-being.

MALPRACTICE DEFENSES

Over the years, the law has developed special doctrines, or theories, to apply to cases involving subordinate-superior relationships. These doctrines may be used in an NP's defense during a lawsuit. Exactly how much protection they offer, however, depends on the circumstances of the case and the development of the law in the NP's state.

Respondeat superior

One of the most important malpractice defenses is the doctrine of **respondeat superior** (Latin for "let the master answer"), also called the theory of vicarious liability.

This doctrine holds that when an employee is found negligent, the employer accepts responsibility if the employee was acting within the course and scope of his employment. The doctrine applies to all occupations, not just health care — a utility company, for instance, is liable for injuries that result if one of its on-duty truck drivers negligently hits a pedestrian.

To the extent that an NP is working as the facility's functionary, she can claim some protection under this theory. This is also true when working for **health maintenance organizations (HMOs),** clinics, community agencies, hospitals, physicians, and schools. This doctrine is attractive to **plaintiffs** as well as employees, because hospitals and health care facilities usually have much more money available to pay claims than NPs do (a reality known as the "deep pocket" doctrine).

Borrowed servant

A concept closely related to *respondeat superior* is the **borrowed-servant** or **captain-of-the-ship doctrine.** It's still applied in malpractice lawsuits, but not as often as in the past. The borrowed-servant doctrine might apply if you, as a hospital employee, commit a negligent act while under the direction or control of someone other than your supervisor, such as a physician. If the court can show that the physician exclusively directed your actions, then you're considered his borrowed servant at the time. If you're sued for malpractice, his liability is vicarious, meaning that even though the physician didn't direct you negligently, he's responsible because he was in control. Courts may apply the borrowed-servant doctrine

(Text continues on page 144.)

Liability in special practice settings

Although errors can be made in virtually any practice setting, nurse practitioners (NPs) who work in certain practice settings are more vulnerable to malpractice charges because their errors usually prove more costly for patients. In addition, the courts may expect a higher standard of practice from an NP who practices in a specialty area.

NPs attained direct Medicare reimbursement in 1997, which also increases their liability. The reimbursement covers all NPs, including obstetric and psychiatric NPs. Keeping up with changes in Medicare laws will help protect you against liability.

Acute care unit

Compared with NPs in other units, acute care NPs spend proportionately more of their time in direct contact with their patients, who typically have highly acute and complex conditions, thus increasing the opportunity for error and the number of potential lawsuits. Because of the many invasive and potentially harmful procedures performed and the multiple medications being ordered in this setting, acute care NPs are especially vulnerable to charges of negligence or battery. If they perform expanded-role duties and complex procedures, they may be accused of practicing medicine without a license. Practice guidelines, hospital protocols, and experience will help guide the NP in this specialty area.

Additional tort claims that may be leveled against acute care NPs include:

● abandonment — the unilateral severance of a professional relationship with a patient without adequate notice and while the patient still needs attention.
● invasion of privacy, intentional infliction of emotional distress, or battery — such cases may involve a patient who was placed on or removed from a life-support system.
● failure to obtain informed consent — this is more likely to occur in a critical care setting because of the inherent pressure and urgency for immediate treatment. Acute care NPs who deny a competent patient the right to refuse treatment — even if lack of

treatment results in the patient's death — expose themselves to charges of various intentional torts.
● failure to provide appropriate or adequate patient interventions or treatment plans.
● failure to provide or establish follow-up care for interventions or treatments provided.
● failure to provide patient education when appropriate.
● failure to monitor medications for potential interactions, adverse effects, and therapeutic effects.
● performance of invasive procedures without an adequate knowledge base, experience, or privileges.

Emergency department

Many of the day-to-day practices of emergency department (ED) NPs fall into a legal gray area because the law's definition of a *true emergency* is open to interpretation; for instance, health care workers who treat a patient for what they regard as a true emergency may be liable for battery or failure to obtain informed consent if the court ultimately concludes that the situation wasn't a true emergency.

Fast track ED, urgent care settings, or triage settings are new areas where NPs are establishing and providing care for the acutely ill. Diagnoses, treatment, procedures, and patient education are all common practices in these settings. This specialty area may be free-standing or part of hospital coverage. NPs themselves or agency NPs may be employed in these areas, with a collaborative agreement or use of hospital protocols for practice. Patient management criteria and practice standards need to be established and agreed upon during employment to form a proper legal basis for practice.

All too often, the use of high-tech equipment combined with a hectic daily pace increases the potential for lawsuits.

Tort claims made against NPs in the ED may involve:

(continued)

Liability in special practice settings *(continued)*

• failure to instruct a patient adequately before discharge
• discounting complaints of pain from a patient who is mentally impaired by alcohol, medication, or injury
• failure to obtain informed consent, giving rise to claims of battery, false imprisonment, and invasion of privacy
• failure to make appropriate diagnoses and treatment plans
• performing procedures without appropriate education, experience, or privileges.

Psychiatric unit
Over the past few years, the psychiatric NP specialty has flourished, introducing independent or collaborative coverage of psychiatric patients in institutional settings (public and private) as well as in private practices. The psychiatric NP establishes patient assessments, evaluations, diagnoses, and treatment plans in these settings.

Malpractice cases dealing with psychiatric care usually involve failure to obtain informed consent. An NP may wrongly assume she doesn't need informed consent, especially if the patient's condition interferes with his awareness or understanding of the proposed treatment or procedure. Violation of a patient's right to refuse treatment may stem from the mistaken belief that all mentally ill patients are incompetent. (The right to refuse treatment isn't absolute, however, and can be abrogated if medications or treatments are required to prevent serious harm to the patient or others.)

Malpractice charges also can be brought against an NP who reveals personal information about a patient to someone not directly involved in his care. Violation of a patient's right to privacy and confidentiality is a common complaint in lawsuits against psychiatric health care workers, probably because of the stigma still associated with seeking care for mental illness.

False imprisonment is another potential charge for which the psychiatric NP is particularly vulnerable. To protect yourself from such charges, make every effort to perform proper assessments, establish effective treatment plans, use appropriate facility procedures when working with persons who can harm themselves or others, and participate in an ongoing review of cases with your collaborating physicians.

Malpractice allegations may also stem from failing to protect a patient from inflicting foreseeable harm to himself or others. If an NP fails to evaluate or report information given by the patient, even in confidence, that could have prevented the harm, she may be held liable for violating her duty to assess and report his condition.

Obstetric setting
Cases involving obstetric errors have at least two plaintiffs: the mother and the neonate. This specialty has a high potential for litigation. (Because some courts recognize a legal duty owed to the unborn, an obstetric NP also may be charged with violating the rights of a fetus.) Monetary damages tend to be large because of the permanent or long-term injuries that can occur to neonates. NPs work within the obstetrical setting in ways other than as a Certified Nurse Midwife. They're also employed in various settings related to women's health, including physician's offices, Planned Parenthood settings, community health clinics, and HMOs. These settings can be for low risk- or high-risk patient populations.

The obstetric NP also can provide care to a pregnant woman that's unrelated to her pregnancy, such as annual screenings, Papanicolaou smears, health counseling, and birth control issues and management. This can be a highly sensitive and litigious area, because the NP can be sued for damages to both the mother and the fetus if proven negligent.

An obstetric NP may be held liable for negligence through:
• participation in transfusion of incompatible blood, especially in relation to Rh factor incompatibility
• failure to attend to or monitor the mother or the fetus during labor and delivery
• failure to recognize labor symptoms or to provide adequate support and care

Liability in special practice settings *(continued)*

- inappropriate or inadequate assessment, treatment plan, or patient evaluation
- inappropriate pharmacological intervention, especially one that causes fetal harm
- failure to protect the mother or fetus during high-risk interventions and therapies
- failure to provide adequate patient education
- failure to monitor contractions and fetal heart rate, particularly in obstetric units with internal monitoring capabilities
- failure to recognize high-risk labor patients who show signs of preeclampsia or other labor complications
- failure to warn parents of the risks of diagnostic tests — or the consequences of refusing such tests — if the failure contributes to maternal or fetal injury
- abandonment of a patient in active labor
- failure to exercise independent judgment
- failure to ensure that a patient has given informed consent for various procedures or treatments, including physical examinations, administration of a potent medication, type of delivery method, sterilization, and postdelivery surgical procedures.

Other common sources of malpractice suits filed against obstetric NPs include failure to attend to the neonate in distress, failure to monitor equipment, use of defective equipment, failure to monitor oxygen levels, failure to recognize and report neonate jaundice during the immediate postnatal period, and failure to provide appropriate and adequate health promotion and disease prevention education.

In some states, parents can file a *wrongful birth* lawsuit if an NP failed to advise them of contraceptive methods or the methods' potential for failure, potential genetic defects, the availability of amniocentesis to detect defects, or the option of abortion to prevent birth of a defective child. A child with a genetic defect can file a *wrongful life* lawsuit if an NP failed to inform the parents of amniocentesis and the option of abortion. Failure to provide adequate genetic counseling and prenatal testing when the mother has a history of Down syndrome can also result in a wrongful birth or wrongful life lawsuit.

Primary care setting

Primary care NPs provide care for the patient, family, and community. Family NPs, adult NPs, and pediatric NPs all participate in this practice specialty.

Malpractice lawsuits typically arise in the areas of diagnosis, treatment, and patient teaching. Because on-call situations figure prominently in such lawsuits, the primary care NP should carefully document telephone advice, treatment plans, and recommendations for follow-up care.

Individualized treatment plans should be age-appropriate and specific. If parental consent is necessary, the NP should obtain it before initiating treatment. In addition, the NP should carefully consider confidentiality and ethical issues before engaging in patient education and treatment.

Protocols for primary care NPs need to be consulted and followed. Careful documentation is also necessary for future review and liability protection. Collaborative agreements for complex patient care management should be specific and should outline strategies to resolve disagreements.

The primary care NP also must ensure that the patient has signed an informed consent form. Appropriate patient education, risks involved with the procedure, alternatives to the procedure, and outcomes should all be included on the form and in the NP's documentation.

Protocols for "on-call" rotations with a collaborating physician, via telephone or in person, should be in place. Algorithms, care maps, triage plans, and clinical practice guidelines must be updated regularly to ensure that patient care meets the current standards of practice.

Finally, disagreement procedures and resolution procedures should also be available for the NP to access when necessary. These procedures help facilitate patient care and will reduce the NP's liability if a patient chooses not to follow the NP's recommendations.

COURT CASE

NP liability

In many states, malpractice issues vary. Regardless of how the state licensing boards view the working relationship of the nurse practitioner (NP) to the physician (collaborative or supervising), both health care professionals can be sued.

In a rural health care clinic in the south, an NP diagnosed a young woman with gastroenteritis after the woman arrived at the clinic with abdominal cramping, nausea, and vomiting. No laboratory work was performed after the NP's assessment, and the NP told the woman to seek follow-up care if her symptoms worsened or recurred. No physician evaluation was done, but the physician signed the chart. Two days later the patient died. An autopsy revealed peritonitis secondary to a ruptured appendix.

The family sued the NP, the physician, and the clinic. The jury found the clinic and the NP liable and awarded $1 million. In clearing the physician, the jury indicated that the NP's poor judgment in not consulting him was more significant to the case than his supervisory status.

for NPs working in the operating room, emergency department (ED), and labor and delivery rooms and during code situations.

Many states have moved away from strict application of the borrowed-servant theory. One reason for this shift is that health care procedures are becoming so complex that they're beyond the direct control of any one person, thus making it difficult for courts to determine responsibility under the borrowed-servant doctrine.

Comparative negligence

The law attempts to compensate victims for injury caused by another person's actions or negligence. However, if the victim's actions contributed to the injury, or made it worse than it would have been otherwise, this is known as *comparative negligence*. For instance, an NP might be negligent by giving a patient a prescription for tamoxifen after a mastectomy and not teaching the patient how to use it correctly. If the patient believes the tamoxifen is only to reduce swelling and discomfort, and thus not really necessary, she may choose not to fill the prescription she was given. A prudent person might suffer some injury from not taking the tamoxifen until speaking with the NP at the follow-up appointment, whereas a less prudent person who negligently fails to keep the follow-up appointment might incur more severe injuries (such as the development of a malignancy deep in the chest cavity). The doctrine of comparative negligence states that if a person is partially responsible for an injury, any damage award received can be reduced by the extent to which she was responsible. In these cases, a judge or jury must calculate how much each party is at fault. Each state has its own rules for calculating damages that can be recovered when a victim is at least partially to blame for his own injury. In Ohio, for instance, the judge reduces the amount of any damage award by the percentage of the victim's contribution to his injuries, and if the plaintiff was found to be more than 50% negligent, he recovers nothing. If a jury awards $100,000 in damages but decides the plaintiff was 30% at fault, the judge reduces the damage award by 30% to $70,000.

Contributory negligence

A related concept is the doctrine of *contributory negligence*. This concept states that negligent defendants determined to be substantially at fault (generally more than 50%) can be held liable for a proportionate share of damages. Negligent defendants can be found liable for the full amount of the award when their behavior is found to be either malicious or reckless.

Assumption of risk

This doctrine is used when the defense contends that the plaintiff knew a particular activity was dangerous and thus bears all responsibility for any injury that resulted. When a patient declines a recommended treatment or signs himself out of a health care facility *against medical advice,* he assumes the risk for his care and the NP isn't liable for any negative outcome related to the patient's choice to forego care.

Other defenses

Other malpractice defenses include "defense of the fact," in which there is no connection between the NP's actions and the negative outcome (such as when an NP treats a patient for epistaxis and 1 week later breaks his nose while skateboarding) and "unavoidable accident," in which there is no cause or fault for the accident (such as when the plaintiff slips on an unobstructed dry floor in a well-lit area).

RES IPSA LOQUITUR

The Latin phrase **res ipsa loquitur** literally means "The thing speaks for itself." *Res ipsa loquitur* is a rule of evidence designed to equalize the plaintiff's and the defendant's positions in court, when otherwise the plaintiff could be at a disadvantage in proving his case — a disadvantage not of his own making. Essentially, the rule of *res ipsa loquitur* allows a plaintiff to prove negligence with *circumstantial evidence*, when the defendant has the primary, and sometimes the only, knowledge of what happened to cause the plaintiff's injury.

Res ipsa loquitur derives from a 19th-century English case, *Byrne v. Boadle* (1863). In that case, the injured person had been struck by a flour barrel that fell from a second-floor window of a warehouse. In the ensuing lawsuit, the plaintiff wasn't able to show which warehouse employee had been negligent in allowing the barrel to fall. The court applied the concept of *res ipsa loquitur* to the warehouse owners, who were found liable in the absence of proof that the employees weren't responsible for the plaintiff's injury.

Applying *res ipsa loquitur*

In medical malpractice cases, the plaintiff has the responsibility for proving every element of his case against the defendant; until he does, the court presumes that the defendant met the applicable *standard of care.* However, when a court applies the *res ipsa loquitur* rule, the burden of proof shifts from the plaintiff to the defendant. The defendant must show that the injury was caused by something other than his negligence. Most cases using this rule of evidence concern unconscious patients, including patients in the operating room, in code situations, and comatose patients and infants.

For the *res ipsa loquitur* rule to apply to an NP, three circumstances must be met:
● The act that caused the plaintiff's injury was exclusively in the NP's control.
● The injury wouldn't have happened in the absence of the defendant-NP's negligence.
● No negligence on the plaintiff's part contributed to his injury.

Incidents associated with *res ipsa loquitur*

Perhaps the most common incident associated with the *res ipsa loquitur* rule is the foreign-object case, in which a sponge, needle, pin, or other object is

Challenging a malpractice suit

If your attorney can establish one of the following malpractice defenses, the court will either dismiss the allegations or reduce the damages for which you're liable.

DEFENSE	RATIONALE
False allegations	Does the plaintiff have legally sufficient proof that your actions caused his injuries? If he doesn't, the court may rule that the allegations against you are false and dismiss the case.
Contributory negligence	Did the plaintiff, through carelessness, contribute to his injury? If he did, some states permit the court to charge the plaintiff with failing to meet the standards of a reasonably prudent patient. Such a ruling may prevent the plaintiff from recovering any damages. A few states permit the court to apportion liability, which prevents the plaintiff from recovering some, but not all, of the damages he claims.
Comparative negligence	Has more than one defendant been named in the lawsuit? In most states, the court may apportion liability according to the negligence of the defendants involved, with the total damages divided among them in proportion to the fault of each.
Assumption of risk	Did the plaintiff understand the risk involved in the treatment, procedure, or action that allegedly caused his injury? Did he give proper informed consent and so voluntarily expose himself to that risk? If so, the court may rule that the plaintiff assumed the risk, knowingly disregarded the danger, and so relieved you of liability.

left inside the patient after surgery. Courts have also been willing to invoke the rule because of injuries to a plaintiff involving body parts completely unrelated to the plaintiff's surgery. NPs who perform surgical procedures in the ED, obstetrical units, clinics, and office settings are vulnerable to these types of lawsuits.

Consider the Wisconsin malpractice case *Beaudoin v. Watertown Memorial Hospital* (1966). A patient suffered second-degree burns on the buttocks during vaginal surgery. She brought suit, claiming negligence. The court applied the *res ipsa loquitur* rule on the basis that injury to an area unrelated to surgery automatically results from failure to exercise due care.

For and against *res ipsa loquitur*

Critics of the *res ipsa loquitur* rule call it "the rule of sympathy" and believe the courts have been too lenient in allowing plaintiffs to use it. **Health care professionals** usually contend that the rule places them at an unfair disadvantage during a malpractice defense. They feel that, by assigning them the **burden of proof,** the court singles them out for more negligence liability than other types of defendants. Also, invoking the rule may eliminate the plaintiff's responsibility to introduce expert testimony.

Supporters of the rule feel that it draws attention to the fact that a plaintiff's unusual or rare injury is, in itself, sufficient to raise suspicion that the defendant was negligent.

State interpretations

In some states, courts can't apply the *res ipsa loquitur* rule. Several states, however, do allow courts to apply some form of it. For example, neither Michigan nor South Carolina uses the rule by name, but both permit circumstantial evidence of negligence, which is, in effect, the same concept. (See *Challenging a malpractice suit.*)

Understanding statutes of limitation

A statute of limitation specifies a particular number of years within which one party can sue another. For malpractice lawsuits, the statute of limitation is specified in each state's code, often in the medical malpractice law section. These limits vary widely from state to state, and it's important to know the limits in your state. Contact the attorney, lobbyist, or legislative committee members of your state nurses' association for information about the statutes of limitation in your state. (For a list of state nurses' associations, see pages 6 to 9.)

PURPOSE OF STATUTES OF LIMITATION

Statutes of limitation are useful because, as time passes, evidence vanishes, witnesses' memories fail, and witnesses become incompetent or unavailable. A time limit for bringing a lawsuit ensures that enough relevant evidence exists for a judge or jury to decide a case fairly.

Statutes of limitation for general negligence usually give a person 3 years to sue another for damages. Defendants may invoke these limits as a defense in general personal-injury lawsuits. In response to pressure from medical and insurance groups, states established shorter statutes of limitation for professions that require independent judgments and incur frequent risks. The statutes of limitation of medical malpractice laws, for example, usually give the patient 2 years or less to sue for damages.

DETERMINING WHICH STATUTE APPLIES

In many states, only physicians and dentists are expressly subject to medical malpractice statutes of limitation, although the growing trend is to include NPs in the statute. NPs are held legally accountable for their own actions and are responsible for exercising independent and rational judgment based on competent assessments of their patients when rendering care. *Statutory law* has established that the NP has the legal authority to practice under her individual nurse's license and that her authority doesn't flow from a physician's or any other health care provider's license.

If an NP alleges a patient's claim is invalid because he didn't file suit until after the statute of limitation had expired, the court must determine which applies: the statute of limitation for state medical malpractice law or the statute of limitation for general personal-injury lawsuits. (The malpractice law's statute of limitation is usually shorter.) The court bases its decision on how much statute of limitation protection the defendant-nurse practitioner's job warrants. If her job requires her to make many independent patient care judgments, the court may apply a strict, or short, statute of limitation. A short time limit offers more protection for the NP because the patient has less time to initiate a lawsuit.

In an Alaska case, *Pedersen v. Zielski* (1991), the plaintiff argued that a 6-year statute of limitation for controlled claims applied to a health care provider's negligence because the physician had a contract to provide care to him. The Alaska court held that the 2-year statute of limitation was applicable as plaintiff's claims arose in tort or personal injury law, not in contract law.

APPLYING THE STATUTE OF LIMITATION

Suppose a patient files suit after the statute of limitation has expired. Don't think your worries are over. Remember, the patient's attorney knows about the statute of limitation, and he's filing suit anyway. That means he believes the court may set aside the statute of limitation.

Normally, the statute begins to run on the date the plaintiff's injury occurred. What if the plaintiff doesn't know he was injured or doesn't find out he has grounds for a suit until after the statutory limitation period expires? Determining when the applicable statute actually begins to run has become the pivotal question whenever a defense attorney invokes the statute of limitation.

Legislatures and the courts, which are continually struggling with this question, have devised a series of guides to help decide, in individual malpractice cases, when a statute should properly begin to run. When requested by a plaintiff-patient's attorney, a court can apply these rules to extend the applicable statute of limitation beyond the limit written in the law. That means that the NP's use of a statute of limitation as a defense is invalidated, and the plaintiff-patient is still allowed to sue.

Occurrence rule

Under the occurrence rule, the statute of limitation begins to run on the day a patient's injury occurs. The occurrence rule generally leads to the shortest time limit. In several states, the courts have interpreted the occurrence rule strictly, so that even severely injured patients have been prevented from bringing suit after the applicable statute of limitation has expired.

Termination-of-treatment rule

The courts may apply the termination-of-treatment rule when a patient's injury results from a series of treatments extended over time, rather than from a single treatment. The termination-of-treatment rule says that a statute of limitation begins on the date of the last treatment. In devising this rule, the courts reasoned that for the patient, a series of treatments could obscure just how and when the injury occurred.

The Supreme Court of Virginia applied this rule in *Justice v. Natvig* (1989). In this case, a patient filed a lawsuit 8 years after an allegedly negligent operation. The patient had continued to receive treatment during this interval. The defendant-physicians argued that the statute of limitation had lapsed. The court ruled, however, that the statute didn't begin to run until the treatment had ended, so the patient's lawsuit was allowed.

Constructive continuing treatment rule

The constructive continuing treatment rule is essentially the same as the termination-of-treatment rule, but it applies even after the patient leaves an NP's or a physician's care. For example, suppose a patient you cared for is injured later, in someone else's care, and sues. Under the constructive continuing treatment rule, if the subsequent health care providers relied on decisions you made earlier in caring for the patient, the court may extend the statute of limitation in malpractice cases.

Discovery rule

Under the *discovery rule,* the statute of limitation begins to run when a patient discovers the injury. This may take place many years after the injury occurred. The discovery rule considerably extends the time a patient has to file a malpractice lawsuit.

Two types of cases in which the discovery rule is usually applied involve foreign objects and sterilization. When an NP or a surgeon leaves a scalpel, sponge, or clamp inside a patient, the patient might not discover the error until long after his surgery. Under the discovery rule, the applicable statute of limitation wouldn't begin to run until the patient found out about the error.

A court's decision to apply the discovery rule depends on whether it believes that the patient could have discovered the error earlier. If evidence indicates the patient should have recognized that something was wrong (for example, if he had chronic pain for months after the surgery but didn't take legal action until long afterward), the court could apply the termination-of-treatment rule instead.

Time limits for applying the discovery rule in foreign-object cases vary from state to state. Missouri allows the longest period (up to 10 years after discovery of the injury); California, the shortest (1 year after discovery of the injury).

In lawsuits involving tubal ligations or vasectomies, the courts have sometimes allowed the discovery rule to apply when a subsequent pregnancy occurs. In these cases, the courts' reasoning is that a patient can't discover the negligence until the procedure proves unsuccessful, no matter how long after the surgery this proof appears.

Because the discovery rule is so generous to plaintiffs, some states, notably Texas, have restricted its application. A number of states have adopted separate statutes of limitations, one for readily detected injuries and one for injuries discovered later. Other states permit statute of limitation extensions only in foreign-object cases.

Proof of fraud

Courts in most states will extend the limitation period indefinitely if a plaintiff-patient can prove that an NP or physician used *fraud* or falsehood to conceal from the patient information about his injury or its cause. In most cases, the law says that the concealment must be an overt act, not just the omission of an act. The most flagrant frauds involve concealing facts to prevent an inquiry, elude an investigation, or mislead a patient. (See *Extending the statute of limitations,* page 150.)

Consider, for example, *Garcia v. Presbyterian Hospital Center* (1979). In this case, a patient was operated on for cancer of the prostate gland twice in 1972 and once again in 1973. He'd repeatedly asked his physician and attending nurses why the third operation was needed, but he hadn't received any explanation. Some time later, he learned that the third operation had resulted from retention of a catheter in his body during the second operation. The court held that the applicable statute of limitation didn't prevent the patient from bringing suit.

Minor or mentally incompetent patients

In most states, laws give special consideration to *minors* and *mentally incompetent* patients because they lack the legal capacity to sue. Some states postpone applying the statute of limitation to an injured minor until he reaches the *age of majority* — age 18 or 21, depending on the state. Some states have specific rules about how statutes of limitation apply to minors. The general trend today is not to give special considerations to minors.

Cases involving mentally incompetent patients who file after statutes of limitation have expired usually follow the discovery rule or a special law. Most of these special laws state that a statute of limitation doesn't begin until

COURT CASE

Extending the statute of limitation

If a plaintiff-patient can prove that a nurse practitioner or physician willfully deceived him, the court may lengthen the statute of limitation for filing a lawsuit.

Painful overtreatment

Consider the case of *Lopez v. Swyer* (1971). Mary Lopez, age 32, underwent a radical mastectomy after discovering a lump in her breast. Several doctors prescribed postsurgical radiation treatments, which were performed by a radiologist.

These treatments occurred six times a week for more than a month and left painful radiation burns over most of her body. When Mrs. Lopez asked why the complications were so severe, her physician assured her that the burns weren't unusual. The physician never suggested that the treatments could have been too numerous or too long.

Mrs. Lopez's condition worsened. Over the next several years, she was hospitalized 15 times, including twice for reconstructive surgery made necessary by the radiation treatment. She didn't file a malpractice suit until she heard a consulting physician tell other physicians, gathered near her hospital bed, that she was a victim of negligence.

Extra time for the plaintiff

A lower court dismissed the suit because the 2-year statute of limitation for malpractice had expired. An appeals court ruled that the statute of limitation didn't begin to run until Mrs. Lopez learned that her physicians had concealed the truth from her. This effectively lengthened the statute of limitation by nearly 10 years. The appeals court ruling allowed Mrs. Lopez to bring the facts of her case before a jury.

---

the patient recovers from his mental incompetence.

USING THE STATUTE OF LIMITATION DEFENSE

When a defendant-NP and her attorney use a statute of limitation as a defense, they're making, in legal terms, an *affirmative defense.* The defendant must prove that the statute of limitation has expired. If the court decides the statutory time limit has expired, the plaintiff-patient's case is dismissed.

For example, in *Claypool v. Levin* (Wis. 1997), the statute of limitation covering malpractice actions began to run when the plaintiff obtained actual or constructive notice of injury and its cause. The fact that there was more than one possible cause doesn't toll (or pause) the statute. Thus, a patient can't argue that the statute is tolled because he sought legal advice that indicated no viable claim.

RETAINING MEDICAL RECORDS

Because a patient may file a malpractice suit years after he claims his injury occurred, accurate *medical records* should be kept on file for years. The complexity of malpractice cases requires you to recall specific clinical facts and procedures. Complete *documentation* of your care is usually found only in the records. These records provide your best defense. Without them, you're legally vulnerable.

Many states have laws setting precise time periods, and legal experts urge hospitals and other health care facilities to maintain medical record files long after patients are discharged. New Jersey, for example, requires hospitals to keep medical records for 7 years.

Some states have adopted the Uniform Business Records Act, which recommends keeping records for no less than 3 years. Some states allow microfilm copies of medical records to be admitted as evidence in malpractice cases; other states insist that only the original records can be used in court.

Avoiding malpractice liability

You can take steps to avoid tort liability by using caution and common sense and by maintaining a heightened awareness of your legal responsibilities. Follow the guidelines described below. (See *Everyday situations that can trigger lawsuits,* pages 152 and 153.)

Know your own strengths and weaknesses

Don't accept responsibilities for which you aren't prepared. For example, if you haven't treated pediatric patients for 10 years, accepting pediatric patients without the appropriate knowledge base only increases your chances of making an error. If you do make an error, claiming you weren't familiar with the treatments, medication dosages, or procedures won't protect you against liability.

As an NP, you shouldn't accept a situation if you can't perform as a *reasonably prudent NP* would in that setting. Courts may, however, be more lenient if the case involved an NP who was working under emergency conditions, such as a fire or flood.

Evaluate your workload for liability

You must work within your scope of practice or education, as designated by your state's nurse practice act and your professional organizations. Scope of practice in each state covers health promotion, disease prevention, and

health assessment. Your degree of autonomy, prescriptive authority, and access to patient populations can vary from state to state.

Keep abreast of new treatments, medications, and technology. However, practice should be research-based and not simply following the latest trends. For example, troglitazone, a drug used to treat diabetes mellitus, quickly gained widespread popularity but had unacceptable risks (fatalities related to severe hepatic reactions) and was later withdrawn. Consider ways to share information with your colleagues, such as by participating in lunchtime in-service workshops and subscribing to free Web-based e-mailing lists. Another way to view current standards of care for specific disorders is to review online evidence-based clinical practice guidelines on government Web sites.

If you're being pressured to function outside the parameters of your *collaborative practice agreement* (for example, by assessing patients outside your area of expertise), speak to the physician involved and work together to maintain the collaborative agreement, or request additional education and a skills update to meet the current needs of the practice.

Above all, develop and maintain a grievance process for patient care situations. If a patient has a problem and either can't determine who should address it or feels the issue isn't being taken seriously, he will likely seek outside assistance in resolving the matter. This often takes the form of litigation by the patient or a third-party payer.

Delegate carefully

As an NP, you'll be delegating patient care to several levels of providers. You may be held responsible if you inappropriately delegate an order. An example would be to order a medical assistant with no medication knowledge

Everyday situations that can trigger lawsuits

Everyday clinical situations present many legal hazards. The following examples of nursing liability, based on actual court decisions, show how deviating from accepted standards can harm a patient and result in lawsuits. By being aware of how certain common situations can cause legal entanglements, you can avoid making similar mistakes.

Failing to perform a thorough assessment

A 1985 California case was brought by a 34-year-old attorney who experienced brief chest pain while he was riding his bicycle to work and similar pain the next day while jogging; 2 days later, he experienced another episode while walking after lunch. When the chest pain returned while he was working at his office that evening, he called his physician the next morning for an appointment. He was evaluated by the nurse practitioner (NP), who diagnosed him with muscle spasm and prescribed Valium after she consulted with the physician.

He was awakened that night with chest pain and went to the emergency department (ED), where a physician confirmed the diagnosis of muscle spasm and ordered meperidine and codeine. He again experienced severe chest pain the next day at noon and went to the ED, where an electrocardiogram showed a myocardial infarction. He recovered, but lost 18 months of pay.

What the NP can learn

Develop a thorough differential diagnosis and rule out all possible causes that have severe consequences before rendering a working diagnosis. (*Fein v. Permanente Medical Group* [1985]).

Failing to take appropriate precautions

In this 1996 Louisiana case, the patient sued for a *Clostridium* infection linked to a lapse of aseptic technique by the ED nurses. The patient's left ring finger was de-gloved from his hand in a combine repair accident. The ED physician cleaned and debrided the wound and called in an orthopedic surgeon to reattach the finger. The ED nurses cut back the patient's shirt to the elbow, but didn't completely clean the hand or the arm. The reattachment surgery was successful, but he was treated with antibiotics postoperatively for the *Clostridium* infection caused by a lapse in aseptic technique by the ED nurses and physician. The patient was awarded damages for subsequent surgeries, medical expenses, and pain and suffering.

What the NP can learn

Infections can be costly for you and your patients. Make sure to fully expose and clean any wound from end to end and to its depths. (*Roberts v. Lowry* [1996]). Also, provide adequate follow-up care or tell the patient when to return to you for further assessments.

Failing to monitor symptoms

In a Virginia case, a patient complained of scabbing and discharge from one of her nipples. The NP ordered antibiotics and a mammogram, which was read as negative. The patient returned several months later with the same complaints, and the NP referred her to a dermatologist, whom the patient didn't visit. Several months later, the patient saw her gynecologist, who assured her she didn't have breast cancer and treated her with antibiotics. The patient continued seeing the NP for other complaints; 18 months after the first visit, masses were noted in the patient's breasts and she was referred to a surgical oncologist, who diagnosed her with Paget's disease. The cancer metastasized and the patient died. In the subsequent wrongful death claim, the patient's family recovered damages against the NP, the family practitioner, and the gynecologist.

Everyday situations that can trigger lawsuits *(continued)*

What the NP can learn

The NP must follow up on all symptoms and reconsider the original diagnosis if symptoms persist. (*Jenkins v. Payne* [Virginia 1996]).

Failure to refer to a specialist

In this 1980 Massachusetts case, an NP, a physician, and a health plan were sued by a patient who had a Dalkon Shield intrauterine device (IUD) placed in 1972. The patient told the physician that she was having vaginal bleeding and that she had read an article in *The New York Times* about the Dalkon Shield causing vaginal bleeding. The physician reassured her that the bleeding wasn't related to the Dalkon Shield. In 1975 the patient reported to the NP she was having a foul vaginal order like a dead fish. The NP advised her to take a yogurt douche. One week later the patient reported to the NP that she was having severe abdominal pain, similar to labor pain. The NP told her the pain was probably due to a GI flu and to call back if she became febrile. A week later she reported to the clinic for a scheduled appointment, and she could hardly walk. The IUD was removed, and she was given antibiotics and pain killers and told to return in 3 days, at which time she was diagnosed with multiple abscesses. Three days later she underwent a total hysterectomy. The appellate court determined that the patient presented sufficient evidence to the medical malpractice tribunal and raised a legitimate question of liability appropriate for judicial inquiry.

What the NP can learn

The NP should always document patient encounters and watch for a pattern of complaints that could lead to a more complete picture of the patient's condition rather than a quick snapshot view. If symptoms don't resolve, consult with or refer to a physician or specialist. The NP should also adhere to acceptable standards of care for all patients. Avoid using treatment methods that aren't considered acceptable practice. (*Gugino v. Harvard Community Health Plan* [1980]).

Failure to provide patient education

In this 1996 Pennsylvania case, parents sued over the death of their newborn, who had been infected by cytomegalovirus (CMV) in utero. The pregnant patient frequently helped her friend feed and bathe the friend's newborn, who was born with abnormalities due to CMV. The friend and baby both had tested positive for CMV. Six months after visiting her friend, the pregnant patient first learned that CMV was highly contagious and caused birth defects and that she herself had become infected with CMV while pregnant.

The court determined that health care professionals have a legal duty to warn patients who have contagious diseases such as CMV, hepatitis C, and human immunodeficiency virus of the possibility of spreading the diseases to others.

What the NP can learn

An NP has a duty to advise patients with contagious diseases that they pose risks to others. A person who contracts a highly contagious disease from a patient who wasn't so instructed has a cause of action against the NP for failure to warn of the danger of the contagion. (*Troxel v. A.P. Dupont Institute* [1996]).

---

to administer an immunization injection. If the medication is administered in the wrong dose or by the wrong route, you could be held liable. It's also your duty to report any incompetent health care personnel to superiors through the facility's chain of command.

Prescribe medications carefully

When prescribing medications, you must use your knowledge of pathophysiology, adverse effects, drug interactions, and precautions related to age, pregnancy, and breast-feeding. You can be held liable for errors in any of the preceding areas if you don't take the proper precautions and consider patient-related factors.

For example, the Centers for Disease Control and Prevention has learned of numerous cases of inadequate treatment of syphilis with Bicillin C-R (1.2 million units each of penicillin G benzathine and penicillin G procaine). Instead, Bicillin (penicillin G benzathine) 2.4 million units should be used. Bicillin has a longer half-life, which is essential for effective syphilis treatment because it yields the sustained spirocheticidal levels needed to treat the slowly reproducing *Treponema pallidum.*

Another troublesome practice is dosing by dropperful — it's both ambiguous and dangerous. Ordering a drug such as liquid ferrous sulfate, used to treat iron deficiency in children, by the dropperful easily leads to errors. One person might correctly consider the dropper full when the liquid meets the upper calibration mark; another might incorrectly fill the entire length of the dropper. Parents or caregivers administering the drug at home might use a different dropper, which could significantly alter the dose.

Dosing directions for liquid drugs must be expressed as weight per volume, such as 15 mg (0.6 ml). The correct dosage should be verified, and parents or caregivers should be taught to use only the dropper that has been provided to them. They should be shown the mark on the dropper that indicates a full dose and then they should demonstrate the proper technique to you.

In addition, your handwriting on prescriptions — as well as any drug information that you write on patient-teaching aids — must be legible to prevent medication errors. Clear handwriting and patient education are essential. (See *Providing clear patient instructions.*)

As a public service, the Food and Drug Administration (FDA) and the Consumer Healthcare Products Association provide a free brochure to teach patients about safe use of over-the-counter drugs. Titled *Nonprescription Medication: What's Right for You,* the brochure discusses label interpretation, drug interactions, medicine cabinet safety, considerations for children and pregnant or breast-feeding women, and protection against tampering. You can provide the following information to your patients as an added precautionary measure: brochures are available by calling 1-888-878-3256 or writing to the Consumer Information Center, Item 548F, Pueblo, CO 81009. Patients may also read the brochure on the FDA's Web site, *www.fda.gov/opacom/what'sright.*

Maintain a rapport with the patient

The importance of finely honed communication skills can't be understated. While listening to the patient's reason for seeking care, also be alert to any hesitancy in stating additional concerns. These areas must be probed more deeply while completing the patient's history and physical examination. Give feedback to the patient, stating your understanding of his problem and your concerns for his health. Assess his understanding and state your plan of care. Ask directly if this is acceptable to him. If not, explore his concerns and attempt to fine-tune the plan of care to meet the patient's medical and emotional needs. Portray a nonjudgmental attitude and an acceptance of his choices. Document if he rejects a treatment and his rationale. This provides a reminder if the situation is revisited at a later time or as evidence for the defense if litigation occurs.

Don't offer personal details about your life or similar problems or complaints to the patient; this may cause the patient to doubt your ability to keep confidences or make it difficult for the patient to view you strictly as a professional. Studies have shown that patients prefer the NP to verbalize in a positive manner but exhibit a serious demeanor when the patient's health or health problems are being discussed.

Involve the patient in his care

After completing your history and physical examination, you arrive at a working diagnosis. List your differential diagnoses in the notes, and address them through assessment findings or diagnostic testing, or note to consider them on follow-up if signs or symptoms don't resolve. Although it isn't necessary to share all your knowledge with the patient, it's important to let him know what you're considering and what might change your opinion. For instance, although his GI symptoms may appear benign, persistent pain or bloody stools would indicate something different, and you should encourage him to contact you immediately. This allows the patient to be an active member of the team, able to assume responsibility for his care.

Don't pass judgment

Avoid making any statement that could be perceived by the patient as an admission of fault or error. Don't criticize other health care professionals or the care they provide in front of the patient, nor discuss with the patient or visitors that members of the health care team are covered by malpractice insurance. Be careful not to discuss a patient's care or personal business with anyone except when doing so is consistent with proper professional care.

Providing clear patient instructions

A 3-month-old infant underwent surgery to correct a ventricular septal defect. Upon discharge from the hospital, the child's mother received a copy of instructions to administer 25 mcg (0.5 ml) of digoxin pediatric elixir (50 mcg/ml) to the infant twice a day. The mother had trouble reading the instructions, so she rewrote them. Unfortunately, she wrote the dose as 2.5 ml instead of 0.5 ml, so the child received 125 mcg of digoxin twice a day, for a total daily dose of 250 mcg.

After administering the incorrect dose for 7 days, the mother found the infant unconscious and took her to the emergency department. The infant suffered a cardiac arrest and was resuscitated and started on digoxin immune FAB (Digibind) to lower her blood digoxin level. After several days, her digoxin level was normal and she went home without any signs of harm.

What the NP can learn

Instruction sheets given to patients or their caregivers must be clear, legible, and complete. The actual product and delivery device (or mock-up) should be used to teach the patient or caregiver how to administer the drug. Then, the patient or caregiver should demonstrate the technique and explain the instructions in her own words to you. Finally, the patient or caregiver should check the instructions on the medication bottle with the instruction sheet; if they don't agree, you should be immediately notified.

Adapted from Cohen, H., and Cohen, M.R. "Providing Clear Patient Instructions," *The Nurse Practitioner* 25(2):80, February 2000.

Obtain informed consent

Patients are usually under stress and anxious at the time they're required to make medical decisions and give *informed consent.* Furthermore, they may have physical or emotional stresses or impairments that make comprehension and decision making more difficult.

To ensure that you've fully informed your patient, follow these steps for all nonemergency procedures and treatments.

First, if possible, give information to the patient and his family at least 24 hours in advance of when the decision must be made. Be sure that written information is appropriate for the patient's primary language and reading level. Ideally, information should be available in written, audio, and video formats. Seek agency-approved interpretations as necessary. Essential information includes:
● the name and definition of the procedure or treatment in layman's terms, including whether it's primarily diagnostic, therapeutic, palliative, aesthetic, or experimental
● a description of how the procedure or treatment will be performed and by whom (identify by full name and title all persons participating or observing, and identify students who will be performing or assisting)
● indications and contraindications
● expected outcomes, including duration of pain, loss of function or sensation, and resolution of original complaint
● success rate for:
–the procedure
–the procedure performed at this facility
–the procedure as performed by this practitioner
–the procedure for this patient type in particular (for example, cryosurgery has a greater risk of a negative aesthetic outcome for a heavily pigmented patient or a patient with a history of keloids)

● the NP's expectations of the procedure or treatment (such as curative versus palliative treatments)
● alternative procedure or treatments, including the risks and benefits associated with them
● potential risks and complications of the procedure or treatment
● expense to the patient (including the amount for which the patient would be responsible if his third-party payer declines payment).

Second, make sure the patient and his family have time to review and discuss the materials before making a decision. Lastly, make sure you answer any questions or concerns that the patient and family have before starting the procedure or treatment.

Document accurately

From a legal standpoint, documented care is as important as actual care. If a procedure wasn't documented, the courts assume it wasn't performed. Documentation of observations, decisions, and actions is considered much more solid evidence than oral testimony.

The NP must document accurately. Retrieval of the medical records in a future lawsuit should reflect your assessments, treatments, and plan of care that was established in your patient encounter. Legible handwriting will also help you when trying to reconstruct your clinical situation. Illegible handwriting may create problems for you if the court can't understand or read your entries. Computer-generated or typed chart entries are more easily read and help provide a quicker and more accurate scenario.

As an NP, you must provide detailed documentation concerning all elements of your patient's care. This includes the history and physical components, the differential diagnoses, the treatment plan developed, and patient education. Document all educational materials you give to the patient; note whether the patient demonstrated the procedure and verbalized pertinent information, such as potential adverse effects of medication and when to return or call you in the future. Be sure to include the risks of nonadherence with the recommended treatment plan on the patient instruction sheet. In addition, include signs and symptoms the patient should report, and tell the patient that you want him to contact you within a specific time frame if his symptoms aren't improving or if he starts feeling worse.

Avoid using abbreviations or technical language on the patient instruction sheet. Review the sheet with the patient, verifying that he understands your written instructions. These components help provide evidence and support for your clinical decision making in the future.

If the patient is a minor, be sure to document the legal guardian who received your instructions. Patients who are elderly, psychologically impaired, or clinically unstable should also have someone present when receiving instructions. Documentation of this person's presence and understanding will help your defense in the future.

The patient's chart, introduced into the court case, is an NP's best evidence of the care given. The chart should follow the "FACT" rule: be *F*actual, *A*ccurate, *C*omplete, and *T*imely.

DOCUMENTATION TIPS. Special situations routinely arise that require specific management in order to effectively minimize your risk for litigation. You should always:
● proactively handle the potential for informed consent disputes. (Even when the facility's informed consent form has been signed, lack of addressing the discussion in your progress notes may lead to a dispute of informed consent. To minimize this risk, write something concise but complete, such as "procedure, risks, and benefits discussed at length; patient requests procedure be done.")
● ensure that communication is accurate and complete. (When the patient's primary language is not English, it's your responsibility — not the patient's — to access a translator. If no one on location can translate, consult one of the phone services that provide around-the-clock translation.)
● ensure that your assessment of the chart is complete. (Be sure to review assessments or testing performed by other health care professionals, such as paramedics, consultants, or nursing staff. Acknowledge that you reviewed a note or finding in your documentation.)
● enhance the likelihood that the patient will adhere with recommended follow-up care or interventions. (To do this, have a reminder system in place to minimize the number of patients lost to follow-up. For example, maintain a file for each month of the year, with preprinted patient-addressed postcards that remind the patient to schedule an appointment or test. The office assistant can mail the cards monthly.)
● guarantee that you'll remember what authorities were notified, particularly for mandatory reporting situations, by writing this information in the chart. (This includes legal or public health concerns such as child abuse and tuberculosis.)
● provide the patient with instructions regarding referral to a specialist or collaborating physician that include the physician's name, phone number, and address, along with the reason for referral.
● use **incident reports** to identify and report any accidents, errors, or injuries to a patient. Give incident reports directly to your facility's **risk manager.** A long period may lapse between an incident and subsequent court pro-

ceedings; this documentation may be the only proof of what actually happened.

● Don't ever correct or revise a patient's medical record after he's filed a lawsuit. (The case of *Carr v. St. Paul Fire and Marine Insurance Co.* [1974] illustrates the liability a hospital may incur when nurses or other employees alter or destroy patient records. The case of *Sweet v. Providence Hospital* [1995] held that a rebuttable presumption of negligence arises if a health care facility's records are unavailable to a plaintiff and the plaintiff can demonstrate that the missing records are necessary to prove his negligence claim.)

Exercise caution with procedures
Don't perform or assist with a surgical procedures unless you're satisfied the patient has given proper informed consent and you've been adequately educated to assist. Never force a patient to accept treatment he's expressly refused. Don't use equipment you aren't familiar with or not trained to use or that seems to be functioning improperly.

Provide a safe environment
When providing care, never use faulty equipment. If you encounter faulty equipment, clearly mark the equipment as defective and unusable. Even after repairs are done, don't use the repaired equipment until technicians demonstrate that it's operating properly. Document steps you took to handle problems with faulty equipment to show that you followed the facility's policy and procedures. This should be done wherever you may work, whether in an HMO, a hospital, a clinic, or a private office.

If a patient receives an injury as a result of any faulty equipment, you could be held liable for his injury. As more procedures and clinical and of-

fice surgeries are performed today by the NP, this area of prevention must not be neglected.

Document the use of restraints
Restraints need to be ordered, applied correctly, and checked according to hospital or health facility policy and procedure. Documentation must be exact about the need, the amount and kind of restraint used, and the status of the restrained patient, and if any medications are used to assist with restraining. An omission or failure to monitor a restrained patient may result in a malpractice claim. Incorrect application of restraints may also trigger malpractice claims.

Know when to refer
As an NP, you must stay within your scope of practice and refer patients for whom care exceeds these boundaries. Failing to refer poses the threat of liability. Consulting with your supervising or collaborating physician may be necessary to decide on the need for referral and to whom the patient should be referred. If you have an independent practice, you should have established consultative agreements with specialists in your geographic area so that the patient can be referred in a timely manner. A supervising or collaborating physician will also have agreements with specialists to whom the patient may be referred.

In certain situations, referral must be made while there is still time to safely transport the patient to another facility or hospital setting. For example, you identify that a mother who has been admitted to your birthing center now needs a high-risk obstetrician. If delivery isn't imminent, transport to the appropriate facility must occur immediately. To avoid liability, always ensure that your assessment of the patient is competent, consider all differential diagnoses from the most to least probable, and consider referral when you believe that the patient will soon exceed the scope of your practice area. If you have a supervising or collaborating physician, seek his advice as soon as you realize that your scope of practice may be inadequate to care for a patient.

Take steps to prevent patient injury

Patient falls are a common area of liability. Patients who are elderly, infirm, sedated, or mentally incapacitated are the most likely to fall. Appropriately monitor medication usage, interactions, and patient responses when prescribing medications.

Comply with laws about advance directives

The Patient's Self-Determination Act, a federal law, requires that every patient, on admission to a hospital, clinic, or other health care agency, be given information concerning *advance directives.* Follow your health care facility's policy and procedure for providing the required information. As one of the patient's health care providers, don't witness a living will or a *durable power of attorney* because this will invalidate the directive. You should also be aware of state laws concerning living wills and advance directives. As an NP, you need to be aware of your patients who have living wills or advance directives when you're establishing treatment plans and to honor their wishes.

Follow facility policies and procedures

You have a responsibility to be familiar with the policies and procedures of the facility where you work. If the policies and procedures are sound and you follow them carefully, they can protect you against a malpractice claim. The court in *Roach v. Springfield Clinic*

(1992) held that "hospital policies are admissible as standards of care for the treatment of patients within that hospital."

Inexperienced NPs are high liability risks. You must be able to recognize your limitations and work with them. If you don't know how to perform a function or procedure, or don't understand the reason for a particular treatment, it's your duty to refrain from performing the procedures and allow another professional with the skill to perform the procedure. You must also obtain assistance or collaborate with a colleague or physician in a timely and appropriate manner.

Use practice guidelines or protocols

Clinical practice guidelines, also referred to as practice parameters or protocols, are statements or algorithms developed by authoritative bodies regarding the assessment, evaluation, and treatment appropriate for a specific symptom or diagnosis. The overall goal of practice guidelines is to determine the "best practices" (those treatment plans with the best outcomes) and make that information available to all health care professionals, thus enhancing patient outcomes on a larger scale. It's expected that practice guidelines will improve patient outcomes as well as reduce nonsupportive testing and treatment, thereby reducing time delays before appropriate care is given.

While developing practice guidelines on which to base your care, make sure that the source of your information or practice guideline is a recognized authority. One source for such practice guidelines is the National Guideline Clearinghouse. This U.S. government Web site identifies and describes generally recommended courses of intervention for specific disorders. These practice guidelines can be adapted or used directly (obtaining permission as indicated on the individual practice guideline) to meet the needs of your practice setting.

Participate in health care research

Be aware of any implications from participation in research with patients, particularly experimental research on patients, because it's strictly mandated by federal guidelines. Make sure that the researcher has received approval from a facility's Committee for the Protection of Human Subjects and Institutional Review Board (IRB).

Essentially, research in health care settings is an extension of the informed consent doctrine. The patient or family member must be fully aware of the purpose of the study, risks, and potential benefits involved; the duration of his participation in the study; a description of the procedure to be followed; and identification of any experimental procedures. The researcher must also inform the patient of appropriate alternative procedures or courses of treatment, compensation (if applicable), measures to preserve confidentiality, who to contact for questions, and a statement that the research is voluntary, that refusal to participate won't affect the patient's care, and that the patient may withdraw from the study at any time. Research with children and vulnerable populations, such as the frail elderly, patients with acquired immunodeficiency syndrome or human immunodeficiency virus, and mentally ill persons, are even more strictly regulated.

If you desire to be involved in patient research, you should seek assistance from the IRB of the facility in which the research will be conducted. While this isn't an area that many NPs are now actively engaged in, such research is essential to an evidence-based practice.

Liability insurance

Your expanded clinical and health care role makes having **professional liability** coverage crucial. In any work setting, you're at risk for malpractice suits. The risk increases if you work as an NP in a specialized setting, such as the **intensive care unit (ICU)**, or in obstetrical and women's health. A million dollars of liability coverage is reasonable today — more if you're an NP in areas where lawsuits are more prevalent, such as in women's health care and acute care.

Some NPs may wonder whether purchasing professional liability insurance makes them a more attractive target for compensation claims and increases their chances of being sued. They also may question whether they're protected by *respondeat superior* and the employer's insurance policy. Given the legal risks inherent in the profession and the litigious society we live in, you can't afford to be without professional liability insurance. Check with your malpractice carrier for details about expanding your insurance coverage. (See *Choosing liability insurance,* pages 161 and 162.)

UNDERSTANDING INSURANCE COVERAGE

To protect your NP practice, you must be covered by malpractice insurance. Some specialty areas, such as acute care, won't allow NPs to practice without proper coverage. When you or your employer buy professional liability insurance, you get protection under the contract for a designated period of time from the financial consequences of certain professional errors. The type of insurance policy you buy determines the amount that the insurance company will pay if the judgment is against you in a lawsuit.

You may purchase a policy designated with "single limits" or "double lim-

Choosing liability insurance

To find the professional liability coverage that fits your needs, compare the features of a number of policies. Understanding insurance policy basics will enable you to shop more aggressively and intelligently for the coverage you need. You should work with an insurance agent who's experienced in this type of insurance. If you already have professional liability insurance, the information below may help you better evaluate your coverage.

The American Nurses Association (ANA) or your state nurse's association is one place to look for a professional liability insurance policy. The ANA has made arrangements with an insurance carrier to cover all nurses including nurse practitioners (NPs) and those in private practice. The only nurses not covered by the ANA's insurance carrier are certified registered nurse anesthetists and nurse midwives.

Type of coverage

Ask your insurance agent if the policy only covers claims made before the policy expires (claims-made coverage), or if it covers any negligent act committed during the policy period (occurrence coverage). Keep in mind that an occurrence policy provides more coverage than a claims-made policy.

Coverage limits

All malpractice insurance policies cover professional liability. Some also cover personal liability, medical payments, assault-related bodily injury, and property damage.

The amount of coverage varies, as does your premium. Remember that professional liability coverage is limited to acts and practice settings specified in the policy. Be sure your policy covers your NP role.

Options

Check whether the policy would provide coverage for the following incidents:
- negligence on the part of persons under your supervision
- misuse of equipment

- errors in diagnosis and treatment
- failure to properly teach patients
- errors in prescribing and administering medication
- negligence while providing care in an emergency setting or outside your employment setting.

Also ask if the policy provides protection if your employer or your collaborating physician sues you.

Definition of terms

Definition of terms can vary from policy to policy. If your policy includes any restrictive definitions, you won't be covered for any actions outside those guidelines. For the best protection, seek the broadest definitions possible and ask the agent for examples of actions the company hasn't covered.

Duration of coverage

Insurance is an annual contract that can be renewed or canceled each year. The policy usually specifies how it can be canceled — in writing either by you or the insurance company. Some contracts require a 30-day notice for cancellation. If the company is canceling the policy, you'll probably be given at least 10 days' notice.

Exclusions

Ask your agent about exclusions — areas not covered by the insurance policy. For example, "this policy does not apply to injury arising out of performance of the insured or a criminal act" or "this policy does not apply to nurse anesthetists."

Other insurance clauses

All professional liability insurance policies contain "other insurance" clauses that address payment obligations when a nurse is covered by more than one insurance policy, such as the facility's policy and the nurse's personal liability policy:
- The *pro rata* clause states that two or more policies in effect at the same time will

(continued)

Choosing liability insurance *(continued)*

pay any claims in accordance with a proportion established in the individual policies.

• The *in excess* clause states that the primary policy will pay all fees and damages up to its limits, at which point the second policy will pay any additional fees or damages up to its limits.

• The *escape clause* relieves an insurance company of all liability for fees or damages if another insurance policy is in effect at the same time; in effect, the clause states that the other company is responsible for all liability.

If you're covered by more than one policy, be alert for "other insurance" clauses and avoid purchasing a policy with an escape clause for liability.

Additional tips

Here is some additional information that will guide you in the purchase of professional liability insurance.

• The insurance application is a legal document. If you provide any false information, it may void the policy.

• If you're involved in specialized practice, nontraditional nursing practice, education, or research, be especially careful in selecting a policy because many policies may not cover these activities.

• After selecting a policy that ensures adequate coverage, stay with the same policy and insurer, if possible, to avoid potential lapses in coverage that could occur when changing insurers.

• No insurance policy will cover you for acts outside of your scope of practice or licensure, nor will the insurance policy cover you if punitive damages are assessed by the court.

• Be prepared to uphold all obligations specified in the policy; failure to do so may void the policy and cause personal liability for any damages. Remember that any act of willful wrongdoing on your part renders the policy null and void and may lead to a breach of contract lawsuit.

• Check out the insurance company by calling your state division of insurance to inquire about the company's financial condition.

---

its." In a single-limits policy, you buy protection in set dollar increments; for example, $100,000, $300,000, or $1,000,000. The stipulated amount will shield you if a judgment, arising out of a single nursing malpractice occurrence, goes against you.

In the double-limits policy, you buy protection in a combination package, such as $100,000/$300,000, $300,000/$500,000, or $1,000,000/$3,000,000. The smaller sum is what your insurance company will make available to protect you from any one injury arising out of a single nursing malpractice occurrence. The larger sum is the maximum amount that will be paid for all claims under that policy in a given year. Although the single-limits policy will also protect you against injuries to

more than one patient, the double-limits policy makes considerably more money available to protect you if you're involved in multiple lawsuits.

Occurrence and claims-made policies

Professional liability insurance may cover either the time the malpractice occurred *(occurrence policy)* or when a lawsuit is filed *(claims-made policy)*.

An occurrence policy protects you against any incidents occurring during a policy period, regardless of when the patient files a claim against you — even after the policy ends.

The claims-made policy protects you only against claims made against you during the policy period. A claims-made policy is often less expensive than an occurrence policy because the insurance company is at risk only for the duration of the policy. However, you can purchase an extended-reporting endorsement, or tail coverage, which in effect turns your claims-made policy into an occurrence policy.

Excess judgment

You're personally responsible for any excess judgment; that is, a judgment exceeding the policy limits. Depending on the laws in your state, several means can be used to satisfy the uninsured portion of a judgment. These means include forcing the sale of property not protected by homestead rights; liquidation of savings accounts and selected retirement accounts; liquidation of personal property, such as jewelry, coin or stamp collections, and pieces of art; and garnishment of future earnings. Your attorney can explain which means of satisfying a judgment are involved in your state of residence.

SUBROGATION

Subrogation is defined as the act of substituting another (that is, a second creditor) with regard to a legal right or claim. Employers (or other defendants such as physicians) who've been found liable for damages can subsequently sue another involved in the incident to recoup their losses.

Insurance costs

Fortunately, premiums for insurance coverage of $1 million aren't much greater than they are for smaller limits. That is because a substantial part of the premium pays for the insurance company's assumption of risk; higher limits don't increase the premium disproportionately.

In recent years, NPs specializing in obstetrics usually have paid the highest insurance premium rates, in part because of the large number of law-suits filed in obstetric cases that ended in negative outcomes, regardless of whether there was practitioner error. Other areas of higher cost insurance for NPs include emergency, acute care, trauma, and surgery.

Insurance companies offer a variety of liability insurance policies. If possible, choose an agent who's experienced in professional liability coverage. Organizations such as the ANA and your state nurse's association offer group plans at attractive premiums. You need to review the extent of coverage with your agent to make sure it's adequate for your needs. Many NPs purchase individual malpractice insurance with total coverage equaling $5 million and $1 million coverage per occurrence.

INSURER'S ROLE IN A LAWSUIT

Professional liability insurance can supply you with more than just financial protection. The insurance company may also provide a defense counsel to represent you for the entire course of litigation. Insurance companies aren't in business to lose money; they'll retain highly experienced attorneys with considerable experience in defending nursing malpractice lawsuits. When applying for NP insurance, be sure to know the insurer's role if a lawsuit is pursued against you.

When preparing your defense, attorneys will investigate the subject of the lawsuit; obtain **expert witnesses;** handle motions throughout the case; and prepare medical and nursing models, transparencies, photographs, and other court exhibits, if necessary. The cost incurred in preparing a defense is covered by your insurance. The full extent of defense coverage needs to be addressed before purchasing insurance so that you won't incur future financial burden if you're sued.

Out-of-court settlements

During litigation, and perhaps even before a lawsuit is actually filed in court, your insurance company may seek an out-of-court *settlement* from the patient's attorneys. Although this saves time and money, it may not be in your best professional interests. In the United States, if you believe your professional reputation is at stake, you can refuse to agree to an out-of-court settlement if your policy mandates that you're consulted in such decisions. Read the policy carefully, ensuring that it doesn't allow the insurer the right to make decisions without consulting you.

You have a right to be kept advised of every step of the case. Most insurers will keep you informed. After all, the insurer knows that a successful defense depends in part on the defendant's cooperation. Also, you can sue the insurance agency if it fails to provide a competent defense.

If you lose a malpractice lawsuit, the insurance company will cover you for jury-awarded general and special damages. In the United States, juries award *general damages* to compensate for:
● pain and suffering
● worsening change in lifestyle.

Juries award *special damages* to relieve:
● present and future medical expenses
● past and future loss of earnings
● decreased earning capacity.

Punitive damages

The court may award *punitive damages* to punish actions that involve malice or reckless disregard for another. Historically, insurance companies haven't had to pay punitive damages. Recently, however, courts have been forcing insurers to pay punitive damages if the policy states that the company will pay "all sums that the insured shall become legally obligated to pay as damages." The courts have also directed insurers to expressly exclude punitive damages from coverage when writing the policy, if that is the insurer's intent.

MULTIPLE INSURERS

You may have more than one insurance policy that covers a patient's claim against you. For example, you might have malpractice coverage through the facility where you work and through membership in a professional organization as well as your own insurance policy. All three insurance companies might well become involved in settling a lawsuit. Determining who pays is complex. However, you must be sure to promptly notify every insurance company you have a policy with that you're the target of a malpractice lawsuit. That will prevent any of the companies from using the *policy defense* of lack of notice or late notice. Such policy defenses frequently enable the insurance company to successfully avoid responsibility for providing coverage.

INDEMNIFICATION SUITS

If several insurance companies are representing different parties in a malpractice lawsuit, they'll typically file counteractions against the other parties, seeking compensation, or *indemnification,* for all or part of any damages the jury awards.

Many states now permit damages to be apportioned among multiple defendants, the extent of liability depending on the jury's determination of each defendant's relative contribution to the harm done. This is called comparative negligence.

A plaintiff's acts or omissions may also be considered by a jury in determining where liability lies. Any judgment would be reduced by the plaintiff's own negligence. If one of the codefendants (for example, the surgeon) decided that he'd been judged negligent only because of your negligence, he could instruct his insurance attorneys to file a new, separate lawsuit in his name against you.

Indemnification suits are becoming increasingly common. Your own facility, a fellow NP, or a laboratory technician — as long as each has individual professional liability insurance — can file an indemnification suit against you. This possibility strengthens the argument for having your own professional liability insurance.

CONTROLLING LIABILITY COSTS

Many states are taking steps to decrease malpractice litigation. In addition to establishing special statutes of limitation, some states have imposed a maximum limit on how much a jury can award in general damages. That restriction, however, has been challenged as being unconstitutional.

Medical associations and insurance companies are also trying to limit malpractice awards in other ways: by forcing malpractice claims into **arbitration**, thus removing them from the province of **lay juries**, and by requiring that claims be screened by a medical malpractice screening panel. A few states, such as Ohio, provide for submission to nonbinding arbitration panels if all parties agree. State laws may also provide for binding arbitration if specified by a written contract between a patient and the physician or hospital.

If a malpractice screening panel decides that the plaintiff's claim isn't valid, the plaintiff can't file suit unless he posts a bond to cover his defense costs in advance. More than half the states have set up screening panels, although the panels have been criticized by consumer groups and plaintiffs' attorneys and challenged in court as being unconstitutional. The Alaska

courts have upheld the constitutionality of screening panels. (*Hayes v. Humana Hospital* [1986].)

YOUR EMPLOYER'S INSURANCE

Virtually all health care facilities carry insurance to protect against their liability for an employee's mistakes. Without professional liability insurance, the facility would have to pay damages awarded in a lawsuit out of its own funds, which could lead to bankruptcy.

You should make a point of finding out the degree of professional and financial protection you're entitled to under your employer's liability insurance. This information will help you to more wisely assess your own professional liability insurance needs.

Consider obtaining a copy of the facility's insurance policy from your employer and letting your professional liability insurance agent review it. Your agent, usually without a fee, should be willing to determine the extent, limits, and exclusions of your employer's insurance coverage. In some states, collaborating with physicians will require you to have additional coverage; this is because a collaborating physician is required by the state nurse practice act.

Coverage limits

Each health care facility's professional liability insurance policy has a maximum dollar coverage limit. Your employer can purchase coverage that exceeds the basic limit; many hospitals do so for extra protection.

Coverage is limited to losses incurred from acts or omissions arising out of the practice of nursing. Thus, you must practice within the scope of practice as defined by your state's nurse practice act. If allegations of practicing medicine are alleged, the insurer may not be required to defend those claims or pay an ultimate judgment against the insured.

Carefully read the policy to see if allegations of defamation will be covered by the policy, and if there are any limitations on that coverage. Most policies provide coverage for intentional torts, such as assault and battery, unless there is willful or specific intent to do harm. Violations of criminal statutes or ordinances won't be covered by most policies. Also not covered are actions brought by the state board of nursing against a practitioner because such actions come under the definition of violation of the nurse practice act (a statute).

Threshold limit

Most health care facilities demand control over when an insurer can settle a case. To gain this control, the employer normally sets a threshold limit, usually $3,000. The insurer can settle a case below the threshold without the employer's permission. To settle a case above the threshold, however, the insurer must have the insured's permission. If professional liability insurance is provided by your employer, you must be individually listed on the insurance policy as a named insured. Should the threshold limit be exceeded, your permission is then required in order to settle the case out-of-court.

Provisions for your defense

If you're sued and your employer's insurance covers you, the insurer has a duty to provide a complete defense, including assigning an attorney to handle the entire case. The insurer will pay the attorney fees as well as any investigation costs and expert witness fees.

Keep in mind that you're a player in the lawsuit but the defense counsel defends the facility first and the NP incidentally. If you're sued for malpractice, you need your own attorney, one who will be concerned with your defense. This attorney may work closely

with the facility counsel, but his loyalty is to you. He'll provide you with an opportunity to confer with him and give you your side of the story.

If your employer grants written consent to settle the case, the insurer may do so, or it may decide to try the case in court if its legal advisors overrule the employer. If the plaintiff wins the lawsuit, the insurer is obliged to pay damages awarded to the patient up to the insurance policy's coverage limit.

Stipulations for denying coverage

Insurance companies that provide professional liability coverage for hospitals and other health care facilities reduce the risk they assume under *respondeat superior* in several ways. One way is by stipulating a precise coverage period, typically 1 year. Another way is by defining the type of coverage they'll provide, whether, for example, it's an occurrence or claims-made policy.

A third way is by putting exclusions into malpractice policies. These exclusions vary considerably from policy to policy, but all list specific acts, situations, or personnel that the insurance doesn't cover.

In addition to exclusions, insurers may deny coverage to you or your employer because of other circumstances, such as:

● the insurance policy lapses because your employer failed to pay the premiums.

● your employer refuses to cooperate with the insurance company, for whatever reason.

● the insurer discovers that your employer made misstatements on the insurance application.

In some malpractice situations, an insurer could agree to provide you with a defense but refuse to pay damages awarded to a patient. The insurer agrees to defend you in this situation because he doesn't want to be accused of **breach of contract.** But he must notify you of his intention not to pay damages in a **reservation-of-rights letter.** This letter informs you and your employer that the insurer believes the case falls outside what is covered by the insurance policy. When your employer and the insurer disagree about whether insurance coverage exists, the dispute may have to be resolved through separate legal action. Similarly, you have the right to bring such action against your employer's insurance company if it refuses to cover you.

Special considerations
Keep in mind a few more concerns when reviewing your employer's policy. First, is the policy purchased for you as an employee benefit? In that case, the insurer protects you and not the facility.

Second, the policy may only provide coverage for **incidents** that occur while you're on the job. You may be held liable for nursing actions off the job, unless your actions are covered under a **Good Samaritan act**, a state law that protects health care professionals who act in an emergency.

Third, many employers provide only a claims-made policy. If a suit is filed against you after you've stopped working there but for an incident that took place while you were still an employee, you probably won't be covered by your former employer's insurance plan.

Fourth, if you're an independent contractor, such as a consultant, you aren't usually considered by the court to be under the facility's direct supervision and control. Consequently, the facility won't be considered responsible for your actions, and its insurance may not cover you. If the policy is yours, with the facility paying the premiums as an employee benefit, you're still covered.

Liability of the collaborating physician
Rules for collaboration vary from state to state; physicians entering into a collaborative agreement with an NP make themselves more vulnerable to litigation. The physician may be sued under the *respondeat superior* doctrine for care that he wasn't personally involved with as the NP's collaborator. Because of this increased professional risk, it's imperative to develop protocols directing when the physician should be consulted, when to refer patients to specialists, and how quality assurance activities and periodic joint documentation reviews will be conducted. You must ensure that all consultation is fully documented and that patients were referred in a timely manner as indicated. In addition, monthly patient care conferences should be held to ensure that all patient issues are thoroughly addressed and that protocols are being followed, quality assurance activities are being carried out, and documentation reflects quality patient care.

Defending yourself in a lawsuit

Imagine you're at the office when a stranger approaches and asks for you. He thrusts some legal papers into your hands and starts to walk away. Baffled, you ask, "What's this all about?" He replies, "You've just been sued."

As you look over the papers, you recognize the name of a former patient listed as the plaintiff, and you see your name listed as the defendant. You learn that you've been accused of "errors and omissions." A nagging worry for most NPs has just become reality for you: You've been sued for malpractice.

Failing to respond to the complaint could result in a default judgment against you. You need to act immedi-

Responding to a malpractice summons

If you ever receive a summons notifying you that you're being sued, your response early on can have a significant effect on the outcome of the suit.

You should immediately cease communication with the plaintiff, his family, and his attorney. If you're insured, notify the company promptly and submit copies of the summons.

Be prepared to maintain your separate file on the case. Ask for copies of all relevant documents and reports from the claims adjuster, your attorney, and the patient's attorney. Check the status of your case regularly.

Selecting a defense attorney

One of your first concerns will be finding a qualified attorney to represent you if you don't have professional liability insurance.

If the patient names your facility in the lawsuit, the facility's insurance company may have an attorney to defend you as the facility's employee. If you're uninsured, you'll have to find an attorney on your own. If the facility's attorney is representing the facility's interest in the lawsuit, you should have a separate attorney to represent your interest. Ideally, two codefendants shouldn't have the same attorney.

Shop around

When seeking a qualified attorney, consider:
- consulting with your facility's legal services department
- consulting with your state nurses' association or other appropriate professional organization

- asking friends or relatives with legal experience whose judgments you can trust
- calling your local bar association, which is listed in the Yellow Pages.

When you meet with a prospective attorney, ask him about his experience with malpractice cases. If he has too little experience, or if he has an enormous case load, consider finding another attorney to represent you.

Working with your attorney

Establishing a good working relationship with your attorney is crucial. It's your job to educate the attorney to the nursing and medical information he needs to defend you. Be prepared to spend many hours reviewing charts, licensing requirements, facility procedures, journals, and texts, as well as your professional qualifications and the details of the case. Do the following:
- Provide your attorney and claims adjuster with all the information you can about the case, including anything relevant you remember that may not appear in the record.
- Supply your attorney with the nursing practice standards for your specialty.
- Discuss advantages and disadvantages in settling out of court with your attorney.
- Develop a list of experts qualified to testify on the standards of care in your specialty and present it to your attorney. Avoid recommending friends, because the jury will believe them to be less objective.
- Review all available records, including those obtained by your attorney that are normally inaccessible to you.

---

ately. Your next step depends on whether you have professional liability insurance. (See *Responding to a malpractice summons.*)

CONTACTING APPROPRIATE PERSONNEL

If you're covered through your employer's insurance, immediately contact your legal services administrators at your work. They'll tell you how to proceed.

If you have your own professional liability insurance, consult your policy and read the section that tells you what to do when you're sued. Every policy describes who you should notify and how much time you have to do it.

Immediately telephone this representative and tell him you've been sued. Document the time, his name, and his instructions. Then, hand deliver the lawsuit papers to him, if possible, and get a signed, dated receipt. Alternatively, send lawsuit papers by certified mail, return receipt requested, so you're assured of a signed receipt.

If you don't contact the appropriate representative within the specified time, the insurance company can refuse to cover you. To protect yourself, act quickly, document your actions, and get a receipt.

In addition, contact the National Nurses Claims Data Bank established by the ANA. Provide a full report of the incident in question, including the date, time, and persons involved. This contact will give you access to national data that may support your case, and your data will, in turn, help other nurses who are involved in lawsuits. Your name and address will be kept confidential.

Insurance company considerations

When you notify your insurance company that you've been sued, it will first consider whether it must cover you at all. The insurer does this by checking for any policy violations you may have committed. For example, your insurance company will check whether you gave late notice of the lawsuit, gave false information on your insurance application, or failed to pay a premium on time. If the company is sure you've committed such a violation, it will use this violation as a policy defense, and it can simply refuse to cover you. If the company thinks you've committed such a violation but isn't sure it has evidence to support a policy defense, it will probably send you a letter by certified mail informing you that the company may not have to defend you, but that it will do so while reserving the right to deny coverage later, withdraw

from the case, or take other actions. Meanwhile, the company will seek a declaration of its rights from the court. If the court decides the company doesn't have to defend you, the company will withdraw from the case.

Usually, however, an insurance company takes this action only after careful consideration. That is because denying coverage may provide you with grounds for suing the company. If you receive such a letter, employ your own attorney to defend you in the lawsuit and to advise you in your dealings with the insurance company. If your case against the insurance company is sound, he may suggest that you sue the insurer.

If your insurance company doesn't assert a policy defense, your company representative will select and retain an attorney or a law firm specializing in medical malpractice cases as your ***attorney of record*** in the lawsuit. Once so designated, this attorney is legally bound to do all that is necessary to defend you.

Your employer will almost certainly be named as a codefendant in the lawsuit. Even if that isn't the case, notify your employer that you're being sued. Your insurance company may try to involve your employer as a defendant.

FINDING AN ATTORNEY

If you don't have insurance (your own or your employer's), you'll have to find your own attorney. Don't even consider trying to defend yourself. You need an attorney who is experienced in nursing and medical malpractice, because the case will be complex and the opposition will be composed of experienced attorneys. Your attorney should be familiar with NP practice and litigation. Some attorneys have a nursing background while others employ nurses as legal assistants in their offices. Such clinical background and expertise can enhance your defense.

Make appointments with a few attorneys who seem qualified to defend you. In most cases, you won't be charged for this initial consultation. When you meet with each one, ask how long he thinks the lawsuit will take and how much money he'll charge. Also, try to get a feel for the attorney's understanding of the issues in your case. Then choose one as your attorney of record. Do this as soon as possible.

PREPARING YOUR DEFENSE

Your attorney will file the appropriate legal documents in response to the papers you were served. He'll ask you for help in preparing your defense. He should give you a chance to present your position in detail. Remember, all discussions between you and your attorney are *privileged communication*, meaning that your attorney can't disclose this information without your permission. Your attorney will also obtain complete copies of the pertinent medical records and any other documents our defense.

Interrogatories, depositions, and examinations

Your attorney will use *discovery tools* to uncover every pertinent detail about the case against you. Discovery tools are legal procedures for obtaining information; these may include:

● *interrogatories* — questions written to the other party that require answers under oath

● *depositions* — oral cross-examination of the other party, lay witnesses to the event, and expert witnesses under oath and before a court reporter

● *defense medical examination* — a medical examination of the injured party by a physician selected by your attorney or insurance company.

The plaintiff-patient's attorney will also use discovery tools, so you may have to answer interrogatories and appear for a deposition as well. Your attorney will carefully prepare you for these procedures.

Neither the interrogatory nor the deposition should be taken lightly. Don't speculate in answering any question. Work closely with your attorney in preparing your written answers to the interrogatory.

That doesn't mean, however, that you must say or do anything he asks. If you feel your attorney is asking you to do or say things that aren't in your best interest, tell him so. You have the right to change attorneys at any time. If you believe an attorney selected by your insurance company is more interested in protecting the company than in protecting you, discuss the problem with a company representative. Then, if you still feel that he isn't defending you properly, hire your own attorney. You may have grounds for subsequently suing the insurance company and the company-appointed attorney.

PREPARING FOR COURT

Plan on spending a considerable amount of time preparing your case before you appear in the courtroom.

Don't talk about the case

Don't try to placate the person suing you by calling him and discussing the case. Your chances of talking him into dropping his lawsuit are very slim. And every word you say to him can be used against you in court. In fact, before the trial, don't discuss the lawsuit with anyone except your attorney. That will help prevent information leaks that could compromise your case. To protect your professional reputation, don't even mention to your colleagues that you've been sued.

Study copies of the medical records

Your attorney will ask you to study relevant medical records as soon as possible. Examine the complete medical chart, including history and physical examination, laboratory reports, and treatment orders. If you must, on a separate sheet of paper, make appropriate notes on key entries or omissions concerning the records, but don't make any changes on the records. Such an action will hurt your case by undermining your credibility. Remember, you aren't the only person with a copy of these records. Also remember that your notes may be used as evidence against you after being acquired by the plaintiff. Only your attorney's notes are safe from discovery.

Create your own legal file

Ask your attorney to send you copies of all documents and correspondence pertaining to the case. Try to maintain a file that is as complete as your attorney's. Also, make sure you understand all the items in your file. If you receive a document that you don't understand, ask your attorney to explain it. Maintaining such a file should keep you current on the status of your case and prevent unpleasant surprises in court.

Take steps to protect your property

Many states have **homestead laws** that protect a substantial part of the equity in your house, as well as other property, from any judgment against you. Ask your attorney about the law in your state or province. If you don't have insurance or if damages awarded to the plaintiff exceed your insurance coverage, these particulars may be considered in deciding to either defend the case or settle it out of court.

Events leading to trial

While your attorney prepares your defense, he'll also explore the desirability of reaching an out-of-court settlement. If he decides an out-of-court settlement is in your best interest, he'll try

to achieve it before your trial date. (See *Settling out of court,* page 172.)

If your case does go to trial, your attorney will participate in selecting the jury. During this process, attorneys for both sides will question prospective jurors, and your attorney will ask your opinion on their suitability. Either attorney may reject a small number of prospective jurors without any reason *(a peremptory challenge).* Either attorney may reject an unlimited number of jurors for specific reasons. For instance, an attorney may reject someone who knows the plaintiff or someone who has a personal interest in the lawsuit *(challenge for cause).*

To help prepare you to testify, your attorney will ask you to review the complete medical record, your interrogatory answers, and your deposition. In addition, you should review the entire legal file you've been keeping, to make sure you understand all aspects of the case.

Deposition

Before the trial, you'll probably be called to testify at a deposition. (If you've been called to testify as an expert witness at another professional's trial, you should be aware that some states don't permit expert witnesses to give pretrial depositions.) Where you give the deposition can vary. It can take place in an attorney's office or in a special room in the courthouse set aside for that purpose. The deposition takes place in a less formal atmosphere than a courtroom provides, but don't forget that a court reporter will be transcribing every word you and the attorneys say. At the trial, the plaintiff's and the defendant's attorneys have the right to use your pretrial testimony to bolster their respective cases. Therefore, you should prepare thoroughly with counsel for your deposition.

Settling out of court

Approximately 15% to 20% of malpractice suits that are filed actually go to court; of those, about half end with a final judgment. The rest are settled out of court.

Making a compromise

Settling your case out of court isn't an admission of wrongdoing. The law regards settlement as a compromise between two parties to end a lawsuit and to avoid further expense. You may choose to pay a settlement rather than incur the possibly greater expense, both financial and emotional, of defending your innocence at trial.

Determining your settlement rights

If you're covered by professional liability insurance, the terms of your policy will determine whether you and your attorney or the insurance company can control the settlement. Some policies don't permit the NP to settle a case without the consent of the insurance company.

Review your policy to determine your settlement rights. If the policy isn't clear on this point, call the insurance company representative and ask for clarification.

Evaluating a possible settlement

Offer your attorney and your insurance company's representative all the information you can about the case, so they can evaluate not only your liabilities but also a possible settlement with the plaintiff. You may be in the best position to provide crucial observations concerning the patient's state of mind; in many cases, this is the basis of a successful settlement.

TRIAL

Be prepared for your trial to last several days or even weeks. After all the witnesses have given their testimony, the jury, not the judge, will decide if you're liable. If the jury finds you liable, it will also assess damages against you. (See *The trial process: Step by-step.*) In some instances, an arbitration proceeding is used instead of a jury trial, but that is the exception and not the rule.

Testifying in court

When you're called to testify in a malpractice lawsuit as a defendant (or as an expert witness in another defendant's trial), you may be expected to respond quickly to a confusing presentation of claims, *counterclaims*, allegations, and contradictory evidence. You can use a number of techniques to help reduce stress and enhance the value of your testimony.

Courtroom demeanor

How you come across to the jury from the witness stand is very important. The jury may form its first, and sometimes lasting, impression of your credibility while you're testifying.

Your attorney will help prepare you to testify at the trial. He'll tell you how to dress (conservatively, as if you were going to an important job interview) and how to act. Your attorney may recommend, for example, that you sit with both feet on the floor with your hands folded in front of you and pay polite attention to other speakers. Keep in mind that the purpose of these instructions is to help win the case. Remember also that your failure to cooperate with an attorney provided by an insurance company can be used by the insurance company to deny coverage.

Malpractice lawsuits are notoriously slow-moving. Interruptions occur in the form of recesses, attorneys' lengthy

The trial process: Step-by-step

This chart summarizes the basic trial process from complaint to execution of judgment. If you're ever involved in a lawsuit, your attorney will explain the specific procedures that your case requires.

Pretrial preparation

1. Complaint
Plaintiff files a complaint stating his charges against the defendant.

2. Summons
Court issues defendant a summons stating plaintiff's charges.

3. Answer or counterclaim
Defendant files an answer and may add a counterclaim to plaintiff's allegations or those of other defendants.

4. Discovery
Plaintiff's and defendant's attorneys develop their cases by gathering information via depositions and interrogatories and by reviewing documents and other evidence.

5. Pretrial hearing
Court hears statements from both parties and tries to narrow the issues.

6. Negotiation by settlement
Both parties meet to try to resolve the case outside the court.

Trial

7. Opening statements
Plaintiff's and defendant's attorneys present facts as they apply to their cases.

8. Plaintiff presents case
Plaintiff's witnesses testify, explaining what they saw, heard, and know. Expert witnesses review any documentation and give their opinions about specific aspects of the case.

9. Cross-examination
Defendant's attorney questions plaintiff's witnesses.

10. Plaintiff closes case
Defendant's attorney may make a motion to dismiss the case, claiming plaintiff's evidence is insufficient.

11. Defendant presents case
Defendant's witnesses testify, explaining what they saw, heard, and know. Expert witnesses review any documentation and give their opinions about specific aspects of the case.

12. Cross-examination
Plaintiff's attorney questions defendant's witnesses.

13. Defendant closes case
Defendant's attorney may claim plaintiff hasn't presented an issue for the jury to decide.

14. Closing statements
Each attorney summarizes his case for the jury.

15. Jury instruction
Judge instructs the jury in points of law that apply in this particular case.

16. Jury deliberation and verdict
Jury reviews facts and votes on verdict. Jury announces verdict before judge and both parties.

17. Appeal (optional)
Attorneys review transcripts. The party against whom the court ruled may appeal if he feels the judge didn't interpret the law properly, instruct the jury properly, or conduct the trial properly.

18. Execution of judgment
Appeals process is completed and the case is settled.

---

arguments in judges' chambers, and the calling of multiple witnesses out of turn. Be patient no matter what happens. When you're asked to appear, be prompt. You may not score points by your punctuality, but you'll definitely lose a few if you aren't in court when you're called to testify.

When you testify, the jury doesn't expect you to be letter-perfect or to have instant or total recall. If you don't know the answer, say so. Listen closely to questions, and answer only what the questioner has asked. Always answer the questions simply and in lay terms, and never elaborate or volunteer infor-

Courtroom controversy: Nurse practitioners as expert witnesses

Testimony by experts is an essential ingredient in malpractice cases for both plaintiff and defendant. In lawsuits against nurse practitioners (NPs), the court's position holds that an NP is the appropriate expert witness when dealing with the actions or decisions of an NP.

Qualifications of an expert

An NP expert witness testifying for the plaintiff in a negligence case must be able to describe the relevant standard of care, detail how the NP deviated from the acceptable standard, and explain how failure to meet acceptable nursing standards caused or contributed to the patient's injury. Defense counsel will also provide an NP expert who will testify to the standard and whether the defendant-NP met the standard.

An NP must meet certain criteria to be considered an expert witness. The first and only absolute criterion is current licensure to practice nursing within the state. In addition, the expert witness' credentials should match or exceed the defendant's. This includes clinical expertise in that specialty area, certification in the clinical specialty, and recent education relevant to the nursing specialty at issue. Another criterion is a lack of bias, for the expert witness can have no relationship, professional or personal, with any parties or agencies involved in the suit.

There is a difference between being a legal consultant and an expert witness. A legal consultant may be an expert, but her name and the information and opinions she gives aren't disclosed to the opposition. When an NP agrees to become an expert witness, she must understand that her name will be given to opposing counsel and that she may have to testify in court. In addition, any comments, notes, or reports she makes may be discovered and reviewed by opposing counsel.

The NP expert witness faces two possible dilemmas: being held to a different standard of care and being trapped into saying that only one opinion is correct. The applicable standard of care will be the one appropriate to NPs at the time the incident occurred. In addition, when there is more than one acceptable choice, the expert witness must repeatedly emphasize that more than one approach could have been selected and still be appropriate.

---

mation. If you're going to be describing a piece of equipment that is unfamiliar to a lay audience, get your attorney's approval to bring it to the courtroom and show it to the jury.

Above all, be honest. Especially when your testimony must be critical of a colleague or of your facility's policies, you may be tempted to bend the truth a little. Don't.

During the trial, your professional reputation will be at stake. Project a positive attitude at all times, suggesting that you feel confident about the trial's outcome. Never disparage the plaintiff inside or outside the courtroom. Characterizing him as a gold digger, for instance, can only generate bad feelings that may interfere with the settlement. You won't want to speak to him during the trial, but if you do, always be polite and dignified.

Cross-examination

During *cross-examination*, the opposing attorney will try to discredit your testimony. This may take the form of an attack on your credentials, experience, or education, especially if you're testifying as an expert witness. Don't take the attacks personally or allow them to fluster you. (See *Courtroom controversy: Nurse practitioners as expert witnesses.*)

Another way of discrediting expert testimony is by the "hired gun" insinuation. The cross-examining attorney may imply that because you accept payment for your testimony, you're being unethical. Just remember that as an expert witness you have the right to expect compensation for the time you spend on behalf of the case in and out of the courtroom, just as the attorney does.

Another ploy the opposing attorney can use to discredit your testimony is the "hedge." He may try to get you to change or qualify an answer you gave previously on **direct examination** or at the deposition. He may also try to confuse the issue by asking you a similar, but hypothetical, question with a slightly different — but significant — slant. Just remember that a simple but sincere "I don't know" often reinforces a jury's belief in your honesty and competence. Your best protection against cross-examination jitters is adequate preparation and allowing yourself time to think about your answer before verbalizing it.

Selected references

Bowman, P. "Role of the Legal Nurse Consultant in Litigation," *Journal of Nursing Law* 5(4):35-41, 1998.

Kelly, L.Y., and Joel, L.A. *Dimensions of Professional Nursing*, 8th ed. New York: McGraw-Hill Book Co., 1999.

Laughlin, S. "Nursing Case Law Update," *Journal of Nursing Law* 5(2):65-74, 1998.

Mason, D.J., and Leavitt, J.K. *Policy and Politics in Nursing and Health Care*, 3rd ed. Philadelphia: W.B. Saunders Co., 1998.

National Guideline Clearinghouse: www.guideline.gov.

Chapter Six

LEGAL ASPECTS OF DOCUMENTATION

The **medical record** chronologically documents all facts pertinent to a patient's care — findings and observations about the patient's health history, physical examination, tests and treatments, outcomes, and evaluation of treatment. It's the principal tool used by all members of the health care team to plan, coordinate, and document the care given to each patient.

In this chapter, you'll learn about the legal significance of the medical record. You'll read about the importance of accurate documentation, examine several court cases in which documentation quality affected the outcome, and review guidelines for avoiding errors. Finally, you'll discover the legal implications of telephone triage and computerized medical records.

Purpose and value of accurate documentation

Changes in health care delivery have led to patients being assessed, cared for, and treated by more health care professionals than ever before. Complete, accurate, and timely documentation is

crucial to the continuity of each patient's care. The medical record is a legal and business record with many uses. If you have your own practice or clinic, you'll be required by state and federal law to maintain the medical records. If you're receiving federal funds for the patients you see, you must comply with federal regulations regarding the establishment and safekeeping of medical records. The state health department will also specify how you maintain patient records. A well-documented medical record should:

● be complete and legible.
● reflect the patient care given.
● reflect if care has not been given (for example, because of canceled or missed appointments).
● show telephone triage information.
● demonstrate the results of treatment.
● help health care professionals to plan, coordinate, and evaluate the care they provide.
● demonstrate telephone conferences, referrals, and other interactions with specialists to coordinate patient care.
● show a record of telemedicine.
● allow interdisciplinary exchange of information about the patient.

● provide evidence of the **nurse practitioner's (NP's)** legal responsibilities toward the patient.
● supply information for analysis of cost-to-benefit reduction.
● reflect professional and ethical conduct and responsibility.
● furnish data for a variety of uses — continuing education; risk management; diagnosis-related group assignment and reimbursement; Medicare and Medicaid reimbursement; local, state, and national health care research; performance improvement; case management monitoring; and outcomes research.
● identify prescriptive patterns of patients or providers.
● aid state and federal authorities investigating communicable disease.
● protect your professional reputation and licensure.

Keep in mind that the medical record also can serve as a court document in medical malpractice actions against you or other providers; in civil cases such as child custody battles; and in such criminal cases as spousal abuse, child abuse, elder abuse, assaults, rape, drug use or overdoses, and even murder.

Legal significance of the medical record

Documentation is so vital to health care that, from a legal standpoint, the documentation of care has become equivalent to the care itself. Documenting in an inadequate, inaccurate, or incomplete manner may result in legal liability. Missing information can lead the court to conclude that the patient didn't receive proper care. For example, lack of information about a patient's changing signs and symptoms could suggest that this information was either not detected or not communicated to other health care providers. (See *Documentation tips,* page 178.)

The medical record provides legal proof of the nature and quality of care that the patient received. The weight it carries in legal proceedings can't be overemphasized. The record may be the focus of inquiry in personal injury, professional **malpractice**, or product liability claims, as well as in **workers' compensation** claims, employment disputes, and insurance benefits cases. It also may be integral in child custody and criminal cases, such as those involving child or spousal abuse, assault, or rape.

A factual, consistent, timely, and complete record defends you against allegations of negligence, improper treatment, and omissions in care. NPs have a legal duty to maintain the medical record in accordance with clinical practice standards and state and federal laws. Inadequate documentation of care may result in **liability** or nonreimbursement by third-party payers.

The medical record may also be used for fact-finding during the discovery phase of litigation. Health care provided to a patient is sometimes complex, and he may see numerous providers during hospitalization or as an outpatient. If an incident occurs and the patient decides to pursue litigation, his attorney may not know which provider or combination of providers breached the standard of care and caused the damage. As a result, the attorney will name all providers who may have played a role in the alleged outcome (including the physician, the NP, and other employees or staff of the medical center or clinic), and he'll count on the medical record and depositions to provide the facts surrounding the event in question.

State and federal agencies such as the General Accounting Office and the Health Care Financing Administration (HCFA) are increasingly using medical records in audits to substantiate third-party payments. These agencies have

Documentation tips

If you're ever involved in a malpractice lawsuit, how you documented, what you documented, and what you didn't document will heavily influence the jury and the outcome of the trial. Following these important tips can ensure that your records don't tip the scales of justice against you.

How to document

- Use the appropriate form, and document in ink.
- Record the patient's name and identification number on every page of his chart.
- Record the complete date and time of each entry.
- Be specific. Avoid general terms and vague expressions.
- Use only standard abbreviations.
- Use a medical term only if you're sure of its meaning.
- Document symptoms by using the patient's own words.
- Document objectively.
- Write legibly.

What to document

- Document the patient's history, allergies, prior surgeries, and illnesses.
- Document the patient's family history.
- Document your assessment.
- Document your plans, including diagnostic testing, procedures, and referrals.
- Include laboratory findings, electrocardiogram strips, fetal monitor strips, computed tomography scans, photographs, and videotapes where applicable, and mention them in your progress notes.
- Document your diagnoses.
- Document your actions.
- Document referrals and consultations whether within your clinic or organization or outside of it — including letters, telephone calls, facsimiles, and e-mails.
- Document your conversation with the patient or family — in person, by facsimile, or by telephone.

- Document patient education.
- Document informed consent and informed refusal (declining any options).
- Document medications you have administered or ordered.
- Document the patient's response to medications and other treatments.
- Document the prognosis and plans of action.
- Document research protocols.
- Document safeguards you use to protect the patient. For example, "Cautioned not to drive while taking prescribed narcotic."
- Document any incident in two places: in your progress notes and in an incident report. Don't mention the report in the patient's record, unless your facility or state requires it.
- Document procedures and tests after you perform them, never in advance.
- Write on every line. Don't insert notes between lines or leave empty spaces for someone else to insert a note. Draw a line from your last entry to the bottom of the page.
- Sign every entry with your full name and title. Add your prescriptive code where applicable.
- Chart an omission as a new entry. Never backdate or add to previously written entries. Within the body of the note, reference the time and date of omission.
- Draw a thin line through an error and mark "error" above it, with the date and your full name. Never erase or obliterate an erroneous entry.
- Document only the care you provide. Never document for anyone else.
- Understand and follow the documentation standards of your organization and your state. These standards are usually defined in state nurse practice acts and in state administrative codes (the rules and regulations governing nurse practitioners and their practice).

found considerable evidence of fraud. Recent studies have also shown that fraudulent data have been entered into patients' records in order to make them eligible for care that a health maintenance organization would otherwise not permit.

CONTENTS OF THE MEDICAL RECORD

Federal and state regulations, such as those governing *Medicare* and *Medicaid* reimbursement, partially determine the form and content of the medical record. Although state laws vary in their stringency and specificity, all states require health care facilities to maintain the medical record in sufficient detail and stipulate how long the record should be kept — how long it should be archived and when it can safely be destroyed (if ever). In addition, rules have been established for the distribution of personal health information. (See *Protected health information,* page 180.)

For evaluation and management services, the nature and amount of documentation varies by the type and place of service and the patient's status. The documentation of each patient encounter may be modified for these variables but generally should include:
- the reason for the encounter and relevant history (including health risk factors)
- physical examination findings
- assessment findings
- diagnostic test results
- clinical impression or diagnosis
- plan for care
- date and a verifiable, legible identification of the health care professional who provided the service
- rationale for ordering diagnostic and other ancillary services (if not specifically documented, it should be easily inferred)
- past and present diagnoses and conditions

- patient's progress
- response to and changes in treatment
- planned follow-up care and instructions
- documentation to support the CPT and ICD-9 codes reported on the health insurance claim form.

Additionally, the medical record may include:
- copies of the patient's care from other providers or prior hospitalizations
- the patient's medication record, including allergies and over-the-counter medications
- photographs or videotapes, as relevant
- operative and other treatment reports
- product information (manufacturer, identification number, and date of medical products, such as a pacemaker or birth control device)
- research protocols
- copies of facsimiles and e-mails sent and received
- discharge summary
- referral summaries
- informed *consent forms* and documentation of informed refusal of care
- other legal documents, including *advance directives, living wills,* do-not-resuscitate orders, and evidence of appointment of a health care proxy or legal guardian, either appointed with a power of attorney to make all legal decisions for the patient or an individual appointed to make health care decisions
- billing records.

FAILURE TO PROPERLY MAINTAIN THE MEDICAL RECORD

As a general rule, the medical record is presumed to be accurate if there is no evidence of *fraud*, alteration, destruction, or other tampering. Evidence of tampering can cause the record to be ruled inadmissible as evidence in

Protected health information

The Department of Health and Human Services recently released final regulations dealing with the confidentiality of an individual's health information. The Health Insurance Portability and Accountability Act (HIPAA), which will be fully implemented by 2002, applies to health insurers and virtually all health care providers and clearinghouses. The new regulation is designed to enhance the protections afforded by many existing state laws. In circumstances where federal rules and state laws are in conflict, the stronger privacy protection would prevail. The standards apply to all consumers, whether they're privately insured or uninsured or whether they participate in public programs such as Medicare or Medicaid.

The act will give consumers more control over and access to their health information, set boundaries on the use and release of health records, safeguard that information, establish accountability for inappropriate use and release, and balance privacy protections with public safety.

Consumer control
The regulation provides consumers with critical new rights to control the release of their medical information, including the right to:
- give advance consent for most disclosures of health information
- see a copy of their health records
- request a correction to their health records
- obtain documentation of disclosures of their health information
- receive an explanation of their privacy rights and how their information may be used or disclosed.

Boundaries
Health care providers and plans often release a patient's entire medical record even if an employer or other entity only needs specific information, such as the information necessary to process a worker's compensation claim. Under the new regulation, providers must disclose only the minimum information needed for the purpose of the disclosure.

Accountability
Under the HIPAA, for the first time, specific federal penalties will be imposed on those who violate a patient's right to privacy. Noncriminal violations of the privacy standards, including disclosures made in error, can result in civil monetary penalties of $100 per violation up to $25,000 per year per standard. In addition, the HIPAA will impose criminal penalties for certain types of violations committed knowingly: up to $50,000 and 1 year in prison for obtaining or disclosing protected health information; up to $100,000 and up to 5 years in prison for obtaining or disclosing protected health information under "false pretenses"; and up to $250,000 and up to 10 years in prison for obtaining protected health information with the intent to sell, transfer, or use it for commercial advantage, personal gain, or malicious harm.

Public responsibility
The new standards reflect the need to balance privacy protections with the public responsibility to support such national priorities as protecting public health, conducting medical research, improving the quality of care, and fighting health care fraud and abuse. For example, when there is an infectious disease outbreak, public health agencies need to obtain important information to better protect the public. The new regulation provides standards for how such information should be released to balance privacy and public health needs.

Security
The final regulation requires covered organizations to establish clear procedures to protect patients' privacy, including designating an official to establish and monitor the entity's privacy practices and training. It also extends the coverage to personal medical records in all forms, including oral, paper, and electronic communications.

court. In fact, under the legal doctrine called *spoliation of evidence*, it may shift the *burden of proof* to you if the patient's attorney can prove that records were deliberately or negligently lost, altered, or destroyed. In addition, a court may issue sanctions (such as hefty fines) against you if records are lost, destroyed, altered, or missing.

Medical records may be corrected if the portion in error remains legible; deleting or rendering the entry illegible can impose liability. An addendum to the medical record is usually acceptable if it's dated the day the information is added and clearly marked as a late entry. Loss of the medical record raises a *rebuttable presumption* of negligence (which may be overcome by contrary evidence).

A pitfall that many honest and professional care providers fall into is the urge to add information to the record once a suit has been filed. For instance, you may recall that you asked about specific details of the patient's history, or took vital signs, and forgot to document this information. In *good faith,* you add this information to the record. This may give you momentary peace of mind, until the patient's attorney produces a document specialist who will testify that the ink, the paper, or both (including photocopies) are of a different age than the original documentation. An incident like this can destroy a totally defensible case because the jury will think the record was altered to change the information.

By the time you receive notice that you're being sued, the patient's attorney will already have obtained a complete copy of the patient's medical record. Any change you make will stand out immediately. Also, many patients obtain copies of their medical records for various reasons and may even have copies before the lawsuit is filed. For instance, members of the military and their families who see civilian providers typically keep copies of their medical records in case they're transferred.

NP documentation

Your documentation must be complete, accurate, and timely to foster continuity of care. It should cover the following:
● initial assessment
● NP actions
● variations from the assessment and plan and justifications for these actions, such as NP decisions or patient preferences
● notation of care by other disciplines
● patient education
● procedures
● diagnostic tests, such as fetal monitoring strips, electrocardiograms, and EEG strips, which should all be dated with identifiable times
● outcomes, such as the patient's response to therapy
● patient comfort and safety measures
● referral summaries
● discharge summary. (See *Documenting discharge planning,* page 182.)

SOURCES OF DOCUMENTATION DUTIES AND STANDARDS
Factors that influence documentation *standards* include:
● federal statutes and regulations
● state regulations and statutes, including licensing statutes and nurse practice acts
● state business record statutes (if you have your own clinic or practice)
● custom
● accrediting bodies
● standards of practice issued by professional organizations
● facility *policies* and procedures.

Professional organizations and accrediting bodies have developed and refined recommendations and standards of practice for documentation. Sometimes these standards are more

Documenting discharge planning

When planning a patient's discharge, be sure to document in his chart that he and his family are aware that treatment and care will be discontinued on a specific date. Also document the alternative resources and specific plans that must be organized to ensure continuity of care.

Writing a discharge summary
The final document in each patient's record, the discharge summary highlights the patient's condition, treatment, status at discharge, discharge diagnoses, all medications, and future plans, such as clinic appointments, testing, and physical therapy. It should also include a home care instruction sheet; documentation that the family and the patient know how to provide home follow-up care; information on agency home health visits; the name of an escort from the facility; the patient's discharge address; how he leaves the facility (ambulatory, in a wheelchair, or otherwise); and his mode of transportation to home or elsewhere.

Taking it step-by-step
When preparing a discharge summary, take the following steps:
● First, review the patient's diagnoses or problem list, care plan, flow sheets, and progress notes to develop an overall impression of his facility stay.
● Follow your facility's policies regarding the format and content of the summary.
● Include any exceptional details or unusual findings.
● Outline all patient teaching and provide, as a record, written instructions in a language the patient understands. Your clinic or organization may have developed specific discharge handouts for the patient's condition. If so, include a sample in the chart.

Reviewing the summary
Make sure that the discharge summary:
● outlines the patient's care
● provides useful information for further teaching, evaluation, and readmission
● indicates that the patient has the information needed to provide self-care or to get further help
● shows that you've met Joint Commission on Accreditation of Healthcare Organizations documentation requirements for collaboration with other disciplines and for patient teaching
● helps safeguard you and your clinic or organization against malpractice charges.

---

stringent than those required by state law.

The ***American Nurses Association (ANA)*** has included documentation in its Standards of Nursing Practice. The ANA says documentation must be systematic, continuous, accessible, communicated, recorded, and readily available to all health care team members.

The ***Joint Commission on Accreditation of Healthcare Organizations (JCAHO)*** also sets standards. Current standards stress a change from source-oriented documentation to a fully integrated, multidisciplinary approach.

Documentation should reflect the collaborative planning and provision of care and treatment. JCAHO doesn't specify a format for medical record documentation. Therefore, patient care, treatment, and rehabilitation may involve many forms, from preprinted forms to handwritten reports to electronic formats, which may include decision algorithms and care pathways. (See *Managed care: Implications for documentation.*)

The HCFA and the ***American Medical Association (AMA)*** jointly have developed guidelines to give health care providers and claims reviewers direction about preparing or reviewing documentation for evaluation and management services for patients. The guidelines provide direction for the three key components of service — history, examination, and medical decision making. (See *Evaluation and management documentation guidelines*, pages 184 to 186.)

HAZARDS OF IMPROPER DOCUMENTATION

All health care providers have the potential to make documentation errors or omissions that can significantly contribute to the legal outcome of a case. Faulty record keeping, absence of information, charting after the fact, missing records, and poor charting are all situations that can lead the jury to determine that a case isn't valid based on prevailing standards of documentation. To avoid litigation, ensure that your documentation skills are up-to-date with current standards and that you take steps to prevent improper documentation.

Faulty record keeping

Accurate, factual, consistent, and legible records will defend you against allegations of negligence. When keeping records, always identify that you're documenting the right information on the right chart. Take care not to document or add diagnostic results to the wrong chart. Incomplete, incorrect, and illegible records lead to discrepancies in care and put you in legal jeopardy.

Absence of information

In a 1985 landmark North Carolina case, an NP, a physician, and a community health center were sued for wrongful life by a child born with Down syndrome (*Azzolino v. Dingfelder*). The defendants were accused of negligently failing to inform the child's parents about amniocente-

---

Managed care: Implications for documentation

Because managed care balances the importance of a medical procedure or treatment against its cost, it requires greater standardization of plans of care as well as continuous monitoring of health care outcomes. To improve outcomes, several tools have been developed.

Clinical practice guidelines are standards developed to help nurse practitioners (NPs) and patients make decisions regarding appropriate care in specific clinical circumstances.

Practice parameters are educational tools that enable NPs to obtain the advice of clinical experts, keep abreast of the latest clinical research, and assess the clinical significance of often conflicting research findings.

Clinical pathways and *practice protocols* are clinical management tools that help to organize, sequence, price, and time the major interventions of NPs, physicians, and other health care providers for a particular case type, subset, or condition.

Care maps are elaborate clinical pathways that show the relationships of sets of interventions to sets of intermediate outcomes along a timeline. They merge standards of care with standards of practice in a cause-and-effect relationship.

---

sis and the availability of genetic counseling, thereby depriving the parents of their choice to avoid the child's birth. The parents claimed that if they had been properly advised, they would have discovered that the unborn child had Down syndrome and would have legally terminated the pregnancy by abortion. The documentation in the record was incomplete and didn't indi-

(Text continues on page 186.)

Evaluation and management documentation guidelines

Patient visits that occur primarily for counseling or coordination of care require documentation in three key areas: history, examination, and medical decision making. Documentation guidelines for each area are indicated below.

History

Documentation of the history should include the reason for seeking care, history of present illness (HPI), review of systems (ROS), and past, family, and social history (PFSH). The extent of the HPI, ROS, and PFSH that is obtained depends on your clinical judgment and the nature of the presenting problem. Specific documentation guidelines include the following:
- The reason for seeking care, ROS, and PFSH may be listed as separate elements of history, or they may be included in the description of the history of the present illness.
- An ROS or a PFSH obtained during an earlier encounter doesn't need to be rerecorded if there's evidence that the provider reviewed and updated the previous information. The review and update may be documented by describing any new ROS or PFSH information or by noting the date and location of the previous ROS or PFSH and confirming that the information on it hasn't changed.
- The ROS or PFSH may be recorded by ancillary staff or on a form completed by the patient. To document that the provider reviewed the information, there must be a notation supplementing or confirming the information recorded by others.
- The provider should document efforts made to obtain a history from the patient, accompanying family members, friends or attendants, or emergency personnel or from available medical records (such as previous hospital records, nursing facility records, ambulance records).
- The medical record should clearly reflect the reason for seeking care.
- A brief HPI consists of documentation of the reason for seeking care as well as one to three pertinent details about the presenting problem or the status of one chronic or inactive condition.
- An extended HPI documents the reason for seeking care as well as four or more details about at least one presenting problem.
- A brief ROS inquires about the systems directly related to the presenting problems. Generally, a brief ROS consists of one or two organ systems.
- An extended ROS includes a brief ROS as well as a review of additional organ systems; generally, an extended ROS consists of three to eight organ systems including the system directly related to the presenting problem.
- A complete ROS includes a review of nine or more organ systems including the system directly related to the presenting problem.
- All positive findings must be described; negative findings don't need to be individually documented except as appropriate for patient care: a notation indicating a system was negative is sufficient; the name of each system reviewed must be documented.
- At least one specific item from any of the three history areas must be documented for a pertinent PFSH.
- At least one specific item from two of the three history areas must be documented for a complete PFSH for office or other outpatient services (established patient), emergency department, subsequent nursing facility care, domiciliary care (established patient), and home care (established patient).
- At least one specific item from each of the three history areas must be documented for a complete PFSH for office or other outpatient services (new patient), hospital observation services, hospital inpatient services (initial care), consultations, comprehensive nursing facility assessments, domiciliary care (new patient), and home care (new patient).

Evaluation and management documentation guidelines *(continued)*

Examination

The extent of the examination performed and documented depends on your clinical judgment and the nature of the presenting problem. It may range from limited examinations of single body areas to general multisystem or complete single organ examinations. Specific documentation are listed below.

- The medical record for multisystem examinations should be documented as follows:
  – A brief examination should include findings from one or two body areas or organ systems.
  – A detailed examination should include findings from three to eight body areas or organ systems.
  – A comprehensive multisystem examination should include findings from nine or more of the seven body areas or 13 organ systems, or at least three constitutional findings comparable to one body area or organ system.
- Specific abnormal and relevant negative findings of the examination of the affected or symptomatic body areas or organ systems should be documented. A notation of "abnormal" without elaboration is insufficient.
- Abnormal or unexpected findings of the examination of the unaffected or asymptomatic body areas or organ systems should be described.
- A brief statement or notation indicating "negative" or "normal" is sufficient to document normal findings related to unaffected areas or asymptomatic organ systems.

Medical decision making

To determine the level of decision making, the medical record should include documentation of an assessment and plan for each problem evaluated during the encounter. The assessment and plan for each problem should include documentation of the status, severity, and urgency of the problems, including the risk of complications

and deterioration; the amount and complexity of data reviewed and differential diagnosis; and the diagnostic and therapeutic tests, procedures, and interventions ordered and the treatment plan. Specific documentation guidelines include the following:

- For each encounter, an assessment, clinical impression, or diagnosis should be documented. It may be explicitly stated or implied in documented decisions regarding management plans or further evaluation.
- For a presenting problem with an established diagnosis, the record should reflect whether the problem is improved, well controlled, resolving or resolved, or inadequately controlled, worsening, or failing to change as expected.
- For a presenting problem without an established diagnosis, the assessment or clinical impression may be stated in the form of a differential diagnosis or as "possible," "probable," or "rule out" diagnoses.
- The initiation of, or changes in, treatment should be documented. Treatment includes a wide range of management options, such as patient instructions, nursing instructions, therapies, and medications. This is particularly important for patients on multiple medications and for those whose primary reason for the visit is medication management.
- When consultations are requested or advice sought, the record should indicate to whom or where the consultation is made or from whom the advice is requested.
- If a diagnostic test or procedure is ordered, planned, scheduled, or performed at the time of the encounter, the type of service should be documented.
- The review of laboratory, radiology, or other diagnostic tests should be documented. An entry in a progress note such as "WBC elevated" or "chest X-ray unremarkable" is acceptable. Alternatively, the review may be documented by initialing and dating the report containing the test results.
- A decision to obtain old records or to obtain additional history from the family, care-

(continued)

Evaluation and management documentation guidelines *(continued)*

taker, or other source to supplement that obtained from the patient should be documented.

- Relevant findings from the review of old records, or the receipt of additional history from the family, caretaker, or other source should be documented. If there's no relevant information beyond that already obtained, that fact should be documented. A notation of "Old records reviewed" or "Addi-

tional history obtained from family" without elaboration is insufficient.

- The results of discussion of laboratory, radiology, or other diagnostic tests with the physician who performed or interpreted the study should be documented.
- The direct visualization and independent interpretation of an image, tracing, or specimen previously or subsequently interpreted by another physician should be documented.

---

cate that the parents were informed about the results of the amniocentesis. The court awarded damages to cover the extraordinary expenses that would be incurred during the child's lifetime by reason of his impairment.

You must inform your patients about all of their options for diagnostic studies. Make sure that you document this and the patient's understanding of the information you've provided.

Charting after the fact

In *Thor v. Boska* (1974), a rewritten copy of a patient's record was suspected of being altered. This lawsuit involved a woman who had seen her doctor several times because of a breast lump. Each time, the doctor examined her and made a record of her visit. After 2 years, the woman sought a second opinion and learned that she had breast cancer. She sued her first doctor. Rather than producing his records in court, the doctor brought copies of the records, and said he had copied the originals for legibility. The court reasoned that he was withholding incriminating evidence and held in favor of the plaintiff.

If you're asked to produce a patient's medical record, you must present originals. In a suspected case of notes written after litigation, the plaintiff's attor-

ney will retain document forensics experts who can determine when portions of the medical record were written. Any alteration in the record can make a defensible case indefensible.

Missing records

The case of *Battocchi v. Washington Hosp. Center* (1990) underscores the significance of missing records. In this case, parents brought a medical malpractice suit against the hospital and a physician for injury to their son during forceps delivery. The nurse had immediately documented the delivery and posted the record in the chart.

Later, the hospital's risk management personnel apparently lost the nurse's record. The court ruled in favor of the hospital and physician, saying the jury couldn't presume negligence and causation simply because the hospital lost the nurse's notes. The appeals court sent the case back to the trial court to determine whether loss of the record stemmed from negligence or impropriety.

Good charting, poor communication

Although thorough documentation is crucial, it isn't always enough. Unless you act on any significant findings, exemplary charting can be worthless. This includes failure to act on the findings of another health care professional's assessment. After reviewing notes from other health care professionals, such as paramedics, nurses, physical therapists, and other specialists, acknowledge that you reviewed the note in your documentation. This action supports your position that you considered the information contained in the note.

Documenting informed consent

An *informed consent* should include the specific benefits and risks associated with the procedure. It's advisable to write in the notes that the procedure was discussed with the patient at length and that the patient has no more questions at this time and wants to proceed. To ensure that the patient is aware of your findings and to provide documentation of preexisting conditions, specify abnormal findings, such as limited range of motion or neurosensory impairment, directly on the consent form, and have the patient initial this as well as sign at the indicated location.

AVOIDING DOCUMENTATION ERRORS

In addition to their potential impact on patient care, charting errors or omissions, even if seemingly harmless, will be devastating to your credibility in court. Be sure to avoid the following potential pitfalls.

Omissions

Include all significant facts that other providers will need to treat the patient. Otherwise, a court may conclude that you failed to perform an action missing from the record or tried to hide evidence. Remember to document related information such as diagnostic test results and referrals. In instances where reporting is mandatory (such as in suspected child abuse, elder abuse, or hu-

> ## Guidelines for follow-up care
>
> Standards of care established by professional organizations and state licensing agencies should be used when determining when to see a patient for follow-up care. Some suggested guidelines are listed below.
>
> - Infants less than age 3 months with a borderline fever without meningitis should be reevaluated in less than 12 hours for signs and symptoms of meningitis.
> - Patients with abdominal pain that is severe or of questionable origin require evaluation within 8 hours and must be seen in person if not significantly improved.
> - Patients with chest pain of undetermined etiology who are at low risk must be reevaluated in person within 24 hours.
> - Patients with wounds should be evaluated in 2 days for signs of infection and neurovascular compromise; this allows time for specialist intervention if the wound is worse than first suspected.

man immunodeficiency virus), note to whom you reported this information (including agency name, person's name, and position in the agency).

Also indicate any follow-up instructions and when the patient should be seen again. You may be increasing your risk of litigation if your follow-up contact is scheduled later than the established guidelines or standards indicate. (See *Guidelines for follow-up care.*)

Personal opinions

Don't enter personal opinions. (See *Distinguishing between subjective and objective charting,* page 188.) Record only factual and objective observations and the patient's statements.

Distinguishing between subjective and objective charting

A common error in charting is writing value judgments and opinions — subjective information — rather than factual, or objective, information. Subjective information reflects how the nurse practitioner feels about the patient's condition, not the patient's actual condition. Here are some subjective entries, with their objective alternatives.

SUBJECTIVE CHARTING	OBJECTIVE CHARTING
She is drinking well.	Drank 1,500 ml liquids between 7 a.m. and noon.
She reported good relief from Demerol.	Pain in R hip decreasing, now described as "like a dull toothache."
Dorsalis pedis pulse present. Good pedal pulses.	Peripheral pulses in legs 2+/4+ bilaterally.
Moves legs and feet well.	Leg strength 5+/5+ bilaterally all major muscle groups. Sensation intact to light touch, pin; denies numbness or tingling. Skin warm and dry. No edema.
Patient is nervous.	Patient repeatedly asks about length of expected discomfort and time off from work.
Breath sounds normal.	Breath sounds clear to auscultation all lobes. Chest expansion symmetrical — no cough. Nail beds pink.
Bowel sounds normal.	Bowel sound present all quadrants — abdomen flat. States NPO since midnight.

Vague entries

Imprecise or hurried charting is often interpreted as an indication that the care was also hurried and imprecise. Instead of "wound cleaned," chart "wound was cleaned and explored to its base."

Late entries

If a late entry is necessary, identify it as such, and sign and date it. Reference the date and time you're relating back to.

Improper corrections

Never erase or obliterate an error. Instead, draw a single line through it, label it "error," and sign and date it. (See *Adverse drug reaction.*)

Erroneous or vague abbreviations

Use only standard abbreviations, and follow your facility's policies.

Illegibility and lack of clarity

Write so that others can read your entry. Use a dictionary if you're unsure of spelling or usage. Recent cases have held physicians liable for illegible handwriting.

SIGNING YOUR DOCUMENTATION

Sign all notes with your full name and title. Place your signature on the right side of the page as proof that you entered all the information between the previous entry and your own. Draw lines through empty or remaining spaces on that page to prevent subsequent amendments or additions. (See *Countersigning: Important guidelines,* page 190.)

AVOIDING SUSPICIOUS CHANGES

In the event of a legal challenge, or if the medical record has been requested for examination in a trial, avoid making changes, corrections, or additions. To do so would raise suspicion, even if you have legitimate reasons and the best intentions.

Many lawyers advise against keeping personal notes about a questionable patient care incident. Often those notes are written when the NP is less than objective and may convey a far different message than was intended. Personal notes you use to prepare for a deposition or trial can be obtained by the plaintiff's attorney in a subsequent trial. If you deny using them to refresh your memory, you're perjuring yourself. If you admit you did use personal notes, the notes may be used to incriminate you or other defendants. Simply put, avoid any written or oral statements without first consulting your attorney.

DOCUMENTING ORDERS OF NPS AND PHYSICIANS

Orders fall into three groups: correct as written, ambiguous, and apparently erroneous. Follow your facility's policy for clarification of orders that are vague or possibly in error. If your office or organization lacks a policy and you have questions about the order of a supervising physician, contact the prescribing physician, and make sure you always document your actions. Advise the staff who will be carrying out your orders how to reach you if they question an order or need clarification. Then work toward establishing a policy

---

COURT CASE

Adverse drug reaction

This 1996 Louisiana case involved a neurologist who performed a Tensilon diagnostic test for myasthenia gravis for a stroke victim. The neurologist administered the anticholinesterase and observed the patient to determine whether her drooping eyelids would subside. Soon afterwards, the patient became nauseated, vomited, and began to sweat, indicating an adverse drug reaction or toxicity. Phenergan I.M. was administered by the nurse at the physician's direction. For the next 15 minutes, the physician remained with the patient until the adverse reaction appeared to subside. The nurse then charted the pulse rate at 88 before the Tensilon was administered, and then at 58 after the physician left the patient. Then the nurse left the patient with two nursing assistants. A short time later the patient experienced a cardiac arrest and eventually died. Substantial monetary damages were awarded to the patient's family and apportioned at 70% for the nurse and 30% for the physician. The evidence presented in court by a handwriting expert indicated that a pulse rate of 58 was changed to 88 sometime after the fact, apparently to correspond to the pulse rate of 88 that the nurse charted before the Tensilon was administered. It wasn't determined who attempted to alter the chart.

What the NP can learn

Medical records should never be altered. If a mistake in documentation is made, it should be corrected according to facility policy. *Cagnolatti v. Hightower,* 692 7So. 2d 1104 (La. App., 1996).

---

in accordance with ***nurse practice*** acts so that, if possible errors arise, you'll know what to do.

Countersigning: Important guidelines

If your facility or clinical practice setting requires your orders or entries to be countersigned by a supervising physician, you need to ensure that mechanisms are in place for this to happen.

Meaning of your signature

To protect yourself, begin by finding out what your facility policy and state nurse practice act say about countersigning. Does the facility interpret countersigning to mean that you performed your actions in the presence of the countersigning physician? If so, don't perform those functions unless the physician is present.

If your facility or clinic acknowledges that you don't necessarily have time to be observed, then the physician's countersignature implies that:
- the notes describe care that you had the authority and competence to perform
- the physician is also accountable for the care provided.

Legal risks of signing another provider's notes

What should you do if another nurse practitioner (NP) or physician asks you to document her care or sign her notes? In a word, "Don't." Unless your facility or clinic's policy authorizes or requires you to witness someone else's notes, your signature will make you fully responsible for anything in those notes.

Supervising student NPs

When you supervise student NPs as a preceptor or faculty member and co-sign their signatures, you're validating that the judgments they're making are correct and that the procedures or patient interactions they've performed are appropriate and within the standard of care. Patients are entitled to the standard of care of a fully licensed NP. It's advisable, therefore, that you be fully aware of the patient's condition and the actions and decisions of any students you supervise when co-signing medical records or orders.

Correct-as-written orders

If the order is correct as written, initial and check mark each line. Below the physician's signature, sign your name, the date, and the time. Expect the same from your subordinates or staff with respect to your orders.

An order may be correct when issued but improper later because of changes in the patient's status. If you're aware that the patient's condition has changed, amend your order in person or by telephone as soon as possible. If you're on the receiving end of an order that appears inappropriate due to changes in the patient's condition, delay the treatment until you've contacted the supervising physician and clarified the situation. Be sure to document all attempts to contact the physician or another on-call physician

if the primary provider isn't available. Numerous lawsuits are settled in favor of the patient when nurses, NPs, and supervising physicians fail to thoroughly document that they've communicated with one another. For instance, one provider may document calling an NP or a physician but may neglect to indicate either the time of the call or the eventual outcome. When this goes to trial, the health care provider contacted will testify that he wasn't called until much later — when it was too late to intervene in the patient's care. This literally turns into finger pointing; frequently, the jury won't believe either provider and will return a judgment against both of them.

Ambiguous orders

Ambiguous orders, whether issued by you or a physician, must be clarified before they can be carried out. If you've received ambiguous orders, document your efforts to clarify the order and whether or not the order was carried out. If a nurse or provider contacts you because your orders appear ambiguous, clarify the order and document this clarification immediately.

Apparently erroneous orders

If you believe a supervising physician's order is in error, you have a duty to refuse to carry it out. Make a record of your refusal together with the reasons and an account of all communication with the physician. Be prepared also for this to happen with an order you've issued. The nurse or provider must communicate this refusal to you, and you're ultimately responsible for ensuring the patient's best interests after that point.

Handling verbal orders

As a general rule, verbal and telephone orders are acceptable only under acute or emergency circumstances, when the practitioner can't promptly attend to the patient, or according to facility policy. Record the order on the order sheet, note the date and time of the order, and record the order verbatim. On the following line, write "v.o." for verbal order or "t.o." for telephone order and record the physician's name, followed by your signature and the time. To avoid liability, be certain the supervising physician *countersigns* the order within the time specified by facility policy.

Preprinted *standing orders* or *protocols* and standing order admission sheets are usually check marked and signed by the physician or NP, cosigned by the nurse or NP, and retained in the chart according to facility policy.

CONTROLLED SUBSTANCES

You're responsible for proper storage, prescription, and administration of *controlled substances* in your clinic, as well as for maintaining detailed records of each dose dispensed and the remaining quantities.

The legal consequences of improper charting have added significance when ordering and administering narcotics and other controlled substances. Be familiar with your state laws, state nurse practice act, and facility policy when ordering and *dispensing* these drugs. Also be aware of controlled substance acts (federal and state laws that control the distribution, classification, sale, and use of drugs). Consult your facility's policies or contact your state board of nursing for information about these laws. If you have a specific question about the propriety of a policy or procedure in your clinic or facility, talk to your attorney or your facility's attorney or write to your state board of nursing and request a formal board opinion or a declaratory ruling.

Telephone triage

Every day, health care providers receive phone calls from patients seeking help and advice over the phone. These encounters are increasingly the cause of litigation. (See *Triage encounters*, page 192.)

GIVING APPROPRIATE ADVICE

If you're answering triage calls, protocols or algorithms can give you specific guidelines that allow you to gather the information you need, offer appropriate advice to the caller (usually the patient or a family member), and protect yourself and the practice from liability. Specifically, the way the caller answers a question determines what you'll ask next. Then, based on the information you gather, you should be able to do two things: first, assess the patient's

COURT
CASE

Triage encounters

Any health care provider who gives advice over the telephone must accurately chart that advice in the patient's medical record. As a nurse practitioner, you must strive to keep an accurate account of all telephone triage encounters.

In the case of *Snyder v. Kaiser Permanente Hospital*, a 27-year-old woman was diagnosed with giardia (abdominal parasites) and was prescribed Atabrine by her primary physician at the hospital. The patient began the drug on a Monday and quickly experienced hallucinations (a known adverse effect). She claimed she called her physician the next day, but he denied that she reported experiencing hallucinations. The patient then called the emergency department (ED) and spoke to a triage nurse, who noted that the patient sounded "very bizarre" and stated that the nurse "had been chosen by God to help her." Although aware that the patient had been seen at Kaiser, the nurse made no further assessment, asked no further questions, and hung up the phone, as documented in the medical record. Meanwhile, the patient got in her car with her two children, ages 3 and 4, unbelted. She drove at 100 miles per hour and rear-ended another vehicle. The mother and children suffered multiple fractures. The suit claimed that if the triage nurse had identified the patient's hallucinations and notified authorities, the police or emergency personnel could have gone to her home and prevented her from driving or warned her not to drive. A $367,893 arbitration award was made on behalf of the patient and her children.

In another telephone triage case, a couple took their 6-month-old baby to the Junction Boulevard Medical Clinic in Queens, where he was diagnosed with a respiratory infection. Neo-Synephrine and liquid Tylenol were prescribed. Three days later, his condition worsened and his fever rose to 104° F. The infant began to vomit his medications. The following day, the mother took him to the physician, who diagnosed a left inner ear infection and prescribed Ceclor and Tylenol. The next day his temperature was still at 104° F and he continued to vomit. The parents called the clinic; the physician wasn't available, so the nurse advised them to continue with the antibiotic and Tylenol. The nurse didn't document the type of vomiting in the medical record. The infant's condition worsened and he had a seizure. The parents brought him to the ED, where he was diagnosed with meningitis; no inner ear infection was found. The infant developed hydrocephalus and required extensive care at home by his parents. Eventually he was placed in a facility, where he was cared for until his death at age 3 years and 9 months. A New York jury awarded a verdict of $1 million. *Laszio and Luz Marine Turscany v. Dr. Paul Grunfeld*, Queens County (NY) Supreme Court Case No. 132/87, 1997.

---

symptoms and classify them as an emergency or an urgent or nonurgent situation and, second, determine the appropriate disposition or outcome — specifically, the recommended level of care, education, and follow-up the caller needs.

Ideally, using protocols increases consistency in the assessment and disposition of calls regardless of which provider takes the call. That's why a practice should have comprehensive, current, user-friendly, symptom-based, and readily available written guidelines. To increase the quality of care, the partners in a practice should periodically review calls to identify weaknesses in the protocols.

The type of protocol you're following affects what advice you can give. More conservative protocols typically result in more patients being advised to go to their ***primary care provider's (PCP's)*** office or to the emergency department (ED). Less conservative protocols allow you and other providers to use more judgment, which may result in fewer office or ED visits; such protocols help contain costs but may result in greater legal vulnerability. You also need to consider whether a caller falls into a high-risk group (such as juveniles, pregnant women, or the elderly) when giving advice. If in doubt, or if you can't accurately determine the patient's condition during a telephone call, insist that the patient be seen in person.

When advising callers, make sure that following a protocol doesn't require you to function outside of your scope of practice and license. Your state's nurse practice act should provide guidance for independent decision making and assessment.

Giving appropriate advice to your callers also requires you to phrase both questions and suggestions carefully, avoiding diagnosing over the phone. For instance, you might say, "Is there anything else going on that I haven't asked about? From what you're describing, this is what concerns me, _____. Because of that, I recommend _____." Or, "From what you're describing, it sounds like there are some things I can suggest to make your child more comfortable. I also want to tell you a few things to watch for. Please call back if they occur or if you have any other questions or concerns." Try to provide the level of care that offers the caller the most comfort and peace of mind, given the diagnostic possibilities his symptoms suggest.

THREE BASICS OF TRIAGE

Telephone triage won't work effectively unless three essential elements are in place: quick access to health care professionals, detailed documentation, and call recording.

COURT CASE

Explore complaints fully

A 1996 Ohio case ruled that the Court of Appeals could reverse the trial court's decision to enter judgment in favor of the hospital and remanded the case for a new trial. This case involved parents who sued both as individuals and on behalf of their brain-damaged child. The patient was pregnant with her fourth child after delivering the first three by cesarean section. She presented to the emergency department (ED) believing she was in labor, was assured that she wasn't, and was sent home. Six days later she returned to the ED believing she was in labor again and was sent home. She returned to the ED later that afternoon and was sent home again, when she began experiencing vaginal bleeding. The patient then telephoned another hospital, and the nurse and her supervisor there told her to remain at home and wait until the bleeding stopped. Later she called her physician and received the same advice. Finally, she went back to the ED and a cesarean delivery was performed; it was found that her uterus had ruptured and the child was brain damaged from lack of oxygen. The court determined that the health care providers were negligent in failing to make the correct assessment.

What the NP can learn

The NP must carefully listen to the patient's specific description of complaints and explore the patient's full history. *McCrystal v. Turnbull Memorial Hospital,* 115 Ohio App., 3d 73, 684 N.E. 2d 721 (1996)

Quick access

Quick access to a health care professional is measured in seconds, not minutes. Someone must have the authority to decide what calls are emergent (and be able to act on that infor-

Telephone triage log

Date/Time: _3/15/01 9pm_ Phone# Current: _610-522-1137_ Home: _610-237-0148_
Patient Name: _Heather Cardell_ Caller: _Christine Cardell_ Relation: _Mother_
Address: _230 Garvin Blvd. Sharon Hill, PA 19079_
Patient DOB/Age: _8/29/00_ SS#: _555-416-0382_ Wt (< 18 y.o.): _18 lbs_
Allergies: _NKDA_
PMH: _Denies_

Current med list, including herbals/supplements: _Multivitamin with fluoride_

Chief complaint: _____
Symptoms/Assessment: _Fever 101.2 F (po)_
(OLDCART acronym) Onset: _Just now_ Location: _Systemic_
Duration: _Unknown_ Characteristics: _Cranky but distractible_
Aggravated by: _Unknown_ Relieved by: _Nothing tried_
Treatments tried/Time seeking treatment (why now?): _Wants antibiotics now because_
going out of town tomorrow
Protocol used: _Fever_
Recommended: _Self-care measures_ Caller Accepted: ⟨Yes⟩/No
Endpoint accepted by patient:
Call 911 ED _____
Specialist (for example, Poison Control/Ophthalmologist): _____
PCP: _Victor Los_ Call/See in: < 4 hr < 24 hr (specify) _⟨PRN⟩_
Self-care advice given on: _Fever_
Per protocol/reference: _Fever_
Potential complications of nontreatment: _____
Caller agreed to follow-up phone call: ⟨Yes⟩/No
Callback scheduled for: (time/person) _3/16/01 before noon_
Notes: _Advised of rationale for no antibiotics at this time & S/S of concern._

Practitioner signature: _Victor Los, PNP_

mation by having the patient activate the emergency medical system or route the caller to a health care professional) at the first point of contact. A health care professional must answer or return all calls as soon as possible. A delay in getting back to a caller may result in the aggravation of an injury or evaluation of a complaint that doesn't sound serious — and increase the risk of negative outcomes and litigation. Although it may need to be performed quickly, a thorough assessment (as time permits in emergency situations) helps avoid negative outcomes. (See *Explore complaints fully,* page 193.)

Detailed documentation

Call documentation serves several functions. Thorough documentation can provide the caller's PCP with information about that patient's complaint, possibly identifying a problem the PCP didn't know about. It also can provide other team members with information about the call if the caller should phone back for affirmation or more detailed assistance. Finally, it can serve as protection against legal liability, working as well as a system of taping calls if the documentation is thorough enough.

Such documentation works best if documentation forms aren't only thorough, but also easy to use. (See *Telephone triage log.*) This encourages all providers to document completely (unfortunately, many practitioners don't document thoroughly, leaving themselves and the practice open to liability). Forms for documentation can be designed to work by exclusion or inclusion of abnormal findings and need to be retained for up to 10 years, depending on your state's statute of limitations. The caller should also either have the right not to have his PCP informed or be told at the beginning of the call that his PCP will get a record of the call.

Call recording

One way to keep track of calls is to record them on tape. Although expensive, keeping an audiotape of all calls helps control risk by providing a record of what both the provider and the caller said. However, if no audiotape exists, it becomes the caller's word against the NP's word. Quality assurance can be monitored even if only some calls are taped. The practice can establish a standard of care and a record of following a set policy. Review of call tapes can help detect weaknesses in the system, allowing the practice to enhance training and algorithms.

MAKING PROTOCOLS WORK

Telephone triage protocols help ensure that all providers deliver consistent and accurate health care information to callers. Ways to make protocols more effective include:
● promoting staff involvement in refining protocols
● using resource books that outline telephone advice protocols
● customizing commercial protocols for specific use
● making protocols physically convenient (for instance, having them in a three-ring binder alphabetized by signs and symptoms or in a computer program that searches for key words and includes space for documenting calls)
● having protocols readily available
● ensuring that all practitioners know where protocols are and how they're organized.

Computerized medical records

As with the manual record system, the computerized medical record provides a detailed account of the patient's clinical status, diagnostic tests, treatments, and medical history. Unlike the manual system, however, the computerized record stores all the patient's medical data in a single, easily accessible source.

Using computers to maintain and access records dramatically increases efficiency and precision. Computerization helps to improve the quality and accuracy of the documentation, to make the patient record more complete, and to keep patient information more current in a "real-time" sense. The computerized record also allows NPs to rely less on human recall, which helps to increase accuracy. Computers prove especially useful in areas that benefit from automated patient monitoring, such as the ***intensive care unit*** and the ***coronary care unit.***

FACILITY COMPUTER SYSTEMS

Health care administrators usually introduce computers for the sake of controlling health care costs. A network computer system typically consists of a large, centralized computer to store information, linked to smaller video display terminals (VDTs) in each office. Ideally, there should be at least one VDT in each work area.

To use the system, an NP signs in by typing onto the keyboard a signature code, or password, that gives her access to a patient's records. The computer recognizes by the signature code that she has authorized access to the information stored in its memory. After a patient's ***code*** number is entered, the computer displays the patient's records on the screen. The NP may access care plans, vital signs, medication records, general progress notes, laboratory and diagnostic test results, assessment findings, discharge plans, and other information. She can also order a printed copy of the patient's record.

Benefits of a computerized system

Just how computer technology will change the profession for NPs remains to be seen. Some experts predict a paperless chart. Health care reform may further transform the documentation process, with the creation of a universal medical record that follows a patient through life. Many companies are organizing patient medical records on the Internet for patient read-only access. Hopefully, integrating computers into your practice will free you to spend more time meeting the needs of your patients. The computerized medical record can save time spent filing, searching for, and retrieving information about a patient. By improving legibility, computers greatly reduce the

risk of misinterpretation. Computers also reduce misinterpretation by offering standardized, structured input formats and mandatory charting fields for assessment reports, flow charts, and care plans. In addition, time stamping can minimize scheduling errors. Correct spelling and legibility are also major advantages. Computerized systems can be especially beneficial to patients who travel.

Facilities must show, however, that their computer systems are trustworthy enough to be used in court. For example, they should use software that automatically records the date and time of each entry and each correction, as well as the name of the author or anyone who modifies a record. When an error is corrected, the software should preserve both the original and corrected versions and identify each author.

Challenging a computer record in court

In 1977, a patient in New York charged that a computerized record system was an invasion of his privacy. In *Whalen v. Roe*, the patient challenged the constitutionality of a state law that required patients buying certain prescription drugs to list their name, address, age, the drug, dosage, and prescribing physician's name for a state database. The state then entered all the information into a computer. The Supreme Court upheld the law but acknowledged the threat to privacy implicit in the system. The Court reasoned that central storage and easy accessibility of computerized data vastly increased the potential for abuse of that information. Numerous subsequent rulings have upheld this decision.

In fact, a documentation system is only as good as the providers who use it. When all members of the health care team sign in and use the documentation system in your organization or clinic, communication and efficiency will be enhanced. Otherwise, there will be poor communication, makeshift documentation, decreased efficiency, and a heightened exposure to liability.

Disadvantages and concerns
Many critics fear that computers will diminish the personal satisfaction that NPs derive from practicing their profession. They argue that technical advances tend to have a dehumanizing effect on the workplace. Relying on computers may mean less opportunity for interaction and communication with coworkers and patients. In addition, patients may be less truthful in providing medical histories and details about illnesses if they know that the information is going into a computer, which could be used to improperly divulge their medical information to insurers, employers, coworkers, and unauthorized sources. Some patients are concerned that genetic information or information relative to serious diseases or illnesses may prevent them from gaining employment, securing a marriage license, serving in the military, adopting children, or obtaining such items as life insurance, a motor vehicle license, or a home mortgage.

Some systems provide you with a selection of words and phrases you can choose from to quickly create a complete narrative note. Use of an incorrect descriptive prompt or phrase can give a misleading assessment. If the prompts aren't exactly descriptive, then it's important to type or write out your assessment.

One major disadvantage of a ***computerized medical record system*** is the need for backup records in case computers break down, making information unavailable. Ensuring completeness and continuity in charting requires a backup system. However, this also creates the appearance of two sets of books and could be risky in court. Poorly designed computer systems or human error can also scramble entries and spread flawed data. Obviously, the key is that all members of the health care team know how to use the system.

Another disadvantage of computerized medical records is that some systems allow the provider to reenter files and change progress notes, orders, and diagnoses, which is tantamount to record altering.

Verifying computerized records
Verification is one way of reducing errors in the computerized record. To use verification, the unit secretary enters the provider's order into the computer. The order is held in a "suspense file" until an NP reviews the entry, verifies the order, and adds it to the active record file.

Legal concerns: the 21st century

The legal implications of computerized medical records are evolving. (See *Computer charting: Minimizing your legal risks*, page 198.) Most computer records are legitimate substitutes for manual records. Some state laws, however, require written records as well.

The most pressing legal questions concern the threat to patient ***privacy*** and ***confidentiality.*** With traditional records, information is restricted simply by keeping the record on the unit; computer records can be called up at any terminal in the facility. The primary safeguard is the signature code, limiting access to the records. For example, an NP's code would call up a patient's entire record, but a technician's code would produce only a portion of the record.

Various laws protect the privacy of a patient's medical records. The Federal

Computer charting: Minimizing your legal risks

Your liability when working with computer documentation is exactly the same as when working with a manual system. You may be liable for any patient injuries associated with charting errors or omissions.

To minimize your legal risks:
- Always double-check all patient information.
- Don't divulge signature codes.
- Inform appropriate authorities if you suspect that someone is using your code or anyone else's code.
- Indicate whether your orders are written or oral (and whether given in person or by telephone) and when the entry was made.
- Know your state's rules and regulations and the facility's policies and procedures regarding privileged data, confidentiality, and disclosure. To learn about state rules and regulations, consult your organization or facility's policy and procedure manual, check with your facility's attorney, and consult your state board of nursing or the state statutory and administrative codes for nurse practitioners.

Privacy Act of 1974 protects the confidential medical information of patients in veterans' hospitals, and some state nurse practice acts impose an ethical *duty* to guard patients' privacy. However, no one can fully guarantee that unauthorized persons won't gain access to computerized records.

Newer methods of communication have undoubtedly saved time and allowed for unprecedented ease of communication across cities, states, and countries — all these new modalities promise better patient care. However, they bring with them the added need for documentation and systems to ensure privacy and confidentiality.

Facsimiles
Care must also be taken to safeguard patient information sent by facsimile machine. In particular, policies and procedures should be established to prevent confidential patient information, such as a positive human immunodeficiency virus report, from being transmitted by facsimile machine — especially one that's centrally located and easily seen by many staff members.

Facsimiles should have qualifying statements to the effect that they're sensitive, confidential patient information, intended for a specific recipient and, if inadvertently received by another person, should be destroyed or returned to the sender and that the sender should be immediately notified. Your health care attorney can assist you with guidelines to sending facsimiles. Also, it's important to confirm that you've received or sent a facsimile.

E-mails
As an NP, you also need to take precautions when e-mailing information to patients and other providers. Your e-mails should have a disclaimer regarding patient confidentiality. Your facility's computer system should have firewalls and encryption to prevent e-mails from being sent to the wrong address or from being "hacked." Keep in mind that e-mails can be archived and retrieved — this is being done daily in trials around the country. Just because you send information about a patient's care in an e-mail doesn't mean that the information won't end up in a courtroom. Forensic scientists can readily retrieve e-mails. With e-mails and facsimiles, consider printing a copy of what you've communicated, and add it to the patient's chart.

Telemedicine

Telemedicine is a rapidly evolving international method of delivering health care that involves two-way, interactive, network video interaction with other heath care providers or patients. As this technology develops, clinics and organizations will need to examine their documentation systems in order to meet the challenges of patient confidentiality and privacy.

Selected references

Allen, J., et al. "Legal Documentation: A Case Study in Basic Concepts," *Advance for Nurse Practitioners* 8(1):67-68, January 2000.

Arent Fox Telemedicine and the Law: *www.arentfox.com/telemedicine.html.*

Boldreghini, S., and Larrabee, J.H. "Difference In Nursing Documentation Before and After Computerization: A Pilot Study," *Online Journal of Nursing Informatics* 2(1), Winter 1998.

Brent, N.J. "Home Care Fraud and Abuse: Dishonest Documentation," *Home Healthcare Nurse* 16(3):196-98, March 1998.

Enzman-Hagedorn, M.I., and Gardner, S.L. "Legal Issues in Neonatal Nursing: Considerations for Staff Nurses and Advanced Practice Nurses," *Journal of Obstetric, Gynecologic & Neonatal Nursing* 28(3):320-330, May/June, 1999.

Health Care Financing Administration: www.hcfa.gov.

Huston, J.L. "Telemedical Record Documentation," *Topics in Health Information Management* 19(3):59-65, February 1999.

Knightlinger, R. "Sloppy Records: The Kiss of Death for a Malpractice Defense," *Medical Economics* 76(11):171-174, June 1999.

McElhaney, R., and Beare, P.G. "Expert Witness/Legal Consultant: The Importance of Data Collection," *Clinical Nurse Specialist* 12(3):117-20, May 1998.

Rapsilber, L.M., and Anderson, E.H. "Understanding the Reimbursement Process," *The Nurse Practitioner* 25(5):36-46, May 2000.

Veronesi, J.F. "Ethical Issues in Computerized Medical Records," *Critical Care Nursing Quarterly* 22(3):75-80, November 1999.

Chapter Seven

ETHICAL DECISION MAKING

Working as interdependent members of the health care team, *nurse practitioners (NPs)* make ethical decisions in their practice every day. These decisions, many of which are unique to the role of an NP, may involve patient care, actions related to coworkers, or nurse-physician relations. At times, you may find yourself trapped in the middle of an ethical dilemma, caught among conflicting *duties* and responsibilities to your patient, to your employer, and to yourself. Even after you make a decision, you may wonder, "Did I do the right thing?"

There are no automatic guidelines for solving all ethical conflicts. Although such conflicts may be painful and confusing, particularly in advanced nursing, you don't have to be a philosopher to act ethically or to make decisions that fall within NP *standards* of practice and ethical *codes.* Nonetheless, you do need to understand the principles of ethics that guide your practice. Legally, NPs are responsible for using their knowledge and skills within the scope of their licensure and state law. Ethically, NPs are responsible, as patient advocates, for safeguard-

ing their patients' rights. The traditional biomedical methodology approaches an ethical decision with detachment and objectivity. However, moral dilemmas of NPs may require an expanded ethical framework to include the unique aspects of advocacy and caring.

To be an effective advocate, an NP not only must know the ethical and legal principles of informed consent but also must understand that the patient's consent isn't valid unless he understands his condition, the proposed treatment, treatment alternatives, probable risks and benefits, and relative chances of success or failure.

Definitions

A familiarization with the language of ethics ensures uniformity and consistency when you're communicating with your colleagues, ethics committee, and patients. The following is a list of frequently used terms and definitions in ethics:

● *Ethics* is the area of philosophic study that examines values, actions, and choices to determine right and wrong.

- **Normative ethics** presents standards of right or good action for the guidance and evaluation of conduct.
- **Descriptive ethics** is a factual investigation of moral behavior and beliefs.
- **Laws** are binding rules of conduct enforced by formal authority such as legislatures, courts, and governmental agencies.
- **Rights** are entitlements that one deserves according to just claims, legal guarantees, or moral principles. For every right there is a correlative duty or obligation.
- **Values** are ideals or concepts that give meaning to the individual's life and are most commonly derived from societal norms, religion, and family orientation.
- **Morals** are fundamental standards of right and wrong that an individual learns and internalizes. An individual's moral orientation is generally based on religious beliefs and personal beliefs.
- **Moral dilemmas** arise when two or more clear ethical principles apply, but they support mutually inconsistent courses of action.

Ethical theories

As the basis for professional codes of ethics, ethical theories attempt to provide a system of principles and rules for resolving ethical dilemmas. Ethical theories consist of arguments or reasons for justifying what is and isn't permissible and propose reasons for maintaining those beliefs.

TELEOLOGY AND DEONTOLOGY
Two types of ethical theories — **teleology** and **deontology** — are used frequently as guides in ethical decision making.

Teleologic ethical theories determine what is right or wrong based on an action's consequences. One such teleologic theory, called utilitarian ethics, requires decision makers to determine and choose those actions that will result in maximized good — that is, the greatest good for the greatest number of people.

In teleologic theories, ethical decisions most often are made through a process called risk-benefit analysis. For example, you may help patients and their families evaluate several courses of treatment to decide which one will produce the greatest amount of relief (benefit) with the least danger of suffering (risk). The fact that teleologic theory assumes that good and harm can be quantified and evaluated can make it a less-than-ideal approach to resolving health care issues. Determining the "greatest good" is highly subjective and can result in inconsistent decisions.

Deontologic ethical theories emphasize moral obligation or **commitment.** One such deontologic theory, called Kantian ethics, is formulated on the ethical premises of Immanuel Kant. Kantian ethics are based on the categorical imperative: "I ought never to act except in such a way that I can also will that my maxim becomes a universal law." Kant's imperative is often compared to the Golden Rule "do unto others as you would have them do unto you."

Deontologic theories give most weight to obeying moral laws such as "Always tell the truth" and "Never harm a patient." According to deontologic theories, honoring ethical obligations ensures good, even though actions may be difficult and consequences painful. Because deontology centers on duty or obligation to others, many experts consider it the only acceptable theory for ethical decision making in health care. Nevertheless, complications can arise when duties conflict.

For example, suppose someone proposes keeping a brain-dead patient on a ventilator while recipients for a kidney transplant are found. Several staff members object because the patient had expressed a wish to die naturally, without artificial support.

On the one hand, you may favor maintaining the patient on a ventilator because you recognize how useful his kidneys will be to others. On the other hand, if you resolve this dilemma by deciding which course of action best supports the patient's rights, you'd probably give more weight to his right of self-determination. This would lead you to oppose maintaining the patient on a ventilator. As you can see from this example, duties can conflict, and you'll have to determine which duty takes precedence.

Aspects of both teleologic and deontologic theories are used when making ethical decisions. To avoid becoming confused, you should develop orderly, systematic, objective decision-making methods. Otherwise, your decision making becomes subjective and arbitrary and results in moral relativism. Additionally, you may want to consider alternative ethical theories and incorporate them into your decision-making process.

ALTERNATIVE THEORIES
Besides teleology and deontology, other ethical theories may help guide ethical decision making.

Egoism
Egoism considers self-interest and self-preservation as the only proper goals of all human actions, insisting that the only right decision is the one that maximizes the autonomy of the decision maker.

Obligationism
Obligationism attempts to resolve ethical dilemmas by balancing *distributive justice* (dividing equally among all) with beneficence (doing good and not harm). This theory holds that benefits and burdens should be distributed equally, according to merits and needs.

Social contract theory
Social contract theory is based on the concept of original position. The least advantaged people (such as children and the handicapped) are considered the norm. Whether an act is right or wrong is determined from the norm's point of view.

Theological ethics
Ethical theories and moral-legal principles can be based in religious traditions — for instance, *Good Samaritan acts* based on the biblical concept of altruism and selflessness.

Ethics of care
Ethics of care emphasizes traits valued in intimate personal relationships, such as sympathy, compassion, fidelity, discernment, and love. Unlike Kantian universal rules, impartial utilitarian calculations, and individual rights, this theory focuses on relationships involving care, responsibility, trust, fidelity, and sensitivity. The ethics of care examines how actions are performed, the underlying motives, and whether such actions promote or frustrate positive relationships.

Communitarianism
Communitarian theories deem the essentials of ethics as deriving from communal values, the common good, social goals, traditional practices, and the cooperative virtues. The communitarian places heightened value on the community as opposed to the individual, which is dissimilar to the traditional teleological and deontological theories that focus on individual rights.

Character ethics
Character ethics — also known as virtue ethics — emphasizes the agents who perform actions and make choices. Some have defined moral virtue as a disposition to act harmoniously with moral principles, obligations, or ideals.

In many ethical situations judgments of personal virtue and character are possible. "An action can be right without being virtuous . . . but an action can be virtuous only if performed from the right state of mind of the person. Both right action and right motive should be present in a virtuous action."

Moral relativism

Are certain values intrinsically best, or are values always a matter of personal interpretation? A theory of ethics known as ***moral relativism*** holds that there are no ethical absolutes, that whatever a person believes is right, is right for him at that moment.

Consider what would happen if everyone practiced moral relativism.
● There would be no objective way to resolve moral dilemmas.
● A person could never question or disapprove of another's moral judgment.
● Professional standards, such as nursing standards, would become meaningless.
● Law and order in society would disappear.
● People and cultures would be unable to grow morally.

Although different people and cultures have different values, moral relativism doesn't provide an adequate basis for ethical decision making. Because you'll probably face numerous moral conflicts in the course of your career, you need to develop consistent ethical standards to guide your behavior.

Law vs. ethics

Ethics is the area of philosophic study that examines values, actions, and choices to determine right and wrong. Laws are binding rules of conduct enforced by authority. In many situations, laws and ethics overlap. When they diverge, you have to identify and examine the fine lines that separate them.

Relationship between law and ethics

When a law is challenged as unjust or unfair, the challenge usually reflects some underlying ethical principle. That is because, ideally, laws are based on what is right and good. Realistically, though, the relation between law and ethics is complex. Most NPs realize that a majority of malpractice suits result from patients' dissatisfaction with care they received. When patients believe they haven't been treated with respect and dignity or that their rights have been ignored or violated, they're more likely to initiate legal action. There's a strong connection between ethics and law, in regard to the NP's role as a patient advocate. (See *Nursing ethics and the law,* page 204.)

Moral dilemmas

An NP confronted with parents who refuse to immunize their child faces a moral dilemma — an ethical problem caused by conflicts of rights, responsibilities, and values.

Such a dilemma carries with it a great deal of stress. As you grapple with the situation, trying to decide what to do, you'll probably experience internal psychological and emotional stress, such as fear or guilt. In addition, you may experience stress caused by external factors that are political or interpersonal.

Moral dilemmas call for ethical choices in the face of profound uncertainty. At times, you may not know what the right or ethical course of action should be. At other times, you may believe completely that a particular action is morally right and yet, for various reasons, find it difficult to act.

A moral dilemma may be further complicated by psychological pressures and personal emotions, especially when any choice is a forced one at best and, in many cases, one that results in an un-

Nursing ethics and the law

When you make decisions, your choices and actions should consider and (ideally) fulfill *three* criteria:
- They should be the best practice *clinically.*
- They should be *legally* within the scope of policies, procedures, and practice acts.
- They should be the right thing to do *morally.*

Sometimes ethics, law, and best practice don't always agree. Certain actions may be considered by some people to be morally or legally ambiguous. Each type of situation shown below can present potential moral dilemmas for nurse practitioners (NPs).

Nursing choices, decisions, and actions

	ETHICAL	UNETHICAL
LEGAL	**Type 1: Actions of this type are the ideal; they're both ethical and legal, although not always without complications and inconveniences.** Example: A young adolescent comes into the NP's clinic requesting a pregnancy test. The test results confirm the adolescent's pregnancy. The NP discusses the possibility of informing her parents as well as other potential support systems. The adolescent chooses not to inform her parents, opting for other means of safe and adequate support. Respecting her informed decision, the NP doesn't disclose the pregnancy to the adolescent's parents.	**Type 2: Actions of this type might be considered unethical but are nevertheless legal.** Example: An NP caring for a 12-year-old with cancer learns that he has accepted the fact that he's dying and wants to stop chemotherapy. His parents have consented to try a new, very aggressive course of chemotherapy. The NP goes ahead and administers the chemotherapy as ordered by the oncologist.
ILLEGAL	**Type 3: Actions of this type might be considered ethical by some but are nevertheless illegal.** Example: After diagnosing a child with otitis media, an NP attempts to write a prescription for amoxicillin. The child's medical assistance card is outdated and can't be used to obtain the medication. A sibling has a current medical assistance card. The NP writes the prescription using the sibling's medical assistance card.	**Type 4: Actions of this type are neither legal nor ethical.** Example: A dying patient comes to the NP seeking assisted suicide advice. The controlling law in the NP's jurisdiction states that every person who deliberately aids, advises, or encourages another to commit suicide is guilty of a felony. The patient discloses his plan to commit suicide and requests a prescription to facilitate his action. Knowing that the patient intends to attempt suicide, the NP willfully prescribes a sufficient quantity of medication to enable the patient to administer a lethal dose. (This example doesn't consider current Oregon law, which permits NP participation in assisted suicide in some measure, nor does it consider varying state law on prescription privileges.)

Ethical principles in conflict

Nurse practitioners (NPs) often identify ethical principles such as beneficence, nonmaleficence, autonomy, justice, and fidelity and strive to honor them in making ethical decisions and choosing courses of action. This way of making ethical decisions is called *principlism*. It's effective only as long as ethical principles aren't in conflict. In the reality of an NP's daily responsibilities, however, ethical principles can and often do conflict with each other.

ETHICAL PRINCIPLES	ETHICAL ISSUE
Beneficence	An NP sees an infant with a brachial plexus injury (Erb's palsy) for routine health maintenance in a health maintenance organization (HMO). After the infant has had an initial evaluation by a pediatric neurologist in the newborn period and prescribed occupational therapy, follow-up by the pediatric neurologist is requested. The NP authorizes the referral and the infant is reevaluated by the subspecialist. The parents have investigated treatment for Erb's palsy and are convinced that surgery performed in a distant state offers the most hope for recovery for their child. The subspecialist concurs and documents his support for this out-of-plan course of treatment.
Conflict between beneficence, autonomy, and justice	The NP and the associate physician must decide if the referral for out-of-plan treatment serves the best interests of the patient as well as the interests of all other patients in the same plan. If the child was treated by a local surgeon who is in the network, the cost to the HMO would be much less than if the child were treated by the out-of-plan surgeon. Yet the parents and the pediatric neurologist see a qualitative difference between the local surgeon and the out-of-plan surgeon, who is a national expert in this particular type of surgery. The NP supports the parents' decision and, acting as their advocate, sends a request to the medical director to authorize an out-of-plan referral. The NP is able to reason that the cost-benefit ratio favors out-of-plan treatment, thus reducing the likelihood of increased costs over an extended time. Reduced health care costs for this one patient will benefit all other patients in the plan. Upon the medical director's denial of the request, the NP faces another complex decision: Should she inform the family that the request was denied and that they must bear the costs of the surgery, or should she appeal the decision? Does she risk unpleasant consequences in terms of loss of year-end bonuses, salary, or benefits increases? Might she be dismissed from the health care plan for incurring a huge expense to the plan?

comfortable compromise. Many moral dilemmas involve choices about justice or fairness, when scant resources (such as medication) must be divided among patients with equal needs. In other cases, a choice must be made quickly because the patient's condition is fluctuating or rapidly deteriorating. Often, NPs who are compelled to make ethical decisions don't have the luxury of time.

TYPES OF DILEMMAS
Most moral dilemmas fall into one of the following classifications:
- Dilemmas of **beneficence** involve deciding what is good as opposed to what is harmful. Such dilemmas often

Principles yardstick

In situations involving conflicting ethical principles, it's helpful to avoid the trap of "either/or" thinking. Instead, think of ethical principles as yardsticks and strive for compromise rather than sacrificing one principle for another. For example, the principles yardstick would look like this:

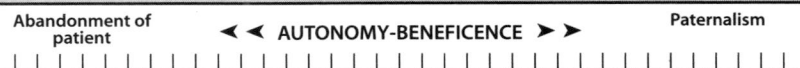

| Abandonment of patient | ◄ ◄ AUTONOMY-BENEFICENCE ► ► | Paternalism |

If we move too far toward emphasizing autonomy without balancing it with beneficence, the result is abandoning the patient. If we move too far in the other direction by emphasizing doing good without balancing it with respect for the patient's autonomy, the result is paternalism.

occur when health care providers, patients, or family members disagree about what course of action is "in the patient's best interest."

● Dilemmas of ***nonmaleficence*** involve the avoidance of harm. These issues often relate to an NP's responsibility to "blow the whistle" if she sees others compromising the patient's safety.

● Dilemmas of ***autonomy*** center on deciding which course of action maximizes the patient's right of self-determination. Autonomy issues are often closely related to beneficence issues, especially when individuals other than the patient must determine (or attempt to determine) what is best for the patient.

● Dilemmas of ***justice*** pertain to ethical issues of fairness and equality, such as those that involve dividing limited health care resources fairly.

● Dilemmas of ***fidelity*** relate to honoring promises. These may include the extent and limits of an NP's role and duties to a patient that might conflict with other duties, such as to the employer, facility, insurer, colleagues, or physicians.

Fidelity involves ***confidentiality,*** respecting privileged information. The

patient's right to privacy must be balanced against society's right to be informed of potential threats to public health.

Fidelity also involves a commitment to ***veracity;*** that is, telling the truth, or fully informing a patient of his medical condition. (See *Ethical principles in conflict,* page 205.)

TYPES OF DECISIONS

In any moral dilemma, the decisions facing NPs usually can be grouped into one of four categories:

● Active decisions represent moral judgments that lead directly to action and bring about change.

● Passive decisions deny, delay, or avoid action; they maintain the status quo by denying or shifting responsibility to avoid change.

● Programmed decisions use precedents, established guidelines, procedures, and ***rules*** to resolve anticipated, routine, and expected types of moral dilemmas.

● Nonprogrammed decisions require a unique response to complex and unexpected moral dilemmas.

Most commonly, an NP's programmed decisions also are active ones. For example, when you tell a patient what to expect from a procedure and then ask him to sign a **consent form**, you're participating in a programmed decision process that involves ethical and legal practices (such as truth-telling) as well as patients' rights (such as self-determination).

The patient facing the procedure, perhaps feeling unprepared to make a complex decision, may respond passively, saying, "I don't know what's best. Should I risk the complications of having the procedure or the danger of not having it? I'll do whatever you tell me."

In such a situation, you must make a choice. You must either relieve the patient's stress by telling him what is "best" for him or ensure his autonomy by removing yourself from the decision-making process. By providing education and assistance to the patient throughout the process of informed consent (or refusal of consent), you're able to balance the principles of autonomy and beneficence without "taking over" the decision for the patient. (See *Principles yardstick.*)

Whenever you're faced with a moral dilemma, you must make moral judgments that lead to decisions about right and wrong courses of action. Even passive decisions — for example, deciding to protect oneself by remaining silent or not taking a stand on an issue — are based on moral judgments. (See *Approaching ethical decisions.*)

Essential features of moral reasoning

In approaching any moral dilemma, you should be aware of five features associated with moral reasoning — contextual framework, values, influencing factors, recognition of the dilemma, and outcomes. An interrelationship exists among these essential features in the moral reasoning process. Identifying them will facilitate a better understanding of the moral dilemma. All five play a role in decision making.

Approaching ethical decisions

When faced with an ethical dilemma, consider the following questions:
- What health issues are involved?
- What ethical issues are involved?
- What further information is necessary before a judgment can be made?
- Who will be affected by this decision? (Include the decision maker and other caregivers if they'll be affected emotionally or professionally.)
- What are the values and opinions of the people involved?
- What conflicts exist between the values and ethical standards of the people involved?
- Must a decision be made and, if so, who should make it?
- What alternatives are available?
- For each alternative, what are the ethical justifications?
- For each alternative, what are the possible outcomes?

● The contextual framework illustrates the specific characteristics of the settings or surroundings, the NP's role, and other persons present in the environment where the ethical dilemma occurs.

● Values are strongly held personal and professional beliefs about worth and importance. Clarifying your own values is an important part of developing a professional ethic. You may become more aware of your values by consciously examining your statements and behavior.

● Influencing factors include variables that intervene and influence the situation to change it from an ordinary clinical encounter to a moral dilemma. These influencing factors can include the work setting, the participants, considerations in the decision-making process, and catalysts to the dilemma.

● Recognition of the dilemma is, simply put, the moment when the NP realizes that the clinical situation is posing a moral dilemma.

● Outcomes are the responses induced by the moral dilemma, including the decision to act as well as affective, cognitive, and evaluative responses.

Basis of ethical decisions

Ethical decision-making most commonly involves reflection on:

● available options or courses of action
● options that seem unavailable
● consequences, both good and bad, of all possible options (teleology)
● rules, obligations, and values that should direct choices (deontology)
● who should make the choices
● desired goal or outcome.

Equally important is the process of self-reflection. This involves uncovering, sharing, and discussing:

● personal and professional values relevant to the situation (values clarification)
● prejudices or biases that affect objectivity
● previous experiences with similar situations and decisions
● limitations that affect skills or understanding
● motives and intentions, particularly those of self-interest and convenience.

All these elements should come together when you're making an ethical decision. The best way to ensure this may be to use a method with which every NP is familiar: the *nursing process,* adapted to ethical decision making.

APPLYING THE NURSING PROCESS TO ETHICAL DECISION MAKING

The nursing process is a continuous, interdependent, systematic organization of cognitive behaviors designed to resolve problems and promote well-being. The essential steps of the nursing process include assessment, planning, *implementation,* and *evaluation.*

Assessment begins with the NP's initial contact with a patient. It involves collecting systematic data, identifying the patient's needs, performing or ordering preventive and diagnostic procedures based on the patient's age and history, and identifying health and medical risk factors.

Planning includes making a diagnosis and formulating a treatment plan. In collaboration with the patient and the family, the NP establishes a mutually acceptable cost-effective treatment plan that maximizes health.

Implementation involves an individualized appropriate plan of care based on scientific principles, theoretical knowledge, and clinical expertise. The NP conducts and interprets diagnostic tests, prescribes pharmacological agents and therapies, provides relevant patient education, and makes appropriate referrals to other health professionals and community agencies.

Evaluation includes systematic follow-up by determining outcomes against outcome criteria, and reassessing and modifying the management plan as necessary to achieve health and medical goals.

You can effectively use the same continuous, systematic, and rational approach when making ethical decisions.

Assessment

● Gather facts, perceptions, and opinions about the ethical problem. Read the patient's chart. Talk with the patient and his family, other health care providers, and anyone who may be familiar with the patient's values.

● Identify the people involved in the problem and assess their roles, responsibilities, authority, and decision-making abilities.

● Identify available resources. These may include the ethics committee, chaplain, nurse ethicist, counselors, and facilitators. Resources also may include hospital policies, as well as literature on similar cases.

● Help clarify values for all participants.

Planning

● Identify the types of moral dilemmas involved — beneficence, autonomy, justice, fidelity, nonmaleficence, confidentiality, or veracity. Identify the specific issues involved by examining the rights, duties, and values that are in conflict.

● Identify possible courses of action, along with their probable and possible risks and benefits (teleology).

● Formulate and assign priorities to the ethical goals or objectives desired by the people involved.

● Determine the ethical obligations of those involved and the ethical principles that shape their actions (deontology).

Implementation

● Develop an ethical goal that maximizes the good, working with others involved, as appropriate.

● Determine the course of action that will produce results closest to those of the ethical ideal.

● Determine if that course of action violates legal or moral principles. If so, modify or change the course of action until it doesn't do so.

● Carry out the agreed-upon course of action.

Evaluation

● Determine if the results approximate the ethical ideal.

● If the results fall short of the ideal, determine what new moral dilemmas have been created.

● Reenter the decision process in the assessment phase to resolve additional moral dilemmas.

Although this process imposes the structure and objectivity necessary for resolving a moral dilemma, it doesn't provide all the answers. Because human beings are fallible, it's impossible for anyone to gather all the facts or to be completely without bias. Psychological and emotional factors can play havoc with fairness and impartiality. (See *The nurse practitioner's role on the ethics committee,* page 210.)

COMMUNICATION SKILLS

When it's time to make fair and ethical decisions, personality conflicts, political forces, and power plays can sabotage even the best intentions. For this reason, you should use communication skills and management techniques to help promote collaboration and prevent divisiveness. In addition, you should observe the following rules of behavior:

● Act within professional bounds, following the appropriate codes of ethics. (See *Ethical codes for nurse practitioners,* pages 211 and 212.)

● Don't make ethical decisions alone. Seek counsel and advice from other professionals.

● Validate information. Don't base ethical decisions on rumors, innuendo, hearsay, first impressions, or snap judgments.

● If religious faith and spiritual values are important to you or others involved in the ethical dilemma, include prayer in the decision-making process.

ACTING AS A PATIENT ADVOCATE

One of your most important moral obligations is your role as a *patient advocate.* When a patient must make an

The nurse practitioner's role on the ethics committee

If your organization doesn't have an ethics committee, you may be able to help start one. If one already exists, you may be able to play a vital role by serving as a committee member and by educating patients, residents, and their families about the existence and work of the ethics committee. It's of little value for an organization to have an ethics committee if patients, residents, and their families don't know how the committee can help them.

When your organization informs those it serves about their rights as patients or residents, make sure it also tells them about their right to access an ethics committee for help in making difficult choices about care and treatment. At the very least, all patients or residents should receive a simple paragraph like this:

"The ethics committee is available to help you and your family as you deal with difficult decisions about your care and what is right and fair. There is no charge for this service. To find out more about the ethics committee, ask your nurse practitioner."

The ethics committee

The ethics committee is usually multidisciplinary. Membership includes nurses, physicians, allied health care professionals, other key members of the care team (respiratory therapists, registered dietitians, licensed clinical social workers, chaplains), administrators, attorneys, ethics experts (like a nurse ethicist), and a community representative who is familiar with the role of the ethics committee and can be a strong patient advocate. Nurse members should include staff, NPs or clinical experts, and nurse administrators.

Key committee functions

The ethics committee has three key functions:
● Develop and revise policies and procedures relevant to ethics (such as policies or procedures on patient rights, advance directives, confidentiality, informed consent, foregoing treatment and resuscitation, and organization ethics.)
● Educate committee members to develop a level of competency consistent with the guidelines of the American Society for Bioethics and Humanities Core Competencies for Health Care Ethics Consultation, and then educate staff, administration, trustees, patients, families, and the community about issues of importance in health care ethics.
● Develop a team to provide case consultation through facilitation, discussion, research, negotiation, resolution, and documentation of difficult cases and evaluation of outcomes to monitor and improve quality.

ethical decision, you should help him resolve his moral dilemma in ways that enhance personal values, priorities, freedom, dignity, and *quality of life.*

As an advocate, you must never impose personal agendas or values on a patient. By listening carefully to him and asking thoughtful questions, you may be able to help the patient and his family make ethical decisions. Consider asking the patient to describe the problem to you, and then ask him the following questions to help him clarify his thoughts.
● What have other health care professionals told you about the situation?
● What options are you considering?
● Have you considered making a list of the best and worst things for each option you're considering?
● What else would it help you to know as you're making the decision?
● Is there anyone you'd like to speak with about this decision (for example,

Ethical codes for nurse practitioners

One of the most important ethical codes for nurses is the American Nurses Association (ANA) code. The International Council of Nurses (ICN), an organization based in Geneva, Switzerland, that seeks to improve the standards and status of nursing worldwide, has also published a code of ethics.

ANA code of ethics

The ANA views both nurses and patients as individuals who possess basic rights and responsibilities and whose values and circumstances should command respect at all times. The ANA code provides guidance for carrying out nursing responsibilities consistent with the ethical obligations of the profession.

According to the ANA code, the nurse:
● provides services with respect for human dignity and the uniqueness of the patient, unrestricted by considerations of social or economic status, personal attributes, or the nature of health problems
● safeguards the patient's right to privacy by judiciously protecting information of a confidential nature
● acts to safeguard the patient and the public when health and safety are affected by incompetent, unethical, or illegal practice of any person
● assumes responsibility and accountability for individual nursing judgments and actions
● maintains competence in nursing
● exercises informed judgment and uses individual competence and qualifications as criteria in seeking consultation, accepting responsibilities, and delegating nursing activities to others
● participates in activities that contribute to the ongoing development of the profession's body of knowledge
● participates in the profession's efforts to implement and improve standards of nursing
● participates in the profession's efforts to establish and maintain conditions of employment conducive to high-quality nursing care
● collaborates with members of the health professions and other citizens in promoting community and national efforts to meet the health needs of the public.

ICN code of ethics

According to the ICN, the fundamental responsibility of the nurse is fourfold: to promote health, to prevent illness, to restore health, and to alleviate suffering.

The ICN further states that the need for nursing is universal. Inherent in nursing is respect for life, dignity, and the rights of man. It's unrestricted by considerations of nationality, race, color, age, sex, politics, or social status.

Nurses and people
● The nurse's primary responsibility is to people who require nursing care.
● The nurse, in providing care, respects the beliefs, values, and customs of the individual.
● The nurse holds personal information in confidence and uses judgment in sharing this information.

Nurses and practice
● The nurse carries personal responsibility for nursing practice and for maintaining competence by continual learning.
● The nurse maintains the highest standards of nursing possible within the reality of a specific situation.
● The nurse uses good judgment in relation to individual competence when accepting and delegating responsibilities.
● The nurse, when acting in a professional capacity, should at all times maintain standards of personal conduct that would reflect credit upon the profession.

Nurses and society
● The nurse shares with other citizens the responsibility for initiating and supporting

(continued)

Ethical codes for nurse practitioners *(continued)*

action to meet the health and social needs of the public.

Nurses and coworkers
● The nurse sustains a cooperative relationship with coworkers in nursing and other fields.
● The nurse takes appropriate action to safeguard the patient when his care is endangered by a coworker or any other person.

Nurses and the profession
● The nurse plays the major role in determining and implementing desirable standards of nursing practice and nursing education.
● The nurse is active in developing a core of professional knowledge.
● The nurse, acting through the professional organization, participates in establishing and maintaining equitable social and economic working conditions in nursing.

---

clergy, counselor, social worker, trusted friend, or lawyer)?
● What is the hardest part about coping with this decision?
● What things in the past have helped you cope with difficult decisions or situations?
● What would make it easier for you and your family to talk about this situation?
● What do you think is the best thing to do?

Selected references

American Society for Bioethics and Humanities: *www.asbh.org*

Banja, J. "Ethical Decision Making: Origins, Process, and Applications to Case Management." *The Case Manager* 10(5):41-47, September-October 1999.

Botes, A. "A comparison Between the Ethics of Justice and the Ethics of Care," *Journal of Advanced Nursing* 32(5):1071-75, November 2000.

Botes, A. "An Integrated Approach to Ethical Decision-Making in the Health Team," *Journal of Advanced Nursing* 32(5): 1076-82, November 2000.

Butz, A.M., et al. "Ethical Conflicts Experienced by Certified Pediatric Nurse Practitioners in Ambulatory Settings," *Journal of Pediatric Health Care*, 12(4):183-90, July-August 1998.

Carter, M.A. "A Synthetic Approach to Bioethical Inquiry," *Theoretical Medicine and Bioethics* 21(3):217-34, 2000.

Furrow, B.R., et al. *Bioethics: Health Care Law and Ethics*, 3rd ed. St. Paul, Minn.: Westgroup, 1997.

Gold, M.F. "Pain Management: The Ethical Dilemma," *Provider* 24(5):44-46, 48, 50, May 1998.

Hinman, L.H., ed. Ethics Updates: *http:ethics.acusd.edu.*

Hoffman, P.B. "Improving Ethics Committee Effectiveness," *Healthcare Executive* 16(1):58-59, January-February 2001.

Howe, E.G. "Ethics and Alzheimer's Disease," *Journal of Clinical Ethics* 9(1):3-96, Spring 1998.

Meisel, A., et al. "Seven Legal Barriers to End-of-Life Care: Myths, Realities, and Grains of Truth," *JAMA* 284(19):2495-2501, November 2000.

National Institutes of Health: *www.nih.gov/sigs/bioethics.*

Chapter Eight

ETHICAL CONFLICTS IN CLINICAL PRACTICE

As the number of *nurse practitioners (NPs)* has increased in our health care system, so too have their responsibilities and exposure to ethical conflicts. Not only are NPs faced with the same rapid advances in medical research and technology as all health care providers, but they're also faced with the seemingly daily changes in and expansions of their *scope of practice.* Ethical decision making for NPs is further complicated by the wide range of clinical areas of practice and the services they render, including taking histories; conducting physical examinations; ordering, performing, and interpreting a range of diagnostic tests; prescribing and monitoring the effects of medications; and often acting as the sole health care providers for specific patient populations.

This chapter discusses six major areas of ethical conflict in which you, as an NP, may become involved — the right to die, organ transplantation, critically ill neonates, acquired immunodeficiency syndrome (AIDS), abortion and reproductive technology, and genetic engineering and screening.

Ethical dilemmas resist easy resolution. The choice you have to make is often between two equally desirable or two equally undesirable alternatives. By learning as much as possible about the underlying ethical principles, you'll be better equipped to make ethically sound and defensible decisions. The more you practice ethical thinking, the more confident you'll become in your ability to make decisions.

GETTING HELP

It's unrealistic to think that you can solve every problem. When difficult ethical problems arise in your practice area, discuss them candidly with other members of the health care team, including the patient's physician, social workers, psychologists, the clergy, and ethics committee members. By learning as much as possible, you can facilitate the decision-making process for the patient, his family, and his physician. (See *The ethics committee,* page 214.)

213

The ethics committee

A facility's ethics committee addresses ethical issues regarding the clinical aspects of patient care. It provides a forum for patient, family, and health care providers to resolve difficult conflicts.

The functions of an ethics committee may include:

- policy development (such as developing policies to guide deliberations over individual cases)
- education (such as inviting guest speakers to visit the hospital and discuss ethical concerns)
- case consultation (such as debating the extent of care for a home health care patient who is in a persistent vegetative state)
- addressing a single issue (for instance, reviewing all cases involving nurse practitioners [NPs] who reported suspected child abuse at a clinic)
- addressing problems of a specific group in the population (for example, the American Academy of Pediatrics recommends that hospitals have a standing committee called the "infant bioethical review committee").

Pros and cons

Properly run, an ethics committee provides a safe outlet for venting opposing views on emotionally charged ethical conflicts. The committee process can help to lessen the bias that interferes with rational decision making. It allows for members of disparate disciplines, including doctors, NPs, nurses, clergy, social workers, hospital administrators, and ethicists, to express their views on treatment decisions.

Critics of the ethics committee think that committee decision making is too bureaucratic and slow to be useful in clinical crises. They also point out that one dominating

committee member may intimidate others with opposing views. Furthermore, they contend that doctors may view the committee as a threat to their autonomy in patient care decisions.

Selection of committee members

Committee members should be selected for their ability to work cooperatively in a group. The American Hospital Association recommends the following ratio of committee members: one-third physicians, one-third NPs/nurses, and one-third others, including lay persons, clergy, and other health professionals. Regulations of the Joint Commission on Accreditation of Healthcare Organizations require that nursing staff members participate on the ethics committee.

NP's role on ethics committees

Because of the NP's close contact with the patient, family, and other members of the health care team, she frequently is in a position to identify ethical dilemmas, such as when a family is considering donating an organ from one child to another. In many cases, the NP is the first to recognize potential conflicts among family members or between the doctor and the patient or family.

Before ethics committees were widely used, nurses and NPs had no official outlet for voicing their opinions in ethical debates. In many situations, physicians made ethical decisions about patient care behind closed doors. Now, ethics committees provide NPs with a means to express their views, hear the opinions of others, and understand more deeply the rationale behind ethical decisions.

Right to die

One of the most difficult ethical decisions you may become involved in is whether to initiate or to withhold life-sustaining treatment for patients who

are irreversibly comatose, vegetative, or suffering with end-stage terminal illness. Treatment decisions for these patients are often emotionally troubling. The patient, his family, and the health care team may be asked to choose between a painful and expensive extension of life or immediate and irreversible death. Surrogate decision makers — people who are designated to act when a patient is no longer capable of deciding his own fate — also face tremendous moral and emotional pressures.

As a primary care provider, you may be asked by family members to disregard the patient's expressed wishes, either verbally or in an advanced directive, to withhold life-sustaining treatment. Caught in the middle, you may become frustrated and demoralized and may have difficulty deciding on your responsibilities to an unresponsive patient.

DEFINING DEATH

Complicating the issue is the lack of consensus about what exactly constitutes death. Some people define death as the loss of all vital functions, whereas others look to neurologic criteria such as *brain death* — the irreversible cessation of brain functioning accompanied by ongoing biological functioning in all other parts of the body, maintained by life-support measures.

Some people maintain a strong ethical belief in the absolute sanctity of life. Others argue that it's morally wrong and wasteful of scarce resources to continue life support when a patient's life is devoid of quality or dignity. To provide high quality care for patients facing death, you'll need to become aware of your personal feelings about death and quality-of-life issues.

ORDINARY VS. EXTRAORDINARY TREATMENT

Ordinary means of medical treatment are medications, procedures, and surgeries that offer the patient some hope of benefit without incurring excessive pain or expense. In contrast, extraordinary means, sometimes called heroic measures, merely maintain or prolong

a patient's life, usually at great expense and suffering. Because of the continuing advances in medicine and technology, the distinction between "ordinary" and "extraordinary" treatments is becoming less and less well defined.

The current basis for the definition of "ordinary" and "extraordinary" treatments comes from the 1983 President's Commission for the Study of Ethical Problems in Medicine and Behavioral Research: "The Commission believes that extraordinary treatment is that which, in the patient's view, entails significantly greater burdens than benefits and is therefore undesirable and not obligatory, while ordinary treatment is that which, in the patient's view, produces greater benefits than burdens."

The commission further stated that *health care professionals* aren't obligated to provide treatment that is considered useless or futile.

Discontinuing treatment

Despite the commission's recommendations, countless terminally ill patients continue to receive treatment that is unlikely to do more than prolong a painful death. Determining whether a particular treatment is futile is highly subjective. Not only are many such decisions based on incomplete information, but they may also involve value judgments about quality of life. Although still considered experimental, a computerized mortality prediction system called Acute Physiology and Chronic Health Evaluation (APACHE) can provide essential data to help make these otherwise highly subjective decisions. (See *Understanding APACHE*, page 216.)

Health care providers face incredible emotional pressure when attempting to decide whether to terminate life-sustaining treatment; a patient can't be brought back after all treatment stops. Because of your close relationship with patients and the strong feelings of trust

Understanding APACHE

The Acute Physiology and Chronic Health Evaluation (APACHE) system is a validated prognostic indicator. To help with highly subjective treatment decisions, APACHE, APACHE II, and APACHE III provide objective data regarding a patient's chance of survival. The purpose of the APACHE system is to classify patients and predict the probability of mortality.

APACHE is composed of two parts:
● A physiological score represents the severity of the patient's acute illness; it's determined by ranking (on a 0 to 4 scale) various elements of the sickness of one or more body systems. Patients with 31 or more points have a 70% chance of mortality before discharge from the hospital. (Patients with acute myocardial infarction or burns are evaluated by a separate classification system.)
● The second criterion is the patient's previous health. As expected, age extremes (the very young and very old) and chronic medical problems are associated with a reduced physiological reserve.

APACHE and its revisions have been validated in clinical practice. APACHE II is simpler than the original APACHE, reducing the number of physiological variables measured from 34 to 12. APACHE III compares each individual's medical profile against nearly 18,000 cases in its database before reaching a prognosis with a predictive value of 95%.

that patients have in NPs, you can help them make decisions about their future care by educating them about their right to refuse extraordinary treatment.

RIGHT TO REFUSE TREATMENT
The ethics of the patient's right to refuse treatment is grounded in the principle of respect for the *autonomy*

of the individual. This principle of autonomy has led to the concept of informed consent — the obligation of health care providers to inform the patient of the risks and benefits of a procedure and to obtain permission before the procedure is carried out. Terminally ill patients who receive life-sustaining treatment have an equal right to informed consent. (See *A question of judgment.*)

Because the NP's primary orientation is towards saving and prolonging lives, you may find it difficult to accept a patient's decision not to use life-sustaining treatment. Keep in mind that limiting treatment doesn't mean abandoning the patient. Supportive measures aren't considered extraordinary treatment. A patient who has chosen to forgo life-sustaining treatment still has the right to receive care that preserves his comfort, hygiene, and dignity. As an NP with prescriptive authority, you have a substantial ethical obligation to fulfill the patient's right to adequate pain control, particularly in terminal diseases.

Health care workers' rights
Although patients have the right to decide whether to accept or forgo heroic measures, they don't have the right to insist on treatments that provide no medical benefit. If you believe that you'll violate your own *values* by implementing a certain treatment, you have an obligation to arrange for the transfer of the patient's care to another provider. Likewise, if you believe that you'll be violating your values by withholding treatment, you should also request the transfer. This right is called the "conscience clause" and applies to several situations, including refusing to assist in abortions and the noninitiation or withdrawal of life-sustaining treatment.

A question of judgment

COURT CASE

In this 1999 Massachusetts case, a 29-year-old patient with asthma was brought to Massachusetts General Hospital's emergency department (ED) by her older sister for treatment of an acute asthmatic attack. Over the years the patient had received ample patient teaching about her condition.

Initially, the patient was placed on an oxygen mask and her blood gases were monitored. The physician decided that she needed to be intubated. Both the patient and her sister disagreed with the intubation plan and decided to run from the ED. They were chased and caught by the hospital security guards and physician, and the patient was returned to the ED. Despite her protests, the patient was then placed in four-point restraints and forcibly intubated. She recovered from her asthmatic attack and was discharged.

Approximately 2 years later, the woman died after refusing to go to the hospital for another acute asthmatic attack. A wrongful death suit was filed by her family, alleging that her death was attributed to her fear and mistrust of hospitals, physicians, and nurses as a result of the trauma from the forced intubation incident. The family's right to sue for wrongful death was upheld by the court. The court determined that a medical emergency justifies nonconsensual treatment only when it isn't possible or feasible to obtain informed consent from a person legally entitled to provide or withhold the consent. Even in a life-threatening situation, the judgment of the health care provider can't substitute for that of a mentally competent adult patient or family member.

What the NP can learn

A mentally competent adult patient or his family member's judgment is upheld even if the decision differs from medical advice. *Shine v. Vega,* 709 N.E. 2d 58 (Mass., 1999).

DOCUMENTING A PATIENT'S WISHES

A patient who has a strong desire to request or reject aggressive treatment measures should document his wishes. He should also designate a surrogate decision maker to speak for him if he can no longer make his own health care decisions. Statements that indicate a patient's wishes in the event he loses his decision-making capability are known as *advance directives,* the patient's best means of ensuring that his wishes will be respected. The advance directive includes a *living will,* which goes into effect when the patient can't make decisions, and the *durable power of attorney,* which authorizes another person to make those decisions. If a patient has both, the person with durable power should be in complete support of the patient's wishes. No family member or health care provider can then override the person with the durable power of attorney.

Although specific treatments can be requested in an advance directive, most people execute a living will to ensure that no extraordinary procedures are used to sustain or prolong life. A durable power of attorney designates a surrogate decision maker who will have full authority to carry out the patient's wishes regarding health care decisions. The authority of this surrogate decision maker is based on the principle of substituted judgment — allowing the surrogate to make the same decisions the patient would, if he were able.

Advance directives, while useful, haven't ended the controversy over a patient's right to limit treatment. Critics contend that they represent the

When family members contest a living will

A living will isn't a guarantee that the patient's expressed wishes will be honored. The language in many living wills is vague and unclear. Patients who have added specific requests to a standardized form (for example, requesting termination of tube feedings) may not realize that such requests may conflict with state law. Physicians, nurse practitioners (NPs), and nurses sometimes find it difficult to carry out wishes expressed years ago, before more modern treatment options became available.

The family's response to the living will also can create problems. Family members may not know about the living will or may choose to ignore it in their turmoil over "letting go." As the following case history demonstrates, all health care workers, including NPs, can be caught in the crossfire.

Conflicting demands

Esther Summerson was brought to the emergency department (ED) in respiratory distress after a long history of chronic obstructive pulmonary disease (COPD). The ED staff asked Mrs. Summerson if she wanted help breathing, but they couldn't get a clear response before she lost consciousness. She was intubated and transferred to the intensive care unit.

When Mrs. Summerson's older daughter, Jean, arrived at the hospital, she was upset to find that her mother had been placed on a ventilator. She showed the staff a copy of her mother's living will, specifying that her mother not be placed on a ventilator or receive supplementary nutrition. Miss Summerson also produced a form giving her durable power of attorney. As her mother's designated decision maker, she demanded that her mother be removed from the ventilator.

Susan Johnson, Mrs. Summerson's younger daughter, reached the hospital about an hour after her sister. Although her mother was still unresponsive, Mrs. Johnson didn't want her removed from the ventilator. "I don't know what I'd do without Mom," she sobbed. "I want you to do everything you can for her."

Implementing facility policy

Fortunately, the facility had developed procedures for resolving this sort of conflict. Mrs. Summerson's NP, pulmonary specialist, primary nurse, priest, and a representative of the facility's ethics committee called a meeting with Miss Summerson, Mrs. Johnson, and Mrs. Johnson's husband. They explained the living will and Miss Summerson's role as the surrogate decision maker, emphasizing that Mrs. Summerson's living will clearly specified her opposition to the ventilator. Without the ventilator, their mother might breathe on her own or she might die. If she did die, it would be from lung damage caused by her long-standing COPD, not from their desire to honor her living will. Each step of the procedure was carefully reviewed.

As a result of this discussion, Mrs. Johnson changed her mind and agreed to removal of the ventilator. All three family members decided to be present when this occurred. After they had a chance to talk to Mrs. Summerson and express their love for her, the balloon was deflated and the tube removed. Mrs. Summerson died quietly 2 days later, with her daughters and her son-in-law by her side.

first step toward active *euthanasia,* or "mercy killing." These people believe that advance directives such as living wills should be restricted to a narrow range of circumstances. (See *When family members contest a living will.*)

Many states have enacted so-called natural death acts to encourage practitioners to abide by a living will by granting statutory enforcement. These laws vary from state to state; several require a "reasonable effort by the physician" to transfer the patient to a physician who will abide by the living will.

Helping the patient plan ahead

Like other professionals who care for the critically ill, NPs have the opportunity to act as *patient advocates.* The patient may look to you as a primary source for guidance. As a primary care provider, you may be in a position to make the ultimate medical decisions to initiate or limit treatment. You can also help the patient express his wishes concerning his health care and guide him in translating these desires into advance directives.

When you're discussing limiting treatment with a patient, consider these suggestions:

● Present options such as do-not-resuscitate (DNR) orders in a realistic but positive context. Reassure the patient that he'll continue to receive supportive care and pain medication.

● Pay attention to the patient's questions and misunderstandings. Be especially alert for unexpressed fears.

● During your discussions with the patient, note his nonverbal cues and emotional responses.

Despite your best efforts to provide objective advice, the patient may not be able to reach a decision about initiating or terminating care. Remember that you must respect the patient's explicit refusal to participate in health care decisions.

WHEN THE PATIENT SHOULDN'T DECIDE

At times, you may question whether a particular patient should be allowed to decide to refuse life-sustaining treatment. Consider whether the patients described below are capable of making life-and-death decisions.

● Joe Ryan suffered a stroke 2 years ago that left him paralyzed on the right side and unable to speak. He was admitted to the hospital with sepsis caused by infected stasis ulcers of his lower legs. Mr. Ryan's physician recommended bilateral above-the-knee amputations. As he was being prepared for the surgery, Mr. Ryan became visibly agitated.

● Mary Kane suffered a severe head injury in a traffic accident that also left her a quadriplegic and dependent on a ventilator. Three months after the accident, she insisted that the ventilator be removed. A hospital psychiatrist determined that Mrs. Kane was seriously depressed.

● George Bowen has Alzheimer's disease. He can't remember a recent conversation, the names of his three children, or how to find his bedroom, although he's still continent and responsive. When Mr. Bowen was admitted to the hospital with his third heart attack, his wife told the physician he had begged to be allowed to "meet his maker."

The concept of *informed consent* creates ethical dilemmas in situations in which the patient's ability to make an informed judgment about his treatment options is questionable. If the patient is nonverbal, depressed, demented, or semiconscious, can he truly consent to or refuse life-sustaining treatment?

It's important to remember that some patients may remain capable of expressing health care preferences even when they can't manage in other areas, such as personal care, eating, or speaking.

Standards for judging decision-making ability

Commonly used standards for judging decision-making capability include:

● the ability to indicate a choice

● a clear understanding of the issues at hand

● the ability to reason based on the information given

● an appreciation of the true nature of the situation.

If a patient is incapable of making a decision, it becomes the duty of a surrogate decision maker or the health care team to act in his best interest.

MAKING DECISIONS FOR THE PATIENT

Two ethical principles can be used in making decisions for an incapacitated patient. The **substituted judgment** test professes to make the same decision the patient would, if he were capable (the principle of autonomy). Alternatively, the decision may be based on the best interest standard, or deciding what is best for the patient, given his current circumstances (the principle of **beneficence**). Both principles are ethically valid. If the two are at odds, they can create dilemmas for family members, physicians, and NPs.

FOSTERING COMMUNICATION

Effective communication is essential when helping families to decide whether to limit or withhold treatment. If you're helping family members or surrogates while they're making life-and-death decisions, the following guidelines can improve communication.
● Create a quiet, private, and unhurried environment — keep all communication simple, factual, and direct.
● Encourage and allow enough time for questions.
● Express medical information in simple, clear language.
● Ask decision makers to summarize and check their responses.
● Clarify missing or misunderstood information.

Keep in mind that this may be the most heart-rending decision family members or surrogates will ever be asked to make. They need plenty of time, care, and understanding.

MERCY KILLING

Euthanasia (a term that means painless death) and assisted suicide further confuse the right-to-die issue. Although DNR orders and other decisions to limit treatment sometimes are referred to as passive euthanasia, the term euthanasia usually refers to active intervention, such as lethal injection to bring about death (mercy killing). The issue of whether physicians, NPs, or other health care professionals can ever ethically assist in taking a life is hotly debated in professional journals and the mass media.

In 1994, Oregon voters legalized physician-assisted suicide. Enactment of the law was delayed in the courts, but similar bills were introduced in other states. The Oregon law states (with qualifying safeguards) that a terminally ill person can ask a primary care provider to prescribe a lethal, oral medication to take when the patient deems it appropriate. Although assisted-suicide laws remain on the books in Oregon and several other states, the federal Assisted Suicide Funding Restriction Act of 1997 has, to a large extent, negated the effects of these laws. This act forbids the use of federal funds to cause or assist suicide or mercy killing. Several states considering assisted-suicide legislation have dropped it, and other states that had passed assisted-suicide laws have since withdrawn them. Check with your state board of nursing about the legal status of assisted suicide in your state and about the role of the NP in such cases.

Proponents of euthanasia and assisted suicide base their argument on the right to self-determination. They argue that if a terminally ill patient is in unendurable pain that can't be controlled, physician-assisted suicide might be seen as a more humane alternative. Public reaction to highly publicized cases of assisted suicide indicates that many people support a patient's right to control his own fate. Dr. Jack Kevorkian, who during his career assisted the suicide of more than 130 terminally ill people, still has numerous supporters, including juries who have acquitted him of criminal charges brought over the years by the state of Michigan. However, in the fall of 1998, Dr. Kevorkian raised the legal and ethical stakes.

On the nationally broadcast network news show *60 Minutes,* Dr. Kevorkian not only admitted to administering a lethal medication to a patient without the patient's assistance but also made and played a videotape that showed the incident. The patient, who had amyotrophic lateral sclerosis (Lou Gehrig disease), had requested that Dr. Kevorkian kill him and had signed a consent form and release. Dr. Kevorkian admitted that his motivation for the act was for him to be tried in a test case for active euthanasia. He was convicted of second-degree murder and in April 1999 was sentenced to up to 25 years in prison. (See *Hemlock Society: Euthanasia advocates.*)

Many health care providers, however, find the mercy killing concept repugnant. While many NPs would agree with allowing the family of a comatose patient to withdraw food and fluids, most oppose more active forms of euthanasia. Allowing euthanasia, many argue, eventually would lead to patients being selectively put to death without consent. The potential object of mercy killing — a patient with Alzheimer's disease or a patient in a **persistent vegetative state,** for example — has lost the capacity to express his wishes. Family members and health care providers don't know if the patient truly desires to die nor do they have the moral right to make this decision for him.

All major professional nursing and medical organizations have taken positions against assisted suicide. The **American Nurses Association (ANA)** has reaffirmed this position repeatedly through its publications. On its Web site, the **American Medical Association (AMA)** has the following statement about assisted suicide: "While the

> ## Hemlock Society: Euthanasia advocates
>
> The Hemlock Society supports the option of active voluntary euthanasia for patients with advanced terminal or severe, incurable illnesses. Founded in 1980, the group now claims over 30,000 members. Its goals include promoting a climate of public opinion tolerant of the terminally ill person's right to end his own life in a planned manner. It also seeks to improve existing laws on assisted suicide.
>
> The Hemlock Society doesn't encourage suicide for any primary emotional, traumatic, or financial reasons in the absence of terminal illness. The group, in fact, approves of suicide-prevention work. To obtain further information, contact the Hemlock Society at (503) 342-5748.

AMA supports the right to remove life-sustaining medical treatment — including artificial feeding — from dying patients or those in irreversible comas, it firmly states that a physician should never intentionally cause death."

COST CONSIDERATIONS
You may be offended by the mention of cost considerations in the context of limiting treatment for the terminally ill patient. Such considerations, however, are ethically legitimate. The necessity of conserving resources eventually will force the public to consider this issue. Health care resources — including organs available for transplantation, beds in the **intensive care unit,** and experimental drugs — are costly and limited in quantity. Some individuals have begun to debate the equity of giving a disproportionate share of the most expensive medical treatments and procedures to elderly patients who are gravely ill. **Medicare** pays out over $21

billion, or about 30% of its budget, for bills incurred in the final year of life. Some policy makers believe that the patient's age should be a valid ethical consideration in the delivery of medical care, especially when so much money is spent to achieve relatively small gains in life expectancy.

Health care in the United States is already rationed to a degree, through policies that discourage the poor from seeking medical attention. Unaffordably high insurance rates, underfinanced state medical programs, and crowded clinics, in effect, ration care.

Deciding how to ration lifesaving technology is an ethical dilemma of huge proportion. Ultimately, it will have to be resolved by society at large through laws based on the ethical principle of distributive justice.

Organ transplantation

The benefits of organ transplantation are widely recognized by health care professionals and the general public. Nevertheless, organ transplantation poses serious ethical concerns. Transplant procedures affect families of the donor and the recipient, nurses, NPs, physicians, and even ambulance attendants at the deepest emotional level. In such a highly charged atmosphere, conflicts of rights easily can develop.
● If the potential donor is a child, questions may arise as to the validity of informed consent.
● Controversy may occur over when to declare a potential donor dead.
● The wishes of a potential donor's family may conflict with the needs of a transplant patient.
● Because the number of available donor organs is limited, difficult choices must be made about which patients should receive transplants.
● Many transplants are prohibitively expensive; questions arise as to

whether subsidizing the procedure is a just allocation of health care resources.
● In light of the limited number of available donor organs and the high cost of the procedure, questions arise as to the patient's right to multiple transplants.

NPs usually aren't responsible for the ultimate medical decisions about an organ transplant; however, you can play a critical role in resolving ethical conflicts.

PROTECTING THE RIGHTS OF POTENTIAL DONORS

Some transplantation procedures pose few ethical problems. An autograft, in which tissue is transplanted from one part of the patient's body to another (such as a skin graft to treat a third-degree burn), is a good example. Certain types of transplants from one person to another (allograft), including blood transfusions and cornea or bone marrow transplants, also are widely accepted and untainted by ethical concerns.

The most difficult ethical issues surround the procurement of vital organs, such as hearts, kidneys, livers, and lungs. In these instances, organ procurement remains ethical only if steps are taken to ensure that the donor's life and functional integrity aren't compromised.

Nonmaleficence

At first glance, removing an organ from a healthy person who has nothing to gain from the procedure seems to violate the ethical principle of **nonmaleficence** — the obligation to "do no harm." However, when providing care, the NP encounters many instances in which the principle of nonmaleficence can't be strictly applied. Some harm, in the form of an invasive or a potentially risky procedure, must be incurred in diagnosing and treating many diseases.

When a living person donates the organ, the key issue is informed consent. From both an ethical and a legal standpoint, informed consent requires the donor to be fully aware of all risks and benefits that can result from the transplant procedure. Because relatives, particularly identical twins or full siblings, typically provide the closest match for a transplanted organ, a great deal of emotional pressure can be exerted on a potential donor. Extreme feelings of guilt and emotional distress may disturb a potential donor's ability to render informed consent.

Child donors

Special problems arise when the potential donor is a child. Because, in most cases, a **minor's** consent is legally invalid, the parents or **legal guardians** must give substitute consent. Sometimes the wishes of the child and the parents are clearly the same. A 13-year-old girl whose parents support her wish to donate a kidney to her 5-year-old brother can probably give valid informed consent. But what about a 3-year-old child who doesn't understand and can't realistically be expected to express his opinion about organ donation? Can his parents ethically "volunteer" this child to donate one of his kidneys to a brother or sister in renal failure? Parents have a moral obligation to protect the life and well-being of all their children. Sometimes it's unclear how to best uphold this obligation. Which are more important — the rights of the healthy child or the rights of the child who needs the kidney?

In a widely publicized 1991 incident, physicians at the City of Hope Medical Center, in Duarte, Calif., transplanted bone marrow into Anissa Ayala, a 19-year-old woman with potentially fatal leukemia. The marrow came from her infant sister, Marissa. The parents said that they conceived Marissa to provide bone marrow to save Anissa's life. This marked the first time that a family publicly admitted to conceiving a child to serve as an organ or tissue donor.

The incident raised troubling ethical questions. Does conceiving a child as a source of donated organs violate the principle that children should be brought into the world and cherished for their own sake and no other motive? If prenatal tests indicate that the fetus has the wrong tissue type to serve as a donor, is an abortion justifiable? Selling organs is both unethical and illegal in many countries, but the legal and ethical status of conceiving potential donors remains unclear.

CADAVERIC DONORS

Harvesting organs from a deceased donor poses a different set of ethical problems. Perhaps the most fundamental issue involves the actual definition of death. Although some organs and tissues, such as bone, skin, cornea, and even kidneys, can be transplanted after complete cardiac arrest, other organs, including the heart, lungs, liver, and pancreas, aren't viable unless they're taken from a brain-dead, or "beating heart," cadaver.

Most states recognize the definition of brain death set forth by the Uniform Determination of Death Act as the legal definition of death. In general terms, a patient is pronounced brain-dead when all functional activity in every area of the brain, including the brain stem, stops. Significantly, this definition of death isn't universally accepted by health care workers, ethicists, or lay people. Many find it difficult to declare death when other aspects of bodily function continue, even if by artificial support.

The issue of declaring brain death must be approached cautiously. The determination that a person is brain-dead should be made by neurologic consult and never by a physician who

National Organ Transplant Act

In response to widespread public interest in organ transplantation, Congress enacted the National Organ Transplant Act of 1984 (PL 98-507). This act:
● prohibits the sale of organs
● provides funding for grants to organ procurement agencies
● establishes a national organ-sharing system.

Task Force on Organ Transplantation

This act also convened a 25-member Task Force on Organ Transplantation with members representing medicine, law, theology, ethics, allied health, the health insurance industry, and the general public. Representatives from the Office of the Surgeon General, the National Institutes of Health, the Food and Drug Administration, and the Health Care Financing Administration also were appointed to the task force. This task force examined the medical, legal, ethical, economic, and social issues created by organ transplantation.

In its final report, the task force concluded that the best way to close the gap between the small number of organ donors and the large number of potential transplant recipients was to actively solicit donations from bereaved families. As a result, the task force recommended that all state legislatures introduce and enact legislation requiring health care professionals to present organ donation as an option to families ("required request").

Assertive approach

Required request policies are legally mandated in many states. This assertive approach to organ procurement has proved highly successful; as many as 80% of families given the option to become donor families ultimately do so. Significantly, studies show that organ donation can facilitate the grieving process and speed recovery for the bereaved family.

is involved in organ removal. No request for organ donation should be made until the family understands the finality of brain death.

Informed consent

The Uniform Anatomical Gift Act allows a person to donate specific organs or even his entire body for organ transplantation. A patient who before death indicated his willingness to be an organ donor could be considered to have given informed consent. True informed consent, however, requires that the patient have the option to withdraw consent at any time before a medical procedure. Therefore, the final decision is left up to the potential donor's family, even if it results in the loss of an organ donation.

Approaching a potential donor's family

All states have enacted required request acts. These laws require hospitals to ask families of potential organ donors to permit donation. The required request laws are intended to increase organ availability. (See *National Organ Transplant Act.*)

Most required request laws are fair to the families of potential donors. Family members are under no compulsion to grant permission to donate organs. Most required request acts grant an exclusion if the request will cause the family severe emotional distress.

These laws may create serious ethical conflicts, however, for an NP who opposes organ transplantation or who finds the idea of approaching a grieving family offensive. Should you be forced to request organ donation regardless of your feelings? One solution to this dilemma is assigning the job of approaching the donor's family to a specially trained organ procurement team.

Some tips to keep in mind when making a request for an organ donation from a patient's family:
● Approach family members tactfully.
● Make sure you know enough about transplantation to answer their questions.
● Explain the potential good that can result from organ donation.
● Remember that the family's decision must be respected.

Caring for a potential donor

If you're directing the care for a patient who's a potential donor, your ethical responsibility includes maintaining his dignity as a human being even after he's declared brain-dead. You'll also need to adhere to your facility's policies and procedures for discontinuing medication and avoiding procedures or medications that could damage organs to be used for transplant.

Maintaining a brain-dead patient until preparations for the transplant are complete raises additional ethical questions. If death is defined as brain death, doesn't the patient have the right to die when this determination is made? If not, how long can he be ethically maintained on a life-support system? One day? One week? Is this a justifiable allocation of resources? Some feel that the effort and money spent to maintain a brain-dead organ donor for any appreciable period might be better spent helping living patients.

USING ORGANS FROM ANENCEPHALIC INFANTS

Anencephaly is the congenital absence of most or all of the cerebral hemispheres. Many anencephalic infants are stillborn, but others have a func-

tional brain stem and live for a short time after birth.

Anencephalic infants might seem to be ideal organ donors. Their immune systems are still immature, reducing the chance of rejection. In addition, their small organs can be readily used in children, who commonly encounter the most trouble locating a suitable donor.

The anencephalic infant, however, doesn't meet the criteria for brain death. Although severely debilitated and with a very limited life expectancy, anencephalic infants have a functioning brain stem and, by law, are considered to be in a persistent vegetative state or a coma, rather than brain-dead. Until an anencephalic infant meets the clinical criteria for brain death, his organs can't ethically, or legally, be used for transplantation.

Laws have been proposed that would increase the supply of organs available for donation from anencephalic infants by broadening the definition of brain death (to discount brain stem function). Another, called presumed consent, would presume every person would donate unless they carried a card stating otherwise. (See *Organ donation and the concept of consent*, page 226.)

SELECTING TRANSPLANT RECIPIENTS

The number of potential transplant recipients far exceeds the number of available donors. How should one determine who receives a transplant and who is turned down?

Medical and physical factors rule out some matches. For example, the donor and the recipient must have compatible blood and tissue types and be fairly close in size and age (it would be impossible to place a 30-year-old accident victim's heart in the chest cavity of a 5-year-old patient). Beyond these limitations, the selection of

Organ donation and the concept of consent

Recent legislative initiatives to increase the supply of organs available for donation have sought to broaden the definition of consent. One recent proposal is based on the concept of presumed consent — the assumption that all sane and rational persons would consent to donate organs if they had the chance to do so.

Under this legislation, every person would be considered an organ donor unless they carried a card stating they did *not* want to donate their organs. Rather than being asked if they wished to have their loved one's organs transplanted, family members would be asked if they had any objections to transplantation.

A violation of informed consent?

Although the doctrine of presumed consent is applied to other aspects of health care law, when applied to organ donation, presumed consent is a controversial idea. Opponents argue that it's coercive and violates the right to informed consent. It contradicts the widely held belief that an individual should have free choice in all decisions related to his own body.

Recipients with unhealthy lifestyles

Another concern is transplanting organs into people whose unhealthy lifestyles have destroyed their health. Mickey Mantle's 1995 liver transplant is a case in point. He had admitted causing damage through years of alcohol and drug abuse. When he died quickly of lung cancer, his long-term smoking became an issue, too. Considering his lifestyle, should he have been a successful transplant candidate?

Ethically, the principle of distributive justice could work both ways in lifestyle cases. Underlying the principle is the belief in equal treatment, which suggests that Mr. Mantle should have had an even chance at a new liver. In the other view, distributive justice applied to scarce resources says the organs should go to people more likely to sustain them with a healthy lifestyle.

To ensure that transplant recipients are selected as fairly as possible, most medical centers have adopted the following guidelines.

Coordinating transplants

A regional organ donation center should coordinate the matching of transplant recipients and potential donors. The principle of "first come, first served" should form one criterion for selection.

All transplant decisions should be made by a committee under the auspices of an impartial organization such as the ***Red Cross*** and include a physician, an NP or a nurse, a lawyer, a religious leader, and a well-informed layperson.

Determining need

The selection procedure should be based on need as well as the potential for survival. Patients with the greatest need (those closest to death) and best survival potential are assigned the highest priority.

transplant recipients depends entirely on value judgments. As a result, the potential for serious value conflicts and unethical behavior is tremendous. For example, the high cost of transplantation raises questions about the fair distribution of organs. Should a wealthy or well-insured patient be given priority over an indigent patient with a similar need? (See *Choosing between potential transplant recipients.*)

Choosing between potential transplant recipients

CASE STUDY IN ETHICS

One concern about organ transplantation is the potential for elitism when choosing one recipient over another. Consider the following situation, in which the committee on organ donation and transplantation at a major teaching hospital had to choose between two potential liver recipients.

Patron's daughter

Jodi Morgan, a 5-year-old girl, had received a liver transplant 18 months earlier. Although her initial response was promising, she'd recently been hospitalized again with signs of irreversible hepatic failure.

Jodi was born with multiple birth defects. Besides biliary atresia, which led to her need for a transplant, she had only one functioning kidney and a cyanotic heart defect. She was mildly retarded, still unable to speak, and had only recently mastered toilet training.

Jodi's father, Jack, was a prominent local businessman, politician, and a patron of the hospital. He wanted Jodi placed at the head of the transplant registry for a second liver transplant. She had spent 4 months on the registry before her first transplant. Nonetheless, rumors had spread that Mr. Morgan had "bought" Jodi's first transplant by making a sizable donation to the hospital's new cardiology wing.

Mother of three

Brenda DeStefano, a 22-year-old mother of three young children, headed the list of potential liver recipients. In chronic hepatic failure for nearly 2 years, she had been on the transplant list most of that time and was now near death. She was unemployed and had no health insurance. Because the federal government won't reimburse for liver transplants, the hospital stood little chance of being paid for her surgery.

Committee decision

According to state law, Jodi couldn't receive a second transplant unless she was returned to the registry. But should she be placed at the head of the list?

The committee struggled with many ethical questions:

- Mr. Morgan would probably exert a great deal of political and financial pressure on the hospital. Could committee members realistically ignore this factor?
- How might past rumors that Mr. Morgan bought Jodi's first transplant influence the present thinking of committee members?
- Mrs. DeStefano's inability to pay would probably create a financial hardship for the hospital. Should this influence their decision?
- Do risk-benefit calculations justify another procedure for Jodi Morgan? Because of her underlying cardiac pathology and renal dysfunction, even if the transplant is successful, her prognosis is poor. The potential for success of the transplant is less than it would be for healthier patients.
- Should a child like Jodi be given automatic preference over an adult? What about Mrs. DeStefano's children? Should their right to have a mother be an overriding consideration?

After much debate, the committee decided to return Jodi to the transplant list, behind Mrs. DeStefano. After a donor was found for Mrs. DeStefano, Jodi could have a second chance at life.

Determining potential for survival

Survival is a more complex issue than need. For example, the potential for survival doesn't necessarily decrease as a patient ages. A health-conscious elderly patient may represent a better transplant risk than a younger patient who has neglected his health.

A patient's willingness to comply with lifestyle changes, medication regimens, and dietary restrictions also can influence survival. Lifestyle factors may raise questions about a patient's suitability as a transplant recipient. Should a heavy smoker who refuses to quit be given a heart-lung transplant? Because of the controversy created by Mickey Mantle's liver transplant and subsequent debate over the fairness of organ donation, the United Network for Organ Sharing (UNOS) began, in 1998, to develop a new system, including a way to make donor livers available nationwide.

UNOS has moved from a local to a regional allocation system. In 1998, categories of potential recipients were revised: status 4 was eliminated, and status 2 was divided into 2A and 2B. The 1999 naturalistic data on regional and state sharing reveal that:
● sharing increases status 1 transplantation rates
● sharing decreases status 2B pre-transplantation mortality rates
● sharing decreases the rate of transplantation of status 3 patients, thereby providing more organs for seriously ill patients
● sharing, which decreased transplantation rates for status 3 patients, didn't provide a concomitant increase in mortality of status 3 patients.

Determining potential value to the community
The selection procedure also can take into account a potential recipient's value to the community. A good case could be made for assigning a higher priority to a mother of two young children than to a convicted drug dealer. Note that value is the last criterion — to be used only if a decision can't be made based on need or potential for survival.

Avoiding manipulation
Neither the donor nor his family ought to play a role in the selection procedure. Because of the potential for ma-nipulation (a payoff by the recipient), such participation isn't compatible with an ethical selection procedure.

Last resort
When other criteria fail to establish priority, the final selection should be made by lot. Although not perfect, this method is unbiased.

Cost considerations
Organ transplants can be prohibitively expensive. A kidney transplant costs about $40,000; a heart transplant may exceed $150,000. Either procedure is much more affordable than a liver or pancreas transplant. The federal government will pay up to 80% of the costs for kidney and heart transplants but refuses to subsidize liver or pancreas transplants, which are still considered experimental. For the patient whose life depends on receiving a liver transplant, the current reimbursement policy would appear unjust.

Along the same line, one might pose an even more challenging question: Is it fair for one person to receive that great a share of the limited funds available for health care? The $150,000 cost of a heart transplant would finance inoculations for several thousand children or prenatal care for hundreds of women. Utilitarian ethical theory would claim that the rights of hundreds of potential patients to a quality life exceed the right of one person to a heart transplant.

Multiple transplants
The issue of multiple transplants is closely related to the concept of *distributive justice.* At first glance, it might seem unethical, or at least unfair, for the same person to receive three or four transplants. The nurses and physicians caring for a transplant recipient, however, may believe that everything possible must be done to

keep the patient alive, including another transplant.

Perhaps the most equitable course of action is to place a repeat-transplant patient back on the regional transplant center register for a fair evaluation.

Transplant appendages

A new wrinkle has been added to the ethical debate over transplant ethics. In January 1999, a man in the United States had a hand transplant to replace the one he lost 13 years before due to a firecracker accident. A man in Italy underwent a testicular transplant in the spring of the same year. After one year, both procedures have been deemed successful; however, it's still much too early to determine the long-term outcome of these transplants.

The ethical issues involved in appendage transplantation revolve around beneficence and maleficence. Prior to the procedures, these transplant recipients were healthy. It's accepted that all surgeries have risks, but transplant surgeries are riskier than most because of their duration and the possible damage they may cause to the vascular system. In addition, there are many possible complications, including emboli formation in the attached appendage, infection due to the use of antirejection medications after transplantation, and the transmission of diseases, such as hepatitis and the human immunodeficiency virus (HIV).

The fundamental question becomes: "Does the health care provider violate the principle of beneficence by changing an otherwise healthy person (who is missing a hand or other body part) into an immunocompromised patient who will need to take antirejection medications for the rest of his life?" We justify the dangers of transplantation and antirejection medications in kidney, heart, and liver transplants because these transplants are performed for life-threatening conditions. However, missing a hand or a set of testicles, while inconvenient, is definitely not life-threatening.

Perinatal ethics

Twenty years ago, an infant born at 26 weeks' gestation had almost no chance of surviving. Today, barring other complications, over 50% of these infants survive. Thanks to spectacular advances in neonatology, such as intrauterine surgery, synthetic lung surfactant, and new antibiotics, physicians can save increasingly smaller and sicker infants.

Many people argue that this lifesaving technology has gone too far. Health care providers who treat critically ill neonates, they say, act too aggressively, frequently overriding the wishes of the infant's parents. Some believe that this type of treatment leads to even greater suffering for the infant and places an enormous financial burden on society. Ethical questions are complicated by lack of knowledge about the long-term outcome of heroic measures.

SANCTITY OF LIFE VS. QUALITY OF LIFE

Without life, other values are irrelevant. As a result, society holds the sanctity of life in high regard. The belief that all human lives have meaning and ought to be respected supports the notion that a critically ill infant should be kept alive at any cost.

But what about the *quality of life?* A utilitarian ethic would support a decision to withhold treatment for a severely handicapped newborn when the prospect for an acceptable quality of life is poor. But what is an "acceptable quality of life"?

One measure of the value of a person's life is his ability to achieve certain goals. Thus, if an infant has little hope of achieving anything but sheer survival, from a utilitarian viewpoint, it's ethically acceptable to terminate treatment.

The "best interest" criterion is another measure of the quality of life. Unfortunately, not everyone agrees on the exact meaning of "best interest." Is death ever in anyone's best interest?

Still another definition considers the patient's potential to establish some type of human relationship. According to this view, an infant who has little chance of recognizing and relating to his family has such a poor quality of life that withholding treatment is both compassionate and ethical. There are two objections to the "human relationship" standard. First, this criterion suggests that medical treatment be withheld from adults who have a limited capacity for human relationships, yet you'd almost certainly find it morally unacceptable to refuse to perform an emergency appendectomy on a psychotic patient or to withhold medication from a comatose automobile accident victim. Second, some experts argue that the infant isn't the only one with a right to an acceptable quality of life. The financial and emotional cost of sophisticated perinatal technology places an enormous burden on the family as well as society in general. Is this too great a price for a few extra months or years of life?

WHO SHOULD DECIDE

The best-qualified person to make a quality-of-life decision is the patient himself. But who's best qualified to give *proxy* consent for a premature infant born at 25 weeks' gestation?

Parents

Although no one knows the infant's true desires, legal and ethical precedent suggests that his parents ought to be the chief decision makers. Others argue that the parents' ability to make a wise and rational decision on short notice in such an emotionally charged atmosphere is limited. In addition, few parents have the necessary medical knowledge to make an informed decision. The combination of time pressures, ignorance, prejudice, and religious or moral beliefs can force parents into a decision that is at odds with the opinions of the medical team caring for their infant.

Health care team

Not only are members of the health care team more objective, but they're also better informed about the potential outcomes of the various treatment options. Ethically, however, this paternalistic approach is unacceptable. After all, the health care team won't bear the burden of raising the child.

Hospital ethics committee

Unfortunately, the slow pace of most committee decisions isn't compatible with the rapid decisions required when treating seriously ill neonates. In addition, using this approach might simply substitute the biases of the committee members for the biases of the parents, physicians, and nurses.

Courts

As the designated protector of individual rights, the legal system typically takes a narrow, although inconsistent, view of the issues. For example, up to the time of birth, greater weight is generally given to the rights of the mother. However, when a pregnant woman is murdered and the fetus also dies, the perpetrator is usually charged with double homicide. Also, during or after birth, the courts often have decided that the rights of the infant supersede those of the parents.

"BABY DOE" REGULATIONS

Court-mandated settlements to perinatal ethical conflicts have created significant debate. The best-known case involved an infant born with Down syndrome and a tracheoesophageal fis-

Critically ill neonate

CASE STUDY IN ETHICS

If you care for extremely premature or severely handicapped infants or their mothers, family members will look to you to assist them in life-and-death decisions. Consider the role of the nurse practitioner (NP) in the case study discussed below.

Grim prognosis

Matthew Klein, a microcephalic infant with transposition of the great arteries, was born more than 6 weeks prematurely. He also had spina bifida. The news of his condition was devastating to his parents, an older professional couple who had eagerly anticipated the birth of their child.

The on-call pediatrician asked a noted neurosurgeon and a pediatric cardiologist to consult on Matthew's case. These experts concurred that without immediate corrective surgery, he might live as long as 1 month on life support. Even with surgery, he probably wouldn't live past age 20. During that time, the doctors explained to Mrs. and Mrs. Klein, Matthew could be expected to suffer from seizure disorders, paralysis, and episodes of heart failure. He'd be highly susceptible to infection and severely retarded. In fact, he faced a grave risk just from the surgery.

Treatment options

Mr. and Mrs. Klein were given two options. They could choose aggressive surgical intervention for their child. If Matthew survived, he'd need additional surgery at age 4 and again at age 10. Alternatively, the Kleins could elect a conservative treatment plan, which included antibiotics, nutrition, and comfort measures but no heroic treatment.

Angelica Perez, a pediatric NP with more than 3 years of experience in caring for seriously ill newborns, had worked with the Kleins in caring for a previous premature infant. Ms. Perez recognized that Matthew's parents were overwhelmed. She knew that, as a result, their decision-making ability was compromised.

Ms. Perez strongly believed in the sanctity of life, but her practical experience gave her an appreciation for quality-of-life issues. In her professional opinion, the quality of Matthew's life was likely to be poor, and the conservative treatment option would be the best.

She carefully reviewed both treatment plans with Matthew's parents, analyzing the possible outcomes and explaining unfamiliar medical terms. Ms. Perez pointed out that even with surgical intervention, Matthew might be too severely brain damaged to ever recognize or interact with them. Mrs. Klein would have to quit her job to care for Matthew, and his medical expenses would pose an enormous financial burden. Eventually, he was almost certain to require institutional care.

Ms. Perez recognized that the conservative option presented problems for the Kleins as well. Deeply religious, both husband and wife strongly opposed mercy killing. They had difficulty seeing the distinction between allowing their son to die and actually causing his death.

Even after extensive counseling, the Kleins couldn't reach a decision. At this point, Ms. Perez suggested that the couple discuss their feelings with the physician, a social worker, and their minister. As a result of these discussions, Mr. and Mrs. Klein accepted the conclusion that conservative treatment was best for Matthew. The baby survived 2 weeks and died in his mother's arms.

tula. The family opted to forgo surgical treatment of the fistula and withhold supplemental nutrition, reasoning that the child's quality of life was too severely compromised. A nurse caring for the child disagreed. She contacted the authorities, but during the ensuing legal battle, the infant died.

On the basis of this and similar cases, the federal government instituted regulations standardizing the care of critically ill or severely handicapped newborns. Enacted under the umbrella of the Child Abuse Protection and Treatment Act, these "Baby Doe" regulations prohibited physicians and nurses from denying treatment to disabled infants. The only exceptions were infants in an irreversible coma; those for whom treatment would prolong dying, not life; and those for whom treatment would be futile or even inhumane. Violators, including health care providers, could be prosecuted for **negligence** or **malpractice.**

Some lawmakers opposed the constitutionality of the Baby Doe regulations. The Supreme Court agreed and, in June 1986, struck down federal laws requiring the treatment of all handicapped newborns. In addition, it reinforced the right to **privacy** by denying access to Baby Doe's **medical records.** Unfortunately, because many states also passed their own Baby Doe regulations before the federal law was reversed, it's still possible to be prosecuted for withholding treatment. Check with your state concerning Baby Doe regulations.

The major ethical problem with these regulations is their failure to address the quality-of-life issue. In addition, they're based on the mistaken assumption that a set of rigid laws can take the place of the ethical decision-making process.

NP'S ROLE
If anything, the Supreme Court's repeal of federal Baby Doe regulations have further confused the ethical issues surrounding the care of critically ill infants by creating a conflict between federal, state, and local laws. NPs who work with premature infants must be knowledgeable about their individual state's laws.

One of your primary roles as an NP is to help the parents of an extremely premature or critically ill neonate reach ethically sound decisions about care options. Education and understanding are the keys. You'll need to present all available options in a compassionate, unbiased manner, using simple terms. By carefully reviewing the pros and cons of both initiating and withholding treatment, you can help family members come to terms with their child's condition and reach a decision with which they'll be able to live. (See *Critically ill neonate,* page 231.)

AIDS

The nursing profession has always honored its professional responsibility to care for all patients regardless of personal attributes, lifestyle, or nature of the illness. Today, AIDS challenges this long-standing professional ethic. No other contagious illness incites such emotionally charged ethical debate.

AIDS touches on two highly controversial social issues: sexuality and drug use. It isn't surprising that many nurses experience value conflicts when working to meet their professional obligations. (See *Ethical issues and AIDS: Where do you stand?*)

Prejudice, fear, and misunderstanding surround AIDS. An HIV-positive test result often means the loss of a job, medical insurance, financial security, and even housing. Family, friends, and even the public may shun the AIDS patient. As a result, maintaining **confidentiality** is a serious concern for people with AIDS.

MANDATORY TESTING
Although there has been a major effort to educate the public about HIV transmission, the Centers for Disease Control and Prevention (CDC) estimates that most of the 1.5 million Americans infected with HIV don't know about it. Lack of awareness can seriously undermine both patient care and prevention efforts.

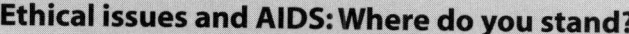

Ethical issues and AIDS: Where do you stand?

Acquired immunodeficiency syndrome (AIDS) raises numerous ethical issues for nurse practitioners (NPs) and other health care professionals. These issues range from personal safety to societal obligations. Read and answer the questions below to help you articulate your ethical positions on AIDS.

- Should all health care professionals be tested for human immunodeficiency virus (HIV) as a requirement for employment?
- Should states pass laws that prevent health care professionals who test positive for HIV to stop performing exposure-prone procedures?
- Does an HIV-positive patient have a right to claim disability under the Americans with Disabilities Act?
- Should all health care professionals have the right to refuse to treat HIV-positive patients?
- Should AIDS patients receive "heroic" life-sustaining treatments?
- Should pregnant HIV-positive patients have abortions rather than risk the chance of passing the virus to their unborn children?
- Should health departments obtain lists of all sexual contacts of people diagnosed as HIV-positive and notify those on the lists of their risk of exposure?
- Should the U.S. government provide free medical insurance to HIV-positive patients who are no longer able to buy health insurance?
- Should pregnant drug abusers who acquire HIV and infect their infants be charged with child abuse?
- Should costly and limited resources in the intensive care unit (ICU), neonatal ICU, and pediatric ICU be tied up in the care of AIDS patients if other patients with better prognoses for survival are being deprived?
- Should hospitals and nursing homes test all current and new employees for HIV infection?
- Should states and jurisdictions enact special laws allowing terminally ill AIDS patients to request and receive a painless lethal injection?

Some institutions, including the military and prisons, and many insurance companies insist on mandatory testing. Several states attempted to institute mandatory testing to obtain a marriage license and then abandoned the policy because of high costs and the low percentage of positive results. Most states now mandate written consent for testing as well as pretest and posttest counseling. All blood donors and potential organ donors are now tested for HIV, along with a number of other blood-borne diseases.

Does mandatory testing violate the ethical principles of autonomy (the patient's right to control his own fate) and justice (his right to be treated fairly)? Does it violate his right to privacy? Many nurses believe that it doesn't. Health care workers, they argue, have

a right to protect themselves and need a complete picture of the patient's health status to deliver quality care.

Public health officials contend that mandatory testing would improve our understanding of the spread of the disease and aid in prevention. Hospital *administrators* say that knowing a patient's HIV status could lower health care costs by pinpointing those who require standard precautions.

Opponents of mandatory testing emphasize the risk of discrimination and the high cost of screening all patients. They also feel that testing drives away patients who need care, because many people fear being tested. Mandatory testing also can backfire. An exposed person can take 12 weeks or longer to develop HIV antibodies. During this time, he's contagious but seronegative.

Case study

The following example illustrates some of the ethical problems raised by mandatory testing.

Karen Owen, a family NP working in an inner-city clinic, was accidentally exposed to a patient's blood during emergency treatment of a knife wound. Many AIDS patients are treated at the clinic and, as a precautionary measure, clinic **policy** dictated HIV testing of source patients when an employee was exposed to blood or body fluids. Ms. Owen's patient strongly objected; she argued that she was equally likely to have contracted AIDS from Ms. Owens and demanded that Ms. Owens be tested as well.

Is this a legitimate request, and must the clinic honor it? What about Ms. Owen's right to privacy? If she proved HIV-positive, would she lose her job? If she was HIV-negative, did she have to consent to be retested at a later date?

Out of concern for her own health, Ms. Owen agreed to be tested. To provide further reassurance, the clinic noted on the patient's consent form that the test was due to worker exposure, not because she was part of a high-risk group.

PUBLIC'S RIGHT TO KNOW

Many people believe that all health care providers should be routinely tested for HIV. The public, they argue, has the right to know a nurse's or physician's HIV status.

After at least three patients contracted HIV from a Florida dentist, the AMA and the American Dental Association recommended that physicians and dentists who are HIV-positive perform no invasive procedures and tell their patients that they're infected.

State and federal lawmakers have considered proposals to prevent physicians who are HIV-positive from performing surgery and other risky procedures. Such proposals are highly controversial. In April 1991, a New Jersey court upheld the right of a Princeton hospital to prohibit a surgeon with AIDS from performing surgery. Some people question the need for restrictions based on status alone. Rules about impaired health care workers, whether based on addiction, mental status, or physical illness, seem fairer and minimize the chance of HIV-based discrimination.

TESTING GUIDELINES

Following the guidelines below can help ensure that HIV testing is carried out in an ethically responsible manner.
● The sole purpose of any screening program should be to prevent the spread of HIV.
● The confidentiality of the test results must be ensured. If it's necessary to disclose the results (when a blood donor tests positive), only the affected person should be notified.
● The patient should receive adequate pretest and posttest counseling.
● The diagnostic laboratory must be as reliable as possible.
● Informed consent should be obtained before a patient is allowed to participate in a voluntary screening program. (See *Correcting a flawed HIV testing policy.*)

STANDARD PRECAUTIONS

The CDC contends that mandatory testing isn't necessary to protect nurses if health care workers follow standard precautions for all patients. This means using gloves, gowns, and goggles to prevent contact with a patient's blood or body fluids and strictly adhering to safety measures when handling needles, scalpels, or other sharp instruments.

Standard precautions can be time-consuming, expensive, and obstructive. Nonetheless, following these precautions means that health care providers can protect themselves without forcing patients to undergo mandatory testing.

CASE STUDY IN ETHICS

Correcting a flawed HIV testing policy

Regardless of whether human immunodeficiency virus (HIV) testing is voluntary or mandatory, careless procedures can ruin lives and increase liability. Consider the case study discussed below.

Surgeon's request

Mike Robertson, a robust, athletic 25-year-old, suffered a herniated disk in a bicycling accident. When bed rest and anti-inflammatory drugs didn't relieve his pain, he was referred to an orthopedic surgeon. The physician recommended surgery but insisted that Mr. Robertson undergo HIV testing before the operation.

"I don't understand why I need an HIV test," Mr. Robertson told Sherry Water, the nurse practitioner (NP) who performed his preadmission examination and testing.

She explained that the physician's request was legal and that it was probably a routine practice. She reviewed the details of the test procedure, emphasizing that a positive result didn't mean that he had AIDS, although it would mean that he faced a high risk of developing the disease and could infect others. Finally, she pointed out to Mr. Robertson that his test results would remain confidential but, if he preferred, she could refer him to an anonymous testing site.

"No, that's OK," Mr. Robertson replied. "I want to get this done and get my back fixed next week. It's really been killing me."

Devastating results

Mr. Robertson's surgery was scheduled for the following Tuesday. Ms. Water set up an appointment for Monday afternoon to give him the test results. To her dismay, he was HIV-positive. Worse, he didn't keep his appointment. Later that day, he called to reschedule the appointment for the morning of the surgery.

Ms. Water became concerned. Should she tell Mr. Robertson the test results just before surgery, when the information could be dangerously upsetting? Should she wait until after surgery, when he'd still be somewhat sedated and might not really understand?

Ms. Water finally reached Mr. Robertson's surgeon just an hour before the operation. Even though Mr. Robertson had already received preoperative sedation, the physician immediately cancelled surgery. He recommended that Ms. Water explain Mr. Robertson's test results as soon as he woke up. She agreed, knowing that Mr. Robertson would need an explanation for the cancellation.

Mr. Robertson was devastated by the news. He was disappointed and angry that the surgery hadn't taken place and even more upset to learn that he was HIV-positive. He felt that his physician had abandoned him, leaving him with two untreated medical problems: his back and his HIV status.

Changing hospital policy

Ms. Water also was disappointed and angry. Fortunately, she was able to capitalize on her feelings to improve her hospital's HIV testing program. She discussed Mr. Robertson's case with the director of nursing, stressing that in the future she would refuse to carry out a test unless ample time was provided for posttest counseling. In response, the hospital established new guidelines for HIV testing. Physicians who requested the HIV antibody test before any medical procedure had to verify that posttest counseling had taken place before the procedure could be performed. In addition, the physician was required to specify whether he would continue to care for a patient who tested positive. If not, he'd need to designate another physician who would do so.

ANA guidelines: Your obligation to provide care

In 1986, the American Nurses Association (ANA) Committee on Ethics reviewed the nurse's obligation to care for patients with infectious diseases, including acquired immunodeficiency syndrome (AIDS). The committee concluded that a nurse must provide care when four criteria are met:

• The patient is at significant risk for harm, loss, or damage if the nurse doesn't assist.

• The nurse's intervention or care is directly relevant to preventing harm.

• The nurse's care will probably prevent harm, loss, or damage to the patient.

• The benefit to the patient will outweigh any harm the nurse might incur, and providing care doesn't present more than minimal risk to the nurse.

Moral option

The last criterion presents you with a moral option when a particular patient poses a significant risk to your health or emotional well-being. For example, nurse practitioners working in particular settings, such as prisons or emergency departments, have a right to refuse to provide care if the patient is physically abusive or uncooperative. Although you can't abandon such a patient ethically or legally, you can find someone else to care for him or wait until he's sufficiently under control, either by chemical or physical restraint, so that he no longer poses a threat to your safety.

REFUSING TO PROVIDE CARE

Under certain circumstances, the NP can refuse to provide care to a patient, if providing such care would pose a greater risk to the NP than withholding the care would pose to the patient. Consider the following examples.

Dorothy Smith, a family NP, struggled for many months with her prejudices against AIDS patients. Although she was deeply committed to her career, her religion taught that homosexuality and drug use were sins. She also was apprehensive about the danger of contracting AIDS. Finally, she asked her office manager to avoid assigning her to AIDS patients.

Marie James, a pediatric NP in a large teaching hospital, also wanted to avoid AIDS patients, but she had a different reason. She had just learned that she was pregnant, and she wanted to avoid exposure to cytomegalovirus (CMV), a common opportunistic infection in AIDS that can cause severe and overt disease in fetuses.

Ethical solutions

The ANA Code for Nurses states that "the nurse provides services unrestricted by considerations of social or economic status, personal attributes, or the nature of health problems." Thus, Ms. Smith's refusal to care for AIDS patients because this duty conflicts with her religious beliefs isn't ethically viable and not covered under the conscience clause. No matter how strong your personal feelings, you can't allow them to interfere with your moral obligation to provide care.

This obligation isn't absolute, however. If the risk to you is greater than the potential benefit to the patient, you can ethically refuse to take that risk. Mrs. James, for instance, is justified in refusing to treat patients with a CMV infection because of the risk to her unborn child. However, she can't avoid caring for patients with *Pneumocystis carinii* pneumonia, where subclinical infection is common and antibodies are present in 75% of 4-year-olds in the

United States, or Kaposi's sarcoma, which is a cancer and not infectious.

As an NP, you also may refuse to perform procedures on a patient who deliberately puts you at risk. For example, if a patient deliberately moves his arm while you're drawing blood, you have the right to refuse to carry out the procedure. You may even be justified in refusing to care for this patient altogether, but you can't abandon him. Ethically and legally, you're required to find someone else to care for him. (See *ANA guidelines: Your obligation to provide care.*)

What if an AIDS patient becomes violent or threatens to bite you? If the patient's decisional capability is in doubt, the use of chemical or physical restraints may be justified. If the patient makes threats because of anger, warn him that his aggressive behavior must stop or treatment can't continue. You and other staff should document the patient's behavior, stating, if necessary, that because treatment can't be administered at this time, the patient is being discharged.

CONTACT NOTIFICATION

The patient's right to privacy may conflict with your duty to prevent the spread of the disease. The patient may balk when you request that he inform his partner that he's HIV-positive. You must respect the patient's right to confidentiality. You should try to impress on him, however, how crucial it is for the other person to know they've been exposed to HIV. Anonymous contact notification programs may provide assistance. For example, with the patient's consent, you can refer the problem to the county health department, which will attempt to locate and inform contacts of their exposure.

Many married patients are reluctant to notify their spouses, especially if the infection can be traced to an extramarital affair. Legally, you can't compel

> ### Confidentiality
> **COURT CASE**
>
> In this 1995 District of Columbia case, a husband sued a hospital for failing to disclose that his wife had tested positive for the human immunodeficiency virus (HIV). While separated from her husband, the patient was involuntarily committed for mental health treatment at a public health hospital, where she tested positive for HIV. She told her estranged husband she was HIV-negative. On her release from the hospital, the husband and wife reconciled and resumed sexual relations. He later learned that his wife had tested HIV-positive, but there was no evidence presented that he tested HIV-positive. The court dismissed the case, stating that health care professionals have no duty to inform the spouse of a spouse's HIV status.
>
> #### What the NP can learn
> Unless express consent is given by the patient, no disclosure of HIV status can be made to the patient's spouse. *N.O.L. v. District of Columbia*, 674 A. 2d 498 (D.C. App., 1995).

the patient to tell his wife, but you can explore options that may make it easier for him to do so. For example, ask the patient if he would feel more comfortable if a family physician gave her the news. A counselor also could work with the patient to reduce his anxiety about informing his wife as well as to support him when he tells her. (See *Confidentiality.*)

Laws dealing with contact notification continue to evolve and vary widely from state to state. In some states, public health authorities will notify partners of persons diagnosed with HIV. For instance, in Utah, public law R388-803-4 states, "If an individual is tested and found to have an HIV infection, the Utah Department of Health or local health department shall conduct partner notification activities."

Many states charge HIV-infected individuals with murder when they have unprotected sex with partners whom they didn't inform of their infection. In 1991, a man in Oakland, Calif., was sentenced to 3 years in prison for this offense. In Jackson, Fla., a 22-year-old man was convicted of attempted second-degree murder for knowingly engaging in intercourse while infected with HIV. He was sentenced to 4 to 5 years in jail and 13 years of probation.

AIDS AND THE PREGNANT PATIENT

Mandatory testing of pregnant women gained support when it was learned that giving a woman zidovudine (AZT) significantly lessened the chance of HIV transmission to her fetus. Giving AZT to the newborn of an HIV-positive woman also helps the at-risk baby.

Those who favor mandatory testing say the potential reduction in transmission is so important that the woman's autonomy should be set aside. Others condemn forced testing or forced medication and, again, raise the specter of women who fear the test, avoiding prenatal care and harming more babies in the long run.

ECONOMIC BURDEN OF AIDS

With the AIDS population rapidly growing, the cost of providing care will cause society to rethink questions about whether health care is a right or a privilege. Due to their work settings, NPs often provide care regardless of the patient's ability to pay for it. What about the rest of the health care system? Must hospitals and government agencies bear the burden of AIDS patients who can't handle the financial burdens imposed by their illness?

The right to health care is, at best, a tentative and an unenforceable moral right with no legal foundation, although most agree that a patient who enters the health care system has a right to receive treatment appropriate to his illness. Still, health care resources are limited, especially for lower- and middle-income people and the uninsured. In the face of such limitations, the best you can do is to refer patients to the appropriate social service agencies and support legislation that guarantees equal access to health care.

Abortion and reproductive technology

Abortion poses a complex and ethically painful dilemma for health care providers and their patients. Consider the cases described here.

● Ashley Adams, a pregnant 14-year-old, quietly wept with her mother sitting next to her. They were waiting in the short procedure unit for Ashley's turn in the operating room. When the obstetrics/gynecology NP took her aside to talk privately, Ashley began to cry harder. She told the NP that she didn't really want an abortion but her parents had placed so much pressure on her she had no real choice in the decision.

● Loretta Hofmann was pregnant with her fourth child. Recently fired from his job, her husband had begun drinking heavily and on more than one occasion had become emotionally abusive. One of her three children has attention deficit hyperactivity disorder and is having trouble in school. Mrs. Hofmann believed that she couldn't handle another child or cope with going through a pregnancy and placing the child for adoption. To get to the abortion clinic, she had to pass through a picket line of *pro-life* protesters, who harassed and taunted her. During her initial interview with the clinic NP, she's visibly shaken and says that she can no longer cope with the stress in her life.

● Lynnette Mack works in a women's health center that provides general family planning, treatment for vaginal infections, counseling, health care for adolescents, and abortion services. Although she was fervently *pro-choice* when she took the job, over the months her feelings about abortion have changed. She wants to continue working at the center but without participating in abortions. She fears that this would create tension as well as extra work for her colleagues. The primary wage earner for her family, Mrs. Mack is considering resigning for ethical reasons.

The U.S. Supreme Court has handed down more than 20 decisions related to the abortion issue. Court rulings, however, can't answer the ethical questions about abortion that NPs encounter in their daily practice.

IS THE FETUS A HUMAN BEING?

The status of the fetus as a human life is an important element in the abortion controversy. Should the fetus be considered a human being or a potential human being? Even if the early embryo isn't considered a human being (at least not in the same sense as a newborn), does its potential to become a human being guarantee a right to life?

This confusion is complicated by the fact that the age of fetal viability — the age at which a fetus can survive outside the womb — has decreased to 20 to 24 weeks.

Many bioethicists use measurable criteria of human body development, such as fetal movement and the existence of a heart and nervous system, to determine when the fetus is alive, but this hasn't ended the debate.

POLITICAL BATTLE

Abortion has become the focal point of a long and bitter political struggle.

Pro-life position

Opponents of *legal abortion* argue that human life begins at conception and, therefore, abortion is murder. This position is most clearly identified with the Roman Catholic church. In 1869, Pope Pius IX condemned all abortions as a form of murder. Before then, the church had imposed no penalties for abortions within the first 40 days of pregnancy.

Antiabortion groups also contend that tolerance for the murder of unborn children will imply tolerance for assisted suicide, death by neglect, or murder of other categories of "undesirable" people, such as the mentally handicapped, seriously ill, and deformed.

Pro-choice position

Those who support legal abortion argue that an embryo or young fetus represents the potential for human life but shouldn't be considered a human being at the time. They view abortion as a type of surgery necessary for the physical and psychological well-being of certain women. Abortion, they point out, will always be part of human society regardless of whether it's legal. They claim that legal abortions reduce the number of mutilations and deaths associated with *illegal abortions.* Further, they argue that legal abortions help to reduce the number of unwanted children, forced marriages, and economic stress on some families.

Some take a third position: Abortions should be allowed only when the life of the pregnant woman is in danger or in cases of incest or rape.

Continuing debate

The furor over abortion is unlikely to go away anytime soon. However, emergency contraception has helped the issue slip from the front page news. Regular birth control pills administered in higher doses that prevent ovulation, fertilization, and implantation of the egg are now prescribed as emergency contraception. The term "morning-after pill" is misleading because the medication can be taken up to three days after intercourse or contraceptive failure.

An abortion-inducing pill, mifepristone (RU-486, Mifegyne), is also available. Taken in the first 7 weeks of pregnancy, mifepristone blocks progesterone receptors and thus allows prostaglandins to stimulate contractions and detach the conceptus. The drug obtained Food and Drug Administration (FDA) approval for use in 1996 and is widely distributed in clinics by NPs as a "morning-after" birth control pill.

In 1995, two more drugs were found to induce abortion safely and effectively. They're common prescription drugs to fight cancer (methotrexate) and ulcers (misoprostol). Methotrexate is injected and stops the division of cells — malignant or fetal. Then, 5 to 7 days later, a misoprostol suppository is given to induce contractions and expel the fetus. One researcher suggests that the procedure could be supplied by an NP under a physician's supervision, increasing availability and lowering costs of abortion. This treatment regimen received FDA approval in 1997.

Manufacturers may not supply mifepristone for fear of reprisals from anti-choice organizations. However, the cancer- and ulcer-fighting drugs are too valuable to be forced off the market. Antiabortion leaders, meanwhile, have made mifepristone a prime target and won't ignore the newest method.

The ethical principle of autonomy (self-determination) is an important part of the abortion debate. This principle upholds a woman's right to control her own body. From the mother's point of view, that right includes choosing whether to have an abortion. Many women may think that they shouldn't be forced into the physical, emotional, and financial hardships of pregnancy.

Opponents of abortion maintain that pregnancy involves two persons who both have a right to autonomy — the mother and the fetus.

RESOLVING YOUR VIEWS ABOUT ABORTION

As an NP who is ethically or morally opposed to abortion, you can't be forced to participate in the procedure. On the other hand, your employer has a right to insist that you provide nursing to all patients under your care.

To reach your own ethical resolution to the abortion issue, you'll need to examine your views honestly and carefully. You'll also want to periodically re-evaluate your position in light of new medical information and your own experience. If you feel strongly, you should work for a facility that matches your views on abortion.

Postabortion care

Every NP has an ethical obligation to provide competent, compassionate care. Even NPs who strongly oppose abortion shouldn't allow their personal feelings to interfere when caring for a postabortion patient. Nor is it appropriate to impose your values on the patient. If the patient expresses guilt or regrets over her decision, an appropriate therapeutic response might be, "You made a decision that you thought was right. I want to help you live with your decision and rebuild your life." Offering to find a counselor or clergy member is another way to help.

PRENATAL SCREENING

Thanks to advanced diagnostic procedures, such as amniocentesis, three-dimensional ultrasound, alpha-fetoprotein screening, and chorionic villus sampling, it's now possible to detect inherited disorders and congenital abnormalities well before birth. In a few cases, the diagnosis has paved the way for repair of the defect in utero. However, because it's easier to detect genetic disorders than to treat them, prenatal screening often forces a patient to choose between having an abortion or taking on the emotional and financial burden of raising a severely handicapped child.

Even those who are opposed to abortion may waver after seeing a child afflicted with Tay-Sachs disease or Duchenne muscular dystrophy. Is the quality of these children's lives so poor that it would be more compassionate to prevent their birth? Is death ever more beneficial than life?

Some ethicists worry that this line of reasoning could cater to a desire for "perfect" children. How would this affect attitudes toward the handicapped? How severe must a defect be for abortion to be considered an ethically acceptable option? For example, should a fetus with cleft palate, a surgically correctable defect, be aborted because of the handicap? What about a girl conceived by parents who desperately want a boy?

The diagnostic procedures themselves involve some risk to the fetus. Amniocentesis, for example, causes serious complications or death about 0.5% of the time. This risk creates a conflict between the rights of the fetus and the parents' right to know his health status. If testing is to be conducted ethically, patients must understand the associated risks before the procedure.

Patients also must comprehend what the test can and can't tell them as well as all the available options. Thus, just as in HIV testing, effective pretest and posttest counseling are essential

parts of an ethical prenatal screening program.

IN VITRO FERTILIZATION

Infertility can have devastating effects on the emotional well-being of a couple who yearn for children. As a result, many couples will spend time and money to conceive or adopt a child. When medical procedures (such as fertility medications, hysterosalpingoostomy [opening blocked fallopian tubes], and artificial insemination) fail and adoption is impossible, infertile couples may turn to controversial techniques, including in vitro fertilization (IVF).

IVF refers to the process of removing ova from a woman's ovaries, placing them in a petri dish filled with a sterilized growth medium, and covering them with healthy motile spermatozoa for fertilization. Three to five ova are implanted in the woman's uterus 10 to 14 days after fertilization, and the remaining fertilized ova are frozen for future use or discarded.

IVF can use either the husband's sperm (homologous) or a donor's sperm (heterologous) to fertilize either the wife's ova or a donor's ova. A "prefertilized ova" can also be purchased from an ova bank.

Complex and expensive, IVF has resulted in the birth of hundreds of healthy "test-tube babies" since the first successful attempt in 1978. These parents have no doubts about the procedure — they're thankful for the opportunity to have children. Yet, *egoism* isn't an acceptable basis for ethical decision making in health care. Worthy ends don't always justify the means, and many people question the morality of the IVF procedure.

Medical miracle or unnatural act?

Some people hail scientific manipulation of the ova and sperm as a medical miracle, but others denounce it as circumvention of the natural process of procreation. By concentrating on conception, IVF enables couples to sidestep other important aspects of a normal sexual relationship, including pleasure, respect, and love. Many religions maintain that a Supreme Being participates in the act of procreation. People with strong religious beliefs may contend that IVF diminishes the spiritual value of family life.

It's ethically acceptable to modify normal body functions to enhance natural actions. Thus, procedures such as hysterosalpingoostomy or use of fertility medications pose few ethical problems. Is IVF the next logical step in fertility modification, or is it an unnatural act that oversteps the bounds of standard medical intervention?

IVF and conflicts of rights

The long-term effects of IVF on the children, their parents, and society in general represent another serious ethical concern. Human society depends on the strength and integrity of the family. By distancing parents from the physical act of procreation, IVF could have a harmful impact on family life.

LEFTOVER EMBRYOS. IVF would pose fewer ethical problems if only one embryo were needed to guarantee a successful pregnancy. Unfortunately, it doesn't work that way. About 15 to 20 embryos may result from a single fertilization effort, but only 3 to 5 are implanted in the mother's uterus. The question arises: What should be done with the leftover embryos? Is it ethical to discard them, destroy them, or perform experiments on them? Who owns them?

In practice, leftover embryos usually are frozen. This raises questions with regard to parental responsibility for the frozen embryos. In 1989, for example, a divorcing Tennessee couple fought a custody battle over seven fertilized eggs that were frozen at an IVF clinic in Knoxville. Mary Sue Davis wanted custody for future implantation; her estranged husband, Junior Davis, insisted on having a joint say in the future of the embryos because he would have to pay child support for any children born from the ova. In a controversial decision, a circuit court judge ruled that the embryos are people, not property, and should go to the mother.

EFFECTS ON CHILD DEVELOPMENT. There is a danger that parents may feel less responsible for IVF children born with congenital defects or conceived with donor sperm. Test-tube babies themselves may develop identity or adjustment problems after they learn the facts surrounding their conception. They're likely to feel insecure about their position in the family, especially if they have "naturally conceived" siblings.

Sperm and egg banks

One of the results of the widespread use of IVF is an increased number of sperm and egg banks in which to store semen and ova until they're ready for use in the IVF procedure. Sperm banks have existed for many years. In the past, stored semen was primarily used for artificial insemination of women whose husbands were infertile and unable to make adequate quality or amounts of semen to produce fertilization.

Egg banks are a relatively new development. To obtain ova, a woman is given a hormone preparation that hyperstimulates the ovaries to produce 30 times the usual number of mature ova. The ova are then removed by laparoscopy or vaginal ultrasound-guided aspiration. The ova can be fertilized immediately or frozen and stored in an egg bank for later use. Since the increase of IVF procedures, egg banks are experiencing shortages and couples desiring IVF have to wait from weeks to a year.

The ethical and legal issues involved with stored semen and ova are similar to those in the storage of in vitro–fertilized ova. One of the obvious ethicolegal questions is: "Who owns the ova and semen after they're deposited for storage in the bank?" Traditionally, after semen was donated and the donor paid for his services, the semen was considered the property of the storage facility to be sold at a later date to an appropriate customer. The donor couldn't find out the names of the women who used the semen for fertilization.

By similar reasoning, it would seem that women who donate ova to an egg bank and are paid for their services would also lose their possession rights of the ova. But most women undergo the ova stimulation and harvesting procedure for their own IVF, thus retaining ownership of their ova.

Over the years, several complicated legal and ethical dilemmas have surfaced from the storage of semen and ova. In a landmark case, a man who knew he was dying donated semen to a sperm bank. After his death, his wife wanted to be fertilized with his semen to have his children. But the husband's parents, who didn't like the wife, sued to prevent her from becoming pregnant with his semen. The parents claimed that the semen belonged to them because the man was their son and that the wife had no legal right to use it for insemination.

Consider this issue: How long can the semen and ova be stored? Almost indefinitely, with current cryotechnology, but no one knows how long-term storage affects semen and ova. Would it be ethical to fertilize ova that have been stored for a decade or two only to produce children who have major birth defects?

Another question that arises from the procedure is beyond comprehension: Who do the children of stored semen and ova belong to? Obviously, to the couple if their semen and ova are used in IVF. But what about a couple who benefits from semen and ova donated by strangers? If the child has a birth defect, is mentally retarded, or of the wrong sex, the couple could claim that the child really wasn't theirs anyway. What happens to the child? Can they give it back? Does it become a ward of the state, like an abandoned child? Where do we apply the principles of distributive justice in this case?

In some settings, NPs may actually be responsible for the technical process of obtaining semen and ova. However, a more likely responsibility you may have is to teach and counsel patients about the risks and complications involved in the procedures. Assess their awareness and understanding of the ethical and legal issues involved in the process. Equally critical are their feelings about sexuality and reproduction. If they're to receive ova that don't belong to them, how will they feel about the resulting child? Even though the IVF procedure is technical and artificial, the result of the process is hardly so. Producing a child is a human event, not a manufacturing process.

Government regulation

Although the federal government has several proposals for legislation to regulate the use of IVF, none have become law. Several states have proposed regulations, but there seems to be a lack of consensus about what should be included in the regulations. The inability of government agencies to pass laws regulating IVF and sperm and egg banks points to the fact that the legal system is poorly equipped to deal with reproductive ethical issues.

Court decisions made on actual cases involving IVF and reproductive controversies have produced a small amount of case law. However, the cases are dissimilar and the decisions tend to be inconsistent. In some situations, the courts support the property rights of self-determination and choice of the mother or patients. In other cases, the courts uphold the child's right to life and nurturing.

In practice, most decisions about IVF and sperm and egg banks are made outside of the legal system by the couples and their lawyers. Some facilities have developed internal guidelines to determine who would be acceptable candidates for IVF. If you work in a facility that performs IVF or maintains a sperm or egg bank, it's important that, as an NP, you become involved in the development of policies and guidelines based on your knowledge of ethical standards. (See *What would you do?*)

Conversely, if IVF becomes a medically essential procedure, the ethical principle of distributive justice holds that everyone — regardless of socioeconomic status — should have access to it. But the cost of a publicly supported infertility treatment program based on IVF would be astronomical.

CLONING

With the successful birth of Dolly, the sheep, in 1996 in Scotland, and the production of five identical rhesus monkeys in 2000 in the United States, the world has awakened to the reality of cloning as a viable reproductive method. The concept of cloning, however, has existed since the discovery of deoxyribonucleic acid (DNA) by Watson and Crick. It's based on the fact that every cell in an animal's body contains all the genetic information needed to reproduce every other cell in the

body. In the strict scientific meaning of the word, the cloning process occurs when any cell in the animal's body is removed and placed in an appropriate growth environment where it develops into an identical reproduction of the animal from which the cell came. Scientists still don't know what triggers some parts of the DNA strand to become active and reproduce and others to remain dormant. Currently, if a skin cell of a human is removed and placed in a growth medium, it will grow new skin, not another identical person.

Although popularly referred to as cloning, the scientific name for the process used to produce Dolly, the monkeys, and other identical animals (cows and mice) is somatic cell nuclear transfer technique. The process starts by removing unfertilized ova from an animal and then removing all genetic material (DNA) from the ova. Next, the scientists remove the DNA from a cell in the animal they wish to clone and insert it into the unfertilized, DNA-free ova. The ova with the new DNA is then implanted in the uterus of an appropriate animal, where it grows into an identical twin of the DNA donor. In the case of Dolly, the DNA donor was her mother (the sheep in whose uterus she was implanted). That makes Dolly an identical twin of her mother even though she's 6 years younger.

Another technique that is commonly referred to as cloning is really embryo splitting. After an ovum is fertilized by a sperm, naturally or with IVF, a single cell results, called a zygote, that contains a combination of genetic material (DNA), half each from father and mother. Left alone to develop, that single cell will eventually develop into an individual who shares some of the inherited features of both parents due to the combination of DNA. Within 12 hours after the zygote is formed, it begins to divide into 2, then 4, then 8,

What would you do?

CASE STUDY IN ETHICS

Marjie May, an obstetric-gynecologic nurse practitioner (NP), has worked at the Reproductive Sciences Center (RSC) of the University Research Hospital in a large city for 6 years. The RSC has a reputation for using cutting-edge technology and has received many public and private grants for developing innovative procedures and techniques to help couples with infertility problems. The RSC has sperm and egg banks that provide semen and ova for the artificial inseminations and in vitro fertilization (IVF) procedures conducted at the center. As a primary care provider at RSC, Ms. May is involved in all aspects of IVF, including physical examinations, testing, and participating in the IVF procedures. Although initially she had ethical issues regarding IVF and artificial insemination, she resolved those concerns and now feels comfortable with most of the activities at the center.

One day, Ms. May's closest friend, a technician in the IVF laboratory where the eggs are fertilized, tells her that Dr. Floral, head of RSC and the person most responsible for its funding, has been experimenting with somatic cell nuclear transfer technique, and that he is planning to use cloned embryos for one of the IVF procedures that Ms. May is to assist with the next morning. The woman to be implanted with the cloned embryo thinks that she's getting an IVF embryo from one of her own eggs harvested earlier and fertilized by the sperm of an unknown donor. The woman is an admitted lesbian but wants to have a child without having intercourse with a man.

Ms. May hasn't resolved the ethics of cloning humans but generally feels that it's unethical and probably immoral. She also feels that not telling the truth to the woman is a violation of the principle of veracity and informed consent. Before the center closes for the day, Ms. May expresses her concerns about the ethics of the procedure to another NP who also works in the clinic. The second NP states her belief that all forms of unnatural reproduction are basically the same and, if IVF is OK, so is cloning. Because the woman didn't know the semen donor, not knowing it was a cloned embryo was basically the same thing, she reasoned.

The second NP also reminds Ms. May that Dr. Floral is the main authority at the center, and questioning him and going against his wishes by telling the woman the truth might result in Ms. May losing her job. Moreover, revealing the cloning technique's use at RSC may jeopardize the center's funding and close it permanently because the government has banned human cloning. The second NP reasons: "If the Center shuts down, we won't be able to help any of those sad couples who come here with infertility problems. Do you want that to happen?"

What is the basis of Ms. May's ethical dilemma? Are her concerns legitimate? What course of action can Ms. May take? What ethical system seems to guide the second NP's reasoning? Are Dr. Floral's actions ethical? What would you do if you were Ms. May?

---

then 16 identical cells. When it reaches 16 cells, it enters the morula stage.

While the embryo is dividing, up to and including the morula state, the cells can be divided and separated. Because the cells are identical, contain all the genetic material necessary to produce a new individual, and have fully active DNA, each cell is essentially a zygote. After the cells are divided and separated, they can be implanted into several appropriate females and will continue to divide and develop into identical twins, or triplets, or more. Also, when the embryo is in the four- to eight-cell stage, these cells can be separated, the DNA material removed from them, and new genetic material inserted. The cell with the new DNA will then grow into a twin of the animal from which the DNA was taken. It appears that by using the embryo-splitting technique, scientists could produce an unlimited supply of ova for the somatic cell nuclear transfer procedure.

With the IVF procedure, embryo splitting, and DNA transfer, the fertilization and early development process occurs in a petri dish in the laboratory. After the cells begin to develop, they're implanted into an appropriate female for the remainder of the pregnancy. Although the cloning or embryo-splitting process is relatively simple, its success rate is at best marginal. For instance, to produce Dolly, more than 1,000 ova were genetically created. Of these, only 29 began to develop, and only one actually produced Dolly. Although it's theoretically possible to reproduce humans using this technique, so far it has only been used to produce animals.

Legal and ethical issues of cloning

Shortly after the news of Dolly reached the United States, a crucial debate developed over whether cloning of humans was ethical or even legal. The three most troubling ethical issues were the loss of uniqueness of the individual, the potential misuse of the technology by diabolical scientists, and degeneration of society as it now exists. Other, more traditional ethical concerns, such as medical risks to the mother or child (beneficence and non-maleficence), life status of the embryo produced by the procedure, distributive justice issues of cost and availability of technology, and autonomy issues of using humans as incubators or sources of organs for donation, also are part of the debate.

The concern for loss of individuality and uniqueness emanates from the fact that clones are exact copies of their DNA donors. For many people, it conjures up an Orwellian image of rows of tanks where identical babies are being grown and incubated, giving rise to **genetic determinism** and production of inferior humans through mass photocopying.

The belief that genetic determinism will produce individuals who not only look, but also act, identical is flawed. Although every cell in one twin body is genetically identical to that of the other twin body, experience shows that twins develop individual personalities and character traits. Personality development is influenced by a wide range of environmental and experiential elements, not just genetic composition. If and when it happens, cloned human babies born to mothers who live in different situations, although they may look the same, will likely have very different personalities.

Similarly, experience doesn't support the belief that each time an individual is cloned, there is loss in quality. In many cases, photocopies may be of higher quality than the original. However, cloning is more than making photocopies because the process is quite different. The danger of "bad copies" from cloning that may result in inferior-quality offspring, or offspring with congenital defects, arises from the mechanical collection and transfer of the very fragile DNA strands. Damaging even one gene sequence can produce birth defects.

In most ethical dilemmas, motivation is an important element in determining if the act was right or wrong. There are several possible motivations to clone human beings, ranging from egoism to helping an infertile couple have a child.

The egoistic motivation conjures up images of the diabolical scientist or a political leader who wants to create a "superior race" by the repeated cloning of physically and mentally superior individuals. It isn't hard to imagine what Hitler might have done with this technology. How about cloning genius inventors, brilliant leaders, or superb athletes? Could embryo factories be far behind?

A somewhat more altruistic, although no less diabolical motive, is cloning humans for organ donation. In theory, a person who needs a heart transplant could donate his DNA and, after some time, have an individual who has a heart with a perfect genetic match. Most people detest the idea of using cloned children as a means to an end, especially if harvesting the organ (as in a heart transplant) resulted in the child's death. Scientists in Texas have cloned mice without heads whose organs were then transplanted into DNA donor mice. What if human clones could be created without heads? Would these headless beings truly be human? Or would they just be biological storage units for organs to be used for donation when the need arose? At first glance, this practice might seem abhorrent. But is it any different from the sperm, egg, embryo, or organ banks that exist today?

In the past few years, parents have had children for the primary purpose of providing bone marrow for an older child who had leukemia. In many cases, these children were identical six-antigen matches, and the bone marrow was harvested from the infant and transplanted into the sick child who recovered from the disease. Is having children for this purpose different from cloning children for organ transplantation? What if scientists are able to clone one organ or a specific tissue? If a person needed a liver, the DNA from his or her liver could be transferred to an ovum and then a new liver grown in the laboratory. A similar procedure is being used already, without ethical objections, for growing new skin to graft onto burn patients.

Some parents might be tempted to clone a replacement child for one who is dead or dying. These parents could "set aside" a clone through the embryo-splitting technique that could be stored in an embryo bank to be implanted and grown if the child died. The underlying motivation would seem to be very selfish and self-serving, to create a replacement child for the relief of grieving patients. But is the cloned child really a replacement for the child who died? Physical appearance may be identical, but what about personality and temperament, which experience has shown could be radically different.

Similarly, an infertile couple who had tried all other methods and were unable to have a child might seek a cloned embryo as a last resort. Perhaps this motivation could pose the fewest ethical objections. Rather than using semen or ova from strangers, they might provide their own DNA, either from the father or the mother, to produce a child.

SURROGATE MOTHERHOOD

A surrogate mother is a woman who gives birth after carrying the fertilized ovum of another woman or, more commonly, after being artificially inseminated with sperm from the biological father. In this case, the infant is then legally adopted by the wife of the biological father. Since the first surrogate birth in England in 1976, more than 4,500 babies have been born through this arrangement.

Surrogate motherhood offers hope to the 60% to 70% of infertile couples in which the woman is the infertile partner. It's also an option for women whose age or health makes pregnancy risky. A surrogate birth poses no greater risk to the fetus (or the surrogate mother) than does any normal birth.

Orphaned ova

Unanswered questions about in vitro fertilization (IVF) and surrogate motherhood may soon come to haunt society. Consider the case study below, which explores what could happen if a surrogate motherhood arrangement doesn't go as planned.

Orphaned before birth

Howard Belmont, age 39, owned a successful manufacturing company. He and his wife, Marsha, age 35, had been trying to have a baby for 2 years without success. After the Belmonts underwent a battery of infertility tests, their physician concluded that Mrs. Belmont could ovulate and produce mature ova but couldn't conceive or bear children. On the physician's suggestion, the couple began to explore the possibility of IVF and surrogate motherhood.

After lengthy consideration, Mrs. Belmont had her ova fertilized in vitro, using her husband's sperm. When some of the fertilized ova were frozen for implantation, the Belmonts located a surrogate mother, Hazel Towers. Ms. Towers agreed to sign a long-term contract saying that she would bear a total of three children for Mr. and Mrs. Belmont. The contract stated that Ms. Towers would be paid $100,000 for the first child and $75,000 (already placed in trust) for the subsequent two children. Ms. Towers was successfully implanted with Mr. and Mrs. Belmont's fertilized ova. When Ms. Towers was near the end of the first trimester of pregnancy, Mr. and Mrs. Belmont were killed in an automobile accident.

Making an offer

Mr. Belmont's two brothers and one sister stood to inherit his company and assets worth $15 million. However, according to the Belmonts' will, if Ms. Towers had the baby, the child would inherit the estate.

Mr. Belmont's brothers and sister offered Ms. Towers $500,000 if she would abort the fetus and refuse to be implanted with any more fertilized ova. In addition, the brothers and sister offered to make a $1 million donation for the construction of a new pediatric wing to the hospital where the fertilized ova were stored if the administrator agreed to have the ova destroyed.

Ms. Towers' dilemma

Ms. Towers was placed under a great deal of stress. She realized that she could base her actions only on her own ethical principles. The $500,00 offer was a temptation she'd have to ignore; she didn't think that financial gain justified an abortion. According to the contract, she was to surrender the child to Mr. and Mrs. Belmont at its birth. She had serious misgivings, however, about surrendering it to the brothers or sister in light of the offer they made for her to have an abortion.

When they learned that Ms. Towers refused to surrender the child, the bothers and sister accused her of having the child for financial gain. They pointed out that the child would be heir to a large fortune; Ms. Towers would probably benefit from the estate in caring for the child.

Preborn siblings

Questions remained about production of the two other children agreed on in the contract. Was the contract binding after the death of Mr. and Mrs. Belmont? Because the money had already been set aside, could Ms. Towers be implanted with the ova, bear the children, and expect to be paid?

What about the hospital administrator and his role in the destruction of fertilized ova? If he believes that the ova aren't human, he probably wouldn't hesitate to carry out this request. But what if he believes that human life starts at the moment of conception? Then it would be betraying his ethical beliefs to destroy the ova.

Outcome

Over time, Ms. Towers began to think of the child in her womb as her own. She realized that her child would need to be loved and

Orphaned ova *(continued)*

cherished for its own sake. She accepted the fact that she'd probably lose her surrogate mother's fee because the contract stipulated that she must turn the child over to the Belmonts. She decided to raise the child regardless of the financial consequences.

Because of the severe emotional stress she experienced, Ms. Towers decided to forgo having any more fertilized ova implanted. The Belmont family immediately initiat-

ed a legal action contesting her child's inheritance; eventually, an out-of-court settlement was reached.

Ms. Towers experienced a bitter lesson in the moral uncertainty that surrounds in vitro fertilization and surrogate motherhood. Existing laws aren't sufficient to answer the many questions raised by reproductive technology; future court rulings may provide better guidelines.

Surrogate motherhood vs. conventional motherhood

One concern about surrogate motherhood involves the true nature of mothering. Is "motherhood" merely the biological act of bearing children? Many people believe that motherhood also implies a long-term commitment to the care and nurture of the child. By agreeing to give the baby to the contracting couple, is a surrogate mother defaulting on a moral commitment? The advertising of services by potential surrogate mothers, with fees ranging from $50,000 to $150,000, suggests to some that surrogate motherhood represents a form of "baby selling."

Conflicts of rights

Surrogate motherhood also can produce conflicts among the rights of the surrogate mother, the infertile couple, the fetus, and society.

The basic dispute revolves around who has the strongest claim to the child. Is it the surrogate mother by virtue of her biological connection? Or does the surrogate contract guarantee the infertile couple the right to the child? Courts of law usually have ruled in favor of the couple.

Surrogate mother contracts seemingly violate adoption laws, which pro-

hibit a mother from surrendering parental rights before the infant is born. Such laws, enacted to protect a biological mother from undue pressure, typically specify an initial waiting period of a few days. In many cases, she can't terminate all parental rights until 6 months after the birth.

What if no one wants the child? This can become an issue if the infant is born with a handicap. Can the infertile couple or the surrogate mother refuse to take responsibility for such a child? What if the defect isn't apparent until the child is 4 years old? Can the infertile couple return the child to his biological mother?

Clearly, the rights of the child to a normal family life must not be lost in the debate over custody. (See *Orphaned ova.*)

Exploitation

Both the infertile couple and the surrogate mother are highly vulnerable to exploitation. The couple, blinded by a longing for a child, is an easy victim for financial and emotional blackmail. On the other hand, surrogate motherhood can be used to exploit poor women, who have few marketable skills other than their ability to bear children. "Womb renting" is as ethically unacceptable as "baby selling."

NP ROLE IN IVF AND SURROGATE MOTHERHOOD

Given the broad scope of practice for NPs in some states, you could be directly involved in an IVF procedure. The surrogate mother contracts are usually handled by lawyers; however, you may have patients who choose the surrogate mother option. Before you can effectively counsel these patients, you'll need to examine your views on these controversial procedures and become familiar with the legal and ethical pitfalls they present.

You can't be forced to participate in procedures you find ethically and morally objectionable. But, according to the ANA Code for Nurses, you're obligated to care for all patients assigned to you regardless of your beliefs or feelings. In any event, you have an ethical obligation to be aware of and report abuses of IVF or surrogate motherhood.

Genetic engineering and screening

Genetic engineering continues to contribute significantly to medical progress. Scientists are discovering new ways to identify and manipulate the genetic material of everything from single-celled organisms to human beings.

By removing or adding DNA, scientists can program the cell or the entire organism to carry out new functions. Such manipulation can be highly beneficial. For example, it has yielded new antibiotics and hormones (such as human insulin) and increased our understanding of cancer cells. But genetic manipulation also gives researchers the potential to alter the gene pool in unethical ways or to create terrifying new biological weapons.

Each of the estimated 100,000 genes found in nearly every human cell codes for a single protein involved in a specific body function. Even a small error in the gene produces a defective protein that can result in disease or deformity. More than 4,000 inherited disorders result from such genetic mistakes. Gene therapy, the introduction of healthy genes to overcome an inherited defect, may someday provide cures for such diseases as cystic fibrosis, muscular dystrophy, and hemophilia.

The identification of the genes responsible for inherited diseases and congenital malformations has spurred the development of screening tests. Genetic testing is now a fairly common component of prenatal care, facilitating the identification of fetuses with disorders including Down syndrome and Tay-Sachs disease. The screening of newborns for phenylketonuria is legally required by most states.

Potential for discrimination

Researchers also have identified the genes responsible for adult-onset disorders such as Huntington's disease, polycystic kidney disease, and some forms of cancer. Ideally, the results of genetic screening could encourage patients to make lifestyle changes that reduce their risk of developing the disease. At the very least, the knowledge can help them prepare to deal with the disease. Unfortunately, this information also can lead to genetic discrimination, preventing people from adopting children or obtaining jobs or health or life insurance.

ETHICS OF GENETIC ENGINEERING

Genetic manipulation, or genetic engineering, has a tremendous potential for altering the course of human development. By themselves, genetic engineering techniques, including cloning, somatic alteration, germ cell alteration, recombinant DNA synthesis, and gene therapy, are ethically neutral. It's the application of these techniques that creates ethical problems. (See *Language of genetic manipulation.*)

Control over future generations

Do researchers have a greater obligation to help those currently alive or, alternatively, to protect the interests of future generations? It would appear that the most ethical applications of genetic engineering should do both, and research should concentrate on solving long-term medical and environmental problems, such as hereditary disease, cancer, pollution, and hunger.

Safety

Genetic researchers have a moral obligation to take all necessary precautions to recognize and prevent harmful consequences of their work, such as the accidental release of new pathogens. Patients who participate in gene therapy trials must be fully informed of the potential risks as well as the benefits. For example, the retroviral vectors used to introduce new genes also may increase a patient's risk of developing cancer.

Potentially dehumanizing effects

In the past, medical research has been limited to efforts to repair or halt the damage caused by disease and injury. Genetic engineering gives science the ability to re-create the human body. Is this unethical? If genetic engineering techniques are used to cure disease and improve the quality of life, society does stand to benefit. Imagine a society, however, in which genetically "perfect" children or genetically inferior servants could be created in the laboratory. Such unethical applications clearly violate human dignity and integrity.

Language of genetic manipulation

The following terms are associated with the science of genetic manipulation.

Cloning: production of an entire organism from a single cell

Eugenics: science of improving a species through control of hereditary factors by manipulation of the gene pool

Gene: fragment of deoxyribonucleic acid (DNA) that encodes a single protein

Gene-splicing: technique by which recombinant DNA is produced and made to function in an organism

Gene therapy: insertion of a normal gene into the nucleus of a cell to compensate for a defective one

Genetic marker: dominant gene or trait that serves to identify genes or traits linked with it

Germ cell alteration: changes in DNA structure during the earliest stages of cell growth (before differentiation)

Recombinant DNA synthesis: insertion of DNA segments from one species into the DNA of another species

Restriction fragment length polymorphism: genetically variable DNA fragments usually used as *markers* for a nearby disease gene

Somatic alteration: in vitro isolation of a specific gene that is then synthetically reproduced in the laboratory

---

VOLUNTARY VS. MANDATORY GENETIC SCREENING

Screening for genetic disorders isn't new. Progress in mapping defective genes to particular chromosomes has led to more sophisticated tests, which probe directly for the faulty gene or a nearby "marker" gene. Moreover, scientists are learning more about the genetic basis of diseases, such as diabetes, cancer, and hypertension.

In and of itself, genetic screening is ethically neutral. Applications of this technology, however, may be acceptable. Prenatal, neonatal, or adult screening can be used to improve treatment, guide personal decisions, and initiate prevention programs. Other applications are an ethical Pandora's box.

Mandatory screening

The ethical principle of beneficence requires that a procedure help the patient. Mandatory genetic screening can be beneficial, such as in the case of neonatal screening for phenylketonuria, in which early detection prevents mental retardation. But what about mandatory testing for incurable illnesses such as Huntington's disease? No doubt some patients will want to know this information and can use it constructively. Others, however, could be seriously harmed psychologically. In this instance, voluntary screening is ethically acceptable, and mandatory screening is not.

Creation of a "biological underclass"

Insurance companies have been among the first to be charged with genetic discrimination. From the company's point of view, it's a sound business decision to increase premiums or deny coverage to anyone with a serious medical condition or at high risk for developing such a condition. Unfortunately, predictive tests don't always tell the whole story. A single faulty gene may not cause trouble unless other related genes also are defective, or the gene may never be expressed unless it's set off by an environmental trigger. A patient who's seen as "certain to become disabled" rather than "at risk" could easily join the ranks of the uninsured, with little legal recourse.

Employers represent another source of potential genetic discrimination. In times of increasing health care costs, employers may avoid hiring someone who is likely to incur large medical bills. Industry officials also argue that genetic screening can identify workers who might be especially sensitive to industrial toxins. A more ethical approach would be to clean up the workplace so that all workers face a decreased risk.

Patient confidentiality

Preserving patient confidentiality may help to guard against abuses of genetic information. However, confidentiality isn't an absolute right. The confidentiality of health-related information, in particular, is protected by law only when the health and well-being of others aren't threatened.

It's unclear whether the disclosure of genetic information represents a breach of confidentiality. Certainly, the right to treatment of a child with phenylketonuria supersedes the parents' right to confidentiality. But what about a patient who has a positive test for the Huntington's disease gene? Here, confidentiality should be preserved, but the widespread use of computerized records makes this task increasingly difficult.

JUSTICE AND GENETIC SCREENING

Justice, as an ethical principle in health care, requires equal sharing of the risks and benefits of diagnostic tests and treatments offered to patients. Genetic screening programs haven't always adhered to this principle. When large-scale screening programs for sickle cell carriers were initiated in the 1970s, for example, participants received little or no posttest counseling or follow-up care. In contrast, similar programs set up to screen for Tay-Sachs disease included teaching programs, support groups, and financial aid. All genetic screening programs need to incorporate this sort of thorough follow-up care.

The justice principle also impinges on the issue of health insurance coverage. Because serious chronic diseases raise everyone's premiums, it would seem that justice is best served by asking those who pose a greater risk to bear more than the average share of the cost. The danger is that these people may never develop the disease. If so, they've been unfairly overcharged.

YOUR ROLE IN GENE THERAPY

Genetic manipulation, including gene therapy, is still experimental. As a result, few NPs are directly involved in this aspect of genetic research. Nonetheless, you have an ethical obligation to stay informed and to support efforts to establish legal and technological safeguards.

You're more likely to be involved in genetic screening. If so, you have an important role to play in dealing with the related ethical conflicts. Your ethical responsibilities may involve:
● making sure that the patient understands the procedure and gives informed consent before the test
● thoroughly reviewing options for treatment or prevention of a genetic disease during posttest counseling
● refusing to take part in compulsory screening programs
● refusing to disclose test results to unauthorized people
● actively supporting legislation to prevent genetic discrimination by employers and insurance companies.

RIGHT TO KNOW VS. RIGHT TO SAFETY

Seeking new knowledge is an essential part of human nature. Yet society tends to oppose the scientist's right to uncontrolled experimentation. This is particularly true with regard to genetic research. Many people believe in the sanctity of life and view genetic screening and manipulation as violations of that principle, especially when

human beings are involved. The public also has a right to protection and personal safety. Thus, it seems likely that the federal government will be involved in regulating genetic research.

Scientists will remain suspicious of attempts to control their work, and a large segment of the public will oppose unregulated tinkering with the building blocks of life. Our hope is that both sides will remember that the dignity, value, and worth of human life must be preserved at all costs.

Selected references

AIDS Info, BBS Database: *aidsinfobbs.org*

American Medical Association: *www.ama-assn.org*

Annas, G.J. "Why We Should Ban Human Cloning," *New England Journal of Medicine* 339(2):122-5, July 9, 1998.

Bioethics Discussion Pages: *www-hsc.usc.edu/~mbernste*

Bioethics Online Service: *www.mcw.edu/bioethics/index.html*

Bott, J. "HIV and Women: Health and Childbearing Issues," *British Journal of Midwifery* 8(1):15-19, January 2000.

Bradley, E.H., et al. "The Patient Self-Determination Act and Advanced Directive Completion in Nursing Homes," *Archives of Family Medicine* 7(5): 417-423, September-October 1998.

Burkhardt, M.A., and Nathanial, A.K. *Ethics and Issues in Contemporary Nursing.* Albany, N.Y.: Delmar Pubs., 1998.

Cameron, M.E. "The Slippery Slope of Decision Making for Persons with Dementia," *Journal of Professional Nursing* 14(1):6, January-February 1998.

Campbell, G. "Ethical Principles Must Guide Us," *AACN News* 15(1):2,12, January 1998.

Catalano, J.T. *Nursing Now: Today's Issues, Tomorrow's Trends,* 2nd ed. Philadelphia: F.A. Davis Co., 2000.

Chambers, T. "Centering Bioethics," *Hastings Center Report* 30(1): 22-29, January/February 2000.

Cline, H.S. "Genetic Testing of Children: An Issue of Ethical and Legal Concern," *Pediatric Nursing* 25(1):61-65, 68, January/February 1999.

Cloonan, P.A., et al. "Interdisciplinary Education in Clinical Ethics: A Work in Progress." *Holistic Nursing Practice* 13(2):12-19, January 1999.

Duquette, S.L., et al. "Transplantation. Living-Donor Lobar Lung Transplantation: A Case Study," *Critical Care Nurse* 20(1):69-80, February 2000.

Etzioni, A. "HIV Testing of Infants: Privacy and Public Health," *Health Affairs* 17(4):170-183, July/August 1998.

Fisher, M.A., and Mitchell, G.J. "Patients' Views of Quality of Life: Transforming the Knowledge Base of Nursing," *Clinical Nurse Specialist* 12(3):99-105, May 1998.

Garman, M.E. "Futile Care: At What Point Have We Done Enough," *AACN News* 17(3):5, March 2000.

Gene Letter: *www.geneletter.org*

Guido, G.W. *Legal Issues In Nursing*, 2nd ed. Stanford, Conn.: Appleton & Lange, 1997.

Hawkins, J.W., and Bellig, L.L. "The Evolution of Advanced Practice Nursing in the United States: Caring for Women and Newborns," *Journal of Obstetric, Gynecologic, and Neonatal Nursing* 29(1): 83-89, January/February 2000.

Helix (Genetic Testing): http://healthlinks.washington.edu/helix

HIV Info Web: *www.infoweb.org/infoweb*

Hopkins, P.D. "Bad Copies: How Popular Media Represents Cloning as an Ethical Problem," *The Hasting Center Report* 28(2):6-13, March/April 1998.

Institute for Genomic Research (TIGR): *www.tigr.org*

Kaplow, R. "Use of Nursing Resources and Comfort of Cancer Patients With and Without Do-Not-Resuscitate Orders in the Intensive Care Unit," *American Journal of Critical Care* 9(2): 87-95, March 2000.

Krishnasamy, M. "Nursing, Morality, and Emotions: Phase I and Phase II Clinical Trials and Patients with Cancer," *Cancer Nursing* 22(4):251-59, August 1999.

Mack, K.A., and Bland, S.D. "HIV Testing Behaviors and Attitudes Regarding HIV/Aids of Adults Aged 50-64," *Gerontologist* 39(6):687-94, December 1999.

Meier, D.E., et al. "A National Survey of Physician-Assisted Suicide and Euthanasia in the United States," *New England Journal of Medicine* 338(17):1193-1201, April 23, 1998.

Menzel, L.K. "Is It Worth It? Balancing the Benefit of Extended Life with the Cost of Suffering During Critical Illness," *Critical Care Nurse* 18(4):67-73, August 1998.

Monsen, R.B. "Genetics and Health Care," *Journal of Pediatric Nursing* 14(2):71-72, April 1999.

Munro, N.L. "Apply the Rules of 'People Ethics,'" *AACN News* 15(11):2, 15 November 1998.

National Human Genome Research Institute (NHGRI): *www.nhgri.nih.gov*

Office of Genetics and Disease Prevention: *www.cdc.gov/genetics*

Parks, J.A. "Why Gender Matters to the Euthanasia Debate. On Decisional Capacity and the Rejection of Women's Death Requests," *Hastings Center Report* 30(1):30-36, January/February 2000.

Penticuff, J.H., and Walden, M. "Influence of Practice Environment and Nurse Characteristics on Perinatal Nurses' Responses to Ethical Dilemmas," *Nursing Research* 49(2):64-72, March/April 2000.

Ryden, M.B., et al. "Nursing Home Resuscitation Policies and Practices for Residents without DNR Orders," *Geriatric Nursing* 19(6):315-21, November-December 1998.

Savage, T. "Ethics, The Outpatient Pediatric Nurse, and Managed Care," *Pediatric Nursing* 25(2):197-99, 207, March/April 1999.

Sinclair, B.P. "HIV and Women: Understand Your Responsibilities; Reduce Your Risk," *AWHONN Lifelines* 3(6):35-38, December 1999-January 2000.

Strodtbeck, F., et al. "Coping with Transition: Neonatal Nurse Practitioner Education for the 21st Century," *Journal of Pediatric Nursing* 13(5):272-278, October 1998.

Terry, P.B. "The Practice of Ethics in Critical Care Units," *Journal of Critical Care Illness* 5(3):152-60, March 2000.

Twomey, J.G. "Ethical Voices of Pediatric Mental Health Nurses," *Journal of Pediatric Nursing* 15(1):36-46, February 2000.

Williams, J.K. "Genetic Testing: Implications for Professional Nursing," *Journal of Professional Nursing* 14(3):184-88, May-June 1998.

Wurzbach, M.E. "Acute Care Nurses' Experiences of Moral Certainty," *Journal of Advanced Nursing* 30(2):287-93, August 1999.

Chapter Nine

ETHICAL CONFLICTS IN PROFESSIONAL PRACTICE

The ethical commitment that each *nurse practitioner (NP)* brings to her work affects patients and their families, colleagues, and the entire health care delivery system. As NPs gain power and influence, they're becoming a more visible force in resolving the ethical dilemmas that confront modern health care.

This chapter discusses three ethical responsibilities of the NP: respecting the patient's autonomy, including the right to *confidentiality* and the right to refuse treatment; blowing the whistle on misconduct by colleagues; and responding to the problem of substance abuse among your peers.

Respecting the patient's autonomy

Autonomy is based on the right of self-determination, whereby a patient may refuse any treatment, ordinary or extraordinary. The decision to refuse ordinary treatment, however, presents an especially complex ethical dilemma. This dilemma hinges on the conflict between *beneficence* and autono-

my. If a patient can make an informed decision, he has a right to refuse treatment. But what if his decision doesn't serve his best interests? Which moral principle, autonomy or beneficence, should take precedence? (See *Saying no to rehabilitation,* pages 256 and 257.)

AUTONOMY AND ITS LIMITS

Autonomy gives the patient the right to maintain control over his life and make decisions about his health care. It's one of the cornerstones of ethical decision making. As with many other ethical rights and principles, however, autonomy isn't absolute. It can be limited by external and internal sources.

External sources

The legal system formally places limits on autonomy. It forbids individuals from committing suicide and family members and health care providers from helping patients to commit suicide. Although several states still have assisted-suicide laws on the books, the procedure is rarely used. The legal system can also force patients who have contagious diseases that threaten pub-

Saying no to rehabilitation

One of the rewards of rehabilitation nursing is watching a patient with severe injuries come to terms with an altered body image and eventually go on to live a fulfilling life with a disability. But what happens when a patient turns down the help that nurse practitioners (NPs) and therapists offer? Professional health care providers may experience a bitter ethical conflict between the principle of patient autonomy, which includes the right to refuse treatment, and the principle of beneficence. Consider the case of Philip Munson, a young quadriplegic who refused rehabilitative treatment, deciding that he preferred to die.

Wanting to die

Philip Munson, 30, was left a C3 quadriplegic after he broke his neck in an automobile accident. First admitted to the intensive care unit (ICU), Mr. Munson was totally dependent on others for all activities and all aspects of his care. His only relatives were a brother and a sister-in-law, who visited regularly and planned to have him live with them after rehabilitation.

During his month in the ICU, Philip told his health care providers that he wanted to live. Shortly after being transferred to the rehabilitation unit, however, he changed his mind. He wanted to die and insisted on discontinuing his rehabilitation program. His brother made it clear that he wanted Mr. Munson's wishes respected. A psychiatrist evaluated Mr. Munson and concluded that he was competent and showed no evidence of psychosis or thought disorder.

Mr. Munson understood his condition and his prognosis; he was aware that after rehabilitation he would be able to operate a wheelchair and a computer. He also understood that he would be paralyzed from the neck down and would always need assistance with activities of daily living. Mr. Munson said that he wasn't afraid of death and wanted no heroic measures taken. His brother helped him draft an extensive legal statement establishing the right to refuse specific treatments, including antibiotic and I.V. therapy. Plans were made to discharge him to a nursing home.

Ethical considerations

Many of the health care providers on the rehabilitation unit were distressed by the decision to stop Mr. Munson's program. Depression, anger, and refusal of treatment are common among young accident victims, and these health care professionals were skilled at encouraging, bargaining with, and even coercing patients to comply. They argued that Mr. Munson's decision was misguided and that there was justification for intervention based on the principles of paternalism and beneficence.

Jim DiFrancesco, RN, FNP, on the rehabilitation team, pointed out that there was a significant difference between a young, recently injured quadriplegic and a terminal cancer patient who finally decides to "pull the plug." He believed that Mr. Munson was under too much stress from the initial impact of the injury and would probably later change his mind and view life as worth living once again. He pointed out to members of the health care team that many patients reverse their decision to die. For example, Elizabeth Bouvia, a young woman incapacitated by cerebral palsy, received national publicity when she requested that the hospital discontinue her tube feedings and allow her to starve herself to death, but she later changed her mind and stated that she wanted to live.

Mr. DiFrancesco pointed out that many factors, such as depression, fear of treatment, hidden family dynamics, and ambivalence, complicated Mr. Munson's ability to make an autonomous decision. Furthermore, Mr. Munson was clearly ambivalent about his desire to die. His behavior wasn't always consistent with his expressed wish for death. For example, Mr. Munson was cheerful on many days and took great interest in the positioning of his joints and measures taken to prevent joint contractures.

In fact, for a brief period, Mr. Munson reneged on his wish to die. His best friend

Saying no to rehabilitation *(continued)*

from high school learned about the accident and decided to devote a long visit to helping Philip. When he learned his friend would be arriving soon, Mr. Munson asked to start full therapy again. Although his high school buddy helped out tirelessly and offered to stay even longer, Mr. Munson quickly became overwhelmed by the pain and hardship of his existence and requested that his previous statement outlining his wish to die be reactivated.

Respecting patient autonomy

An RN on the team, Christina Walsh, pointed out that the rehabilitation center's mission was to serve the patient's best interest, not meet the emotional needs of the staff. She believed that members of the health care team had their own vested interest in keeping Mr. Munson alive. For example, the occupational therapist was excited about experimenting with the latest wheelchair control devices. Many of her coworkers, accustomed to seeing their patients readjust to life, couldn't accept that they would inevitably fail some of their patients. It wasn't right, asserted Ms. Walsh, to pursue every technological intervention regardless of the cost or burden to the patient.

An ethical struggle

During the time Mr. Munson remained on the rehabilitation unit, the professionals caring for him experienced an intense ethical struggle. It was difficult to agree not to perform routine tracheostomy care or range-of-motion exercises or to care for the pressure ulcer that developed on the back of Mr. Munson's head. It also was difficult, however, to do these things in good conscience for a patient who asked that they not be done. It seemed like a total usurpation of what little power and control Mr. Munson still had. Each nurse had to struggle with questions about the rights of a patient who doesn't have the ability to leave the hospital against medical advice, protest his treatment, or even verbally complain without the assistance of another person.

Mr. Munson's ordeal finally came to an end when he was transported to a nursing home near the residence of his brother's family. After 2 months, he slipped into a coma and died. His existence was a lesson to the rehabilitation team: Most patients are grateful for the opportunity for a second chance at life; for some, however, the pain is too great. Ultimately, the decision to accept treatment belongs to the patient.

---

lic safety to be treated, even if that treatment requires incarceration.

Additionally, family members and health care providers can exert appreciable, however informal, influence on a patient's decisions. Typically, this influence takes the form of persuasion or encouragement. Infrequently, it takes the form of coercion, in which the patient comes to believe he has no free choice.

NP-patient relationships are inherently imbalanced. As an NP, you possess knowledge, skill, and authority, whereas the patient possesses fear, doubt, and a need for care. Because the patient has a health care need, he as-

sumes a dependent and potentially vulnerable position. He must trust you, yet he may feel that being assertive or questioning your advice isn't appropriate. You can counteract this feeling by encouraging the patient to be informed and to ask questions.

Internal sources

The patient's feelings of self-doubt, his lack of knowledge, and his illness all combine to reduce his autonomy. For instance, the patient may see himself as too ignorant to make crucial decisions about his health. One way you can counter this belief is to bolster his self-esteem by assuring him that it's appropriate to take an active role in decision making, and then support him in his efforts. The patient's signs and symptoms, such as dyspnea, nausea, or pain, may distract him. You should use appropriate medications and treatments to relieve them so the patient can make more autonomous decisions.

BENEFICENCE

When you're caring for children, the mentally incompetent, or other patients who are unable to make informed decisions, the principle of beneficence supersedes the right to autonomy. Young children, for instance, don't understand the implications of not being vaccinated for measles or mumps; they would simply prefer to avoid the pain of an injection.

For competent patients who can make their own informed decision, applying the principle of beneficence is more ethically demanding. The ***burden of proof*** for using beneficence in place of autonomy lies with the health care provider. Arguments that the NP can use to support the use of beneficence over autonomy include the following:
● The patient is under excessive stress and can't think rationally.
● The patient may change his mind later, when little or nothing can be done to restore his health.
● The patient needs to be protected from acting irrationally as a result of emotion or anxiety.

These arguments must be used with caution and only in selected situations to avoid the trap of paternalism (the belief that, because the health care provider possesses superior medical knowledge, the patient should follow any advice given without question). Years ago, paternalism was a common element of health care. The current health care system generally rejects the principle of paternalism; health care providers who attempt to practice it run the risk of violating the legal principle of ***informed consent.***

FUTILITY

Medical futility refers to treatment that can't benefit a patient, not necessarily because the treatment itself has no merit, but more frequently because the patient's condition makes the medical action futile. A futile intervention differs from one that is harmful, ineffective, or impossible, and it shouldn't be equated with hopelessness. Hope may be maintained by patients even in impossible situations.

A futile treatment differs from an ineffective or highly improbable treatment in that it often may achieve a short-term gain (such as relieving pain in a cancer patient or improving carbon dioxide excretion in a ventilated patient who has chronic obstructive pulmonary disease), but it remains fruitless because it doesn't lead to a true personal benefit (restoration of health).

Often, health care providers feel strongly about rendering care that they deem futile. With the growing emphasis on patient autonomy and self-determination, however, health care providers are less likely to make these decisions independently. Patients believe they have a right to determine what constitutes a "benefit" to them. At the same time, health care providers believe that they're better able to judge when a treatment is futile, based on their knowledge of the treatment and the likely outcome on the patient's quality of life. Another complicating factor in today's era of ***managed care*** is that the third-party payer may have an influence on what course of action is to be taken. Indirectly, the patient's right to choose his treatment may be limited by the health care provider who feels a duty to provide the best care possible and by the health care payer who has an obligation to allocate scarce resources equitably.

Ethicists argue that, while autonomy and self-determination give the patient the right to refuse treatment or to choose from medically justifiable options, the patient nevertheless doesn't have a right to demand any and all possible treatment. Furthermore, with growing emphasis on **cost containment,** it's likely that futile treatment won't even be offered as a patient option in the future. In some **health maintenance organizations,** medical treatment is already becoming a function of statistical measurement of probable benefits to patients.

Helga Wanglie represents a classic case in futility. This 85-year-old woman was unconscious and connected to a mechanical ventilator at a hospital after suffering a heart attack at the long-term care facility where she resided for the past 10 years. The physicians wanted to withdraw the life-sustaining support they deemed to be futile, but her husband objected and had her transferred to another medical center, where she was diagnosed as being in a **persistent vegetative state.** The physician at the second hospital concurred and suggested removing the ventilator.

The family ultimately asked the courts to decide if the physicians could be compelled to provide treatment they believed to be of little benefit to a patient with no hope of recovery. The courts appointed the husband conservator and decided to honor his request for life support. This decision reflects a recurrent problem in attempting to resolve ethical dilemmas in courts of law. The judge's decision wasn't based on ethical principles or medical values but, rather, on the legal mandate that the husband as the legal surrogate had the right to make any and all decisions about the patient's health care. In this case, autonomy, as a legal principle, held precedence over the physicians' professional judgment of the futility of extraordinary treatments.

Confidentiality and the right to privacy

The **American Nurses Association's (ANA's)** Code for Nurses states that, as an NP, you must safeguard the patient's right to **privacy** by judiciously protecting information of a confidential nature. The patient's belief that the health care provider will maintain confidentiality is the basis for the trusting relationship between the health care provider and patient that is necessary for the provision of effective care. A patient must often reveal sensitive or embarrassing information during his assessment if an accurate diagnosis is to be made. The patient must have confidence that this information will be shared in a professional manner and only with those who require it for his care. (See *Right to privacy,* page 260.)

UNDERLYING PRINCIPLES
Underlying confidentiality are two key ethical principles: autonomy and **fidelity.** Autonomy, as discussed previously, is the patient's right to make decisions about his own health care; it includes his right to maintain control over personal information (right to privacy). Fidelity refers to one's faithfulness to obligations that one has accepted. To maintain confidentiality, the NP's ethical belief in the patient's right to maintain autonomy must outweigh the urge to talk about patients in a nonprofessional setting. All health care professionals pledge to keep patient information confidential when they accept the authority granted by licensure. It's a very serious obligation. Without fidelity and respect for confidentiality, meaningful NP-patient relationships can't survive.

BREACHES OF CONFIDENTIALITY
As with autonomy, confidentiality isn't an absolute patient right. Health care providers have an ethical right and, in

Right to privacy

When entering the hospital, most patients tacitly agree to sacrifice a considerable amount of privacy to enable health care professionals to plan and provide care. Occasionally, however, a patient refuses to cooperate. If his resistance hampers your ability to give good care, you may face an ethical dilemma, as the following case study shows.

Hidden medicine bottle

John Gordon is admitted to the hospital with chronic diarrhea. All diagnostic tests have been negative. His primary health care provider, Mary Stein, RN, FNP, suspects that Mr. Gordon is causing the diarrhea by taking laxatives, a charge Mr. Gordon vehemently denies.

Mr. Gordon's nurse, Susan Morrison, is starting to think that Ms. Stein may be right. Yesterday, Mr. Gordon put a medicine bottle in his satchel as she walked into his room. When she asked him what was in the bottle, he became defensive and refused to answer.

Ms. Stein asks Ms. Morrison to "do a little detective work" by searching Mr. Gordon's room for laxatives the next time he receives visitors in the lounge. "After all," she tells her, "we can't help Mr. Gordon until we know for sure what's going on."

Ethical considerations

At first, Ms. Morrison is willing to conduct a search of Mr. Gordon's room. Later, she begins to have doubts about whether such a search would be ethical. She decides to write down her concerns:

• Do we know Mr. Gordon is lying when he denies taking laxatives? Several possible explanations exist for his defensive behavior. Perhaps he doesn't know what a laxative is and is reluctant to reveal his ignorance.

• Why did he hide the medicine bottle? He might be embarrassed to admit he's taking a home remedy. There may be several other reasons. What appears to be a medicine bottle could contain any number of things.

• Even if Mr. Gordon is lying, is a search justified? Can one person's unethical behavior justify another's? Nurse practitioners, after all, are medical authorities, not moral authorities.

• Even if conducting an investigation is necessary, wouldn't openly searching Mr. Gordon's room without his permission be more ethical than conducting a search behind his back?

• What about Ms. Stein's role in this incident? Should I allow her to delegate this distasteful duty to me?

• Even if Mr. Gordon is indeed lying and is taking laxatives, who — besides himself — is he harming? Doesn't he have the right to treat himself with an over-the-counter medication against his physician's advice?

• How would a search affect my nurse-patient relationship with Mr. Gordon? If he thinks that I violated his trust, it will probably destroy it forever.

• Will the search really help us to accomplish our goal — to help Mr. Gordon get better? Unless we find out why he's taking a laxative, he'll probably continue taking it.

Presenting alternatives

Ms. Morrison decides that she has too many ethical misgivings to cooperate with the search. Before telling Ms. Stein about her decision, she outlines the ways in which she is willing to help. Her first recommendation is to call a conference with the patient. She's willing to discuss with Mr. Gordon the need for the health care team to know about all of his medications, including over-the-counter and home remedies, and to again ask him to identify the medication he takes. If Mr. Gordon still refuses to discuss the problem, she'll make it clear that she's willing to listen if he should change his mind.

She's also willing to arrange to be in Mr. Gordon's room during morning care. If, for example, she opens his drawer to get his toothbrush and finds a medicine bottle, she can then ask about it. But that's as far as she'll go. She won't participate in a search without the patient's consent, even in his presence. She realizes that, as Ms. Stein said, this might limit the ability of the health care team to help Mr. Gordon, but a competent patient has the right to forgo help.

some situations, a legal obligation to reveal confidential patient information. Examples include:

- situations in which failure to disclose information could lead to serious physical harm to the patient, his family, hospital staff, or any other third party
- certain types of injuries, such as gunshot wounds or knife stabbings
- infectious diseases that threaten the health of society (such as tuberculosis or sexually transmitted diseases)
- suspected child, spousal, or elder abuse.

Knowing when confidentiality may be appropriately breached, however, isn't always easy. Consider the two case studies below. For each case, decide whether you agree with the ethical decision reached.

Preventing harm to the patient

Kitisha Jefferson, RN, FNP, was providing follow-up care for Will Cooke, a 33-year-old electrician who broke his femur in a fall at a construction site. She had established a good NP-patient relationship with him during his stay in the hospital. However, during her morning rounds for the past 2 days, she noted that Mr. Cooke had seemed bored and edgy. When Ms. Jefferson came to check him on the 3rd day, she found his curtain drawn halfway around his bed. She walked to the open side and saw Mr. Cooke wiping his nose and hurriedly closing a plastic bag that contained white powder. "What are you doing?" she asked him.

"All right," Mr. Cooke replied. "You've taken good care of me, so I'll level with you. I was doing cocaine. I know I shouldn't, but it gets boring when you're in traction with nothing to do but watch the tube. Please, don't tell anybody. If my wife finds out, I'm finished."

Ms. Jefferson patiently explained that cocaine can have severe effects, especially when taken with other drugs. She advised Mr. Cooke to discontinue using cocaine at least while he's hospitalized.

After taking these measures, Ms. Jefferson still faced ethical dilemmas. What should she write in the patient's chart? Should she report it to Mr. Cooke's orthopedic surgeon? Or even report it to the police?

After careful consideration, Ms. Jefferson decided to tell Mr. Cooke that she had an obligation to let the health care team know about his cocaine use. Her decision was based on the ethical principle of beneficence; she believed the risk of cardiac arrest caused by the combination of cocaine and other medications was an overriding factor.

Protecting the patient's family

Jenny Chu, an obstetrics/gynecology NP, works in a busy inner-city clinic and was initiating the preoperative teaching for Susan Schaffer, a 32-year-old mother of five scheduled for a tubal ligation. Jenny wanted to be sure her patient understood the effects of this surgery, so she asked Mrs. Schaffer to explain the procedure. Mrs. Schaffer did so eagerly and added, "I'm so happy I won't have to worry about getting pregnant again. Five kids is more than I can handle as it is."

Ms. Chu felt that Mrs. Schaffer had a good grasp of the procedure so she moved on to other patients waiting to be seen. Later that day, she met Mrs. Schaffer's husband, Matt, at the clinic's front desk. He asked for a box of tissues and said, "I hope the surgery fixes Susan's problem. Did she tell you we've been trying to have another baby for over a year? I really want to have a few more kids."

What should Ms. Chu do — protect Mrs. Schaffer's confidentiality or tell Mr. Schaffer the truth? Ms. Chu felt that her first obligation was to protect Mrs. Schaffer's confidentiality. The urge to tell Mr. Schaffer about his wife's deception was compelling, but he wasn't in danger of physical harm from her action. Ms. Chu felt badly that Mr. and Mrs. Schaffer couldn't talk to each other frankly, but she also felt this wasn't an excuse for breaching confidentiality. Nonetheless, Ms. Chu decided to discuss the matter with the surgeon, especially because hospital policy required a spouse's signature on the **consent form** for a sterilization procedure.

Whistle-blowing

Whistle-blowing refers to the disclosure of illegal, immoral, or incompetent practices by a health care professional. The ANA Code for Nurses outlines the nurse's obligation to report acts of **negligence** or **incompetence** by other health care providers. It states that "the nurse acts to safeguard the patient and public when health care and safety are affected by incompetent, unethical, or illegal practice by any person."

The ANA guidelines on reporting incompetent, unethical, or illegal practices identify helpful parameters for judging problematic conduct. Incompetent practice is measured by standards established by professional organizations; unethical practice is evaluated in light of the Code for Nurses; and illegal practice is identified in terms of violations of the law. As a **patient advocate,** you must be willing to take appropriate action; in short, to blow the whistle on those who aren't meeting the standards of care.

WHEN TO BLOW THE WHISTLE
A health care professional who makes a mistake usually wants to ensure that it won't happen again. Correcting an error usually involves admitting the mistake, expressing honest regret, and completing an **incident report.** At times, though, you may encounter a health care professional who makes repeated mistakes, attempts to cover

them up or minimize them, and engages in suspect or misleading behaviors. To uphold the ethical standards of your profession, you need to report these individuals to the proper authorities. (See *Is whistle-blowing warranted?*)

IMPLICATIONS OF WHISTLE-BLOWING
As a professional, you may equate whistle-blowing with heroic self-sacrifice: a moral victory in the midst of a professional defeat. In fact, some NPs have had their reputations tarnished, lost their jobs, or been named in **libel** suits after reporting professional misconduct. Fortunately, such bitter retaliation is rare. Keep in mind, however, that the higher the professional standing of the health professional who commits misconduct, the greater the risk you face when blowing the whistle. (See *Whistle-blowing: A systematic approach,* page 264.)

REPORTING MISCONDUCT
Usually, facility channels exist through which you can report the misconduct of those you're supervising, such as nurses or nursing assistants, without fear of reprisal. Often, a nurse-manager and the facility personnel office assume joint responsibility for investigating allegations of misconduct. For you, the only drawback is animosity from the affected staff member and, possibly, from her acquaintances or sympathizers. The benefits, though, include correcting an injustice, preventing harm to patients, and strengthening your sense of moral integrity.

REPORTING MEDICAL OR MANAGEMENT MISCONDUCT
If you report the misconduct of a physician, an NP, a nursing supervisor, a nurse manager, or a member of the facility administration, expect stiffer resistance and possibly more severe retaliation, especially if management has cooperated in concealing the miscon-

Is whistle-blowing warranted?

How do you know whether to blow the whistle on a colleague? The decision may require careful deliberation and judgment. Review the two case studies below. Do you think that each nurse practitioner's decision to blow the whistle is justified?

Habitually late colleague

An hour after the pediatric care clinic opened for the day, Sylvia Myers, RN, PNP, can't locate her colleague, Mary Calvo, RN, PNP. She checks the sign-in record, which shows that Ms. Calvo arrived on time. A few minutes later, Ms. Myers sees Ms. Calvo with her coat and gloves on, getting off the elevator.

Ms. Myers approaches Ms. Calvo and asks where she's been. Ms. Calvo impatiently tells her to mind her own business and adds, "You have no idea how hard it is to raise three kids and have to work."

Upset and confused, Ms. Myers decides that she'd better find out what's going on. After some investigation, she realizes that one of the RNs in the clinic, Allison Henkel, a mutual friend, has been signing in for Ms. Calvo. Ms. Henkel tells her that Ms. Calvo arrives up to an hour late two to three times a week. She goes on to say, "Don't worry. I'll keep covering for Ms. Calvo. What's important is that we're helping Ms. Calvo out and no one's getting hurt."

Ms. Myers is faced with an ethical dilemma: Should she report Ms. Calvo's lateness and Ms. Henkel's cover-up? Or should she remain quiet; after all, Ms. Calvo's lateness hasn't affected patient care thus far, and blowing the whistle might undermine her friendship with Ms. Henkel.

After careful consideration, Ms. Myers decides that there is no getting around the fact that Ms. Calvo is jeopardizing her patients' well-being. Ms. Henkel shares partial responsibility. Although sympathetic to Ms. Calvo's child-care problems, Ms. Myers recognizes her overriding obligations to ensure the health and safety of patients.

Ms. Myers decides that her first step is to talk directly to Ms. Calvo about the situation. If Ms. Calvo's behavior persists, Ms. Myers will explain that she's ethically obligated to report Ms. Calvo to the manager. Before taking any action, Ms. Myers is careful to document specific circumstances of Ms. Calvo's lateness.

Questioning medical protocol

Rachel Kirkwood, RN, FNP, is in charge of a small oncology unit that develops treatment protocols for the National Cancer Institute. She has worked for several years on the unit, finds her position rewarding, and enjoys a good relationship with the medical staff. However, the latest protocol of the chief oncologist troubles her. None of the patients are improving with the experimental therapy. Ms. Kirkwood knows from her own extensive clinical experience that patients with the same condition fare much better with conventional therapy.

Ms. Kirkwood decides to share her concerns with the oncologist. He responds curtly, saying only that his research brings a large grant for the unit. He makes it clear that he doesn't want to discuss the matter with her any further.

Ms. Kirkwood is faced with a choice: Should she defer to the oncologist's knowledge and trust his sense of professional responsibility? Or should she pursue her concerns?

Ms. Kirkwood realizes that, at this point, her options are limited. She's in no position to make charges against the chief oncologist, but she can still take steps to correct the situation. She decides to discuss the matter confidentially with another oncologist and see what insight he can provide. In addition, she begins keeping accurate records of each patient's treatment and its results. If the evidence she gathers indicates that the patients are suffering harm and the chief oncologist continues to ignore her, Ms. Kirkwood is ready to blow the whistle.

Ms. Kirkwood is committed to preparing herself for the long haul. She gathers numerous articles on whistle-blowing and arranges to meet with a lawyer experienced in representing whistle-blowers. Aware that her actions may jeopardize her job, she has begun to search for alternative employment, and she also realizes that she must emotionally prepare to deal with the wrath of coworkers, especially those who disagree with her conclusions.

Whistle-blowing: A systematic approach

Like other nursing actions, whistle-blowing can be carried out successfully if it's planned, systematic, and purposeful.

Gathering facts

Begin by gathering all the facts. Then put in writing the misconduct you want to report. Be sure to include the incident's date and time, the person or people involved, and the source of your information. Above all, avoid accusations and personal opinions.

Stating the problem

Clearly state the problem and identify causative factors. Was incompetence or negligence involved? Were supplies adequate? Did equipment malfunction? Was facility policy at fault?

When answering these questions, try to eliminate your personal biases. If possible, review the problem with a trusted colleague.

Determining your objective

State your objective in confronting the problem. For example, you may want to eliminate threats to patient safety; eliminate illegal, immoral, or illegitimate practices; uphold professional ethical standards; or put into effect needed changes in institutional policy.

Confronting the problem

Confront the person who committed the misconduct in a constructive, nonthreatening way. Express your concerns and ask for an explanation of the incident. Seek reassurance that the problem will be addressed.

Deciding whether to blow the whistle

After a reasonable duration, determine if the problem has been corrected. If it hasn't, identify the pros and cons of whistle-blowing. The pros include correction of a harmful or potentially harmful situation, retained moral integrity, and an enhanced sense of moral accountability. The cons include alienation, stress, and possible loss of reputation, professional standing, and job. After you weigh the pros and cons, talk over the issue of whistle-blowing with your lawyer or other knowledgeable person before you proceed.

Next, realistically appraise your situation. Will you be able to cope if you blow the whistle? Are you secure professionally and financially? Do you have the support of your family, colleagues, or administration? How much help can you count on?

Now make your decision based on your analysis of the severity of the incident, the consequences of whistle-blowing, and your resources. If you elect to blow the whistle, carefully devise a strategy that follows institutional channels. If you're fearful of losing your job as a result of your actions, consider taking a position in another institution before you blow the whistle. If you fail to get satisfaction through institutional channels, consider consulting professional organizations, regulatory agencies and, as a last resort, the press. Be sure to document each step you take.

---

duct. Be prepared for a lengthy and hard-fought battle. That is because the accused professional may attempt to discredit you or have you fired rather than face the allegations honestly.

If you risk significant personal losses, you may want to make a thorough moral assessment before taking any action. If these losses extend to your dependents, consider the situation carefully. You may have moral grounds for not blowing the whistle if your dependents could be harmed emotionally, financially, or even physically.

Working through channels

Whistle-blowing can be pursued in one of two ways: by going public or by proceeding through the facility's chain of command. You should make every effort to correct the situation internally before going public. If you work successfully through the chain of command, you'll be able to accomplish your goals with a minimum of exposure. Ethically, you owe management an opportunity to fix the situation before you go public. For your own legal protection, you should maintain a record of your efforts to work through channels before considering more drastic measures.

If you fail to get satisfaction from the facility's chain of command, contact the appropriate regulatory agencies, including state boards of medicine or nursing. Contact the media only as a last resort.

Providing adequate documentation

Document your disclosure carefully. Write a clear, objective summary of the relevant facts. Explain why the information is significant and what needs to be done. Avoid focusing on personalities, and keep personal opinions to a minimum. Personal accusations detract from the disclosure and may invite a lawsuit for libel or ***slander.*** Have other professionals verify the information, if possible. This will lend objectivity to the information and may shield you from retaliation.

Surviving the setbacks

Prepare yourself for possible retaliation. Management often finds it easier to attack the whistle-blower than to address the problem. Colleagues may start giving you the cold shoulder, or you may experience overt harassment. Rumors that you're dishonest or incompetent may spread through the facility. To protect yourself and to maintain pressure on management, meticulously document everything, including continued incidents of incompetence or negligence. Photocopy all

documents, letters, and incident reports you file, and keep them in a secure location away from the facility. Be especially vigilant in your own practice, and document your actions carefully. Your employer may try to distract attention from the disclosure by portraying you as an incompetent worker or a troublemaker. To counteract this tactic, maintain diplomatic relations with as many colleagues as possible.

If you anticipate that whistle-blowing will cause severe personal hardship, consider mapping out a self-protection strategy. Find new employment before you blow the whistle, and retain a lawyer who'll provide you with competent legal advice throughout your ordeal. Seek out friends and colleagues who have the moral integrity to stand behind you.

Substance abuse among practitioners

An estimated 7% of the 2 million nurses in the United States are addicted to alcohol or drugs. In one state study, researchers found that more than 90% of disciplinary hearings for nurses in the state were related to alcohol and drug abuse. These statistics aren't surprising in light of the high stress levels found in today's health care system. In addition, NPs often experience feelings of frustration when trying to act as patient advocates in the face of ***managed care organizations.*** Many NPs shoulder tremendous family and financial obligations while trying to meet the demands of their professional practice. And, of course, NPs aren't immune to the anxieties of modern life. Combined with the availability of ***controlled substances,*** such stressors can easily lead to substance abuse.

PAST ATTITUDES TOWARD SUBSTANCE ABUSE

In the past, nurses who were caught abusing drugs or alcohol were removed from practice and punished. The prevailing ethic held that a nurse who abused drugs violated the public trust and the **standards** of her profession and deserved strong disciplinary action.

Nursing administrators were expected to report suspected substance abusers to their state nursing board. The board would then investigate the allegation and, if it found the nurse guilty, would impose such punishment as revocation of her license, fines, or even jail time.

In practice, though, many administrators didn't report substance abuse but chose instead to fire the offending nurse. In addition, colleagues of a suspected substance abuser commonly didn't report their suspicions because they knew the nurse's job would be in jeopardy. Aware of the harsh treatment that awaited them, nurses who abused drugs or alcohol switched jobs frequently rather than endure the repercussions that would follow an admission of abuse.

Ethical perspectives

From an ethical viewpoint, this punitive approach to substance abuse left much to be desired. Administrators who simply fired a substance abuser neglected their ethical responsibility to help nurses in need. Colleagues who didn't report substance abuse abandoned the best interests of both the addicted nurse and her patients. The substance abuser had little motivation to deal with the addiction, knowing that she was unlikely to receive understanding or rehabilitation.

A MORE ENLIGHTENED VIEW

Fortunately, society is now viewing substance abuse as a treatable disorder, and the emphasis is on rehabilitating chemically dependent nurses. Within the nursing profession, there is a greater understanding of the importance of peer support for the nurse struggling with addiction. **Nurse practice acts** may include provisions that encourage chemically dependent nurses to complete a treatment program. Peer-assistance programs have been established in many states; once a nurse requests entry into the program, all punitive actions are suspended, depending on the long-term results of the program. If the nurse has demonstrated success over a prescribed period of probation, no punitive action is taken against her license.

Many facilities now have policies for dealing with substance abuse among employees, from initial reporting through rehabilitation and returning to work. In addition, treatment programs have become commonplace, and associations for recovering nurses are available to provide needed support.

WHEN YOU SUSPECT SUBSTANCE ABUSE

Because of the high rate of chemical dependency among health care practitioners, chances are you'll encounter this problem sometime during your career. Initially, you may experience confusion, guilt, anger, and remorse if faced with the responsibility of confronting and reporting a colleague with a substance abuse problem. Numerous potential ethical conflicts may arise from this situation:

● You may feel torn between your obligation to protect patients and your loyalty to a fellow NP.

● You may feel that you contributed to the addiction by not acting sooner.

● If you aren't entirely certain your suspicions are correct, you may fear the damage you could do to an innocent professional's reputation and career.

● You may have difficulty accepting the addict's self-destructive behavior as part of her addiction.

- You may feel that you're betraying a friendship.

Although the decision to report a colleague is never an easy one, you have an ethical obligation to intervene if you suspect she's abusing drugs or alcohol. Intervening enables you to fulfill your moral obligation to your colleague. By reporting abuse, you compel her to take the first step toward regaining control over her life and undergoing rehabilitation. You also fulfill your obligation to patients by protecting them from a practitioner whose judgment and care don't meet professional standards.

Recognizing substance abuse

Be aware that allegations of substance abuse are serious and potentially damaging. To make an accurate assessment, you need to be familiar with the signs of substance abuse.

Signs of drug or alcohol abuse may include:
- rapid mood swings, usually from irritability or depression to elation
- frequent absences, lateness, and use of private quarters such as bathrooms
- excessive errors or problems with controlled substances, such as reports of broken vials or spilled drugs
- illogical or sloppy charting
- inability to meet deadlines or minimum job requirements
- avoidance of new and challenging assignments
- increased errors in treatment, particularly in dosage computation
- poor personal hygiene and appearance
- inability to concentrate or remember details
- alcohol on the breath
- slurred speech, unsteady gait, flushed face, or red eyes
- discrepancies in narcotics supplies
- preference for working alone or on the night shift, when supervision is minimal
- social withdrawal

- alcohol-induced complications, including jaundice, bruises (from falls), and delirium.

Reporting substance abuse

If you detect signs of substance abuse, your first step is to document them. Include the time, date, and place of the incident; a description of what happened; and the names of any witnesses. Be sure to leave out personal opinions and judgments. For example, "At 10:15 p.m. on January 15, 2001, I went to the restroom. When I opened the door, I saw June Barrett, NP, injecting some solution into her thigh using a hospital syringe. She told me to get out. I did. We didn't talk about it afterward."

Never confront or accuse the suspected abuser on your own. After you've documented the incident, discuss it with your medical director. He'll need to gather additional information by examining patient charts, medication records (especially for narcotics), and reports from patients and other health care personnel. After the director completes this review, he'll try to determine if the evidence corroborates your incident report.

Confronting the substance abuser

If the medical director concludes that substance abuse is likely, he'll need to confront the abuser with the facts and explain the options. It's hoped that these options will include treatment and perhaps eventual reinstatement in her position. (See *Helping an impaired colleague.*) If you're asked to be present for this confrontation, keep in mind that you best fulfill your moral obligation to the substance abuser by being honest, compassionate, and nonjudgmental and by expressing your willingness to help. Expect that she'll feel threatened, may become hostile, and may attempt to deny her condition even if the facts are fully substantiated.

Helping an impaired colleague

Colleagues can take steps to put a stop to a practitioner-addict's self-destructive behavior. By using an effective, nonpunitive, group-oriented approach, they can break the cycle of addiction. In this approach, group members confront the practitioner-addict, help her to acknowledge her condition, and motivate her to seek rehabilitation before she harms a patient or herself.

Intervention team

The team includes 2 to 10 carefully selected persons who are personal and professional associates of the practitioner-addict. If possible, the team also includes a colleague who has successfully entered rehabilitation and a practitioner who possesses experience in treating drug and alcohol addiction.

Team members must share a nonjudgmental attitude. Each must accept that the practitioner's self-destructive behavior represents an aspect of her illness and doesn't indicate that she's morally deficient. What's more, each should avoid expressing judgments about her.

CONFRONTING THE COLLEAGUE

Team members document all evidence of the practitioner's chemical dependence, including the date, time, and place of relevant incidents. They should be careful not to include any judgmental remarks in their documentation.

▼

The team leader reviews all important documentation, including patient charts, practitioners' notes and orders, narcotic prescriptions and narcotics records (such as for dispensing drug samples), and the impaired practitioner's personnel file.

▼

Team members meet with the impaired practitioner in a private room away from patient areas and the front desk. The group leader explains why the team has gathered. Participants present their evidence, always prefacing their testimony with positive remarks.

▼

The impaired practitioner is given a chance to respond.

▼

The team leader makes clear the options available to the impaired practitioner. The impaired practitioner is given an opportunity to voluntarily enter a treatment program; otherwise, she may lose her job and be reported to the state board of nursing.

▼

Arrangements are made for the team leader to monitor how the practitioner is progressing in therapy.

▼

Events of the meeting are documented.

▼

To ease the tension stirred up by the confrontation, the team leader may arrange for follow-up discussions.

In most substance abuse cases, if the abuser is willing to enter a treatment program and successfully completes it, no disciplinary action will be taken against her. If the abuser refuses to enter treatment, she may be reported to the state board of nursing or medicine, suspended, or dismissed.

The road back

In most instances, the recovering professional is able to return to practice after rehabilitation. She may be placed under a special contract that stipulates conditions for continued employment. These conditions may include:

● attending weekly meetings with a counselor
● participating in a 12-step program and meetings with other recovering professionals
● submitting to random blood and urine screenings
● remaining drug-free.

The medical director, who is responsible for the recovering professional, should carefully document all meetings and keep a copy of all contracts.

The chemically dependent professional's colleagues must use their compassion and training to try to understand her condition. Coworkers play a crucial role in the recovering professional's ultimate success or failure. When recovering from addiction, a person's needs include:

● finding ways to improve self-esteem, including assertiveness training
● developing a stronger support system
● developing stress-management and coping techniques
● learning to come to terms with past traumatic experiences, such as physical or sexual abuse.

Welcoming a recovering professional back to the work setting and offering support during the critical transition period is as important as detecting and reporting signs of abuse. From an ethical point of view, working with a colleague who is a substance abuser can be frustrating and uncomfortable, but helping an NP recognize her problem and begin the process of recovery is an act of significant moral courage and humanity.

Selected references

Agency for Health Care Policy and Research: *www.ahcpr.gov*

American Medical Association (AMA): *www.ama-assn.org*

American Nurses Association: *www.ana.org*

Brown-Saltzman, K. "Living with Ethical Dilemmas: The Art of Compromise," *AACN News* 15(10):2, October 1998.

Campbell, G. "Ethical Principles Must Guide Us," *AACN News* 15(1):2,12, January 1998.

Catalano, J.T. *Nursing Now: Today's Issues, Tomorrow's Trends,* 2nd ed. Philadelphia: F.A. Davis Co., 2000.

Chambers, T. "Centering Bioethics," *Hastings Center Report* 30(1):22-29, January/February 2000.

Cornelison, A.H. "A Profile of Ethical Principles," *Journal of Pediatric Nursing* 13(6):383-86, December 1998.

Crego, P.J., and Lipp, E.J. "Nurse's Knowledge of Advance Directives," *American Journal of Critical Care* 7(3):218-23, May 1998.

Ethics Manual, 4th ed. Philadelphia: American College of Physicians, 1998.

Freidson, E.L. "Professionalism and Institutional Ethics," in *The American Medical Ethics Revolution: How the AMA's Code of Ethics Has Transformed Physicians' Relationships to Patients, Professionals, and Society.* Edited by Baker, R.B., et al. Baltimore: Johns Hopkins University Press, 1999.

Kempski, K. "Discovering Peer Review in Medical Malpractice Cases," *Journal of Nursing Law* 5(3):25-32, March 1998.

Ott, B.B. "Advance Directives: The Emerging Body of Research," *American Journal of Critical Care* 8(1):514-519, January 1999.

Sullivan, M.C. "Ethics Integration Both Clinical and Organizational," *AACN News* 16(1):3, January 1999.

Chapter Ten

PATIENTS' RIGHTS

Patients are more knowledgeable, assertive, and involved in their health care than ever before. They question their diagnoses, seek assurances that their treatment is appropriate, and take action when care doesn't meet their expectations. They demand more education about wellness-related issues, risks, alternatives, and benefits, before consenting to treatment. In addition, patients expect confidentiality to be maintained. When disgruntled with care, patients now may initiate a malpractice suit, a complaint to the state's health professional licensing authority, or a criminal action suit. Therefore, health professionals must be aware of issues involving the "rights" of their patients.

YOUR ROLE IN PATIENTS' RIGHTS

At one time, nurses were forbidden to give patients even the most basic information about their care or health. Only physicians answered questions about a patient's condition.

In the 1960s, attitudes began to change. Demanding more information about their care, patients turned to

nurses to assist them in getting the information.

This chapter will help you apply sound legal principles when confronted with questions regarding patients' rights as you practice as a ***nurse practitioner (NP).*** It begins with a discussion of the evolution of patients' rights and goes on to outline your responsibilities in ensuring *informed consent,* respecting the patient's right to refuse treatment, and upholding his right to *privacy.* You'll find summaries of major U.S. Supreme Court rulings on the right to die and reproductive rights issues. You'll learn what your responsibilities are when you disclose confidential information, what steps to take when the patient leaves the hospital against medical advice, and how to avoid false imprisonment charges. Finally, you'll learn how to take responsibility for upholding the patient's dignity in regard to his decisions about death.

Documents upholding patients' rights

Bills of rights for patients, endorsed by major health care providers and consumer groups, have helped to reinforce the public's expectation of quality care. These documents define a person's rights while receiving health care.

For years, hospitals and extended care facilities have used the published **Patient's Bill of Rights** to inform consumers of some of their rights in the health care setting. These privately drafted bills of rights are designed to protect such basic rights as human dignity, privacy, **confidentiality,** informed consent, and refusal of treatment. They also assert the patient's right to receive a full explanation of the cost of medical care, to be fully informed, and to be required to give consent before participating in experimental treatments, as the patient exercises control over his own health care. These bills emphasize the patient's rights to information about *all aspects* of his care.

EARLY BEGINNINGS OF PATIENTS' RIGHTS

The concept of a formal document setting forth patients' rights has been around since 1959, when the **National League for Nursing (NLN)** issued its position paper outlining a series of seven points to help patients better understand nursing care. "What People Can Expect of Modern Nursing Practice" referred to the patient as a partner in health care, whose ultimate goal was self-care. (See *Landmarks in the evolution of patients' rights,* page 272.) Patients' rights received increasing public support during the 1960s as more people became aware of their rights as consumers. In a 1962 message to Congress, President John F. Kennedy further heightened this awareness when he outlined four basic consumer rights: the right to safety, the right to be in-

formed, the right to choose, and the right to be heard.

In 1973, the **American Hospital Association (AHA)** issued its "Statement on a Patient's Bill of Rights." The statement — the result of a study the AHA had conducted with consumer groups — listed 12 patient rights. (See *AHA patient's bill of rights,* page 273.) That same year, the Pennsylvania Insurance Department (PID) developed the "Citizens Bill of Hospital Rights," the first patient's bill of rights formulated by a government agency. This bill outlined the kinds of treatment a patient should expect in a hospital. It pointed out omissions in the AHA document. The PID also warned that it would enforce the bill by stopping Blue Cross and Blue Shield payments to hospitals and other health care facilities that failed to protect the rights described in the bill. Also in 1973, Minnesota became the first state to make a law protecting a patient's rights. That law required all state health care facilities to post Minnesota's patient's bill of rights conspicuously and to distribute it to their patients.

Since these early milestones, all states, many advocacy groups, and health care organizations have developed their own patient's bills of rights. In 1990, the Advisory Board of Directors of the Hospice Association of America approved a bill of rights for **hospice** patients. (See *ACLU patient's bill of rights,* pages 274 and 275, and *Hospice patient's bill of rights,* page 276.)

Congressional action

In 1973, Congress passed the Rehabilitation Act. This act guarantees the physically or mentally disabled person the right to any service available to a nondisabled person. In 1990, an expanded version of this act, called the Americans with Disabilities Act, was passed. The act prohibits discrimination on the basis of disability by employers with 15 or

(Text continues on page 275.)

Landmarks in the evolution of patients' rights

Due in part to growth in consumer activism, more attention is being paid to the rights of health care consumers. Despite such progress, however, no person is guaranteed an absolute right to health care. The following list highlights some of the landmarks in the evolution of patients' rights.

1959: The National League for Nursing issued the first patient's bill of rights, outlining seven points to help patients understand nursing care.

1973: The American Hospital Association (AHA) drew up a patient's bill of rights, listing 12 patient "rights."

Also in 1973, Minnesota passed a patient's bill of rights, modeled after the AHA bill, becoming the first state to establish a bill of rights as law.

1973 - 1978: The U.S. Congress enacted a series of laws designed to protect the rights of handicapped people. These laws included the Rehabilitation Act of 1973, the Community Mental Health Amendment of 1975, the Education for Handicapped Children Act of 1975, the Developmentally Disabled Assistance Bill of Rights Act, and the Rehabilitation Comprehensive Services and Development Disability Amendment of 1978.

1976: The New Jersey Supreme Court ruled in the *Quinlan* case, granting the parents of Karen Ann Quinlan, who was in a persistent vegetative state, permission to remove her ventilator. This was the first court case to use the constitutional right to privacy as a basis for withdrawing life support.

1980: The U.S. government passed the Mental Health Systems Act (MHSA), which included a bill of rights for patients receiving mental health services. Although much of this statute was later repealed, several states adopted recommendations found in the MHSA bill of rights.

1987: President Ronald Reagan signed the Omnibus Budget Reconciliation Act, which included provisions to protect the rights of patients receiving long-term care. Under the law, nursing homes could be fined up to $10,000 a day for violating a patient's rights.

1990: The Americans with Disabilities Act was signed into law. This wide-ranging legislation was intended to make America more accessible to people with disabilities. Specifically, the act prohibited discrimination on the basis of disability by employers with 15 or more employees and restricted employers' medical testing of employees and job applicants. Other portions of the act guaranteed that services, facilities, and telecommunications available to the general public must be available and accessible to individuals with disabilities.

Also in 1990, the U.S. Supreme Court ruled in the *Cruzan* case. The parents of Nancy Cruzan requested that their daughter's feeding tube be removed after she had spent several years in a persistent vegetative state. The Supreme Court refused their request, saying that, under the Constitution, a state had the right to require clear and convincing evidence that the patient wanted life-sustaining treatment withheld. The ruling implied that, when there was such evidence, the patient's desires would be respected.

1991: The Patient Self-Determination Act went into effect. This federal law called for hospitals, nursing homes, health maintenance organizations (HMOs), hospices, and home health care agencies that participate in Medicare and Medicaid to inform patients of their right (under state law) to draft advance directives, such as living wills, durable powers of attorney for health care, or any other document that states the patient's wishes with regard to health care should he become incapacitated. Facilities must honor the directives within the limits of existing state law.

1999: The U.S. House of Representatives passed a patient's bill of rights, allowing patients to sue their insurers in state court if a benefit is denied or delayed. The bill would let patients take complaints about their insurers to an independent outside panel whose decisions were binding on the health plan. It also would require HMOs or other insurers to pay for needed specialists and for routine patient care as ordered by the specialist. The bill must now be passed by the U.S. Senate.

AHA patient's bill of rights

The document below outlines the rights of the hospitalized patient as defined in 1992 by the American Hospital Association (AHA). Although the patient's bill of rights has no enforcement mechanism, many hospitals use it as a model when establishing guidelines for patient care.

A patient's bill of rights

1. The patient has the right to considerate and respectful care.

2. The patient has the right to obtain from his physician complete, current information about his diagnosis, treatment, and prognosis in terms the patient can be reasonably expected to understand. When it isn't medically advisable to give such information to the patient, it should be made available to an appropriate person in his behalf. He has the right to know, by name, the physician responsible for coordinating his care.

3. The patient has the right to receive from his physician information necessary to give informed consent prior to the start of any procedure or treatment. Except in emergencies, such information for informed consent should include but not necessarily be limited to the specific procedure or treatment, the medically significant risks involved, and the probable duration of incapacitation. Where medically significant alternatives for care or treatment exist, or when the patient requests information concerning medical alternatives, the patient has the right to such information. The patient has the right to know the name of the person responsible for the procedures or treatment.

4. The patient has the right to refuse treatment to the extent permitted by law and to be informed of the medical consequences of his action.

5. The patient has the right to every consideration of his privacy concerning his own medical care program. Case discussion, consultation, examination, and treatment are confidential and should be conducted discreetly. Those not directly involved in his case must have the permission of the patient to be present.

6. The patient has the right to expect that all communications and records pertaining to his care should be treated as confidential.

7. The patient has the right to expect that within its capacity a hospital must make reasonable response to the request of a patient for services. The hospital must provide evaluation, service, or referral as indicated by the urgency of the case. When medically permissible, a patient may be transferred to another facility only after he has received complete information and explanation concerning the needs for and alternatives to such a transfer. The facility to which the patient is to be transferred must first have accepted the patient for transfer.

8. The patient has the right to obtain information as to any relationship of his hospital to other health care and educational facilities insofar as his care is concerned. The patient has the right to obtain information as to the existence of any professional relationships among individuals, by name, who are treating him.

9. The patient has the right to be advised if the hospital proposes to engage in or perform human experimentation affecting his care or treatment. The patient has the right to refuse to participate in such research projects.

10. The patient has the right to expect reasonable continuity of care. He has the right to know in advance what appointment times and physicians are available and where. The patient has the right to expect that the hospital will provide a mechanism whereby his physician or a delegate of the physician informs him of the continuing health care requirements following discharge.

11. The patient has the right to examine and receive an explanation of his bill, regardless of source of payment.

12. The patient has the right to know what hospital rules and regulations apply to his conduct as a patient.

Reprinted with permission from the American Hospital Association.

ACLU patient's bill of rights

The American Civil Liberties Union (ACLU) developed this patient's bill of rights as a model for health care institutions.

Preamble

As you enter this health care facility, it's our duty to remind you that your health care is a cooperative effort between you as a patient and the physicians and hospital staff. During your stay a patient's rights advocate will be available to you. The duty of the advocate is to assist you in all the decisions you must make and in all situations in which your health and welfare are at stake. The advocate's first responsibility is to help you to understand the role of all who'll be working with you, and your rights as a patient. Your advocate can be reached at any time of the day by dialing _____. The following is a list of your rights as a patient. Your advocate's duty is to see to it that you're afforded these rights. You should call your advocate whenever you have any questions or concerns about any of these rights.

Patient rights

• The patient has a legal right to informed participation in all decisions involving his health care program.

• We recognize the right of all potential patients to know what research and experimental protocols are being used in our facility and what alternatives are available in the community.

• The patient has a legal right to privacy regarding the source of payment for treatment and care. The right includes access to the highest degree of care without regard to the source of payment for that treatment and care.

• We recognize the right of a potential patient to complete and accurate information concerning medical care and procedures.

• The patient has a legal right to prompt attention, especially in an emergency situation.

• The patient has a legal right to a clear, concise explanation in layperson's terms of all proposed procedures, including the possibilities of any risk of mortality or serious side effects, problems related to recuperation, and probability of success, and will not be subjected to any procedure without his voluntary, competent, and understanding consent. The specifics of such consent shall be set out in a written consent form, signed by the patient.

• The patient has a legal right to a clear, complete, and accurate evaluation of his condition and prognosis without treatment before being asked to consent to any test or procedure.

• We recognize the right of the patient to know the identity and professional status of all those providing service. All personnel have been instructed to introduce themselves, state their status, and explain their role in the health care of the patient. Part of this right is the right of the patient to know the identity of the physician responsible for his care.

• We recognize the right of any patient who doesn't speak English to have access to an interpreter.

• The patient has a right to all the information contained in his medical record while in the health care facility and to examine the record on request.

• We recognize the right of a patient to discuss his condition with a consultant specialist, at the patient's request and expense.

• The patient has a legal right not to have any test or procedure, designed for educational purposes rather than his direct personal benefit, performed on him.

• The patient has a legal right to refuse any particular drug, test, procedure, or treatment.

• The patient has a legal right to privacy of both person and information with respect to hospital staff, other physicians, residents, interns, medical students, researchers, nurses, other hospital personnel, and other patients.

• We recognize the patient's right of access to people outside the health care facility by means of visitors and the telephone. Parents may stay with their children and relatives may stay with terminally ill patients 24 hours a day.

ACLU patient's bill of rights *(continued)*

- The patient has a legal right to leave the health care facility regardless of his physical condition or financial status, although the patient may be requested to sign a release stating that he is leaving against the medical judgment of his physician or the hospital.
- The patient has a right not to be transferred to another facility unless he received a complete explanation of the desirability of and need for the transfer. If the patient doesn't agree to transfer, the patient has the right to a consultant's opinion on the desirability of transfer.
- A patient has a right to be notified of his impending discharge at least 1 day before it's accomplished, to insist on a consultation by an expert on the desirability of discharge, and to have a person of the patient's choice notified in advance.
- The patient has a right, regardless of the source of payment, to examine and receive an itemized and detailed explanation of the total bill for services rendered in the facility.
- The patient has a right to competent counseling from the hospital staff to help in obtaining financial assistance from public or private sources to meet the expense of services rendered in the institution.
- The patient has a right to timely prior notice of the termination of his eligibility for reimbursement by any third-party payer for the expense of hospital care.
- At the termination of his stay at the health care facility, we recognize the right of a patient to a complete copy of the information contained in his medical record.
- We recognize the right of all patients to have 24-hour-a-day access to a patient's rights advocate, who may act on behalf of the patient to assert or protect the rights set out in this document.

Reprinted with permission of the American Civil Liberties Union.

---

more employees and restricts employers' medical testing of employees and job applicants.

Other laws passed by Congress to protect the rights of handicapped people include the Community Mental Health Amendment of 1975, the Education for Handicapped Children Act of 1975, the Developmentally Disabled Assistance and Bill of Rights Act, and the Rehabilitation Comprehensive Services and Development Disability Amendment of 1978.

In 1980, Congress enacted the Mental Health Systems Act (MHSA), a comprehensive federal law on mental health services. Although much of this statute was later repealed, the MHSA Patient's Bill of Rights, which recommended that states review their mental health laws in light of patients' rights, survived. Since then, the bill has been used as a model by several states when revising their laws concerning the rights of patients suffering from mental illness.

LEGAL STATUS

Bills of rights that have become *laws* or state regulations carry the most authority because they give the patient specific legal recourse. If a patient believes a facility has violated his legal rights, the patient can report the violation to the appropriate legal authority, usually the state health or licensing department. If an investigation shows that the facility violated the patient's rights, the state will demand that the facility modify its practices to conform to state law.

Bills of rights issued by health care facilities and professional associations aren't legally binding. But hospitals

Hospice patient's bill of rights

In 1990, the Hospice Association of America issued a bill of rights for hospice patients.

Introduction

Patients have a right to be notified in writing of their rights and obligations before their hospice care begins. Consistent with state laws, the patient's family or guardian may exercise the patient's rights when the patient is unable to do so. Hospice organizations have an obligation to protect and promote the rights of their patients, including the following:

Dignity and respect

Patients and their hospice caregivers have the right to mutual respect and dignity. Caregivers are prohibited from accepting personal gifts and borrowing from patients, families, or primary caregivers. Patients have the right:

- to have relationships with hospice organizations that are based on honesty and ethical standards of conduct
- to be informed of the procedure they can follow to lodge complaints with the hospice organization about the care that is, or fails to be, furnished, and regarding a lack of respect for property (To lodge complaints with us, call _____.)
- to know about the disposition of such complaints
- to voice their grievances without fear of discrimination or reprisal for having done so.

Decision making

Patients have the right:

- to be notified in writing of the care that's to be furnished, the types (disciplines) of caregivers who will furnish the care, and the frequency of the services that are proposed to be furnished
- to be advised of any change in the plan of care before the change is made
- to participate in the planning of care and in planning the changes in the care, and to be advised that they have the right to do so

- to refuse services and to be advised of the consequences of refusing care
- to request a change in caregiver without fear of reprisal or discrimination.

Privacy

Patients have the right:

- to be informed of the extent to which payment may be expected from Medicare, Medicaid, or any other payer known to the hospice organization
- to be informed of any changes that won't be covered by Medicare
- to be informed of the charges for which the patient may be liable
- to receive this information, orally and in writing, within 15 working days of the date the hospice organization becomes aware of any changes in charges
- to have access, upon request, to all bills for the service the patient has received regardless of whether they are paid out-of-pocket or by another party
- to be informed of the hospice's ownership status and its affiliation with any entities to whom the patient is referred.

Quality of care

Patients have the right:

- to receive care of the highest quality
- in general, to be admitted by a hospice organization only if it's assured that all necessary palliative and supportive services will be provided that are necessary to promote the physical, psychological, social, and spiritual well-being of the dying patient; however, an organization with less than optimal resources may nevertheless admit the patient if a more appropriate hospice organization isn't available, but only after fully informing the patient of its limitations and the lack of suitable alternative arrangements
- to be told what to do in case of an emergency.

The hospice organization will assure that:

- all medically related hospice care is provided in accordance with physicians' orders and that a plan of care developed by the

---

Hospice patient's bill of rights *(continued)*

patient's physician and the hospice interdisciplinary group specifies the services to be provided and their frequency and duration
- all medically related personal care is pro

vided by an appropriately trained home-maker-home health aide who is supervised by a nurse or other qualified hospice professional.

Reprinted with permission of the Hospice Association of America.

---

may jeopardize federal funding, such as **Medicare** and **Medicaid** reimbursement or research funding, if they violate federal regulations or the standards of the **Joint Commission on Accreditation of Healthcare Organizations (JCAHO).**

You should regard bills of rights for patients as professionally binding where they exist as a facility's stated policy, and you're required to uphold those rights. You're also expected to uphold the bills of rights published by professional organizations.

GUIDELINES FOR UPHOLDING PATIENTS' RIGHTS

The NLN encourages you to view your patient as a partner in the health care process. In planning your patient's care, recognize his right to participate in decisions. Help him set realistic goals for his health care, and teach him the various approaches he can use to achieve them.

Throughout the decision-making process, keep assessing the patient's understanding of his illness. When he needs and wants more information, first determine whether you or the physician should provide it. Then, let the patient participate in the development of his care plan, which must address that patient's unique needs, as well as his rights.

Added benefits

Upholding patients' rights provides additional benefits, such as opening health care to new ideas. For example, **nurse-midwives** and other maternity nurses have acted as advocates for patients who challenge traditional childbirth practices. As a result, many hospitals have introduced changes, such as:
- using birthing rooms as an alternative to traditional delivery rooms
- using less **intervention** and medication during delivery
- allowing patients to use a birthing chair or to walk at will during labor
- encouraging the company and support of a "coach" — husband, other relative, or friend — during labor and delivery
- allowing families, including other children and grandparents, to participate in or to attend the delivery.

Facilities employ full-time patient advocates, or **ombudsmen,** to mediate between the patient and the facility when a patient is dissatisfied with care. **Patient advocates** may help you uphold your responsibilities to your patient, but advocates don't diminish those responsibilities. As an **advanced practice nurse,** you must respect and safeguard your patient's rights. You can develop and maintain the patient's confidence in you — and possibly prevent a lawsuit — by disclosing important information, such as the options, risks, and benefits of the care you're suggesting and the risks he could incur if no action is taken.

Informed consent and the law

Being adequately informed about proposed treatment, procedures, surgery, or research in order to properly consent is a patient's legal right. It isn't surprising, therefore, that the topic of informed consent appears in all current medical and NP texts, and must be evidenced in the patient's records where invasive or experimental procedures, treatment, or surgery is contemplated.

In the 1960s, physicians were primarily responsible for obtaining the patient's consent. Since then, NPs have also played a role in obtaining informed consent. Generally, it's a basic rule that the responsibility for obtaining a patient's informed consent rests with the person who will carry out the procedure or who is recommending a course of treatment. This procedure may be delegated to an appropriate person under certain circumstances; for example, to the NP that works with the physician who will participate in the procedure.

Informed consent involves the patient, or someone acting on his behalf, having enough information to know what the patient is risking should he decide to undergo the proposed treatment or surgery or the anticipated consequences should consent to the treatment be refused or withdrawn. The NP has the legal responsibility to give the patient such information and must not use coercion to obtain the consent.

Under certain circumstances, persons with mental disorders may be held competent to consent. When there is a question about an individual's capacity to give consent, a legal determination may be sought from the appropriate court (for example, probate court) or an ethics committee of the facility.

The bottom line in determining capacity must be whether or not the person giving consent is impaired in his capacity or judgment so as not to know what he's getting into before the treatment begins.

To assess *capacity* to consent, an NP may need to rely on her instincts, as well as professional judgment. If she believes the patient doesn't understand, she should reassess and discuss the consent issue with the patient, his guardian if applicable, and the collaborating physician before the treatment begins.

INFORMED CONSENT STANDARDS

Generally, informed consent can be viewed legally from two different perspectives. The first is known as the majority rule or malpractice model: what a reasonable medical practitioner would have disclosed to his patient regarding proposed treatment, under the same or similar circumstances. Consider *Nathanson v. Kline* (1960), a case in which the physician allegedly failed to inform the patient of the side effects of cobalt radiation therapy. The court ruled that the physician had a duty to disclose information "which a reasonable medical practitioner would disclose under the same or similar circumstances." Therefore, under the majority rule, the information is viewed from what a reasonable health care professional would tell a patient or patient's family about the procedure.

The second perspective, known as the minority rule, looks at disclosure of the material information that a *reasonable patient* in the situation *would deem important to know* in making a decision to undergo the proposed treatment.

Negligent nondisclosure

Consider *Canterbury v. Spence* (1972). In this case, a patient had a laminectomy and then fell and developed paralysis. The patient sued the physician for failing to warn him of the inherent risks. The court ruled that the physician had a duty to disclose as much information as he knew, or should have known, a reasonable patient would need to make an informed decision.

What should the patient be told? First, it's well accepted that a duty of reasonable disclosure of risks incident to the particular medical diagnosis and treatment is required. Information regarding the likelihood of success of this treatment should be provided as well as viable alternatives to the treatment, if any exist. The patient must be given an opportunity to evaluate the options, alternatives, and risks, and then exercise his choice. In medical malpractice cases involving consent issues, expert testimony is often required to establish whether or not the information given to the patient was reasonable, understandable, presented at a time when the patient was functionally able to process the information (as opposed to being sedated or medicated), and complete enough to allow the patient to knowledgeably agree to proceed. However, not every single or remote risk or benefit must be raised or addressed. It's generally agreed that those risks and benefits that arise frequently or regularly need to be discussed with the patient or the decision maker for the patient. Or, if there are specific consequences known to the health care practitioner to be particularly significant to this patient, those must be discussed before true informed consent may be obtained. Professional judgment must be exercised by all health care practitioners involved at this point. There should also be time given to a discussion on what the consequences may be if the treatment or procedure is refused.

A landmark case, *Karp v. Cooley* (1998), is a good example of how informed consents are raised and added to other allegations in malpractice cases. Mr. Karp was offered a mechanical heart transplant when it was obvious that his medical condition was deteriorating, and he was near death. Many consultants evaluated Mr. Karp. One, Dr. Beasley, wrote in Mr. Karp's chart that he didn't recommend the procedure because he thought the patient wasn't a suitable candidate for the surgery. Dr. Cooley, the surgeon, admitted at trial that he didn't tell Mr. Karp of Dr. Beasley's note, which was made during initial work-ups, and actually was directed and related to Beasley's reservation about the patient's psychological or emotional acceptance of a less-than-perfect outcome.

Mrs. Karp testified to what Mr. Karp's physicians said in her presence. However, Mr. Karp also spoke with his physicians on several occasions about the proposed treatment when his wife wasn't present, and it was Mr. Karp who signed the consent form. The consent form matched the details Dr. Cooley testified to, as being the basis of discussions with Mr. Karp, before he signed the form. No expert testimony was offered to indicate that what Dr. Cooley discussed with Mr. Karp was inadequate or breached Dr. Cooley's duty to obtain informed consent.

The court dismissed the informed consent issue on that basis, and also raised the issue that the plaintiff, the estate of Mr. Karp, didn't present substantial evidence that there was any causal connection between their claimed lack of informed consent and Mr. Karp's death. To address this proximate cause relationship, the court looked at Texas case law (previous cases on this issue) and noted that for a finding of proximate causation between the alleged omissions of in-

formed consent and injury (in this case death), certain things must exist.
● A hidden risk that should have been made known, and wasn't, must materialize.
● The hidden risk must be harmful to the patient.
● Causality exists only when disclosures of significant risks incidental to treatment would have resulted in the patient's decision against the treatment.

What the court relied upon, then, in discussing the case on the proximate cause issue was testimony that Mr. Karp was near death prior to the wedge excision operation, to which he gave consent. There was no dispute by Mrs. Karp about the validity of that consent. After the excision, Mr. Karp was also near death. Therefore, no one testified that to a reasonable degree of medical certainty the mechanical heart caused Mr. Karp's death. Finally, there was no proof offered at trial that Mr. Karp wouldn't have agreed to proceed with the mechanical heart surgery had alleged undisclosed material risks been disclosed. On appeal, the dismissal on the informed consent issue was upheld.

Another scenario: Suppose a patient is scheduled for surgery. He's talked to his physician and signed the consent form. But the night before surgery, he doesn't seem to understand the implications of the procedure. If you're the NP caring for this patient and preparing him for surgery, what would you do?

Basic elements of informed consent

The basics of informed consent should include:
● a description of the treatment or procedure
● a description of inherent risks and benefits that occur with frequency or regularity or specific consequences known by the health care practitioner to be particularly significant to this patient or his designated decision maker

● an explanation of the potential for death or serious harm (such as brain damage, stroke, paralysis, or disfiguring scars) or for discomforting side effects during or after the treatment or procedure
● an explanation and description of alternative treatments or procedures
● the name and qualifications of the person who'll perform the treatment or procedure
● a discussion of the possible effects of not having the treatment or procedure.

Patients must also be told that they have a right to refuse the treatment or procedures without having other care or support withdrawn and that they can withdraw consent after giving it. (See *Informed consent: A landmark ruling.*)

If you witness a patient's signature on a consent form, you attest to three things:
● The patient voluntarily consented.
● The signature of the patient or the patient's designated decision maker is authentic.
● The patient appears to be competent to give consent.

There are many consent and privacy issues now, particularly due to such procedures as human immunodeficiency virus (HIV) testing, drug and alcohol treatment, and sterilization. Your facility's **risk manager** should define your responsibilities, your employer's policies, and your state's legal requirements. Each state has specific statues governing informed consent issues that are subject to change as tort reform evolves and as case law interprets existing statutes or legal concepts.

Informed consent under state law

Many state legislatures have passed laws supporting the standards of informed consent set by the courts. States have procedural laws on informed consent — laws that describe, for example, the tort of **negligent**

Informed consent: A landmark ruling

COURT CASE

The right of informed consent didn't exist at the beginning of the century. A patient had no legal right to information about his medical treatment. If a doctor performed surgery without the patient's consent, the patient could sue for battery — legally defined as one person touching another without consent. A patient could claim battery only if he'd refused consent or hadn't been asked to give it, but not if he hadn't had enough information to make an appropriate decision.

Rare exceptions

Most battery lawsuits were unsuccessful because courts usually took the physician's word over the patient's. Two cases that patients did win were *Mohr v. Williams* (1905), in which the patient consented to surgery on one ear, but the doctor performed it on both, and *Schloendorff v. Society of New York Hospitals* (1914), in which the patient consented to an abdominal examination, but the doctor performed abdominal surgery.

Establishing a patient right

The right to receive informed consent wasn't expressed legally until 1957, when the California Supreme Court introduced the theory in the case of *Salgo v. Leland Stanford, Jr. Univ. Board of Trustees*. This case involved a patient who had acute arterial insufficiency in his legs. The physician recommended diagnostic tests but failed to describe the tests or their risks. The day after the patient underwent aortography, his legs became permanently paralyzed. The court found the physician negligent for failing to explain the potential risks of aortography.

This decision established a basic rule: A health care provider violates "his duty to his patient and subjects himself to liability if he withholds any facts that are necessary to form the basis of an intelligent consent by the patient to the proposed treatment."

Since this landmark ruling, a patient can sue for negligent nondisclosure if his health care provider fails to provide enough information to enable him to make an informed decision.

---

nondisclosure. A few states have laws that are substantive, meaning they actually define what must be present for informed consent to have been established. These laws define who is able to give consent and for what, and what type of documentation is required. These laws define exemptions to documented consent and when consent becomes invalid.

INABILITY TO CONSENT

Informed consent relies on an individual's capacity, or ability, to make decisions at a particular time under specific circumstances. To make decisions about his medical care, the patient must possess the capacity and the competence to make such decisions. He

must possess three critical elements of decision making:
● the ability to understand and communicate information relevant to the decision
● the ability to reason and deliberate concerning the decision
● the ability to apply a set of values to the decision.

If you have reason to believe that a patient is incompetent to participate in giving informed consent because medication or sedation is affecting his decision-making capacity, you have an obligation to refrain from obtaining consent at that time (or to seek a guardian or family member to obtain the consent, if appropriate). You should, however, return when the patient can adequately and legally provide informed consent. Why? If you fail to provide adequate information for consent because of the patient's medicated status, the patient may sue you for lack of informed consent due to temporary incapacitation. The courts might hold you responsible if you knowingly did not provide adequate information to a patient. It's better to delay a procedure than to become a defendant in a battery lawsuit because you didn't obtain informed consent.

Incompetent patients

A patient is deemed mentally incompetent if he can't understand the explanations or can't comprehend the results of his decisions. When the patient is incompetent, the NP has two alternatives. She may seek consent from the patient's *next of kin,* usually a spouse. (Legal definition of next of kin varies from state to state.) Alternatively, other interested family members or people, the physician, or the hospital may petition the court to appoint a *legal guardian* for the patient. Sometimes, a Probate Court may decide who the proper legal guardian should be after reviewing petitions and taking testimony. This works well if there is time to appoint a proper guardian. However, that isn't always possible in the case of a potentially dangerous or deadly medical condition. Under those circumstances, the courts will look to the reasonableness of the actions by the health care providers, before proceeding with the treatment, in determining if there was informed consent by a proper party, or whether the informed consent requirement was properly waived.

Mental illness isn't the same as incompetence. Persons suffering from mental illness have been found competent to consent because they're alert and, above all, able to understand the proposed treatment, risks, benefits, and alternatives, as well as the consequences of refusing the treatment. Consider a patient who has been hospitalized involuntarily but who remains alert and oriented. His mental status and education enable him to understand the information presented by the practitioner; he merely lacks freedom from incarceration. Should this patient be allowed to make medical decisions affecting his life or future health? Why should a court-appointed person assume this authority? On the other hand, shouldn't the patient have the right to refuse treatment even if it might ease his mental illness (for example, electroconvulsive shock therapy)?

Since the late 1980s, practitioners have to resolve medical restraint issues that involve elderly, confused, and infirm patients. It's now well established that a confined patient, mentally or physically disabled, may be forcibly medicated only in an emergency when he may cause harm to himself or others. In such cases, documentation in the patient record is critical regarding the actual mental status of the patient and competency to give consent.

Minors

Over the last 25 years, NPs have witnessed a great social and legal challenge involving the rights of minors, especially their right to seek health care. As concerns for the rights of minors regarding consent to health care have arisen, all states have looked at the issue of just who can give consent for minors to receive what care, and what information a minor may keep confidential in regard to that care. Certain rules have evolved.

Generally, the person giving consent for the care and treatment of a minor is a parent or other designated adult. This isn't always the case, however, as you'll see below. The practitioner still must disclose all relevant information to the person giving consent to ensure that the consent is informed.

The patchwork of rights and limitations of the various state laws governing when minors can and can't consent give us alternating perceptions of teenagers. They're viewed as adultlike and childlike, and there is a desire to protect and respect these qualities. For example, although a teenage mother must give consent before her baby can receive treatment, she generally isn't permitted to determine the course of her own health care. Under federal law, adolescents can be tested and treated for HIV without parental involvement; however, in most cases, parental consent is required to set an adolescent's broken arm.

Every state will allow an **emancipated minor** to consent to his own medical care and treatment. So far, state definitions of emancipation vary, but it's generally recognized that to be emancipated, the individual must be a minor by state definition (less than the legal age of majority in that state) and must have obtained a legal declaration of freedom from the custody, care, and control of his parents. In doing so, emancipated minors forgo the right to financial support from their parents as well as any protection from lawsuits. Once declared emancipated, minors gain the right to enter binding contracts, to sue, and to consent to medical, dental, or psychiatric care without parental approval. They also assume all the financial obligations for this care, just as an adult would, if an adult had entered into such contracts. In granting emancipated status to minors, the courts will look for employment, demonstrated fiscal responsibility, other evidence of support systems the minor has available, and the individual circumstances that underlie the request for legal determination of emancipation.

Most states will allow teenagers to consent to treatment, even though they haven't been determined emancipated, in situations involving pregnancy or sexually transmitted disease. Because privacy issues are involved, the NP must understand the specific circumstances allowing a minor to consent as well as the circumstances under which she should contact the parent or legal guardian. Your risk manager should be able to help you. Contact with a parent or legal guardian and disclosure of confidential information have resulted in lawsuits for breach of confidentiality.

An unemancipated minor, in mid-to-late teens, who shows signs of intellectual and emotional maturity is considered a "mature minor." In some cases, a mature minor is allowed to exercise some of the rights regarding health care that are generally reserved for adults. Because there is no consensus about when maturity occurs, and thus, no clear guidelines for those who must make such assessments, the issue of maturity must be decided on a case-by-case basis.

It's an accepted practice to allow children, to the extent they may participate, to be involved in the decision-making process regarding life-sustaining medical treatment. In making the ultimate decisions, there must be a weighing of "the best interests" standards, which involves considering the benefits and the burdens to the child. Some benefits to be considered are prolonging life and improving quality of life following treatment. Some of the burdens of the proposed treatment may be intractable pain, irremediable disability or helplessness, emotional suffering, and invasiveness of the procedure, which could severely detract from the quality of life. Keep in mind that the quality of life to be considered is from the child's perspective, not that of the parent or decision maker, or even health care providers. Without evidence to the contrary, the assumption is that life-sustaining medical treatment will be provided in accordance with existing medical, ethical, and legal norms.

RIGHT TO REFUSE TREATMENT

It's generally held that parents have the right to refuse life-sustaining medical treatment for unemancipated children who lack the capacity or statutory criteria for maturity to make such decisions for themselves.

Decisions to limit, withhold, discontinue, or forgo treatment must be very carefully documented and must be very specific in nature. The collaborative process must occur between patient, parent (or parent's surrogate), and practitioner. Young children deserve to hear the general conclusions of a decision that will affect their survival, especially when the clinician believes treatment no longer will benefit the patient and should be withdrawn.

Emancipated or mature minors are presumed to have the capacity to give consent. Regarding younger children, however, it might be helpful to consider what a Tennessee State Supreme Court did in a 1987 case. It utilized the "Rule of Sevens." The court presumed that up to age 7 the child lacked capacity to consent. From age 7 to 14, the presumption of incapacity can be rebutted (by evidence to demonstrate that the child, in fact, possesses maturity); over age 14, we should presume capacity.

Remember that informed consent is a process, not a document. Hospitals generally address informed consent in policy and procedure manuals to ensure consistency and thorough implementation and documentation. Current JCAHO "hot spots" include issues of informed consent, advance directives, and confidentiality. Regarding informed consent issues, evidence is required that the consent is voluntary and that sufficient information regarding the treatment was given. This includes an explanation of alternatives, differences in effectiveness of alternatives, consequences of not having the proposed treatment, risk and benefits, impact on daily living, likelihood of success, responsible practitioners, and any possible conflicts of interest. In addition, this information must be presented in a manner that the patient understands, including appropriate language, reading level, cognitive ability, and ethnic orientation. Lastly, the appropriate documentation must be completed properly.

EVIDENCE OF CONSENT

Consent can be demonstrated by a signed, witnessed document; a note in the medical record detailing communications between the physician and patient; or the patient willfully undergoing the procedure by appearing at the appointed time and place. Some states have statutes stating that a signed consent form disclosing the treatment in general terms is deemed conclusive proof of a valid consent. Georgia's law is such a statute. Of course, the validity of the signature may be challenged. But, if the patient is legally competent to sign the form, and does so, he waives the right to a later claim that he didn't. He also waives the right to a later claim that he didn't understand the medical treatment or that the physician didn't explain information presented in the consent form.

Other states take the position that a signed consent form is evidence of informed consent but may be refutable, if the patient offers sufficient evidence to the contrary. The patient may challenge his consent by attacking the substance of the consent form. He may claim that the practitioner didn't explain medical terms in a manner that a patient could understand or (given the medical diagnosis, the patient's condition, or the surgery contemplated) that relevant information significant to the patient wasn't provided.

A signed consent form may not be required in your state. However, there must still be evidence that the patient has been provided with the required information and has given his consent to proceed. This may be done by a notation in the progress notes indicating that the patient has been told of specific risks, benefits, and alternatives; has had an opportunity to have questions answered; and understands and agrees to the procedure. The evidence of informed consent is further enhanced if the medical record documents other family members who were present with the patient when the consent was obtained, such as "Wife present and concurs in patient's decision to proceed with surgery."

If you work in a facility that uses investigational drugs or engages in research, your policies and procedures must state that the patient or surrogate receives a clear explanation of experimental treatment. This includes the procedures to be followed, a clear description of potential discomforts and risks, a list of alternative treatments, and a clear explanation that the patient may refuse to participate in the research project without compromising access to care or treatment.

Most of JCAHO Type 1 Recommendations concerning informed consent result from inadequate or incomplete documentation. (Health care organizations must resolve insufficient or unsatisfactory compliance with standards in a specific performance area within a specific period of time to maintain accreditation.) It's easier to comply with JCAHO standards if forms are user-friendly and include the required criteria, if an audit system is in place to validate that forms are consistently completed appropriately, and if the forms are included in the medical records.

EXCEPTIONS TO OBTAINING INFORMED CONSENT FIRST

Emergency treatment to save a patient's life or to prevent loss of an organ, a limb, or a function may be done without first obtaining consent in specific circumstances. If the patient is unconscious (or is a minor who can't give consent), emergency treatment may be performed. The presumption is that the patient would have consented if he had been able, unless there is reason to believe otherwise. For example, to sustain the life of unconscious patients in the emergency department (ED), intubation has been held to be appropriate even if there is no one to consent to the procedure. Children brought to the ED following serious injury in school whose parents can't be located in time may be provided with emergency medical care without consent while attempts are made to locate the parents. Although consent is presumed in such cases, lawsuits may still occur. For example, giving blood to a severely injured unconscious person may be a life-saving procedure, but the patient or a family member may sue if such action is against their religious convictions. Courts will uphold emergency medical treatment as long as reasonable effort was made to obtain consent and no alternative treatments were available to save life or limb. The courts won't uphold treatment in the absence of informed consent if the practitioner has had prior contact and has been told that such treatment would be refused. If the practitioner has time to locate family members or to obtain proper consent from the patient, that's what the courts will require the practitioner to do.

Before proceeding, a ***reasonably prudent NP*** will make certain that the precise medical emergency has been documented in the medical record, along with the assumptions to obtain proper consent and any information that has been conveyed to the patient.

Right to consent: From birth to adulthood

A person attains more medical rights as he reaches the age of majority, defined as the age when a person is considered legally responsible for his activities and becomes entitled to the legal rights held by citizens generally.

Birth rights
From birth, everyone has medical rights to:
- confidentiality concerning medical records
- privacy during treatment
- reasonable and prudent medical care.

Minors
Anyone under age 18 or 21 (depending on the state in which he lives) has the right to consent to treatment for sexually transmitted diseases, serious communicable diseases, and drug or alcohol abuse (although state law may require that the minor's parents be notified).

Mature minors
In certain instances, a physician or judge may decide that a minor is sufficiently mature (has a sufficiently developed awareness and mental capacity) to consent to medical treatment. If so, the minor has the right to make decisions about medical care.

Adults
Anyone who has reached the age of majority or who is legally emancipated has the right to:
- consent to or refuse medical treatment
- consent to or refuse medical treatment for his children (in most circumstances).

Patients may also waive their rights to additional information by appointing someone else as their medical decision maker. Advance directives are one way to have another person participate and be responsible for one's medical care and treatment. If this has been decided beforehand, proper documentation must appear in the medical record.

WHEN INFORMED CONSENT BECOMES INVALID
Informed consent can become invalid if the change in the patient's medical status alters the risks and benefits of treatment. In such situations, the practitioner must explain the new risks and benefits to make sure the patient will consent to the treatment.

To summarize, the controversy over informed consent centers on medical and surgical treatments and procedures that are invasive, risky, or experimental or that have low likelihood for successful outcome. We've come a long way since the concept of silence, or ***therapeutic privilege.*** In that situation, the physician was allowed to withhold information from a patient at the sole discretion of the physician and the patient's family, who believed that the information would jeopardize the patient's health. In some instances, patients weren't told that they were dying or that the treatment would have no benefit. Now, therapeutic privilege is viewed narrowly; withholding of significant information from patients or their designated decision makers is frowned upon by the courts because of a patient's right to self-determination, a right that the NP is charged with protecting. (See *Right to consent: From birth to adulthood.*)

The patient who refuses treatment

Any mentally competent adult may legally refuse treatment if he's fully informed about his medical condition and about the likely consequences of his refusal. As a professional, you must respect that decision.

When your patient refuses treatment, you must understand more than his rights and your responsibilities. (See *When a patient says no,* page 288.)

RIGHT TO REFUSE TREATMENT

Most court cases related to the right to refuse treatment have involved patients with a terminal illness, or their families, who want to discontinue life support. In one of the best known cases, Karen Ann Quinlan's parents argued that unwanted treatment violated their comatose daughter's constitutional right to privacy. In 1976, the Quinlans successfully petitioned the New Jersey Supreme Court to discontinue her life support.

In another landmark case, *Cruzan v. Director, Mo. Dept. of Health* (1990), the parents of Nancy Cruzan petitioned to have their comatose daughter's tube feedings discontinued. In 1990, the U.S. Supreme Court held that the state of Missouri has the constitutional right to refuse to permit termination of life-sustaining treatment *unless "clear and convincing evidence" exists about a patient's wishes.* Because this standard wasn't met, the Court didn't allow removal of the feeding and hydration tube. Significantly, the Court implied that when clear and convincing evidence exists, the patient's wishes will be respected.

Two months after the Supreme Court ruling, the Cruzans petitioned the local court with new evidence. A Missouri judge granted them the right to remove Nancy's feeding and hydration tube. She died shortly thereafter. Publicity about Nancy Cruzan's legal ordeal heightened the awareness of millions of Americans to the need to prepare ahead for critical medical decisions.

More and more, health care providers consider quality end-of-life care as an ethical obligation. But what does end-of-life mean, and how do you measure it? Some researchers have viewed decisions from the patient's perspective based on five domains, or focal points, that study participants viewed as end-of-life issues. By understanding these domains from the patient's perspectives, NPs can improve the quality of end-of-life care.

● The problem with pain and other symptoms is still of concern for some patients. Therefore, greater attention may be warranted to attitudes of NPs toward pain and symptom control. Clearer guidelines are needed that will separate appropriate pain management from euthanasia, thus alleviating the concerns of health care providers as well.

● Many patients feared "being kept alive" after life could no longer be enjoyed, or loss of "dignity in death." This indicates that health care providers need to focus not only on specific treatment decisions but also on consent issues.

● Sense of control is also critical, and some patients are adamant about controlling their end-of-life care decisions.

● Patients tend to seek a psychological outcome rather than a precise treatment decision. For example, some patients feel that loved ones will be relieved of the burden that difficult end-of-life care decisions entail.

● Many patients expressed an overwhelming need to communicate with loved ones at this stage of their life. Dying offers important opportunities for growth, intimacy, reconciliation, and closure.

Using these domains of end-of-life care at the bedside to review and assess the quality of care of dying patients, NPs can clarify treatment goals for the health care team and provide a conceptual framework for teaching the

When a patient says no

A patient must give his consent before you can perform any treatment or procedure. If the patient refuses, take the following steps:
1. Explain the risks involved in not having the treatment or procedure performed. For a patient's refusal to be valid, the patient must have the capacity to refuse, be fully informed of all the facts necessary to make an informed decision, be informed of the risks to himself that could result from his refusal, and understand that treatment can and will continue within the guidelines of his refusal.
2. If the patient understands the risks but still refuses, notify your collaborating physician and discuss whether all reasonable opportunities have been given to the patient to make an informed decision. The patient's ability to refuse treatment can be challenged. The nurse practitioner can attempt to prove that the patient isn't competent to make his own decisions.
3. Record the patient's refusal in the progress notes.

4. Ask the patient to complete a refusal of treatment release form, like the one shown below. The signed form indicates that appropriate treatment would have been given had the patient consented.
5. If the patient refuses to sign the release form, document this in the progress notes as well as on the form itself, by writing "refused to sign" on the patient's signature line. Initial it with your own initials and date it.
6. For additional protection, your facility's policy may require you to get the patient's spouse or closest relative to sign a refusal of treatment form. Document whether or not the spouse or relative does this in the same manner as above.
7. Your facility's policy may require that an incident report be completed to document the events surrounding the patient's refusal of treatment. Complete the form as objectively as possible and send it to the risk management department of your facility.

REFUSAL OF TREATMENT RELEASE FORM

I, _____ , refuse to allow anyone to

_____ [insert treatment].

The risks attendant to my refusal have been fully explained to me, and I fully understand the results for this treatment and that if the same isn't done, my chances for regaining my normal health are seriously reduced and that, in all probability, my refusal for such treatment or procedure will seriously affect my health or recovery.

I hereby release _____
                [name of hospital]
its nurses and employees, together with all physicians in any way connected with me as a patient, from liability for respecting and following my expressed wishes and direction.

_____   _____
Witness   Patient or Legal Guardian

_____   _____
Date   Patient's Date of Birth

care of dying patients to others on the team. The domains can serve as a checklist to review the adequacy of the end-of-life care being provided. NPs may ask themselves: Am I adequately treating pain and other symptoms? Am I inappropriately prolonging life? Am I helping patients achieve a sense of control, relieve burdens on their families, and strengthen relationships with loved ones?

ADVANCE DIRECTIVES
The Patient Self-Determination Act of 1990 ensured the rights of patients to author or execute *advance directives* — written or oral instructions by the patient about his wishes for medical treatment in the event he becomes "incapacitated." Examples include living wills, durable powers of attorney for health care, or any document that states the patient's wishes. JCAHO standard RI.1.2.4 mandates that each hospital ensure patients over the age of 18 the opportunity to initiate an advance directive. The hospital must also honor the directives within the limits of the law and their capabilities.

All advance directives aren't black-and-white and may not address all contingencies or medical situations that a patient may encounter. For example, the patient may not realize that advanced life support may only be necessary for a brief time to help him regain sufficient strength or to support breathing during surgery.

Although the health care proxy (one authorized to act for another) is supposed to be the ultimate decision maker, the practitioner has a legitimate role in the decision-making process and may refuse to comply with any decision that he believes is contrary to the patient's wishes or best interests. If that happens, the proxy may ask that the patient be transferred to a physician or practitioner who will honor the patient's or the proxy's requests. Or the

proxy may request the ethics committee of the facility to mediate. As a last resort, the proxy may seek a court order to stop the unwanted care or treatment.

FREEDOM OF RELIGION
Jehovah's Witnesses may refuse treatment on the grounds of freedom of religion. Members of this sect oppose blood transfusions, based on their interpretation of a biblical passage that forbids "drinking" blood. Some sect members believe that even a lifesaving transfusion given against their will deprives them of everlasting life. The courts usually uphold their right to refuse treatment because of the constitutionally protected right to religious freedom. In the case of *In re Osborne* (1972), for example, the court respected a Jehovah's Witness's right to refuse consent.

Most other religious freedom court cases involve Christian Scientists, who oppose many medical interventions, including medicines. For example, in *Winters v. Miller* (1971), a psychiatric patient claimed she involuntarily received treatment and medications at a New York state hospital. After her discharge, she sued for damages based on a violation of her religious freedom as a Christian Scientist. The trial court dismissed her complaint, but an appeals court ordered a new trial on the grounds that the unwanted treatment might have violated her rights.

Besides court rulings, most *patient's bills of rights* support the right to refuse treatment, starting with the bill of rights adopted by the AHA.

When a Jehovah's Witness refuses blood because of religious beliefs, health care professionals are challenged to provide optimal care without using standard medical treatment. Health care, legal, ethical, and management issues of how to treat blood loss when it occurs must be carefully considered. Some strategies are currently available that minimize blood loss during cardiac surgeries, for example, as well as methods to increase endogenous production. Because Jehovah's Witness number over 3.9 million worldwide, and about 1 million are in the United States, health care providers face situations in which blood transfusion isn't a treatment option.

Using a cardiac-surgery example, some suggested blood-conserving strategies as effective treatments include:

● preoperative adequacy of hemoglobin levels, administration of erythropoietin, and use of iron and folic acid supplements

● intraoperative hemodilution to decrease blood viscosity and to improve systemic and pulmonary circulation, preserving clotting factors and platelets to reduce the likelihood of postoperative bleeding, hypothermia to reduce tissue oxygen requirements and to prevent hypothermia-related coagulopathy, desmopressin to control bleeding in the presence of platelet defects and in patients with decreased level of factor VIII, and aprotinin to reduce blood loss by inhibiting fibrinolysis and the turnover of coagulation factors

● postoperative use of protamine sulfate to bind with heparin and to neutralize the anticoagulant effect; use of aminocaproic acid to enhance fibrinogen activity and clot formation; use of erythropoietin, iron, and folic acid to accelerate erythropoiesis; and use of blood reservoir devices and the collection tubes used for blood sampling in children to minimize the volume of blood lost with phlebotomy and to preserve the hemoglobin level.

The use of blood-conserving techniques during surgery has been validated by several investigations and allows certain patients to adhere to their religious beliefs while resolving the dilemmas associated with the unacceptability of standard and accepted

treatments. Of course, physicians and NPs would have the ethical and legal rights to refuse to care for any patient in a nonemergency when standard medical care isn't acceptable to the patient. Court orders also can be obtained, requiring the patient to undergo the standard treatment against the patient's wishes. Alternatively, health care providers could honor the patient's request under all circumstances.

RIGHT TO DIE

Most states have enacted right-to-die laws (also called *natural death laws* or *living will laws*). These laws recognize the patient's right to choose death by refusing extraordinary treatment when he has no hope of recovery.

Whenever a competent patient expresses his wishes concerning extraordinary treatment, health care providers should attempt to follow them. If the patient is incompetent or unconscious, the decision becomes more difficult.

In some cases, the next of kin may express the patient's desires for him, but whether this is an honest interpretation of the patient's wishes is sometimes uncertain.

Written evidence of the patient's wishes provides the best indication of what treatment he would consent to if he were still able to communicate. This information may be provided through:

● a *living will.* This is an advance directive document that specifies a person's wishes with regard to medical care if he should become unable to communicate. (See *Living will.*) In some states, living wills don't address the issue of discontinuing artificial nutrition and hydration.

● a *durable power of attorney* for health care. In this document, the patient designates a person who will make medical decisions for him if he should become incompetent to do so. This differs from the usual *power of*

Living will

The living will is an advanced care document that specifies a person's wishes with regard to medical care, should he become terminally ill, incompetent, or unable to communicate. The will is often used in combination with the patient's durable power of attorney. All states and the District of Columbia have living will laws that outline the documentation requirements for living wills. A sample living will is shown below.

LIVING WILL

If my attending physician and one other physician who examines me determine, to a reasonable degree of medical certainty and in accordance with reasonable medical standards, that I am in a terminal condition or in a permanently unconscious state, and if my attending physician determines that at that time I no longer am able to make informed decisions regarding the administration of life-sustaining treatment, and that, to a reasonable degree of medical certainty and in accordance with reasonable medical standards, there is no reasonable possibility that I will regain the capacity to make informed decisions regarding the administration of life-sustaining treatment, then I direct my attending physician to withhold or withdraw medical procedures, treatment, interventions, or other measures that serve principally to prolong the process of my dying, rather than diminish my pain or discomfort.

I have used the term "terminal condition" in this declaration to mean an irreversible, incurable, and untreatable condition caused by disease, illness, or injury from which, to a reasonable degree of medical certainty as determined in accordance with reasonable medical standards of my attending physician and one other physician who has examined me, there can be no recovery, and death is likely to occur within a relatively short time if life-sustaining treatment is not administered.

I have used the term "permanently unconscious state" in this declaration to mean a state of permanent unconsciousness that, to a reasonable degree of medical certainty, is determined in accordance with reasonable medical standards by my attending physician and one other physician who has examined me, as characterized by both of the following:
I am irreversibly unaware of myself and my environment.
There is a total loss of cerebral cortical functioning, resulting in my having no capacity to experience pain or suffering.

Nutrition & Hydration
I hereby authorize my attending physician to withhold or withdraw nutrition and hydration from me when I am in a permanent unconscious state if my attending physician and at least one other physician who has examined me determine, to a reasonable degree of medical certainty and in accordance with reasonable medical standards, that nutrition or hydration will not or no longer will serve to provide comfort to me or alleviate my pain.

_____

[Sign here for withdrawal of nutrition or hydration]

(continued)

Living will *(continued)*

I hereby designate:
[Print name of person to decide] _____
as the person who I wish my attending physician to notify at any time that life-sustaining treatment is to be withdrawn or withheld pursuant to this Declaration.

_____   _____
[Sign your name here]   [Today's date]

Witness by:
[Living will person's name] _____
voluntarily signed or directed another individual to sign this Living Will in the presence of the following who each attests that the Declarant appears to be of sound mind and not under or subject to duress, fraud, or undue influence.

_____   _____
[First witness signs here]   [Second witness signs here]

---

attorney, which requires the patient's ongoing consent and deals only with financial issues. (See *Durable power of attorney for health care.*)

Most states recognize living wills as legally valid and have laws authorizing durable powers of attorney for initiating or terminating life-sustaining medical treatment.

PERTINENT LEGISLATION

The Patient Self-Determination Act of 1990 requires that health care facilities ask whether the patient has completed an advance directive. This law includes the following requirements:

● Each patient must be given written information about his rights under state law to make decisions concerning medical care, including the right to accept or refuse medical or surgical treatment and to formulate advance directives.
● The patient's decision whether or not to execute an advance directive must be documented in the medical record.

● The facility must ensure that the patient's decision regarding the execution of an advance directive doesn't influence the provision of care, and health care providers must not discriminate against a patient in any way based on his decision.
● The health care facility must provide education for the staff and community on issues concerning advance directives.

CHALLENGING THE PATIENT'S RIGHT TO REFUSE TREATMENT

There are two grounds for challenging a patient's right to refuse treatment: You can claim that the patient is incompetent, or you can claim that compelling reasons exist to overrule his wishes. (See *Overruling the patient,* page 294.)

The courts consider a patient incompetent when he lacks the mental ability to make a reasoned decision, such as when he's delirious.

Durable power of attorney for health care

The sample document below is an example of a durable power of attorney, which allows a competent patient to delegate to another person the authority to consent to or refuse health care treatment. This helps a patient ensure that his wishes will be carried out if he should become incompetent.

Each state with a durable power of attorney for health care law has specific requirements for executing the document. A sample is shown below.

POWER OF ATTORNEY FOR HEALTH CARE

I appoint _____

whose address is _____

and whose telephone number is _____

as my attorney in fact for health care.

I appoint _____

whose address is _____

and whose telephone number is _____

as my successor attorney in fact for health care.

I authorize my attorney in fact appointed by this document to make health care decisions for me when I am determined to be incapable of making my own health care decisions. I have read the warning that accompanies this document and understand the consequences of executing a power of attorney for health care.

I direct that my attorney in fact comply with the following instructions or limitations: (optional)

I direct that my attorney in fact comply with the following instructions on life-sustaining treatment: (optional)

I direct that my attorney in fact comply with the following instructions on artificially administered nutrition and hydration: (optional)

I have read this power of attorney for health care. I understand that it allows another person to make life and death decisions for me if I am incapable of making such decisions. I also understand that I can revoke this power of attorney for health care at any time by notifying my attorney in fact, my physician, or the facility in which I am a patient or resident. I also understand that I can require in this power of attorney for health care that the fact of my incapacity in the future be confirmed by a second physician.

_____   _____
[Signature of person making designation]   [Date]

Compelling circumstances

The courts also recognize several compelling circumstances that justify overruling a patient's refusal of treatment.

These include:

- when refusing treatment endangers the life of another; for example, a court may overrule a pregnant woman's ob-

Overruling the patient

Even when a patient's decision to refuse treatment rests on constitutionally protected grounds, such as religious beliefs, the court will intervene in certain circumstances. Becoming familiar with court rulings in this area will help you to better cope if you ever get caught between a patient and his family and a court. Here are some delicate legal situations the courts have ruled on. Keep in mind that each case is only binding in its own jurisdiction. A court where you practice may hold differently.

Incapacitated patient

If an adult patient becomes physically or mentally incapacitated, a relative can't always refuse treatment for him. The court reserves the right to overrule even a spouse on the patient's behalf if the decision seems to be medically unreasonable. For example, in *Collins v. Davis* (1964), the court overruled a wife's refusal of surgery for her unconscious husband.

Patient responsible for child

If a patient responsible for the care of a child refuses lifesaving treatment, the court may reverse the patient's decision. In *Application of the President and Directors of*

Georgetown College, Inc. (1964), the New York Supreme Court ordered a blood transfusion for a Jehovah's Witness who was the mother of an infant and who refused to give consent for her own transfusion. In *Melideo* (1976), the court said that it might have ordered a lifesaving transfusion for the patient if she had had a child.

Pregnant patient

If a pregnant patient refuses treatment, thereby threatening not only her own health but also that of her unborn child, the court has reversed the patient's decision. In *Jefferson v. Griffin Spalding County Hospital Authority* (1981), the court awarded temporary custody of an unborn child to a state agency. The mother had a complete placenta previa but had refused to consent to a cesarean delivery. The court's custody award included full authority to give consent for a surgical delivery.

Patient who is a minor

If a patient is a minor, the court will allow his parents or legal guardian to consent to medical treatment, but not allow them to deny him lifesaving treatment. In re *Sampson* (1972) was such a case.

---

jection to treatment if it endangers her unborn child's life.

● when a parent's decision to withhold treatment threatens a child's life; for example, a court may overrule the parents' religious objections to their child's treatment when the child's life is endangered. (When the child's life isn't in danger, the courts are more likely to respect the parents' religious convictions.)

● when, despite refusing treatment, the patient makes statements indicating that he wants to live; for example, some Jehovah's Witnesses who oppose blood transfusions say or imply that they won't prevent the transfusions if a court takes responsibility for the deci-

sion. In *Powell v. Columbia-Presbyterian Medical Center* (1965), the court authorized transfusions when a Jehovah's Witness indicated that she wouldn't object to receiving blood, although she'd refused to give written consent.

● when the public interest outweighs the patient's right; for example, the law requires school-age children (with few exceptions) to receive a polio vaccine before they can attend classes.

RESPONDING TO THE PATIENT'S REQUEST TO STOP TREATMENT

When a patient plans to refuse treatment, you may be the person he tells first. Whether he tells you he's going to refuse treatment or he simply refuses to give consent, stop preparations for any treatment at once. Try to convince the patient to accept treatment or ask him to sign a release form. This form relieves the hospital and the health care team of liability for any consequences the patient suffers by refusing treatment. It doesn't, however, release the health care team from its obligation to continue providing other forms of care.

Don't ignore the patient

Never ignore a patient's request to refuse treatment. A patient can sue you for battery — intentionally touching another person without authorization to do so.

To overrule the patient's decision, the health care provider or your facility must obtain a court order. Only then are you legally authorized to administer the treatment.

If the health care provider or facility tries to convince the court to overrule the patient on the grounds that he's incompetent, they'll need proof that he lacks the mental ability to make a reasoned decision. Your documented observations about your patient's mental status may be used as evidence.

No matter how serious the patient's condition, refusing treatment doesn't constitute evidence of incompetence. In *Lane v. Candura* (1978), for example, a diabetic patient first agreed to have her leg amputated and then changed her mind and refused the surgery. The physicians applied for a court order, arguing that by changing her mind, the patient had shown incompetence. The court disagreed and upheld the patient's right to withdraw her consent.

RIGHT TO REFUSE EMERGENCY TREATMENT

A competent adult has the right to refuse emergency treatment. His family can't overrule his decision, and his health care provider may not give the expressly refused treatment, even if the patient becomes unconscious.

If there are no grounds for overruling your patient's decision, you have an ethical duty to defend his right to refuse treatment in the face of all opposition, even his family's. Try to explain the patient's choice to family members. Emphasize that the decision is his as long as he's competent.

Patient's right to privacy

Obtaining highly personal information from a patient can be uncomfortable and embarrassing. Reassuring the patient that you'll keep information confidential may help to put him at ease.

IS THERE A CONSTITUTIONAL RIGHT TO PRIVACY?

Privacy and confidentiality were first proposed as basic legal rights in 1890 in a *Harvard Law Review* article titled "The Right to Privacy."

The U.S. Constitution doesn't explicitly sanction a right to privacy. In several cases, however, including *Roe v. Wade* (1973), the U.S. Supreme Court cited several constitutional amendments that imply the right.

The right to privacy essentially is the right to make personal choices without outside interference. In the landmark case of *Griswold v. Connecticut* (1965), for example, the Supreme Court recognized a married couple's right to privacy in contraceptive use. In *Eisenstadt v. Baird* (1972), the Supreme Court extended the right to privacy in contraceptive use to include unmarried people. In *Carey v. Population Services International* (1977), the Supreme Court said a state law that prohibited the sale of contraceptives to anyone under age 16 was unconstitutional.

The U.S. Department of Health and Human Services tried to modify the

Carey ruling by publishing a regulation, "Parental Notification Requirements Applicable to Projects for Family Planning Services." Also known as the "squeal rule," this regulation proposed that any federally funded clinic or health agency that gave contraceptives to a minor be required to inform the minor's parents or guardian. A New York federal district court, however, declared that divulging such confidential information invades the minor's privacy and is unconstitutional. (See *Distributing contraceptives in public schools.*)

Right to privacy and abortion law

The Supreme Court ruling in *Roe v. Wade* (1973) protects a woman's right to privacy in a first-trimester abortion. After the first trimester, a state may regulate abortion to protect the mother's health and prohibit an abortion if the fetus is judged viable. However, state legislators have complicated access to abortion services in different ways. In 1999 alone, Texas passed seven laws affecting abortion rights. One law mandates parental involvement and a 48-hour waiting period for minors (SB 30). Another makes it a felony for any adult to take a minor out of state without parental consent (HB 1428). Another law excludes organizations that offer abortion procedures from receiving family planning funding and mandates that funds for prescription contraceptives for minors only be given with parental consent (HB 1); another denies tax-exemption status to not-for-profit organizations that perform, refer for, or assist other organizations that perform or refer for abortion (HB 541). Yet another law prohibits the state Child Health Plan from covering any services that prevent conception or birth (SB 445). Another prohibits school-based health centers from providing reproductive services, counseling, or referrals if they receive certain grants (HB 2202).

Other states, including Virginia, Arizona, Iowa, and Florida, have passed similar laws. Florida passed a law that creates pro-life license plates, the payments for which fund private organizations that provide services and counseling to pregnant women, but fund recipients may not perform, refer for, or counsel about abortion (HB 509).

Contraception and abortion are heavily restricted through legislation. A federal directive issued July 2, 1998, by the Clinton administration specifically mandates payment by Medicaid and insurance companies for the drug sildenafil (Viagra), which treats impotence. There are no laws mandating any type of payment for birth control, and about 50% of large insurance companies won't pay for it.

Restrictions on the abortion right

Since *Roe v. Wade,* the Supreme Court has handed down more than 20 major opinions related to the abortion issue.

A 1989 Supreme Court decision, *Webster v. Reproductive Health Services,* placed certain aspects of *Roe v. Wade* into doubt. Although viability of the fetus remains the guideline, the Supreme Court now appears more willing to allow states to regulate abortion. For example, in 1992, the Supreme Court let stand Pennsylvania's Abortion Control Act of 1989 (*Planned Parenthood of S.E. Pennsylvania v. Casey*). This act requires that a woman wait 24 hours between consenting to and receiving an abortion, except in narrowly defined medical emergencies, and that a woman seeking an abortion be given state-mandated abortion information and offered state-authored materials on fetal development. The Supreme Court struck down the requirement that a married woman inform her husband of her intent to have an abortion. Overall, the decision reaffirmed a woman's right to abortion but suggested that the

Distributing contraceptives in public schools

Making contraceptives readily available in public schools has caused a political uproar. Advocates claim that school-based family planning services effectively counter high pregnancy rates and lower the incidence of sexually transmitted diseases (STDs) among teenagers. Consider these statistics:

- About 12 million (48%) adolescents in the United States are sexually active.
- By age 19, 75% of American girls have had sexual intercourse.
- Girls age 15 to 19 have the highest incidence of pelvic inflammatory disease.
- About 35% of sexually active teens don't use any form of birth control; those who do commonly use it incorrectly, providing inadequate protection against pregnancy and STDs.
- Twenty-six percent of all abortions are performed on teenagers.

In 1986, the National Academy of Sciences (NAS) recommended that adolescents not be forced to seek parental consent for abortion. The NAS also recommended that contraceptives be made available in the schools. These recommendations drew strong opposition. The National Right to Life Committee and then-Secretary of Education William J. Bennett argued that providing contraceptives in schools would contribute to teenage promiscuity and abortion. Local initiatives have been opposed by parents and clergy, who argue that school-based family planning undermines the relationship between parents and adolescents.

Chicago: A case study

The first school-based health clinic to dispense contraceptives in Chicago opened in 1984. Anti-abortion activists picketed the facility; members of the clergy sued, unsuc-

cessfully, to stop it; and conservative activist Phylllis Schlafly backed a bill to outlaw such clinics (the bill was vetoed by the governor of Illinois).

By 1990, three school-based clinics in Chicago were dispensing contraceptives without incident. To use these clinics, students need parental permission, and parents who don't want their children to receive contraceptives can say no.

Thus far, the Chicago clinics apparently haven't reduced pregnancy rates. In one Chicago high school with about 1,000 girls, 30 to 50 pregnancies continue to occur each year. Nevertheless, school officials believe that their clinics help control repeat pregnancies, and that they promote the overall health of the students. In fact, fewer than 20% of the visits to clinics have been for contraceptives. Most are for inoculations, basic medical care, and emergency first aid.

A mixed report

The Chicago experience apparently isn't unusual. There are more than 170 school-based clinics in the United States. Many provide family planning services, as well as counseling on alcohol, smoking, and drug use. To date, school-based family planning services haven't had the impact that advocates hoped for; they also haven't had the effect that opponents feared. Studies by the Center for Population Options, an independent group, have shown that school-based clinics reduce students' use of alcohol and tobacco. They also find that making contraceptives readily available doesn't spur sexual activity. Studies also show that school-based clinics that provide contraceptives haven't had a significant effect on teenage pregnancy rates.

Court had revised its long-standing definition of that right as fundamental.

In May 1991, anti-abortion groups won a victory on another front. In *Rust*

v. Sullivan, the Court upheld federal regulations prohibiting health care workers at more than 4,000 government-subsidized family planning clinics from providing any information about abortion. Under the regulations, if you work in a subsidized clinic, you may not advise a pregnant woman that abortion is a possibility, nor may you help her find a private abortion clinic. You're obligated to refer pregnant women for prenatal care.

Abortion rights for minors

Roe v. Wade played an important role in extending abortion rights to minors. In *Planned Parenthood of Central Missouri v. Danfort* (1976), the Supreme Court overruled a law that prevented first-trimester abortions for minors without parental consent. This decision was based on *Roe v. Wade.*

In *Bellotti v. Baird II* (1979), the Supreme Court acknowledged that the privacy rights of a minor aren't equal to those of an adult. The Court held, however, that a state law requiring a minor to obtain parental consent for an abortion infringed on the minor's rights.

In *H.L. v. Matheson* (1981), the Supreme Court upheld a Utah law requiring a physician to notify the parents of an unemancipated minor before an abortion. More recently, however, in *Hodgson v. Minnesota* (1990), a Minnesota statute that required notification of both biological parents before a minor's abortion, followed by a wait of at least 48 hours, was held unconstitutional. The chief difference between the two cases is that the Utah law required notification of only one parent, where feasible; the Minnesota law required notification of *both* parents, even if they were divorced or separated. In *Hodgson,* the Supreme Court decreed that the rule requiring notification of both parents was too burdensome on the abortion right because it could create exceptional difficulties for one-parent families. The Court also stated that the 48-hour waiting period required under the Minnesota law would not, by itself, render the statute unconstitutional.

By letting stand Pennsylvania's Abortion Control Act in 1992, the Supreme Court allowed the state to require that one parent or guardian give consent in person for a minor seeking an abortion, unless the minor obtains a judicial waiver.

In *Hodgson* and in *Ohio v. Akron Center for Reproductive Health* (1990), the Supreme Court set forth its position on so-called *judicial bypass statutes.* These statutes allow a minor to avoid notifying parents or obtaining consent for an abortion by going before a judge. The Court stated that judicial bypass satisfies the requirement that parents or other third parties can't have an absolute veto over the minor's abortion decision.

STATE LAW AND THE RIGHT TO PRIVACY

The right to privacy has received even more attention at the state level. Ten states — Alaska, Arizona, California, Florida, Hawaii, Illinois, Louisiana, Montana, South Carolina, and Washington — have written a privacy provision into their constitutions. Nearly all states recognize the right to privacy through *statutory law* or *common law.*

PRIVILEGE DOCTRINE

The state courts have been strong in protecting a patient's right to have information kept confidential. Even in court, your patient is protected by the *privilege doctrine.* People who have a protected relationship, such as a physician and a patient, can't be forced, even during legal proceedings, to reveal communication between them unless the person who benefits from the protection agrees to it. This means that the patient must agree before confidential information is revealed in court. The purpose of the privilege doctrine is to encourage the patient to reveal confidential information that may be essential to his treatment. State law determines which relationships are protected by the privilege doctrine. Most states include husband-wife, lawyer-client, and physician-patient relationships. These doctrines have been directly applied to the NP-patient relationships as well.

Extent of privilege

State laws also determine the extent of privilege in protected relationships. In *Hammonds v. Aetna Casualty and Surety Co.* (1965), the court reinforced the privilege doctrine by declaring that protecting a patient's privacy is a physician's legal duty. It further ruled that a patient could sue for damages any unauthorized person who disclosed confidential medical information about him. Similarly, a patient can sue for invasion of privacy any unauthorized personnel, such as NP students, who observe him without his permission. The only hospital personnel who have a right to observe a patient are those involved in his diagnosis, treatment, and related care.

Exceptions

In some states, a patient automatically waives his right to physician-patient privilege when he files a personal injury or **workers' compensation** lawsuit.

A facility or physician can't invoke the privilege doctrine if the motive is self-protection. In *People v. Doe* (1978), a nursing home was being investigated for allegedly mistreating its patients. The court ruled that the nursing home's attempt to invoke patient privilege was unjust, because the issue at hand was the patients' welfare.

The other exception is in life-threatening situations where certain patient information must be released in order to best treat the patient despite the fact that the patient was unable to consent or was unaware of the disclosure of confidential information.

YOUR RESPONSIBILITIES IN PROTECTING PATIENT PRIVACY

Despite legal uncertainties regarding your responsibilities under the privilege doctrine, you have a professional and ethical responsibility to protect your patient's privacy.

This responsibility requires more than keeping secrets. You may have to educate your patients about their privacy rights. Some of them may be unaware of what the right to privacy means, or even that they have such a right. Explain to the patient that he can refuse to allow pictures to be taken of his disorder and its treatment, for example. Tell him that he can choose to have information about his condition withheld from others, including family members. Make every effort to ensure that the patient's wishes are carried out.

WHEN YOU MAY DISCLOSE CONFIDENTIAL INFORMATION

Under certain circumstances, you may lawfully disclose confidential information about your patient. For example, the courts allow disclosure when the welfare of a person or a group of people is at stake. Suppose a patient diagnosed as an epileptic asks you not to tell his family. Depending on the circumstances, you may decide that this isn't in the patient's and his family's best interest, particularly in terms of safety. In that situation, inform the patient's physician; he may then decide to inform the family to protect the patient's well-being. In most states, the physician is required to inform the Department of Motor Vehicles of uncontrolled epilepsy.

You're also protected by law if you disclose confidential information about a patient that's necessary for his continued care or if your patient consents to the disclosure.

Be careful not to exceed the specified limit of a patient's consent. Taking pictures is the largest single cause of invasion of privacy lawsuits. In *Feeney v. Young* (1920), a woman consented to the filming of her cesarean delivery for viewings by medical societies, but the physician incorporated the film into a generally released movie titled *Birth*. The court awarded damages to the woman under the state's privacy law.

Protecting the public
The courts have granted immunity to health care professionals who, in good faith, have disclosed confidential information to prevent public harm. In *Simonsen v. Swenson* (1920), a physician who thought that his patient had syphilis told the owner of the hotel in which the patient was staying about the patient's contagious disease. The court ruled that physicians are privileged to make disclosures that will prevent the spread of disease.

A controversial California case established a physician's right to disclose information that would protect any person whom a patient threatened to harm. In *Tarasoff v. Regents of the University of California* (1976), a woman was murdered by a mentally ill patient who had told his psychotherapist that he intended to kill her. The victim's parents sued the physician for failing to warn their daughter. The Supreme Court found the physician liable because he didn't warn the intended victim. The Court ruled similarly in *McIntosh v. Milano* (1979).

WHEN YOU MUST DISCLOSE CONFIDENTIAL INFORMATION
In some situations, the law requires you to disclose confidential information.

Child abuse
All 50 states and the District of Columbia have **disclosure laws** for **child abuse** cases. Except for Maine and Montana, all states also grant immunity from legal action for a **good faith** report on suspected child abuse. In fact, there may be a criminal penalty for failure to disclose such information.

Courts also may order you to disclose confidential information in cases of child custody and child neglect. One case involving such an order was *D. v. D.* (1969). Despite the physician-patient privilege, the court ordered the physician to turn the mother's **medical records** over to the court for a private inspection. The mother had a history of illness, and the court said that the inspection would help it to decide which parent should be granted custody. The courts made a similar ruling in the custody case of *In re Doe Children* (1978). The court stated that the children's welfare outweighed the parents' right to keep their medical records private.

Criminal cases
Some laws create an exemption to the privilege doctrine in criminal cases so that the courts can have access to all essential information. In states where neither a law nor an exemption to the law exists, the court may find an exemption to the doctrine in criminal cases.

Government requests
Certain government agencies can order you to reveal confidential information, including federal agencies such as the Internal Revenue Service, the Environmental Protection Agency, the Department of Labor, and the Department of Health and Human Services. State agencies that may order you to reveal confidential information include revenue or tax bureaus and public health departments. For example, most state public health departments require reports of all communicable diseases, births and deaths, and gunshot wounds.

Public's right to know
The newsworthiness of an event or person can make disclosure accept-

able. In such circumstances, the public's need for information may outweigh a person's right to keep his medical condition private. For example, newspapers routinely publish the findings of the President's annual physical examination in response to the public's demand for information. Even the First Lady's health may become a matter of public record. In 1990, when Barbara Bush underwent radiation therapy for Graves' disease, the media publicized many details of her treatment.

Other events for which the public's right to know may outweigh the patient's right to privacy include breakthroughs in medical technology (the first successful implantation of an artificial heart) and product tampering cases. In 1991, the national media gave wide exposure to an incident in Washington state in which three people suffered acute onset of cyanide poisoning by taking Sudafed 12-hour capsules.

Even when the public has a right to know about a confidential matter, the courts won't allow public disclosure to undermine a person's dignity. In *Barber v. Time, Inc.* (1942), *TIME* magazine was sued by a woman whose name and photograph were published in an article that revealed she suffered from an illness that caused her to eat as much food as 10 persons could eat. The court ruled that publishing the patient's name and picture was an unnecessary invasion of her privacy and that ethics required keeping such information confidential.

Doe v. Roe (1977) is a similar case. A patient sued his psychiatrist for publishing the patient's biography and thoughts verbatim. Even though the physician didn't use the patient's name, the court stated that the patient was readily identifiable by the article. It found the physician liable for violating the physician-patient privilege.

When the patient demands his records

Suppose the patient says to you, "I'm paying for the tests; I have a right to know the results." Does the patient have the legal right to know what's in his medical records?

Yes. And because patients increasingly want explanations about what's being done to them and why, you should know how to respond when your patient asks to see his medical records.

DISCLOSURE DEBATE

For years, health care experts have debated the merits of letting a patient see his medical records. Proponents argue that knowing the information helps the patient to better understand his condition and care and makes him a more cooperative patient.

Opponents, usually physicians and facilities, argue that the technical jargon and medical abbreviations found in medical records may confuse or even frighten a patient. In addition, opponents claim that opening medical records to a patient will increase the risks of malpractice lawsuits. No evidence exists to support this contention.

The **right-to-access** issue has spawned an important legal debate. The first issue the courts had to answer involved ownership.

Determining ownership

The hospital owns the hospital medical records, and the physician owns his office records, according to court decisions. Most courts have decided that a patient sees a physician for diagnosis and treatment, not to obtain records for his personal use.

Right to access

The second issue the courts had to resolve involved access. While granting ownership of medical records to physicians and facilities, the courts have expressed rights to get the records anytime they need for a case review.

For this reason, any patient in any state can file a lawsuit to **subpoena** his medical records. But some court decisions and some states' laws have given patients the right to direct access. Many states guarantee a patient's right to his medical information.

In *Cannell v. Medical and Surgical Clinic S.C.* (1974), the court ruled that a physician had the duty to disclose medical information to his patient. The court also ruled, however, that physicians and facilities needn't turn over the actual files to the patient. Instead, they need only show the complete medical record — or a copy — to the patient.

The court based the patient's limited right to access on two important concepts:
● A patient has a right to know the details about his medical treatment under common law.
● A patient has a right to the information in his records because he pays for the treatment.

Setting up roadblocks
Despite the laws and court decisions, hospitals don't always make access to records easy. Some facilities discourage a patient from seeing his medical records by putting up bureaucratic barriers. For example, requiring the patient to have an attorney make the request can stifle a patient's attempt to gain access and encourage visits to malpractice lawyers. Other facilities charge high copying fees to discourage patient record requests.

Some states, such as Pennsylvania, have laws that require reasonable copying fees.

HOW TO RESPOND TO YOUR PATIENT'S REQUEST
A patient's request should make you question whether you and your colleagues have done enough to communicate with him. Assess why the patient wants to see his records. He may simply be curious, or his request may reflect hidden fears about his treatment.

Many hospitals have established policies that deal with this issue. These policies may include notifying the nursing supervisor that the patient has asked to see his medical records and notifying the risk manager, if your facility has one, to alert administrative staff and legal counsel, if necessary.

After your patient gets approval to see his records, stay with him while he reads them. Explain to him that state laws prohibit him from changing or erasing information on his records, even information he considers incorrect. Tell him to show you any information he considers incorrect. Offer to answer any of his questions that you can; assure him that his physician will answer questions, too. In fact, encourage the patient to write down specific questions for his physician, and offer to contact his physician for him.

While your patient reads, help him to interpret the abbreviations and jargon used in medical charting. One patient hospitalized for hypertension was greatly relieved when her nurse explained that the "malignant hypertension" notation on her chart had nothing to do with cancer.

Observe how the patient responds while he reads. If he becomes apprehensive, puzzled, or angry, try to provide him with calm, professional explanations about what he's read in his records. He may simply seem relieved. Some patients want to read their records just to be sure you and the physicians aren't hiding any information. For example, one patient who demanded to see her medical records merely flipped through the pages. The facility's willingness to share information about her treatment apparently satisfied her.

WHEN A RELATIVE REQUESTS MEDICAL RECORDS

A relative may see a patient's medical records when:
● the relative or next of kin is the patient's legal guardian, and the patient is incompetent.
● the relative has the patient's approval.

Patient discharge against medical advice

The patient's bill of rights and the laws and regulations based on it give a competent adult the right to refuse treatment for any reason without being punished or having his liberty restricted.

Some states have turned these rights into law. In addition, the courts have cited the bills of rights in their decisions.

The right to refuse treatment includes the right to leave the hospital *against medical advice (AMA)* any time, for any reason. All you can do is try to talk the patient out of it.

RECOGNIZING A POTENTIAL PATIENT WALKOUT

Because you may have more contact with your patient than other health care professionals, you're likely to be one of the first persons to suspect that a patient is contemplating leaving AMA.

Complaints or hostile behavior may indicate the patient's extreme dissatisfaction with hospital routine or with the care he's receiving. By carefully observing, listening to, and talking with him, you may be able to resolve the problems by offering him a fresh perspective and perhaps change his mind about leaving.

If you discover that a specific problem has caused his dissatisfaction, try to resolve it. If the problem lies outside the scope of your practice, call the collaborating physician.

A patient may tell you that he's changed his mind about leaving just to divert your attention. If you suspect this, have the RN check on him more often, and have someone stay with him when he's escorted to another part of the hospital.

WHEN THE PATIENT INSISTS ON LEAVING

If your patient still insists on leaving AMA, and your hospital has a policy on managing the patient who wants to leave, follow it exactly. Following policy will help to protect the hospital, coworkers, and you from charges of unlawful restraint or *false imprisonment.* If your employer doesn't have such a policy, take these steps:
● Contact the patient's family (if he hasn't already called them), and explain that the patient is getting ready to leave. If you can't reach the family, contact the person listed in the patient's records as being responsible for him (or for his body and valuables if he should die).
● Explain the hospital's AMA procedures to the patient if hospital policy delegates this responsibility to you.
● Give the patient the AMA form to sign (see *Documenting a patient's decision to leave AMA,* page 304). His decision to leave is the same as a refusal of treatment. Inform the patient of his medical risks if he leaves the facility, and explain the alternatives available at the facility and at other locations, such as regular visits to the outpatient clinic or admission to another facility. His signature on the AMA form is evidence of his refusal of treatment. You should witness the signature.
● Provide routine discharge care. Even though your patient is leaving AMA, his rights to discharge planning and care are the same as those for a patient who has signed out with medical advice. So if the patient agrees, have him escorted to the door (in a

Documenting a patient's decision to leave AMA

An against-medical-advice (AMA) form is a medical record as well as a legal document. It's designed to protect you, your coworkers, and your facility from liability resulting from the patient's unapproved discharge or escape.

To document an AMA incident, begin by getting your facility's AMA form. The form may look like the one shown below. It clearly states that the patient:

● knows he's leaving against medical advice
● has been advised of, and understands, the risks of leaving
● knows he can come back.

Discuss this form with the patient and ask him to sign it. Don't try to force the patient to sign, if he is unwilling to do so.

Add the AMA form to the patient's medical chart. Then write a detailed description of how you first learned of the patient's plan to leave AMA, what you and the patient said to each other, and what alternatives to the patient's action were discussed.

Also, check your facility's policy concerning incident reports. If the patient leaves without anyone's knowledge, or if he refuses to sign the AMA form, you'll probably be required to file an incident report. Be sure to include the names of any other employees involved in the discovery of the patient's absence. Facility administration or your head nurse also may want to solicit corroborating reports from other employees, including other registered nurses, licensed practical nurses, nurses' assistants, orderlies, and clerical staff.

RESPONSIBILITY RELEASE

This is to certify that I, _____

a patient in _____

am being discharged against the advice of my physician and the facility administration. I acknowledge that I have been informed of the risks involved and hereby release my physician and the hospital from all responsibility for any ill effects that may result from such a discharge. I also understand that I may return to the hospital at any time and have treatment resumed.

_____   _____
[Patient's signature]   [Date]

_____   _____
[Witness' signature]   [Date]

RE: _____   Patient # _____
[Name of patient]

---

wheelchair, if necessary), arrange for medical or nursing follow-up care, and offer other routine health care measures. These procedures will protect the facility as well as the patient.

WHEN THE PATIENT REFUSES TO SIGN OUT

If the patient refuses to sign the AMA form, you should document his refusal in a note stating that all risks have been explained to the patient.

Dealing with an escape

If you discover that a patient is missing from the hospital, notify the nursing supervisor and security immediately. If the patient was in police custody or poses a threat to anyone outside the hospital, the administration should contact the police. The hospital administration subsequently may ask you to notify the patient's family or friends and document the escape in the patient's medical chart and ***incident report.***

FALSE IMPRISONMENT

Never attempt to detain a competent adult who has a right to leave. Any attempt to detain or restrain him may be interpreted as unlawful restraint or false imprisonment, for which you can be sued or prosecuted.

Your facility's policy should reflect state law. It should specifically answer such questions as:
● How long and for what reasons may a patient be detained?
● When can you use forcible restraints?
● Who may order the use of restraints?
● Who may apply the restraints?

Knowing the policies will reduce your liability exposure.

Court cases

Most courts disapprove of detaining a patient arbitrarily or for an unreasonably long time, which may be ruled false imprisonment. (For an example of a case in which the court found a health care facility guilty of false imprisonment, see *Patient or prisoner?*)

Court cases that involve false imprisonment charges have occurred when facilities threatened to hold patients or their personal belongings until bills were paid. In most cases, the courts ruled against the institutions.

COURT CASE

Patient or prisoner?

In false imprisonment cases, two elements must be proven. First, the defendant must have intended to confine or restrict the patient's movement. Second, the patient must have had an awareness of the involuntary confinement. The case of *Big Town Nursing Home v. Newman* (1970) provides a good example of how a health care facility may become vulnerable to charges of false imprisonment.

Mr. Newman, 67, had Parkinson's disease, arthritis, heart trouble, hiatal hernia, a speech impediment, and a history of alcoholism. Four days after his nephew signed him into a nursing home, Mr. Newman decided to leave.

No exit

Employees at the nursing home stopped Mr. Newman, locked away his suitcase and clothes, restricted his use of the phone, and restricted his right to visitors. When Mr. Newman tried to walk off the grounds, employees locked him in a wing with severely emotionally disturbed patients and patients addicted to drugs and alcohol. He made other unsuccessful escape attempts, so the staff tied Mr. Newman to a chair for long periods. Twenty-two days after his admission, Mr. Newman escaped. Eventually, he sued.

The court ruled in favor of Mr. Newman. Despite his physical infirmities, Mr. Newman hadn't legally been declared incompetent and was, therefore, legally entitled to exercise his rights.

A facility or nursing home can delay a patient's discharge, for a reasonable period of time, until routine paperwork is complete. *Bailie v. Miami Valley*

Hospital (1966) was a case in which the court ruled in favor of a facility.

An exception

In a few cases, because of extenuating circumstances, the courts have ruled against patients who sued on grounds of false imprisonment. The case of *Pounders v. Trinity Court Nursing Home* (1979) is one such example.

Mrs. Pounders, 75, was a disabled widow. When her niece and nephew no longer wanted her to live with them, the niece arranged for her to move to Trinity Court Nursing Home. Mrs. Pounders didn't object.

During her 2 months at Trinity Court, Mrs. Pounders complained only once to a nurses' assistant that she wanted to leave. Unfortunately, the assistant failed to report the complaint to anyone in authority at the home.

Mrs. Pounders was finally released, through the aid of an attorney, into another niece's care. She eventually sued the nursing home.

Because Mrs. Pounders couldn't prove she'd been involuntarily detained, the court absolved the nursing home of the false imprisonment charges.

LAWFUL DETENTION

The right to leave the hospital AMA isn't absolute. Certain patients who pose a threat to themselves or to others can't legally leave the hospital. Restraint, when necessary, is lawful with psychiatric patients, prisoners, and violent patients.

Patients from psychiatric hospitals or prisons

If a patient transferred to your hospital for medical care from a prison or psychiatric hospital threatens to escape, notify the custodial institution immediately. They're responsible for sending personnel to guard the patient and for making new arrangements for his care.

Restrain the patient only if his medical condition warrants it or if the police or psychiatric hospital authorities instruct you to do so.

If the prisoner or psychiatric patient escapes, you or your facility or nursing administration should call the authorities at the custodial institution or the police.

Violent patients

If you suspect that a patient with a history of violence or violent threats is planning to leave AMA, notify facility and nursing administrators immediately. If state law allows it, your facility administrators may decide to get police assistance to restrain the patient.

If the violent patient has escaped, notify your nursing or facility administration immediately. They'll contact the police and mental health authorities. If the patient ever expressed an intention to harm a known person, the administration also should contact that person.

When a patient dies

When a patient dies, his rights are transferred to his estate. In recent years, however, legally determining when death occurred has become difficult. That, in turn, complicates your role as an NP.

How can you be sure a patient is legally dead? Who has the right to pronounce death? What are your responsibilities after the patient dies?

CONTROVERSY OVER THE DEFINITION OF DEATH

Determining death used to be simple. When a person's circulation and respiration stopped, he was dead. Advances in medical technology, however, have made death pronouncements more complicated. Because medical equipment — such as ventilators, pacemakers, and intra-aortic balloon pumps —

can maintain respiration and circulation, patients may continue to "live" even after their brains have died.

Criteria for brain death

To help physicians determine death in such cases, an ***ad hoc committee*** at Harvard Medical School published a report in 1968, establishing specific criteria for ***brain death:***
● failure to respond to the most painful stimuli
● absence of spontaneous respirations or muscle movements
● absence of reflexes
● flat EEG.

The committee recommended that all these tests be repeated after 24 hours, and that hypothermia and the presence of central nervous system depressants, such as barbiturates, be ruled out.

In 1981, the American Medical Association, the American Bar Association, and the President's Commission for the Study of Ethical Problems in Medicine and Behavioral Research collaborated to derive a working definition of brain death. The result of this effort, the Uniform Determination of Death Act (UDODA), has gained wide acceptance among the health care and legal communities.

In general terms, the UDODA defines brain death as the cessation of all measurable functions or activity in every area of the brain, including the brain stem. This definition excludes comatose patients as well as those in a persistent vegetative state. Current debate centers on whether to expand the definition to include certain patients who still have brain stem function, such as anencephalic infants.

Court cases

Several court decisions have been based on such definitions.

In *State v. Brown* (1971), an Oregon court was among the first to recognize

brain death. In this case of second-degree murder, the defendant argued that he hadn't caused the victim's death by inflicting a gunshot wound to the brain. Instead, he claimed, a physician killed the victim by removing artificial life support. The court ruled that the defendant caused the victim's death because the gunshot wound resulted in brain death.

In 1975, several New York hospitals initiated a lawsuit to get a legal ruling on the definition of death when the patient was a potential organ donor (*N. Y.C. Health and Hospitals Corporation v. Sulsona* [1975]). Expert testimony showed that the common law definition of death (cessation of circulation and respiration) raised the failure rate of organ transplants. The incidence of renal failure in kidney recipients was about 88%. Using the brain death standard, however, the incidence of renal failure in recipients was only about 15%. (Medical advances have since improved the success rate of almost all types of transplant surgery.)

The court ruled that it would recognize brain death in transplantation cases to encourage anatomic gifts, even though the state had no law defining brain death. Its ruling applied only to transplantation cases, however.

In 1979, a Colorado court also accepted the criteria for brain death. In *Lovato v. Colorado* (1979), a mother was charged with abusing her child. The child was comatose, with a flat EEG and fixed and dilated pupils, and lacked spontaneous respiration or reflexes or responses to painful stimuli. The mother petitioned the court to keep the child on a ventilator. The court ruled that the child was dead because he met the criteria for brain death.

Know your state's law

In states without laws defining death or without judicial precedents, the common law definition of death (cessation of circulation and respiration) is still used. In these states, physicians are understandably reluctant to discontinue artificial life support for brain-dead patients. If you're likely to be involved with patients on life-support equipment, protect yourself by finding out how your state defines death.

PRONOUNCING DEATH

Only a physician or a *coroner* can legally pronounce a person dead. In some health care facilities, such as nursing homes, nurses pronounce death when a physician isn't available. The state board must indicate that this is an appropriate nursing practice. If you work in such a facility, you should understand that pronouncing death typically isn't a nursing responsibility.

The attending physician usually is responsible for signing the death certificate, unless the death comes under the jurisdiction of a medical examiner or coroner. State laws specify when this occurs. The coroner or medical examiner usually has jurisdiction over deaths with violent or suspicious circumstances. These include suspected homicides and suicides and deaths after accidents.

YOUR RESPONSIBILITY WHEN A PATIENT DIES

When a patient dies, you're responsible for accurately and objectively charting all his signs and any actions you take. If you're notified of the death before the patient's physician, you should call the patient's physician and inform him of the death and the circumstances that occurred around it. You or the physician should notify the family.

OBTAINING CONSENT FOR AN AUTOPSY

If a death comes under the jurisdiction of a medical examiner or coroner, the decision to perform an *autopsy* rests

solely with him, despite the family's wishes. In all other cases, the patient's family has a right to give or withhold consent. In some states, the patient can give written consent to an autopsy before he dies.

As the NP involved in the care of the patient, you may be responsible for obtaining consent from the family for an autopsy. Be prepared to explain why the autopsy is needed and how autopsy arrangements are made.

Who may give consent

Most states have laws to specify who has the right to give consent to autopsies. Some laws list which relatives can give consent. Others list relatives in descending order, according to their relationship to the deceased. The usual order is spouse, adult children, parents, brothers or sisters, grandparents, uncles or aunts, and cousins. The person with the right to consent may withhold consent or impose limits on the autopsy. If the autopsy exceeds these limits, the consenting relative may sue.

The relative with the right to consent also may sue if an autopsy is performed without any consent. The grounds for such lawsuits usually are mental or emotional suffering.

EXPERIMENTAL PROCEDURES

The family has a right to give or withhold specific consent to practice medical procedures on a corpse. In teaching hospitals, residents and medical students practice procedures, such as intubation, on corpses. If a hospital doesn't obtain proper consent, however, the family member responsible for consent may sue. In many states, the hospital may even face criminal charges.

RESPONSIBILITY FOR BURIAL

In the United States, the family member who has the right to consent to autopsy usually has the responsibility to bury the body as well.

If no one claims the body, despite the facility's effort to contact the person responsible, a state or county official must dispose of it. Laws in many states direct this official to deliver unclaimed bodies to an appropriate educational or scientific institution, unless the person is a veteran or has died from a contagious disease. In these situations, the state pays for burial or cremation.

Selected references

Friedman, E. "Making Choices: Elective Procedures," *Health Forum Journal.* 43(5):8-11, September-October 2000.

Hickey, J.V., et al. *Advanced Practice Nursing: Changing Roles and Clinical Applications,* 2nd ed. Philadelphia: Lippincott, Williams and Wilkins, 2000.

Lens, V., and Pollack, D. "Advance Directives: Legal Remedies and Psychosocial Interventions," *Death Studies* 24(5):377-99, July-August 2000.

Logan, P. *Principles of Practice for the Acute Care Nurse Practitioner.* Stamford, Conn.: Appleton & Lange, 1999.

Merz, J.F., et al. "Hospital Consent for Disclosure of Medical Records," *Journal of Law, Medicine, and Ethics* 26(3):241-48, Fall 1998.

Reed, S. "Keeping Secrets Secret: Legislation to Secure Patient Privacy and Confidentiality Is Still Needed," *American Journal of Nursing* 100(8):73-74, August 2000.

Renke, W.N. "The Mandatory Reporting of Child Abuse under the Child Welfare Act," *Health Law Journal* 7:91-140, 1999.

Rockett, L.R. "Legal Issues Affecting Confidentiality and Informed Consent in Reproductive Health," *Journal of the American Medical Women's Association* 55(5):257-60, Fall 2000.

Schulmeister, L. "Living Wills, Advance Directives, and Surrogate Decision Making," *Clinical Journal of Oncology Nursing* 2(4):148-50, October 1998.

Silveira, M.J., et al. "Patients' Knowledge of Options at the End of Life: Ignorance in the Face of Death," *Journal of the American Medical Association* 15;284(19):2483-8, November 2000.

Chapter Eleven

NPs IN A CHANGING HEALTH CARE MARKETPLACE

The health care industry is undergoing rapid transformation that will profoundly affect nursing and *nurse practitioners (NPs)*. Not only are the changes affecting each NP's ability to deliver quality patient care, but they also affect the practice areas and the number and type of employment opportunities available to them.

Today, the health care marketplace is revolutionizing the financing and delivery of health care, reshaping our cultural perceptions of nursing and health care, and redefining the mission of NPs. NPs need to think about how they can shape future changes in the health care delivery system and how they can advance their careers in such uncertain times. With all of these simultaneous changes, the NP is in a position to be both a caregiver and a leader in today's changing health care marketplace.

The health care marketplace

In the United States, the health care marketplace remains on the competitive course set forth by the Clinton administration in the 1990s, a course that struggled to provide quality health care at a cost savings to patients. Providing affordable quality care as well as broadening the choices in health care delivery are issues that remain in the forefront of the health care marketplace today.

PAST AND PRESENT

Since the 1800s, the health care marketplace in the United States has undergone three major reorganizations. The first reorganization involved science-based medicine, which focused on improvements in the approach to clinical medicine, such as pharmaceutical advances and the education of physicians. During this time, physicians were perceived as and assumed the role of the unquestioned authority figure.

The second reorganization of health care, which occurred after World War II, revolved around supply. Its focus was to increase the supply of services and specialists, which included advanced education for specialty areas. Federal entitlement programs were initiated. Because there was an increased supply of services and specialists, demand increased and resulted in the growing expense of health care. Employers began to insure their employees, causing the costs of health care to escalate.

The third reorganization began in the 1980s and continues into this new century. Its primary focus has centered on reducing the unacceptable increases that had been established by the second reorganization. The marketplace began to take notice of the skyrocketing growth in health care cost, expenditures, and specialists and decided it demanded immediate attention. Regulations that decreased the oversupply of health care services and education were put into place. Generalists in medicine began to replace specialists. The concept and institution of managed care was introduced. During the first half of the 1990s, health care issues were highlighted with the Clinton administration as it attempted to reform health care. Although the Clinton initiative didn't succeed, it received front line attention that resulted in continued growth of managed care, the introduction of the more complex integrated health care delivery systems, and consumer dissatisfaction with and lack of confidence in providers, insurers, and health care systems.

This current reorganization era brings with it the challenges of competition and the need for the marketplace to retool. Health care joined other businesses in its efforts to downsize, reengineer, restructure, and reorganize. Physicians, nurses, and other health care disciplines were plunged into a world that didn't coincide with their basic philosophy. Health care delivery is now at odds with the business of health care delivery. Health care is no longer exclusively caring for people; it now includes the business of **cost containment** and the bottom line. (See *Trends in insurance coverage,* page 312.)

MANAGED CARE

Although the term itself is of recent vintage, **managed care organizations (MCOs)** have existed in some form for more than 100 years. Puerto Rico, one of the first to develop a managed care system, designed the first **health maintenance organization (HMO).** MCOs have existed in the U.S. for more than 30 years but have only recently received widespread attention and have grown substantially since the mid 1980s.

Managed care relates delivery of care and reimbursement. Before the introduction of managed care, these two constructs were mutually exclusive. The health care industry required an initiative that would address its high percentage of the gross domestic product and the fact that the health care delivery system in the United States had become the most expensive in the world. To prevent a bankruptcy scenario and eventual collapse of the system, delivery and reimbursement had to be incorporated.

Managed care can be defined as a type of health insurance plan, but it can also describe an extensive and comprehensive range of health care and delivery strategies that are designed to minimize costs and ensure quality care. Literally, managed care defines an obligation to manage patient care that is shared by unrelated parties, such as providers, consumers, payers, and government.

Providers include physicians, NPs, facilities, and other health care providers who agree with payers to provide care within a fee schedule. Providers may assume partial or total financial risk for the enrollees assigned to them, creating an environment for delivering cost-effective care.

Consumers seek care according to the rules and regulations of their health care plan. They may have fewer choices and more financial responsibil-

Trends in insurance coverage

• Larger — In the United States, there's a growing trend toward larger health plans. In Colorado, for instance, the 10 largest plans cover 80% of the market. This indicates a decline in competition and a rise in consumer costs.

• More managed care — The U.S. market for insurance coverage is changing. Managed care covered 30 million people in 1990, 75 million in 1999, and about 90 million in 2000. Traditional indemnity insurance coverage continues to shrink; only about 10% of the population has adequate coverage, and 15% of the population remains uninsured. In the managed care industry, preferred provider organizations (PPOs) have become the fastest-growing segment. Unlike health maintenance organizations (HMOs), PPOs provide a wide network of preferred providers but at a higher premium. These plans suggest the market's growing demand for quality, not just cost containment.

• Health care insurance premiums are expected to continue rising for three reasons:

1. Increased demand for quality and choice of health care by employers, plus policies that affect care, such as the 48-hour postpartum rules and the right to sue HMOs

2. New technology and advances in pharmaceuticals, such as chemoprevention (for example, estrogen and Lyme and chickenpox vaccine)

3. No more big discounts anticipated from providers.

• Patients' rights — National leaders have developed minimum standards for health care, called the patient's bill of rights, but many states already mandate the bill's key provisions. State legislators are also responding to consumer demand for quality in health care coverage. Twenty-three states are considering or have already passed (Texas, Missouri, and California) HMO liability legislation laws that provide HMO patients with damages when an insurance company delays or denies medically necessary care.

• Corruption — On another front, a federal antiracketeering law, called Racketeer-Influence and Corrupt Organizations Act (RICO), was invoked against an HMO. The lawsuit (against an HMO in the U.S. District Court in Philadelphia filed on April 19, 1999) alleges that Aetna attracted customers by advertising quality medical care while encouraging systemwide cost-cutting measures undermining medical care.

---

ities in the form of copayments or deductibles. Consumers must learn to manage their health as well as know how to seek care when needed.

Payers manage care through the allocation of their health care dollars. They use benefit design and selective contracting to assist in this endeavor and only reimburse care ordered by the primary care provider that falls within the guidelines of the plan. Some of the financial risk is also shifted to the providers.

State legislatures and the federal government respond to consumer and provider concerns regarding managed care. Their role in managing care is to act as protectors of the public interest. Numerous laws have addressed insurance regulations, quality of care issues, and federal licensure.

TYPES OF MANAGED CARE PLANS

No standard managed care plan exists. Managed care systems have components that address organizational structure, access to providers, risk sharing, utilization management, and quality management. Several different administrative structures are characteristic of managed care arrangements. Some of

Types of HMOs

Health maintenance organization (HMO) models in popular use today include the staff model, the group model, and the independent practice association (IPA) model. Regardless of their structures, the primary purpose of HMOs is to ensure profits by decreasing referrals to specialists, restricting diagnostic studies, decreasing patient hospitalizations, reducing lengths of hospital stays, and using a capitated payment system.

● The staff model HMO uses staff physicians who are employed by the plan. These plans are also known as closed-panel plans because the staff physician provides most of the health care services. In the staff model, employees of the HMO provide health care services and function as administrative personnel to supervise and manage the organization. Most of the income generated by the physician belongs to the plan. Physicians provide outpatient care at ambulatory care sites owned by the health plan.

● Group plans require that the HMO contract with a group of primary or specialty physicians. Outpatient care is provided at the physician's office. The administrative functions are carried out by individuals from the HMO's administrative staff. The group model has three variations:

– The physician group organizes as a separate legal entity and provides care to the members of the HMO with which it has contracted.

– The physician group, which existed before the decision to contract with the HMO, provides care to HMO enrollees and other non-HMO patients (who may be enrolled in other HMO plans or may be fee-for-service patients).

– Two or more groups of physicians are part of a network that contracts selectively with hospitals and other nonphysician providers.

● IPAs are an example of open-panel plans where enrollees have more provider choice. The provider delivers outpatient care in their office. As with group plans, the health plans contract with the IPAs, which are a variation of the traditional HMO within the IPA structure; HMOs contract with nurse practitioners, physicians, and hospitals to provide care for their members. Health care providers are paid on a fee-for-service basis at rates that are usually predetermined and attractive to payers. Fee-for-service means that IPA members are charged for each service at the time care is provided, unlike most HMO plans, in which members pay premiums and aren't charged for each service individually. Similar to traditional HMOs, IPAs don't reimburse for payments to nonmember providers. Finally, hospitals and physicians must adhere to utilization guidelines to contain costs that limit the number of services they can provide.

the more common structures include HMOs, ***preferred provider organizations (PPOs),*** and point-of-service (POS) models. Keep in mind that these systems are in a state of flux, and efforts are continually being made to refine them. To reduce costs, private insurance companies have played a major role in encouraging their development.

HMOs

HMOs are the most common type of managed care plan and have the highest number of people enrolled. The most popular models are the ***staff model HMO,*** the ***group model HMO,*** and the ***independent practice association model HMO.*** (See *Types of HMOs.*)

HMOs include preventive, inpatient, and outpatient services as part of their comprehensive delivery and financing system. HMOs provide these services for an enrolled population for a fixed fee. Most HMOs provide health care services to their covered members through affiliated providers. This differs substantially from traditional fee-for-service insurers that are responsible for reimbursing covered individuals for the cost of their health care.

Under the capitated HMO system, participants pay a flat rate, usually through their employer, to belong to the HMO for a prescribed period of time. Expenses incurred by the HMO in excess of the capitated rate during the contract period are considered financial losses. Amounts that remain after services have been rendered and costs have been covered are profit. In short, health care practitioners (including physicians and NPs) who function within an HMO have strong incentives to keep costs down and ensure profits. The uniqueness of this system is that health care providers share in the financial risk. The ideal HMO is one with a large pool of healthy members who require few services and with a relatively few unhealthy patients who require more services and expensive care.

HMOs appear attractive to patients for two reasons.

● After premiums are paid, care is free or requires only a small copayment if a designated HMO provider is used.

● Cost-containment incentives are in place to keep expenses down.

Less attractive aspects of HMOs include a limited number of providers under contract at any one time. Patients must select a practitioner from a list of providers or a provider panel, which may exclude the patient's preferred clinician. If individuals choose to use providers who aren't included in their HMO's panel, they must pay for those services themselves. The only exception is in emergency situations, such as when an individual is injured in a car accident away from home.

PPOs
PPOs are a type of managed care that fall between traditional fee-for-service programs and HMOs. As with HMOs, there is no standard PPO plan. PPOs use financial incentives to influence consumer and provider behavior. In a PPO, an employer or a health care insurance carrier contracts with a group of preferred or selected participating providers. The providers agree to accept the PPO's reimbursement structure and payment levels, in return for which the PPO limits the size of its participating provider groups and gives incentives for its covered individuals to use the participating providers instead of other providers.

POS plans
A POS plan is either an HMO or a PPO with an additional feature to benefit patients. In a POS plan, patients have the ability and flexibility to decide at the point of service whether to use the provider network or to go outside of the network. If the POS plan is a variation of an HMO, enrollees will use the primary care physician (the gatekeeper) to coordinate all care. If the POS is a variation of a PPO, the patient will be able to opt into the provider network at a lower cost. Because of this flexibility, POS plans are becoming more popular.

DISEASE-MANAGEMENT COMPANIES
Some HMOs are increasingly contracting with disease-management companies, which manage all aspects of treating a specific disease. Major pharmaceutical companies (including Merck, Eli Lilly, and GlaxoSmithKline), major providers of health care (including The Johns Hopkins Hospital, Mayo Clinic, and Memorial Sloan-Kettering Cancer Center), third-party payers, and others have joined forces or have gone into disease management on their own.

In a typical disease-management arrangement, an HMO, employer, or insurance company contracts with a disease-management company for coverage of its enrollees when they are diagnosed with a specific disease such as heart failure. Components of a disease-management program include clinical pathways or treatment guidelines designed to provide the best possible care in the most streamlined environment. Disease-management companies usually guarantee that payments won't exceed a maximum amount. At best, the arrangement has the potential advantage of providing high-quality care at the lowest possible cost.

HEALTH CARE NETWORKS

Conceptually, health care networks are similar to disease-management companies. A typical health care network includes a major hub hospital; several smaller, community-based hospitals; a long-term care facility; and perhaps a rehabilitation center, a home health care agency, and a subacute care center.

In smoothly functioning health care networks, patients benefit from the reduction or elimination of fragmented delivery of care. Such networks can provide a continuum of care from one stage of illness to the next. Duplication of services is limited, and both preventive and outpatient care can be encouraged.

EFFECTS OF MARKETPLACE CHANGES

The radical changes in the last 10 years in the health care marketplace have profound impact. Control and direction are at the core of the changes.

Increased oversight of providers

Until recently, providers were able to control the flow of health care expenditures based largely on what they believed to be the provision of appropriate medical care. However, with the advent of managed care, providers have had to contend with the oversight from third-party payers, other health care professions, and the government.

Greater role for primary care providers

To the extent that providers still have an essential role in controlling the expenditure of health care dollars, it's the primary care provider, not the specialist, who is in control.

Most HMO models won't cover any costs incurred by a patient who sees a specialist unless he's referred to that specialist by a primary care provider "gatekeeper." Additionally, tests and surgery are strictly limited within certain prescribed situations.

Increased reliance on practice guidelines

Disease-management companies and health care networks are increasingly relying on practice guidelines such as clinical pathways. Although guidelines can help reduce costs and streamline care for efficiency sake, they may stir up controversy when not all providers of health care agree on the guidelines and the way they should be implemented.

Questionable effects on patient care

Thirty years ago, in a fee-for-service–indemnity insurance world, a woman having a baby might stay in the hospital with her baby for up to 1 week. Today, however, the stay is usually limited to 48 hours. Reduction in the duration of health care stays is seen across the board from birthing to gallbladder removal to coronary bypass surgery. Advances in medical care are partially responsible for speeding up the process, but concerns over health care costs are also a driving force.

Additionally, medical malpractice and liability lawsuits are on the rise. If MCOs continue to clamp down on the medical care being provided to their enrollees, more enrollees are likely to file claims that they've been injured as a result of receiving too little care.

Continuing competition for health care dollars will force prices down over the near term. At some point, however, the quality of care will be compromised. Then, the pendulum may swing back as the public demands more comprehensive care.

Need for information
With increased reliance on practice guidelines to assist in care management, information is needed to demonstrate value, competency, and outcomes. Measurement of outcomes will provide information needed to evaluate practice guidelines, determine the effectiveness of care, and guide future care delivery changes. Information systems require design, development, and revision to be able to provide this information.

Emphasis on prevention
A positive side benefit to the increased power of HMOs is the promotion of preventive medicine. However, HMOs are in a quandary about preventive health care. Because of the mobility of people and a pattern of job shifting in the last 2 decades, the average time an enrollee spends in an HMO is 18 months to 2 years. HMOs are finding that they're expending significant dollars on preventive care and promoting preventive activities only to see the healthy enrollee move to another health or insurance option. Actuaries who create or recommend costing and pricing for specific populations aren't able to keep up with the fluid enrollee.

Changing facility environment
Hospitals are no longer the dominant provider for health care. The change from *fee for service* and indemnity insurance has in large part contributed to a changing facility environment. Today, the goal is to provide a less expensive ambulatory setting in either outpatient clinics and surgery centers or at home.

Hospitalized patients tend to be sicker on average and require more intensive services than those seen on as outpatients. They're hospitalized only for the most acute episode of their illness and then they're transferred to a less intensive level of care, such as a subacute care or skilled nursing unit in a long-term care facility. Consequently, the length of stay for hospitalized patients has decreased sharply over the past 10 years. These factors have caused a significant decline in hospital census. The combination of fewer patient days and the deep discounts demanded by the payers has caused hospital reimbursement to decline as well.

As a result, hospitals are trying to do more with less. Operating budgets are being slashed. Hospital executives, many of whom don't have a medical background, are calling the shots; with fewer patients and improved technology, they reason, fewer personnel are needed for patient care. Staff physicians aren't needed in the same quantity that they once were and are finding themselves being downsized. Hospital executives, however, may overlook the facts that patients are sicker and that the technology being used to implement care is more complex.

In an effort to contain costs, hospital executives are restructuring the delivery of patient care. In many instances, they've hired consultants to review hospital operations and determine better and more cost-effective ways of delivering patient care.

Managing across care continuums
Because patients are moved rapidly across care continuums, effective mechanisms of communications with-

in the system as well as follow-up are needed to coordinate care. Case management across the continuum is necessary for patients with chronic disease to ensure management of care and patient compliance.

Increased implementation of cost-cutting strategies

Health care providers have adopted a number of strategies in their quest to overhaul and retool patient care, including continuous quality improvement and case management. At the core of these strategies is the desire to reduce failures in health care delivery, minimize unnecessary variations in patient care practices, and enhance collaboration among members of the health care team to produce more cost-effective, higher-quality patient care.

How changes in health care will affect NPs

Rapid changes in health care delivery and in the business of health care delivery have resulted in opportunities for NPs. The number of NPs is growing proportionate to the decline in growth of physician specialists.

INCREASED NUMBERS OF NPS

NPs are becoming powerful forces in today's health care marketplace. The growth of NPs in the health care environment has quadrupled while the supply of physicians is diminishing. (See *The growth of nurse practitioners.*) The number of NPs in clinical practice in 2005 is projected to equal the number of family physicians.

The significance of NP growth goes beyond numbers, however. The meaning of the real and projected statistics extends to the future of strategic planning for NPs as they will share the marketplace not only with physicians but also with an equal number of other

---

The growth of nurse practitioners

The following chart shows the number of nurse practitioner graduates over the past decade, according to the *Journal of the American Medical Association.* An asterisk denotes projected data.

YEAR	NP GRADUATES
1992	1,500
1993	1,750
1994	2,525
1995	3,600
1996	4,800
1997	6,350
1998	6,600
1999*	6,850*
2000*	7,100*
2001*	7,250*

---

disciplines. As a substantial provider, coexisting with other providers in a managed care system or an integrated delivery system, NPs will have to acquire new roles, especially in the areas of business and leadership.

CONTINUED EMPHASIS ON PRIMARY CARE

With the emphasis on health promotion, disease prevention, and care management, most NPs will function as primary care providers in either collaborative or independent practices. Many health care plans and private practices will continue to employ NPs to provide or collaborate in this care. The use of NPs in the arena of prevention optimizes their academic and philosophical background. Additionally, it's cost-effective to use NPs rather than physicians for this role.

In a managed care environment, the NP as a primary care provider not only provides care but also coordinates referrals and ensures that patients have access to wellness and preventive services.

SPECIALIZATION

Although the majority of NPs will continue to work in primary care, changes in the health care system have provided fertile ground where NPs can grow their practice areas of specialization, particularly acute care. The number of resident physicians is declining, with continued shortages projected in metropolitan centers, resulting in the need for more patient care providers in large tertiary hospitals. With a health care focus on coordinated care, improved patient outcomes, and use of appropriate resources, the acute care NP can meet this need within a collaborative model of practice.

INCREASING REGULATION

The Pew Health Professions Commission has issued reports calling for tougher standards to regulate the health care workforce. The Commission proposes that a warning is indicated to strengthen consumer protection because the current professional regulation system contains conflicting policies of protecting consumers while the marketplace is advancing the economic interests of health care professionals. These types of reports and recommendations have an impact on NPs.

The Commission calls for major changes in the regulation of health professions, including the creation of specific competency requirements to

be met throughout a career and an implementation of nationally uniform scopes of practice.

The role of NPs in shaping health care today

In the face of inevitable shifts in NP professions, NPs must become involved in the changes that are taking place in health care delivery to protect their own interests as well as their patients' interests. Today's health care arena is so complex that it has necessitated an acquisition of skills and a mindset that advances beyond clinical proficiency.

Nurses and NPs have a positive image with the public and political leaders. They are seen as being interested in the public good. Through the use of their large numbers and positive image, NPs can use their leadership skills in the political arena to reshape the face of health care delivery. They can refine and implement cost-effective models of care that provide quality patient care.

POLITICAL POWER

Political power is the ability to influence persons, such as government leaders, who have the power to work toward the goals that NPs desire. The political process provides the vehicle for NPs to work for change in government and health policy.

Political power may be increased through political activism. When NPs fail to participate in the political process, individuals who don't have the same interests or issues at stake as the NP may make the decisions. It's crucial for NPs to become dominant political players and work toward change.

It may seem that you don't have much power as an individual NP; however, when you belong to a professional organization, the power potential is increased exponentially by the organization. The dedication to high-quality practice standards and improved methods of practice by the major nursing organizations has led to improved care and increased benefits to the public as a whole.

National nursing organizations need the participation and membership of all nurses, including NPs, in order to claim that they are truly representative of the profession. A large membership allows the organization to speak with one voice when making its values about health care issues known to politicians, physicians' groups, and the general public.

Redefining the role of government in providing care, understanding system thinking, and helping consumers become informed about their own health defines the composition of health policy. The elements of health policy composition are parallel to the elements of the NP's education and practice. NPs can and should consider their contribution to politics.

The NP should educate herself to understand the political process to gain power. Because of the numbers of NPs and the predictions for the discipline's continued growth, they can obtain power and ultimately produce change at their own hands. (See *Increasing your political involvement.*)

YOUR DUTY AS A PATIENT ADVOCATE

As the health care delivery system becomes more cost effective, you may confront ethical conflicts brought on by difficult choices between managing costs and providing care. Designing treatment plans to contain costs without sacrificing patient care is a pressing issue in the delivery of timely, accessible, and quality patient care. Your nursing background and philosophy make you acutely aware of the conse-

---

Increasing your political involvement

As a nurse practitioner, you can increase your political involvement by:

● joining a local or state nursing organization.

● reading a book that describes the political process.

● joining a group that has a public policy agenda.

● using the Internet to visit Web sites of professional nursing organizations, government agencies, and state and local governments.

---

quences of cost containment on patient care. There will be times when you feel that the managed care guidelines or protocols aren't adequate and that they're unable to provide safe and effective patient care. This is an extremely difficult situation for an NP.

Your best response is to use creativity and ingenuity to address and resolve each situation on an individual basis. In a health care system that increasingly stresses the "bottom line," NPs should continuously advocate that the patient must always remain the primary focus in any decision about health care access, quality, and cost.

Advancing your career

Because change is inevitable in health care, NPs need to learn new and more effective ways of adapting to and coping with change. NPs will draw empowerment by accepting the need for change, taking control of the process, and recognizing that it's a matter of personal and professional survival. (See *Strategies to deal with change,* page 320.)

Strategies to deal with change

The best advice on how to deal effectively with change is to change the only thing you can control — your attitude.

● Instead of spending time and energy fighting change, spend your time planning how you'll succeed within the changing environment.

● Be willing to try new ideas and roles; open your mind and expand your horizons.

● Keep your skills and expertise updated and broaden your experience.

● Put yourself in charge of managing the pressure of change. Your own decisions determine your stress level.

● Be flexible; make quick adjustments.

● Accept change and move on; don't act like a victim and wallow in self-pity.

● Study the new situation, figure out how the game is played, and adapt to the new rules.

● Don't look for short-term comfort. Don't spend your time and energy looking for a low-stress organization. Organizations that will survive are the very ones that are going through the painful change process.

● Don't try to control your situation. Generally, it isn't controllable. Accept what can't be changed and learn ways to deal effectively with the change.

● Proactively make changes to your job function — add new activities and eliminate those that don't contribute to the organization's goals. Be seen as part of the solution, not part of the problem.

● Move quickly — adapt to the changes quickly and perform your job more quickly. Speed is a competitive advantage.

● Don't be afraid of the future. Instead of worrying about the bad things that might happen, proactively create your own future.

● Choose your battles — big enough to matter, small enough to win.

● Don't let the stress of change drive a wedge between you and your work. Continue to be committed to your career and profession.

● Develop a tolerance for ambiguity and uncertainty. It's the norm in health care today and will increase in the future.

● Take personal responsibility for stress reduction and use stress-reduction techniques regularly.

The changes in health care provide NPs with opportunities for professional growth and career choices. Your experience and education place you in a perfect position to assume a variety of important roles.

WHERE THE JOBS ARE

NPs are experiencing a wide range of opportunities that have been made available because of the changing health care system. Perceptions and attitude changes have opened clinical and nonclinical doors to NPs. The three "R's" — recognition, respect, and reimbursement — are opening a world of opportunities that weren't a reality for NPs as recently as 20 years ago.

NPs are a growing force in the clinical field. Their continued growth in numbers and independence seems confirmed by a confluence of interests with health care organizations, insurers, legislators, and physicians in clinical areas, such as managed care, occupational health, outpatient and long-term care, and postacute care.

Managed care

The opportunities for NPs in *managed care* are expanding. Reimbursement changes account for this. Until recently, MCOs have focused on nonclinical issues, such as network development and contracting. However, these organizations are starting to manage pa-

NP roles in managed care

Nurse practitioners (NPs) function in a managed care environment at various points in the continuum of care. They can serve as primary care providers, case managers, patient advocates, educators, triage coordinators, and quality improvement specialists.

ROLE	FUNCTIONS
Primary care provider	• Provide primary care for patient problems and disease prevention. • Act as a "gatekeeper" by coordinating referrals.
Case manager	• Manage high-risk, high-cost segments of the total enrollee population. • Manage the use of resources by patients.
Patient advocate	• Resolve clinical and financial problems related to managed care health plans.
Educator	• Provide details to patients on health plan programs for health education and prevention. • Educate and maintain ongoing relationships with network physicians. • Explain rules and act as problem-solvers with participating facilities.
Triage coordinator	• Assess and steer patients according to the guidelines of the health care plan. • Answer enrollee inquiries through a telephone triage system.
Quality improvement specialist	• Identify problems, develop solutions, and communicate results.

tient care with the goal of keeping their patients healthy.

Many MCOs are moving toward providing care within a capitated model. Under **capitation,** incentives change and health care providers are paid to keep people healthy. This transformation in the focus of patient care is good news for NPs who were educated to promote healthy behavior. The foundation of nursing practice that provides the structure for NP practice is based on treating the whole person, not just the illness, and is focused on promoting wellness instead of treating disease.

A number of new employment opportunities are available in MCOs. NPs may provide direct patient care or serve in such areas as case management, utilization management, quality improvement, marketing, information systems, general management, and senior administration. (See *NP roles in managed care.*)

In the managed care setting, NPs have a chance to use their creativity, take initiative, express leadership, and expand their scope of practice. Within managed care, NPs can provide the expertise needed to cope with today's health care system.

Occupational health
Most companies offer a wide range of risk assessment and health screening programs to their employees through the occupational health department. An increasing number of these companies are hiring NPs to facilitate these programs. The NP practices within a

prevention framework and manages a variety of employee health concerns ranging from work-related risks to those involving general health and lifestyle.

Outpatient service and long-term care

Outpatient services — particularly primary and preventive care — continue to grow as do job opportunities for NPs in this area. Opportunities exist in surgical centers, clinics, and community health services. Certain levels of patient care formerly provided exclusively in hospitals, such as I.V. therapy and ventilator care, are being provided in various other settings, including subacute or skilled care.

The concept of long-term care has expanded beyond the traditional custodial care provided in a nursing home to include subacute care, skilled care, rehabilitation services, and more. Patients in long-term care settings now include those with multiple acute care problems.

Postacute care

The role of the NP in postacute care has greatly expanded due to the Balanced Budget Act, allowing for reimbursement of NP services in postacute care settings, including home care, personal care homes, assisted living, and other senior citizen living arrangements. NPs have the expertise to provide services in the management of chronic illness in these environments.

Conclusion

The major challenge facing the health care industry is to find better ways to deliver quality patient care less expensively. NPs have an opportunity to dramatically influence this health care reform. They should embrace the opportunity to help shape the new era. NP participation will be invaluable to the development of a new health care delivery system and invaluable to the profession of nursing.

Selected references

Peters, S. "Lobbyists Vital to NP Success," *Advance for Nurse Practitioners* 7(3):25, March 1999.

Richmond, T.S., et al. "Reimbursement for Acute Care Nurse Practitioner Services," *American Journal of Critical Care* 9(1):52-61, January 2000.

Rowland, R. "Study: Nurse Practitioners Equal to Doctors in Some Cases." *www.cnn.com/2000/HEALTH/01/05/nurses.vs.doctors/index.html*. (January 5, 2000).

Sharp, N. "1999: The Road Ahead for NPs," *Nurse Practitioner* 24(2):120, 123-4, February 1999.

Sharp, N. "The 21st Century Belongs to Nurse Practitioners," *Nurse Practitioner* 25:99-100, April 2000.

Glossary • Appendices • Indexes

Glossary

A

ad hoc committee A committee commissioned for a specific purpose.

adjudicated incompetent Declared incompetent by exercise of judicial authority. Note that a patient who has been adjudicated incompetent may still have the mental capacity to make an informed decision about his medical care. Compare *incompetence* and *mental incompetence*.

administrative law Concerns administrative agencies, boards, and commissions legislated by Congress or the state legislatures. For nurse practitioners, the most important administrative agency is the state board of nursing created under the provisions of each state's nurse practice act.

administrators 1. Persons legally vested with the right of administration of an estate. 2. One who administers business affairs.

adult 1. One who is fully developed and matured and who has attained the intellectual capacity and the emotional and psychological stability characteristic of a mature person. 2. A person who has reached full legal age (in most states, age 18 or 21).

advance directive A document created by a competent individual which serves as a guideline for life-sustaining medical care when that individual has advanced disease or disability and is no longer able to indicate his own wishes.

advanced practice nurse (APN) Individual whose education and certification meet criteria established by each state's board of nursing, including current licensure as a registered nurse and a master's degree or post-basic program certificate in a clinical nursing specialty with national certification.

affirmative defense A denial of guilt or wrongdoing based on new evidence rather than simple denial of a charge. For example, a nurse who pleads immunity under the Good Samaritan law is making an affirmative defense. The defendant bears the burden of proof in an affirmative defense.

against medical advice (AMA) A patient's decision to leave a health care facility against his physician's advice.

age of majority Persons age 18 or 21 years, depending on the laws of each state.

amendment An alteration to an existing law or complaint.

American Hospital Association (AHA) Founded in 1898, the AHA is an association of 45,000 individuals and health care institutions, including hospitals, health care systems, and preacute and postacute health care delivery organizations. The AHA is dedicated to promoting the welfare of the public through its leadership and assistance to its members in the provision of better health services for all people.

American Medical Association (AMA) A professional association including practitioners in all recognized medical specialties as well as general primary care physicians. The AMA is governed by a Board of Trustees and House of Delegates. Trustees and delegates represent various state and local medical associations as well as such government agencies as the Public Health Service and medical departments of the Army, Navy, and Air Force.

American Nurses Association (ANA) The national professional association of registered nurses in the United States. It was founded in 1896 to improve standards of health and the availability of health care given in order to foster high standards for nursing, to promote the professional development of nurses, and to advance the economic and general welfare of nurses. The ANA is made up of 53 constituent associations from 50 states, the District of Columbia, Guam, and the U.S. Virgin Islands, representing more than 900 district associations. Members may join one or more of the five Divisions on Nursing Practice: Community Health, Gerontological, Maternal and Child, Medical-Surgical, and Psychiatric and Mental Health Nursing. These divisions are coordinated by the Congress for Nursing Practice. The Congress evaluates changes in the scope of practice, monitors scientific and educational developments, encourages research, and develops statements that describe ANA policies regarding legislation that affects nursing practice. Other commissions within the association include the Commission on Nursing Education, the Commission on Nursing Services, the Commission on Nursing Research, and the Economic and General Welfare Commission.

American Red Cross A nationwide organization that seeks to reduce human suffering through various health, safety, and disaster relief programs in affiliation with the International Committee of the Red Cross. The Committee and all Red Cross organizations evolved from the Geneva Convention of 1864, following the ex-ample and urging of Swiss humanitarian Jean-Henri Dunant, who aided wounded French and Austrian soldiers at the Battle of Solferino in 1859. The American Red Cross (one of more than 120 national Red Cross organizations) has more than 130 million members in about 3,100 chapters throughout the United States. Volunteers constitute the entire staffs of about 1,700 chapters. Other chapters maintain small paid staffs and some professionals but depend largely on volunteers. See also *International Red Cross Society*.

ANA *abbr* American Nurses Association.

answer The response of a defendant to the claims of a plaintiff. The answer contains a denial of the plaintiff's allegations and may also contain an affirmative defense or a counterclaim. It's the principal pleading on the part of the defense and is prepared in writing, usually by the defense attorney, and submitted to the court.

APN *abbr* advanced practice nurse.

appellate court A court of law that has the power to review the decision of a lower court. An appellate court doesn't make a new determination of the facts of the case; instead, it reviews the way in which the law was applied to the case.

arbitration The settlement of a dispute by an impartial person chosen by the disputing parties.

attorney of record The attorney whose name appears on the legal records for a specific case as the agent of a specific client.

autonomy The principle of self-determination. The right to make decisions about one's own health care.

autopsy A postmortem examination of a body to determine the cause of death.

B

battery The unauthorized touching of a person by another person. For example, a health care professional who treats a patient beyond what the patient has consented to has committed battery.

beneficence The promotion of good and prevention of harm.

borrowed-servant doctrine A legal doctrine that courts may apply in cases in which an employer "lends" his employee's services to another employer who, under this doctrine, becomes solely liable for the employee's wrongful conduct. Also called ostensible agent doctrine. Compare *captain-of-the ship doctrine* and *dual agency doctrine.*

brain death Final cessation of activity in the central nervous system, especially as indicated by a flat electroencephalogram for a predetermined length of time. The cessation of all measurable function or activity in every area of the brain, including the brain stem. Compare *death.*

breach Infraction or violation of a law, obligation, tie, or standard.

breach of contract Neglect or failure to perform all or part of a contracted duty without justification.

breach of duty Neglect or failure to fulfill in a proper manner the duties of an office, job, or position.

burden of proof The duty of proving a disputed assertion or charge.

C

capitation A per-member, monthly payment to a provider that covers contracted services and is paid in advance of delivery. In essence, a provider agrees to provide specified services to enrollees for this fixed payment for a specified term, regardless of how many times the member uses the service.

captain-of-the-ship doctrine A legal doctrine that considers a surgeon responsible for the actions of his assistants when those assistants are under the surgeon's supervision. Compare *borrowed-servant doctrine.*

CCU *abbr* coronary care unit.

certified nurse-midwife (CNM) See *midwife.*

chain of custody Evidentiary rule requiring that each individual having custody of a piece of evidence be identified and that the transfer of evidence from one custodian to another be documented so that all evidence is accounted for. Also called chain of evidence.

challenge for cause A challenge based on a particular reason (such as bias) specified by law or procedure as a reason that a party (or his lawyer) may use to disqualify a prospective juror.

child abuse The physical, sexual, or emotional mistreatment of a child. It may be overt or covert and commonly results in permanent physical or psychological injury, mental impairment or, sometimes, death. Child abuse results from complex factors involving both parents and child, compounded by various stressful environmental circumstances, such as poor socioeconomic conditions, inadequate physical and emotional support within the family, and any major life change or crisis, especially those crises arising from marital strife. Also called battered child syndrome for children under age 3. Compare *child neglect.*

child neglect Failure by parents or guardians to provide for the basic needs of a child by physical or emotional deprivation that interferes with normal growth and development or that places the child in jeopardy. Compare *child abuse.*

circumstantial evidence Testimony based on inference or hearsay rather than actual personal knowledge or observation of the facts in question.

civil defense laws Body of statutory law that is invoked when the juris-

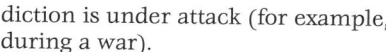

diction is under attack (for example, during a war).

claims-made policy A professional liability insurance policy that covers the insured only for a claim of malpractice made while the policy is in effect.

clinical nurse specialist (CNS) A registered nurse who holds a master of science degree in nursing (MSN) and who has acquired advanced knowledge and clinical skills in a specific area of nursing and health care.

CNM *abbr* certified nurse-midwife. See *midwife*.

CNS *abbr* clinical nurse specialist.

code *1.* A published body of statutes, such as a civil code. *2.* A collection of standards and rules of behavior, such as a dress code. *3.* A symbolic means of representing information for communication or transfer, such as a genetic code. *4. Informal.* A discreet signal used to summon a special team to resuscitate a patient without alarming patients or visitors. See also *no-code order.*

codes A system of assigned terms designed by a medical facility for quick and accurate communication during emergencies or for patient identification.

collaboration *1.* Process in which a nurse practitioner (NP) works with one or more physicians to deliver health services within her scope of professional expertise. *2.* Process in which individuals work jointly toward a common goal.

collaborative practice agreement Process in which a nurse practitioner works with one or more physicians under an agreement that follows the laws and regulations of the state in which the health care services are provided.

collective bargaining A legal process in which representatives of unionized employees negotiate with employers about such matters as wages, hours, and conditions.

commitment *1.* The placement or confinement of an individual in a specialized hospital or other institutional facility. *2.* The legal procedure of admitting a mentally ill person to an institution for psychiatric treatment. The process varies from state to state but usually involves judicial or court action based on medical evidence certifying that the person is mentally ill. *3.* A pledge or contract to fulfill some obligation or agreement, used especially in some forms of psychotherapy or marriage counseling.

common law Law derived from previous court decisions as opposed to law based on legislative enactment (statutes). Also called case law. In the absence of statutory law regarding a subject, the judge-made rules of common law are the law on that subject.

comparative negligence Determination of liability in which damages may be apportioned among multiple defendants. The extent of liability depends on each defendant's relative contribution to the harm done as determined by the jury.

complaint *1.* In a civil case, a pleading by a plaintiff made under oath to initiate a suit. It's a statement of the formal charge and the cause for action against the defendant. In a criminal case, a serious felony prosecution requires an indictment with evidence presented by a state's attorney. *2. Informal.* Any ailment, problem, or symptom identified by the patient, member of the patient's family, or other knowledgeable person. The chief complaint is usually the reason the patient has sought health care.

computerized medical record system A system that stores medical records in the memory bank of a computer.

confidentiality A professional responsibility to keep all privileged information private. In some instances, confidentiality is mandated by state or federal statutes and case law.

consent form A document, prepared for a patient's signature, that discloses his proposed treatment in general terms.

consequential damages See *special damages.*

consultation A deliberation between health care professionals on a case or its treatments.

contract defense An answer to an allegation that a breach of contract has occurred. Compare *impossibility defense.*

contributory negligence Negligence in which defendants who are determined to be substantially at fault can be held liable for a proportionate share of damages. Also, defendants could be found liable for the full amount if their behavior is found to be either malicious or reckless.

controlled substance Any substance that is strictly regulated or outlawed because of its potential for abuse or addiction. Controlled substances include cannabis, depressants, hallucinogens, narcotics, and stimulants. Compare *prescription drug.*

cost containment Control or reduction of inefficiencies in the consumption, allocation, or production of health care services in order to lower health care costs.

coronary care unit (CCU) A specially equipped hospital area designed for the treatment of patients with sudden, life-threatening cardiac conditions. Such units contain resuscitation and monitoring equipment and are staffed by personnel specially trained and skilled in recognizing and immediately responding to cardiac emergencies with cardiopulmonary resuscitation techniques, the administration of anti-arrhythmic drugs, and other appropriate therapeutic measures.

coroner A public official who investigates the causes and circumstances of a death occurring within a specific legal jurisdiction or territory, especially a death that may have resulted from unnatural causes. Also called medical examiner.

counterclaim A claim made by a defendant establishing a cause for action in his favor against the plaintiff. The purpose of a counterclaim is to oppose or detract from the plaintiff's claim or complaint.

countersignature A signature obtained from another health care professional to verify that information is correct and is within the verifier's personal knowledge.

cross-examination The questioning of a witness by the attorney for the opposing party.

D

death 1. The final and irreversible cessation of life as indicated by the absence of heartbeat or respiration. 2. The total absence of meaningful activity in the brain and the central nervous, cardiovascular, and respiratory systems, as observed and declared by a physician. Also called *legal death.* Compare *brain death.*

declared emergency Situation in which a government official formally identifies a state of emergency.

defendant The party that is named in a plaintiff's complaint and against whom the plaintiff's allegations are made. The defendant must respond to the allegations. See also *answer* and *litigant.*

defense independent medical examination In malpractice litigation, a medical examination of the injured party by a physician selected by the defendant's attorney or insurance company. Compare *discovery tool.*

deontology An ethical theory based on moral obligation or commitment to others.

deposition A sworn pretrial testimony given by a witness in response to oral or written questions and cross-examination. The deposition is transcribed and may be used for further pretrial investigation. It may also be presented at the trial if the witness can't be present or changes his testimony. Compare *discovery tool* and *interrogatories*.

descriptive ethics A factual investigation of moral behavior and beliefs.

direct examination The first examination of a witness called to the stand by the attorney for the party the witness is representing.

disclosure laws Legislation requiring that potentially confidential information be reported; for example, laws that mandate nurses report suspected child abuse or neglect.

discovery rule Rule stating that the time period for a statute of limitation begins when a patient discovers the injury. This may take place many years after the injury occurred and after the applicable statute of limitation has formally run out.

discovery tool A pretrial procedure that allows the plaintiff's and defendant's attorneys to examine relevant materials and question all parties to the case. Compare *deposition, defense independent medical examination*, and *interrogatories*.

discretionary powers The freedom of a public officer to choose courses of action within the limits of his authority.

dismiss To discharge or dispose of an action, suit, or trial.

dispense To take a drug from the pharmacy and give or sell it to another person.

distributive justice The principle that advocates allocation of benefits and burdens to everyone as merited.

documentation The preparation or assembly of written records.

drug abuse The use of a drug for a nontherapeutic effect, especially one for which it wasn't prescribed or intended. Some of the most commonly abused substances are amphetamines, barbiturates, tranquilizers, and cocaine. Drug abuse may lead to organ damage, addiction, and disturbed patterns of behavior. Some illicit drugs, such as lysergic acid diethylamide, phencyclidine hydrochloride, and heroin, have no recognized therapeutic effect. Use of these drugs can incur criminal penalties in addition to the potential for physical, social, and psychological harm. See also *drug addiction*.

drug addiction A condition characterized by an overwhelming desire to continue taking a drug to which one has become habituated through repeated consumption because it produces a particular effect, usually an alteration of mental activity, attitude, or outlook. Addiction is usually accompanied by a compulsion to obtain the drug, a tendency to increase the dose, a psychological or physical dependence, and detrimental consequences for the individual and society. Common addictive drugs are barbiturates, cocaine, crack, and morphine and other narcotics, especially heroin, which has slightly greater euphorigenic properties than other opium derivatives.

dual agency doctrine A legal doctrine stating that both the agency and the "borrowing" party may be held liable for the actions of the agent. Under this doctrine, a nurse from a nurses' registry may be held to be the agent of both the registry and the hospital. Compare *borrowed-servant doctrine*.

due process rights Personal rights based on the principle that the government may not deprive an individual of life, liberty, or property unless certain rules and procedures required by law are followed.

durable power of attorney A legal document enabling an individual to designate another person, called an "attorney-in-fact," to act on the individual's behalf, even if the principal person becomes disabled or incapacitated. This power is revoked when the principal person dies. Compare *power of attorney*.

duty A legal obligation owed by one party to another. Duty may be established by statute or another legal process, such as by contract or oath supported by statute, or it may be voluntarily undertaken. Every person has a duty to avoid causing harm or injury to others by negligence.

duty-to-rescue laws Legislation that requires certain people — those who perform rescues as part of their jobs — to rescue people in need. These people include fire fighters, police officers, and emergency medical technicians. Only a few states apply duty-to-rescue laws to nurses.

E

egoism An ethical theory that considers self-interest to be the goal of all human actions.

emancipated minor A minor who is legally considered free from the custody, care, and control of his parents before the age of majority. To be considered emancipated, a minor must meet one of three conditions: be living separate from parents or guardian and managing his or her own financial affairs for any length of time — with or without permission, be married, or be the birth mother of a child. Emancipated minors lose the right to parental support but may gain certain other rights, such as the right to consent to their own medical care and the right to enter into binding contracts.

employee contract An employee contract is a written agreement between the employee (nurse practitioner) and employer that outlines the compensation, working conditions, and rights of the employee. A contract also minimizes misunderstandings and therefore provides protection for the employee and employer.

employee-at-will agreement Unless the employee has entered into a contract, an employee-at-will agreement is in place. As an employee-at-will, the employee has no definite period of employment and employment is terminable either by the employee or employer — at any time without notice for any or no reason.

ethics An area of philosophy that examines values, actions, and choices to determine right and wrong. The study of professional standards of conduct and moral judgments.

euthanasia Deliberately bringing about the death of a person who is suffering from an incurable disease or condition, either actively (for example, by administering a lethal drug) or passively (for example, by withholding treatment).

evaluation Determining the total health status of a patient and the health care services that are necessary.

exclusionary rule A constitutional rule that evidence secured by illegal means and in bad faith cannot be introduced in a criminal trial.

exemplary damages See *punitive damages*.

expert witness A person who has special knowledge of a subject about which a court requests testimony. Special knowledge may be acquired by experience, education, observation, or study and isn't possessed by the average person. An expert witness gives expert testimony or expert evidence. This evidence usually serves to educate the court and the jury about the subject under consideration.

F

False Claims Act In 1986, the United States Congress passed this Act to combat fraud against the federal government such as Medicare fraud.

false imprisonment The act of confining or restraining a person without his consent for no clinical or legal reason.

fee for service 1. A charge made for a professional activity such as a physical examination. 2. A system for the payment of professional services in which the practitioner is paid for the particular service rendered rather than receiving a salary for providing professional services as needed during scheduled hours of work or time on call.

fidelity Faithfulness to agreements that one has accepted.

fraud Intentional deception resulting in damage to another, whether to his person, rights, property, or reputation. Fraud usually consists of a misrepresentation, concealment, or nondisclosure of a material fact, or at least misleading conduct, devices, or contrivance.

G

general damages Compensation for losses that are directly referable to a legal wrong but abstract in nature, such as pain and suffering and a worsening change in lifestyle. Compare *punitive damages* and *special damages*.

genetic determinism The flawed belief that all humans, if cloned, would be determined genetically identical.

good faith Honest intent to act without taking unfair advantage of another person; to fulfill a promise despite a legal technicality.

Good Samaritan One ready and generous in helping those in distress.

Good Samaritan acts State laws that provide civil immunity from negligence lawsuits for individuals who stop and render care in an emergency.

grace period In general, any period specified in a contract during which payment is permitted, without penalty, beyond the due date of the debt.

grievance procedure Steps agreed upon by employees and their employer to settle disputes in an orderly fashion. A labor contract may outline grievance procedures.

gross negligence The flagrant and inexcusable failure to perform a legal duty in reckless disregard for the consequences.

group model HMO A managed-care organization that contracts with a multispecialty group of physicians to provide all physician services to its members. The physicians are employed by the group practice, not the HMO, and may treat other patients.

guardian ad litem A person appointed by the court to safeguard a minor's or other incompetent's legal interest during certain kinds of litigation.

H

health care professional A professional engaged in the delivery of health services who is licensed, practices under an institutional license, and is certified or practices under other authority consistent with the laws of the state.

health maintenance organization (HMO) An organization that provides basic and supplemental health maintenance and treatment services to voluntary enrollees who pay a monthly premium and the HMO will cover their routine visits, hospital stays, emergency care, surgery, checkups, lab tests, X-rays, and therapy — with limited referral to outside specialists. The patient must use the health care professionals and hospitals designated by the HMO.

Health Plan Employer Data Information Sets (HEDIS) A set of standardized performance measures designed to allow reliable comparison of the performance of managed-care organizations. HEDIS enables public- and private-sector buyers, regulators, consumers, and beneficiaries to distinguish among health plans on the basis of comparative quality information. HEDIS measures address issues such as how well preventive care is delivered, how well adults and children in the health plan are cared for, and how accessible care is. The precision of HEDIS specifications ensures that HEDIS results are comparable across health plans.

HMO *abbr* health maintenance organization.

homestead laws Laws protecting any property designated as a homestead (any house, outbuildings, and surrounding land owned and used as a dwelling by the head of the household) from seizure and sale by creditors.

hospice A system of family-centered care designed to assist the chronically ill person to maintain a satisfactory lifestyle through the terminal phases of dying. Hospice care is multidisciplinary and includes home visits, professional medical help available on call, teaching and emotional support of the family, and physical care of the client. Some hospice programs provide care in a center as well as in the home.

I

ICN *abbr* International Council of Nurses.

ICU *abbr* intensive care unit.

illegal abortion Induced termination of a pregnancy under circumstances or at a gestational time prohibited by law. Many illegal abortions are performed under medically unsafe conditions. Also called criminal abortion. Compare *legal abortion* and *therapeutic abortion.*

immunity from liability Exemption by law of a person or institution from a legally imposed penalty.

immunity from suit Exemption by law of a person or institution from being sued.

implementation 1. A deliberate action performed to achieve a goal, as in carrying out a plan in caring for a patient. 2. In the nursing process, a category of nursing behavior in which the actions necessary for accomplishing the health care plan are initiated and completed.

impossibility defense A contract defense that says circumstances rendered the violation of a contract (such as not showing up for work) impossible to avoid. Compare *contract defense.*

incident An event that is inconsistent with ordinary routine, regardless of whether injury occurs.

incident report A formal, written report that informs a health care facility's administration (and its insurance company) about an incident and serves as a contemporary, factual statement of the incident in the event of a lawsuit.

incompetence The inability or lack of legal qualification or fitness to discharge the required duty. Compare *adjudicated incompetent* and *mental incompetence.*

indemnification Repayment or compensation for a loss. A person who has compensated another for injury, loss, or damage caused by a third party may file a suit seeking indemnification from the third party.

independent contractor A self-employed person who renders services to clients and independently determines how the work will be done.

independent practice association (IPA) model HMO A managed-care organization that contracts with an association of physicians to provide physician services to its members. The physicians maintain their independent practices.

independent provider organization (IPO) A hybrid form of managed-care organization with characteristics of both IPAs and medical associations commonly organized by community physicians to provide a

mechanism for evaluating and negotiating participation in HMOs.

informed consent Permission obtained from a patient to perform a
specific test or procedure after the
patient has been fully informed
about the test or procedure.

inpatient *1.* A patient who has been
admitted to health care facility for at
least an overnight stay. *2.* Pertaining
to the treatment of such a patient or
to a health care facility to which a
patient may be admitted for 24-hour
care.

intensive care unit (ICU) A facility
unit in which patients requiring
close monitoring and intensive care
are housed for as long as needed. An
ICU contains highly technical and
sophisticated monitoring devices
and equipment, and the staff in the
unit is educated to give critical care,
as needed by the patients.

International Council of Nurses (ICN)
The oldest international health organization, the ICN is a federation of
nurses' associations from 93 nations
and was one of the first health organizations to develop strict policies
against discrimination based on nationality, race, creed, color, politics,
sex, or social status. The objectives
of the ICN include promoting national associations of nurses, improving
standards of nursing and the competence of nurses, improving the status
of nurses within their countries, and
establishing an authoritative international voice for nurses.

International Red Cross Society An
international philanthropic organization, based in Geneva, concerned
primarily with the humane treatment and welfare of the victims of
war and calamity and with the neu-
trality of hospitals and medical personnel in times of war. See also
American Red Cross.

interrogatories A series of written
questions submitted to a witness or
other person having information of

interest to the court. The answers
are transcribed and are sworn to under oath. Compare *deposition* and
discovery tool.

intervention *1.* Any act performed to
prevent harm from occurring to a
patient or to improve the mental,
emotional, or physical function of a
patient. A physiologic process may
be monitored or enhanced, or a
pathologic process may be arrested
or controlled. *2.* The fourth step of
the nursing process. This step includes nursing actions taken to meet
patient needs as determined by
nursing assessment and diagnosis.

JK

JCAHO *abbr* Joint Commission on Accreditation of Healthcare Organizations.

job description A written statement
describing responsibilities of a specific job and the qualifications an applicant for that job should have.

***Joint Commission on Accreditation of
Healthcare Organizations (JCAHO)***
A private, nongovernmental agency
that establishes guidelines for the
operation of hospitals and other
health care facilities, conducts accreditation programs and surveys,
and encourages the attainment of
high standards of institutional medical care. Members include representatives from the American Medical Association, American College
of Physicians, and American College
of Surgeons.

judicial bypass statutes Statutes that
allow a minor to go before a judge to
avoid a strict requirement of
parental notification or consent to
obtain an abortion.

justice The principle or ideal of just
dealing or right action.

L

law *1.* In a field of study: a rule, standard, or principle that states a fact
or a relationship between factors,

such as Dalton's law regarding partial pressures of gas and Koch's law regarding the specificity of a pathogen. 2. *a.* A rule, principle, or regulation established and promulgated by a government to protect or to restrict the people affected. *b.* The field of study concerned with such laws. *c.* The collected body of the laws of a people derived from custom or from legislation.

lay jury A jury made up of people who aren't from a particular profession. For example, a lay jury in a medical malpractice trial wouldn't contain any physicians, nurses, or other members of medical professions.

lay-midwife See *midwife.*

least restrictive principle Principle that restraint on a patient be used no more than is necessary.

legal abortion Induced termination of pregnancy by a physician before the fetus has developed sufficiently to live outside the uterus. The procedure is performed under medically safe conditions prescribed by law. Compare *illegal abortion* and *therapeutic abortion.*

legal death See *death.*

legal guardian An officer or agent of the court who is appointed to protect the interests of minors or incompetent persons and provide for their welfare, education, and support.

liable Legally bound or obligated to make good any loss or damage; responsible.

liability Legal responsibility for failure to act or action that fails to meet standards of care that causes another person harm.

libel The written or broadcast form of defamation (untrue statements about another which damages his/her reputation) distinguished from slander which is oral defamation. Compare *slander.*

litigant A party to a lawsuit. See also *defendant* and *plaintiff.*

living will A witnessed document indicating a patient's wishes regarding care if a terminal illness occurs. The will applies to decisions that will be made after a terminally ill patient is incompetent and has no reasonable possibility of recovery. Compare *testamentary will.*

living will laws Laws that help to guarantee that a patient's documented wishes regarding terminal illness procedures will be carried out. Living will laws may set forth testator and witness requirements for executing a living will and medical requirements for terminating treatment. Living will laws may also address other issues, such as authorization of a proxy for health care decisions, immunity from liability for following a living will's directives, and the withholding or withdrawal of tube feedings. Also called *natural death laws* and *right-to-die laws.*

M

malpractice A professional person's wrongful conduct, improper discharge of professional duties, or failure to meet standards of care that results in harm to another person.

managed care Methods used to manage costs, use, and quality of the health care system. All health maintenance organizations and participating provider organizations, and many fee-for-service plans, have managed care.

managed-care organizations (MCO) Systems that integrate the financing and delivery of health care services to covered individuals by means of contracts with selected providers.

Medicaid A program that subsidizes medical care for low-income women and children, some men, and people with certain disabilities. Although passed by Congress in 1965, Medicaid is a state-level program, with each state defining income levels and other standards of eligibility and the federal government subsidizing a portion of the expenses.

medical record A written, legal record of every aspect of the patient's care. A record of a person's illnesses and their treatment.

Medicare Federally funded national health insurance authorized by the Social Security Act for persons age 65 and older.

mental incompetence The inability to understand the nature and effect of the action a person is engaged in. A mentally incompetent person is incapable of understanding explanations and is unable to comprehend the results of his decisions. Compare *adjudicated incompetent* and *incompetence*.

midwife *1.* In traditional use: a person who assists women in childbirth. *2.* According to the International Confederation of Midwives, the World Health Organization, and the Federation of International Gynecologists and Obstetricians: "a person who, having been regularly admitted to a midwifery educational program fully recognized in the country in which it's located, has successfully completed the prescribed course of studies in midwifery and has acquired the requisite qualifications to be registered or legally licensed to practice midwifery." Among the responsibilities of the midwife are supervision of pregnancy, labor, delivery, and puerperium. The midwife conducts the delivery independently, cares for the newborn, procures medical assistance when necessary, executes emergency measures as required, and may practice in a hospital, clinic, maternity home, or in a woman's home. Also called *lay-midwife, nurse-midwife, and certified nurse-midwife (CNM)*.

minor A person not of legal age; below the age of majority. Minors may not be able to consent to their own medical treatment unless they are legally emancipated. However, in many jurisdictions, parental consent is no longer necessary for certain types of medical and psychiatric treatment.

misdemeanor An offense that is considered less serious than a felony and carries with it a lesser penalty, usually a fine or imprisonment for less than 1 year.

moral dilemma Situation when two or more clear ethical principles apply, but they support mutually inconsistent courses of action.

moral relativism A view that ethical truths depend on the individuals and groups that hold them. There are no ethical absolutes and whatever an individual feels is right for him at that moment.

morals Fundamental standards of right and wrong that an individual learns and internalizes. An individual's moral orientation is generally based on religious, cultural, and personal beliefs.

N

National Committee for Quality Assurance (NCQA) A private, not-for-profit organization dedicated to improving the quality of health care. The organization's primary activities are assessing and reporting on the quality of the nation's managed care plans and the voluntary accreditation of managed care organizations.

National League for Nursing (NLN) An organization concerned with the improvement of nursing education, nursing service, and the delivery of health care in the United States. Its members include nurses and other health care professionals, nursing educational institutions, agencies, departments of nursing in hospitals and other health care facilities, home and community health services, and community members interested in health. Among its many activities are accreditation of nursing programs at all levels, provision of preadmission and achievement tests for nursing students, and compilation of statistical data on nursing manpower and on trends in health care delivery.

natural death laws See *living will laws.*

negligence Failure to act as an ordinary prudent person would under similar circumstances. Conduct that falls below the standard established by law for the protection of others under the same circumstances.

negligent nondisclosure The failure to completely inform a patient about his treatment.

negotiation A meeting at which an employer and employees confer, discuss, and bargain to reach an agreement or settle a dispute.

network model HMO A managed-care organization that contracts with more than one group practice to provide physician services to its members.

next of kin One or more persons in the nearest degree of relationship to another person.

NLN *abbr* National League for Nursing.

no-code order An order, written in the patient record and signed by a physician, instructing staff not to attempt to resuscitate a patient if he suffers cardiac or respiratory failure.

nonmaleficence An ethical principle based on the obligation to do no harm.

normative ethics Standards of right or good action for the guidance and evaluation of conduct.

NP *abbr* nurse practitioner.

nurse-midwife See *midwife.*

nurse practice act A law enacted by a state's legislature outlining the legal scope of nursing practice within that state.

nurse practitioner (NP) A nurse who, by advanced training and clinical experience in a branch of nursing (as in a master's degree program in

nursing or a certification program), has acquired expert knowledge in a specialized branch of practice.

nursing administrator A nurse who is responsible for overseeing the efficient management of nursing services.

nursing diagnosis Descriptive interpretations of collected and categorized information indicating the problems or needs of a patient that nursing care can affect. According to the North American Nursing Diagnosis Association: "a clinical judgment about individual, community, or family responses to actual or potential health problems or to life processes. Nursing diagnoses provide the basis of selection of nursing interventions for which the nurse is accountable."

nursing process An organizational framework for nursing practice, encompassing all the major steps a nurse takes when caring for a patient. These steps are assessment, diagnosis, planning, implementation, and evaluation.

O

Occupational Safety and Health Administration (OSHA) In 1970, the Occupation Safety and Health Act placed safety and health under this federal agency. OSHA enforces health and safety standards in the workplace without notice, assesses substantial fines, and orders employers to eliminate safety hazards from the workplace.

occurrence policy A professional liability insurance policy that protects against an error of omission occurring during a policy period, regardless of when the claim is made.

ombudsman A person who investigates complaints (as from employees, students, or consumers), reports findings, and helps to achieve equitable settlements.

P

PA *abbr* Parents Anonymous; physician's assistant.

parens patriae A doctrine that appoints the state as the legal guardian of a child or incompetent adult when a person hasn't been appointed as guardian.

Parents Anonymous (PA) An international organization, founded in 1970, dedicated to the prevention and treatment of child abuse.

patient advocate A person such as a nurse practitioner who seeks to protect a patient's rights from infringement by institutional policies.

patient's bill of rights Documents that define a person's rights while receiving health care. Bills of rights for patients are designed to protect such basic rights as human dignity, privacy, confidentiality, informed consent, and refusal of treatment. The American Hospital Association, the National League for Nursing, the American Civil Liberties Union, and other organizations and health care institutions have prepared patient's bills of rights. Concepts expressed in these documents may be incorporated into law. Although bills of rights issued by health care institutions and professional organizations don't have the force of law, nurses should regard them as professionally binding.

peremptory challenge A right given to attorneys at trial to dismiss a prospective juror for no particular reason; the number of times an attorney can invoke this right is usually limited.

persistent vegetative state A state of severe mental impairment in which only involuntary bodily functions are sustained.

physician assistant (PA) A person who is trained in certain aspects of the practice of medicine and provides assistance to a physician. A physician's assistant is trained by physicians and practices under the direction and supervision and within the legal license of a physician. Training programs vary in length from a few months to 2 years. Health care experience or academic preparation may be a prerequisite for admission to some programs. Most PAs are prepared for the practice of primary care but some practice subspecialties, including surgical assisting, dialysis, or radiology. National certification is available to qualified graduates of approved training programs. The national organization is the American Association of Physician's Assistants (AAPA). Also called *physician's associate.*

physician's associate See *physician assistant.*

plaintiff A person who files a civil lawsuit initiating a legal action. In criminal actions, the prosecution is the plaintiff, acting on behalf of the people in the jurisdiction. See also *litigant.*

policy A definite course or method of action selected from among alternatives and in the light of given conditions to guide, and usually determine, present and future decisions. Compare *rule.*

policy defense Rationale for denying coverage given by professional liability insurance carriers when a client submits a claim. Reasons for denial may include failure to pay a premium on time or failure to renew the policy.

power of attorney A legal document enabling an individual to designate another person, called an "attorney-in-fact," to act on the individual's behalf as long as the individual doesn't become disabled or incapacitated. Power of attorney continues to operate only with the continued consent of the person who granted it. If the grantor of the power should become incompetent, the power of attorney is automatically revoked. It's also revoked when the grantor dies. Compare *durable power of attorney.*

PPO *abbr* preferred provider organization.

practicing medicine without a license Practicing activities defined as medical under state law in the medical practice act without the required qualifications.

practicing pharmacy without a license Practicing activities defined as pharmaceutical under state law in the pharmacy practice act without the legal authority to prepare, compound, preserve, and dispense drugs.

practitioner A person qualified to practice in a special professional field such as a nurse practitioner.

preferred provider organization (PPO) A combination of traditional fee-for-service and a health maintenance organization. When the patient uses the health care professionals and hospitals that are part of the participating provider organization, the patient can have a larger part of his medical bills covered. The patient can use other physicians, but at a higher cost.

prescription drug Any drug restricted from over-the-counter regular commercial purchase and sale. Compare *controlled substance.*

primary care provider (PCP) Usually a patient's first contact for health care. A PCP performs the appropriate screening tests, monitors a patient's health, diagnoses and treats minor health problems, provides health education, and refers the patient to specialists if another level of care is needed. The PCP assists the patient in managing his health and coordinating his care over time.

privacy One's private life or personal affairs. The right to privacy refers to the right to be left alone and to be free from unwanted publicity.

privileged communication A conversation in which the speaker intends the information given to remain private between himself and the listener.

privilege doctrine A doctrine that protects the privacy of persons within a fiduciary relationship, such as a husband and wife, a physician and patient, or a nurse and patient. During legal proceedings, a court can't force either party to reveal communications between them unless the party who would benefit from the protection agrees.

pro-choice The philosophy that a woman has the right to choose to either continue or terminate her pregnancy.

problem-oriented medical record A record keeping system in which all members of the health care team combine their information in a special format that goes by the acronym SOAP. Each note combines Subjective data, Objective data, Assessment data, and Plans. Also, the patient's active and inactive problems are documented on a master problem list. See also *SOAP.*

professional liability A legal concept describing the obligation of a professional person to pay a patient or client for damages caused by the professional's act of omission, commission, or negligence, after a court determines that the professional was negligent. Professional liability better describes the responsibility of all professionals to their clients than does the concept of malpractice, but the idea of professional liability is central to malpractice.

professional liability insurance A type of liability insurance that protects professional persons against malpractice claims.

pro-life The philosophy that an unborn fetus has the right to develop to term and to be born.

protocol A code providing and prescribing strict adherence to guidelines for and authorization of particular practice activities.

proxy The recipient of a grant of authority to act or speak for another.

punitive damages Compensation in excess of actual damages that are a form of punishment to the wrongdoer and reparation to the injured party. These damages are awarded only in rare instances of malicious and willful misconduct. Also called *exemplary damages*. Compare *general damages* and *special damages*.

Q

quality of life A legal and ethical standard that is determined by relative suffering or pain, not by the degree of disability.

qui tam actions A lawsuit brought by a private citizen (popularly called a "whistle-blower") against a person or company who is believed to have violated the law in the performance of a contract with the government or in violation of a government regulation when there is a statute which provides for a penalty for such violations.

R

reasonably prudent nurse practitioner (NP) The standard a court uses to judge an NP being sued for negligence. The court considers whether another NP would have acted similarly to the defendant under similar circumstances.

rebuttable presumption A presumption that may be overcome or disputed by contrary evidence.

Red Cross See *American Red Cross* and *International Red Cross Society*.

registered nurse (RN) In the United States, a professional nurse who has completed a course of study at an approved school of nursing, passed the NCLEX-RN, and met the requirements for licensure set forth by the board of nursing in her state. A registered nurse may use the initials RN following her signature. RNs are licensed to practice by individual states.

remuneration A payment made for equivalent services rendered. The payment can be defined to include any type of exchange of something of value.

reservation-of-rights letter Letter written when plaintiff's insurer doesn't intend to pay damages to the plaintiff because the case falls outside of what the insurance company will cover.

res ipsa loquitur Latin phrase meaning "the thing speaks for itself." A legal doctrine that applies when the defendant was solely and exclusively in control at the time the plaintiff's injury occurred, so that the injury wouldn't have occurred if the defendant had exercised due care. In addition, the injured party couldn't have contributed to his own injury. When a court applies this doctrine to a case, the defendant bears the burden of proving that he wasn't negligent.

respondeat superior Latin phrase meaning "let the master answer." A legal doctrine that makes an employer indirectly liable for the consequences of his employee's wrongful conduct while the employee is acting within the scope of his employment.

rights Entitlements that one deserves according to just claims, legal guarantees, or moral principles. For every right there is a correlative duty or obligation.

right-to-access laws Laws that grant a patient the right to see his medical records.

right-to-die law Law that upholds a patient's right to choose death by refusing extraordinary treatment. Also called *living will law* and *natural death law*.

risk management The identification, analysis, evaluation, and elimination — or reduction — to the extent possible — of risk to an organization's patients, visitors, or employees. Risk management programs are involved with both loss prevention and loss control and handle all incidents, claims, and other insurance- and litigation-related tasks.

risk manager A person who identifies, analyzes, evaluates, and eliminates or reduces an organization's potential accidental losses. This job entails systematically and continually answering three questions: "What can go wrong in this situation?" "What are the options?" "Which option minimizes adverse effects for the organization?" Almost always, a risk manager deals with situations in which the only possible outcome is a loss or no change in the status quo. Examples of the responsibilities of a risk manager include purchasing and managing insurance policies, inviting engineering professionals to examine the structural integrity of a building, and examining policies and procedures to eliminate unnecessary risks.

RN abbr registered nurse.

rule A guide for conduct that describes the actions that should or shouldn't be taken in specific situations. Compare policy.

S

scope of practice In nursing, the professional nursing activities defined under state or province law in each state's nurse practice act.

settlement An agreement made between parties to a suit before a judgment is rendered by a court.

slander Spoken words that may damage another person's reputation. Compare libel.

SOAP An acronym for the format used in problem-oriented record keeping; it represents: Subjective data, Objective data, Assessment data, and Plans. See also problem-oriented medical record.

special damages Out-of-pocket costs which directly resulted from the breach of contract, negligence or other wrongful act by the defendant. Special damages can include medical bills, repairs and replacement of property, loss of wages and other damages which are not speculative or subjective. Also called consequential damages. Compare general damages and punitive damages.

specialty standards The standards of care that apply to a given nursing specialty.

spoliation of evidence When records are deliberately or negligently lost, altered, or destroyed.

staff model HMO A managed-care organization in which the physicians who serve the HMO are its salaried employees.

standard 1. A criterion that serves as a basis for comparison for evaluating similar phenomena or substances, such as a standard for the practice of a profession. 2. A pharmaceutical preparation or a chemical substance of known quantity, ingredients, and strength that is used to determine the constituents or the strength of another preparation. 3. Of known value, strength, quality, or ingredients.

standards of care Criteria that serve as a basis of comparison when evaluating the quality of nursing practice. In a malpractice lawsuit, a measure by which the defendant's alleged wrongful conduct is compared — acts performed or omitted that an ordinary, reasonably prudent nurse practitioner, in the defendant's position, would have done or not done.

standing orders A written document containing rules, policies, procedures, regulations, and orders for the conduct of patient care in various stipulated clinical situations.

state of emergency A widespread need for immediate action to counter a threat to the community.

statute of limitation Law that sets forth the length of time within which a person may file a specific type of lawsuit.

statutory law A law passed by a federal or state legislature.

subpoena A writ issued under authority of a court to compel the appearance of a witness at a judicial proceeding; disobedience may be punishable as contempt of court.

substitute judgment A legal term indicating the court's substitution of its own judgment for that of a person the court considers unable to make an informed decision such as an incompetent adult.

TU

teleology An ethical theory that determines right or good based on an action's consequences.

termination The procedure an employer follows to fire an employee.

testamentary will A will whose provisions take effect after death. Compare *living will*.

therapeutic abortion Induced termination of pregnancy to preserve the health, safety, or life of the woman. Compare *illegal abortion* and *legal abortion*.

therapeutic privilege A legal doctrine that permits a physician to withhold information from the patient if he can prove that disclosing it would adversely affect the patient's health.

tort A civil wrong or wrongful act, whether intentional or accidental, from which injury occurs to another.

trial de novo A proceeding in which both issues of law and issues of fact are reconsidered as if the original trial had never taken place. New testimony may be introduced or the matter may be determined a second time on the basis of the evidence already produced.

V

values Strongly held personal, religious, and professional beliefs about worth and importance. The social principles, goals, or standards held by an individual or society.

veracity Devotion to the truth.

vicarious liability Refers to the responsibility one is found to have for the actions of others because a relationship exists between those individuals such as in an employer-employee relationship.

WXYZ

whistle-blower One who reveals something covert or who informs against another.

witness 1. One who gives evidence in a case before a court and who attests or swears to facts or gives testimony under oath. 2. To observe the execution of an act, such as the signing of a document, or to sign one's name to authenticate the observation.

worker's compensation Compensation to an employee for an injury or occupational disease suffered in connection with his employment, paid under a government-supervised insurance system contributed to by employers.

writ of habeas corpus Literally means "you have the body"; a process whereby an individual detained or imprisoned asks the court to rule on the validity of the detainment or imprisonment. If the person is granted the writ, he must be released immediately.

Appendix A
UNDERSTANDING THE JUDICIAL PROCESS

The judicial process in the United States is based on court jurisdiction and consists of state and federal court systems. *Court jurisdiction* refers to a court's authority to hear a case and determine judicial action in a given place at a given time. Jurisdiction is determined by several factors, including the

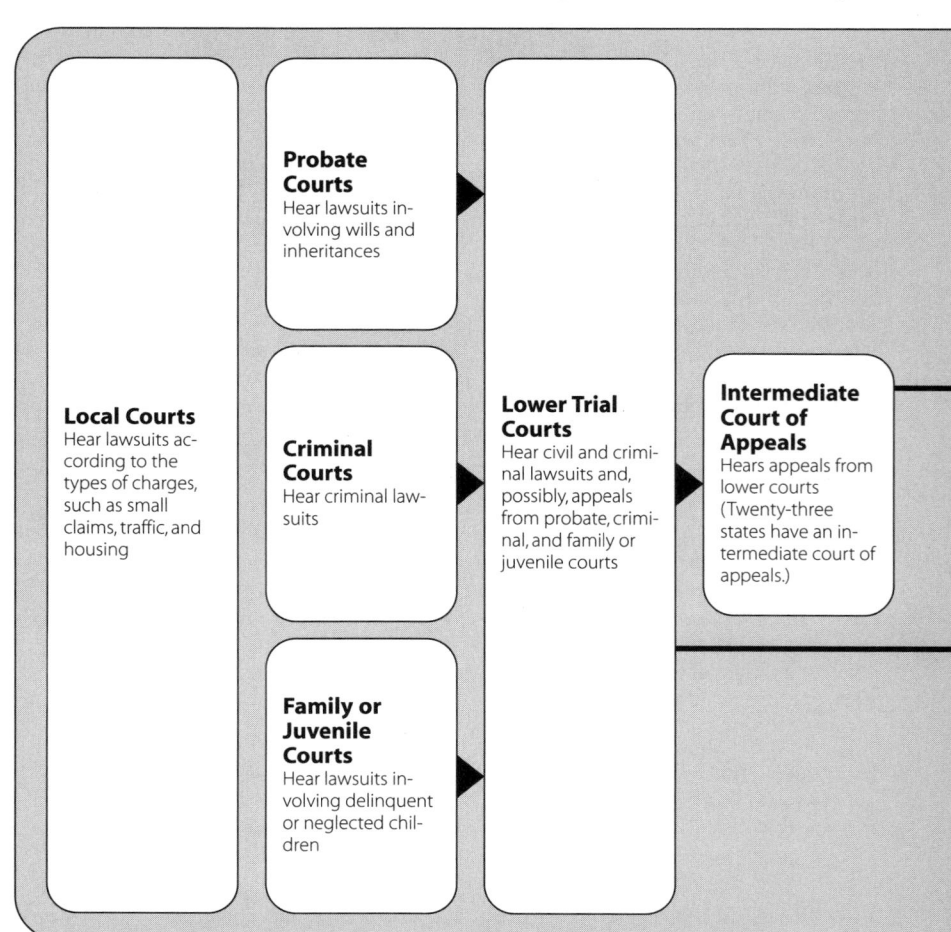

Probate Courts
Hear lawsuits involving wills and inheritances

Local Courts
Hear lawsuits according to the types of charges, such as small claims, traffic, and housing

Criminal Courts
Hear criminal lawsuits

Family or Juvenile Courts
Hear lawsuits involving delinquent or neglected children

Lower Trial Courts
Hear civil and criminal lawsuits and, possibly, appeals from probate, criminal, and family or juvenile courts

Intermediate Court of Appeals
Hears appeals from lower courts (Twenty-three states have an intermediate court of appeals.)

type of case (for example, a tort action or a criminal case) and the location of the transgression or dispute.

Appeal is a legal process whereby a party dissatisfied with the decision of a lower court can seek a more favorable decision from a higher court. Either the plaintiff or the defendant can appeal an unfavorable decision from a lower court.

doesn't include the complete federal court structure and that not all states follow the model depicted here.

COURTS IN THE FEDERAL AND STATE SYSTEMS

The diagram below depicts selected courts within the federal and state judicial systems. The arrows indicate pathways for appeal. Note that this diagram

U.S. Customs Court
Hears lawsuits involving the U.S. Patent and Trademark Office and other federal agencies

U.S. Court of Customs and Patent Appeals
Hears appeals from the U.S. Customs Court

Supreme Court of the United States
Consists of a chief justice and eight associate justices appointed by the President with advice and consent of the U.S. Senate; hears lawsuits between states, appeals from the U.S. Court of Appeals, and appeals from state supreme courts if cases involve federal law or constitutional rights

State Supreme Court
Hears appeals from lower state courts; makes final decisions except when lawsuits involve constitutional rights

U.S. Tax Court
Hears lawsuits involving tax disputes

U.S. Court of Appeals
Hears appeals from the U.S. district courts and the U.S. Tax Court

U.S. District Courts
Hear federal, criminal, and civil lawsuits

U.S. Court of Appeals for the Federal Circuit
Hears appeals from all federal circuit courts

U.S. Court of Claims
Hears lawsuits against the federal government that involve a constitutional right, federal laws or regulations, or government contracts

Appendix B
INTERPRETING LEGAL CITATIONS

You may obtain information on a specific court case or law (statute or regulation) from your county courthouse law library or local law school library. If you're looking for an overview or summary of a court case or law, look up the citation in a standard legal reference, such as a legal encyclopedia *(Corpus Juris Secundum)* and a legal text *(Restatements of Law)*.

If you have a full citation, you can locate the complete text of a court case. A full citation includes the name of the court case and a series of identifying numbers and letters. If you're missing some or all of the identifying information, you can look up the case name in the index of a legal reference.

In the court case citation index of this reference, most of the court cases on the state level will have two complete series of identifying numbers. The first series is the *official citation,* indicating where the case can be found in that state's set of court case decisions. The second series is the *unofficial citation,* indicating where the case can be found in a commercially published set of court case decisions grouped by region. Keep in mind that an "unofficial" legal reference doesn't have any less authority than an "official" legal reference.

Each citation includes an abbreviation for the legal reference that contains the law or case. For example, "U.S.L.W." stands for *United States Law Week.* To find out what the abbreviations used in the *Nurse's Handbook of*

Law and Ethics stand for, see the list of legal reference abbreviations at right. For more information on legal citations, see *A Uniform System of Citation* (The Harvard Law Review Association, 16th ed., 1996).

The number that precedes the abbreviation indicates either a volume number or title classification within the legal reference. A title classification is a body of laws or cases on a particular subject such as malpractice. A title can be one book or many books, depending on the amount of cases that bear on the titles.

Two sets of numbers follow the abbreviation. The first set indicates the page where you'll find the case. The second set, in parentheses, indicates the year of the decision.

344

LAW OR CASE	LEGAL REFERENCE	ABBREVIATION
Federal court decisions	*United States Law Week* (unofficial reporter containing recently issued Supreme Court decisions)	U.S.L.W.
	United States Reports (official reporter containing Supreme Court decisions)	U.S.
	Supreme Court Reporter (unofficial reporter containing Supreme Court decisions)	S. Ct.
	Lawyers Edition, United States Supreme Court (unofficial reporter containing Supreme Court decisions)	L. Ed.
	Federal Reporter (contains court of appeals decisions)	F., F. 2d
	Federal Supplement (contains Federal District Court of Appeals decisions)	F. Supp.
State court decisions	Published state court decisions in official state sets for about two-thirds of U.S. states (The *Uniform System of Citation* lists all state reporters and instructs how to cite them.)	Standard state abbreviations
	Commercially published National Reporter System, which includes all state and group state court decisions by region:	
	North Eastern Reporter	N.E., N.E. 2d
	Atlantic Reporter	A., A.2d
	South Eastern Reporter	S.E., S.E. 2d
	Southern Reporter	So., So. 2d
	North Western Reporter	N.W., N.W. 2d
	South Western Reporter	S.W., S.W. 2d
	Pacific reporter	P., P. 2d
Miscellaneous abbreviations	*New York Supreme Court, appellate division*	A.D.
	New York Miscellaneous Reports	Misc. 2d
	West's New York Supplement	N.Y.S. 2d
	National Labor Relations Board	N.L.R.B.
Federal statutes	*United States Law Week* (contains chronologic list of recently enacted statutes)	U.S.L.W.
	United States Statutes at Large (contains chronological lists of all statutes enacted during a single legislative session)	STAT. Or STAT. AT L.
	United States Code (contains all statutes arranged by title)	U.S.C.
State statutes	Published state statutes in official state sets	Standard state abbreviations
Federal regulations	*Code of Federal Regulations* (contains federal regulations arranged by title)	C.F.R.
	The Federal Register (contains updates to the C.F.R.)	F.R.
State regulations	Published state regulations in official state sets	Standard state abbreviations

Appendix C
TYPES OF LAW

Constitutional, administrative, and criminal law deal with the individual's relationship to the federal government and the state. Contract law, tort law, and protective reporting law deal with relationships between people. Property law deals with interests in land and personal property.

CONSTITUTIONAL LAW

This type of law deals with the individual's rights and responsibilities under federal and state constitutions as interpreted by United States and state courts. A patient's right to self-determination in refusing treatment as well as the right to life, liberty, and religious freedom are founded in constitutional law.

ADMINISTRATIVE LAW

Administrative law concerns administrative agencies, boards, and commissions legislated by Congress or the state legislatures. For nurse practitioners (NPs), the most important administrative agency is the state board of nursing created under the provisions of each state's nurse practice act.

CRIMINAL LAW

Criminal law concerns state and federal criminal statutes, which define criminal actions, such as murder, manslaughter, criminal negligence, theft, and the illegal possession of drugs. NPs risk violating criminal laws when they become involved in such actions as removing life-support systems or failing to nourish or medicate neonates with catastrophic disorders. They may also perform obviously criminal acts such as stealing medications or narcotics.

NPs may also be involved as witnesses in criminal court proceedings if they care for victims of rape, shootings, or other violent crimes.

CONTRACT LAW

Contract law involves agreements between two or more persons to do something for some type of remuneration — a "bargained-for-exchange." In essence, a contract is a promissory agreement that creates, modifies, or destroys a legal relationship. In many situations, an oral agreement is also legally binding.

TORT LAW

Tort law concerns the reparation of civil wrongs or injuries. A tort is a breach of a legal duty that exists by virtue of society's expectations regarding interpersonal conduct (as opposed to a legal duty that exists by virtue of a contractual relationship). More generally, a tort is any action or omission that harms somebody. Common causes of tort litigation include negligence, professional malpractice, assault and battery, invasion of privacy, false imprisonment, and defamation.

PROPERTY LAW

Property laws concern real property and personal property. Real property concerns any interest in land and generally whatever is erected on, growing on, or fastened to it. In health care, real property interests are involved when real estate is purchased or leased to provide health care services. Personal property laws regard interests in movable assets (including animals). An example of a violation of personal property would be loss of or damage to a patient's possessions.

PROTECTIVE REPORTING LAW

This type of law is enacted to protect an individual's health and well-being. Examples include laws requiring NPs to report child abuse or elder abuse, the Federal Privacy Act of 1974, which protects a person's legal right to obtain and correct information held by the government, and the Health Care Quality Im-provement Act of 1986 which estab-lished the National Practitioner Data Bank (implemented in 1990) to collect and disseminate to authorized profes-sional review authorities information concerning medical incompetence. Protective reporting laws may be con-sidered criminal law, depending on how the state has classified them.

The following chart provides examples of these different types of law.

TYPE OF LAW	FEDERAL	STATE
Constitutional	• U.S. Constitution • Civil Rights Act	• State constitution • Health Care Quality Improvement Act of 1986, established the National Practitioner Data Bank (implemented in 1990) as a flagging system to identify health care practitioners who may be involved in incidents of medical incompetence.
Administrative	• Food, Drug, and Cosmetic Act • Social Security Act (Medicare/Medicaid) • National Labor Relations Act	• Nurse Practice Act • Medical Practice Act • Pharmacy Act • Worker's compensation laws • State Labor Relations Act • Employment Security Act
Criminal law or code	• Comprehensive Drug Abuse Prevention and Control Act (Controlled Substance Acts) • Kidnapping laws	• Criminal codes that define murder, manslaughter, criminal negligence, rape, fraud, illegal possession of drugs (and other controlled substances), theft, assault, and battery
Contract	• Laws that govern business or employment relationships with the federal government	• Laws that govern entering into busi-ness or employment contracts • Uniform commercial code (a state statute that governs sales, banking docu-ments, and credit transactions)
Tort law or claims	• Federal Torts Claims Act (allows tort claims against the federal government)	• State and local government tort claims acts (allow tort claims against the state or local government) • Malpractice statutes (establish profes-sional liability) • Other tort claims, such as negligence, assault, battery, false imprisonment, inva-sion of privacy, and libel

(continued)

TYPE OF LAW	FEDERAL	STATE
Property law	● Eminent domain: the power of the government (federal, state, county, or city; school district, hospital district, or other agencies) to take private real estate for public use, with or without the owner's permission.	● Eminent domain; the power of state and local government to take private real estate for public use, with or without the owner's permission.
Protective reporting	● Child Abuse Prevention and Treatment Act of 1984 ● Privacy Act of 1974 (protects the legal right of a U.S. citizen or permanent resident alien to obtain and correct information about him held by the government or governmental agencies)	● Age of consent statutes for obtaining medical treatment ● Privileged communications statute ● Malpractice insurers must report to the data bank all payments made on behalf of individual practitioners. State licensing boards, hospitals, and other health care entities, including professional societies; also must report to the data bank certain adverse licensing and disciplinary actions taken against individual practitioners. ● Abortion statute ● Good Samaritan Act ● Child abuse and neglect statute ● Elderly abuse statute ● Domestic violence statute ● Involuntary hospitalization statute ● Advance directives legislation (laws dealing with living wills and durable powers of attorney for health care)

Court Case
Citation Index

General Index

i refers to an illustration; t refers to a table.

i refers to an illustration; t refers to a table.

i refers to an illustration; t refers to a table.

i refers to an illustration; t refers to a table.

i refers to an illustration; t refers to a table.

Managed care, 117, 258
  employment in, 320, 321t
  types of plans for, 312-314
Managed care organizations, 45, 134, 311
  substance abuse and, 265
Medicaid, 17, 29
Medical practice, definition of, 26
Medical records. *See also* Documentation.
  contents of, 179
  definition of, 176
  improper maintenance of, 179, 181
  legal significance of, 177
  patient's right to access, 301-302
  purpose of, 176-177
  statute of limitation and, 150
Medicare, 17, 27-28, 80-82
Medication labels, 38
Medication log, 39
Medication samples, 35
Mental health care of minor, 61-62
Mental illness
  establishing legal responsibility for, 69
  government action on, 68-69
  informed consent and, 69-70
  involuntary sterilization and, 74
  privacy and, 73
  research participation and, 74
  restraints and, 71-72
  right to treatment for, 73
  sexual rights and, 73-74
  statute of limitations and, 149
  writ of habeas corpus and, 73
Mental illness follow-up, 53
Mercy killing. *See* Euthanasia.
Mifepristone, 240
Minor
  abortion and, 61, 298
  communicable disease and, 61
  contraceptive and, 61
  drug abuse and, 61
  emancipation of, 59
  emergency care for, 60
  guardian *ad litem* for, 59
  informed consent of, 59-60
  mature, 59
  mental health care of, 61-62
  religious beliefs of, 61
  rights of, 58-59, 282-284
  statute of limitations and, 149
Minority rule, 278

Misconduct, reporting of, 262, 264-265
Misdemeanor, 34, 126
Moral dilemmas, 201, 203, 205-208
Moral relativism, 203
Morals, 201
Myocardial infarction, post-care for, 52

N

National Committee for Quality Assurance, 47, 50, 52, 114
National Labor Relations Act, 117
National Labor Relations Board, 119
National League for Nursing, patient's rights and, 271
National Organ Transplant Act, 224
National Practitioner Data Bank, 135-136
Natural death laws, 290
Negligence, 124, 137, 139, 232
  comparative, 144, 146t
  contributory, 144-145, 146t
Negligent nondisclosure, 279, 280-281
Negotiation, 113-114, 115i, 116
Next of kin, 68
  patient's rights and, 282
Nonemancipated minor, 60
Nonmaleficence, 206, 222
Normative ethics, 201
Nurse practice act, 1, 3-17, 31, 43, 136
  substance abuse and, 266
Nurse practitioner
  certification of, 2
  changes in health care market and, 317-322
  donating services of, 130, 131-133
  educational requirements for, 2
  ethical codes for, 211-212
  liability of, 144
  medical practice and, 26
  organizations for, 95-98
  political power of, 318-319
  practice boundaries of, 10
  standards of care for, 1, 17, 18-20t, 21-22
Nurses' associations by state, 6-9t
Nursing administrators, substance abuse and, 266
Nursing diagnosis, 26
Nursing process, ethical decision making and, 208

i refers to an illustration; t refers to a table.

i refers to an illustration; t refers to a table.

i refers to an illustration; t refers to a table.

i refers to an illustration; t refers to a table.

i refers to an illustration; t refers to a table.